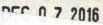

Top Federal Tax Issues for 2017 | CPE Course

Wolters Kluwer Editorial Staff Publication

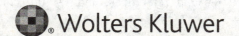
Wolters Kluwer

Contributors

Contributing Editors . . . . David Becker, J.D.;

Elena Eyber, J.D.;

Brant Goldwyn, J.D.;

Daniel C. Johnson, J.D., LL.M;

Robert A. Morse, J.D., LL.M.;

Lawrence A. Perlman, CPA, J.D., LL.M.;

Deborah Petro, J.D., LL.M.;

John W. Roth, J.D., LL.M.;

James Solheim, J.D., LL.M.;

Raymond G. Suelzer Jr., J.D., LL.M.;

George L. Yaksick, Jr., J.D.

Technical Review . . . . George G. Jones, J.D., LL.M.

Production Coordinator . . . . Gabriel E. Santana; Jennifer Schencker;

Vignesh Lakshmikanthan

Production . . . . Lynn J. Brown; Muthuraman Lakshmanan

This publication is designed to provide accurate and authoritative information in regard to the subject matter covered. It is sold with the understanding that the publisher is not engaged in rendering legal, accounting, or other professional service. If legal advice or other expert assistance is required, the services of a competent professional person should be sought.

ISBN: 978-0-8080-4399-7

SUSTAINABLE FORESTRY INITIATIVE

Certified Sourcing

www.sfiprogram.org

SFI-01681

Printed in the United States of America

Introduction

Each year, a handful of tax issues typically require special attention by tax practitioners. The reasons vary, from a particularly complicated new provision in the Internal Revenue Code, to a planning technique opened up by a new regulation or ruling, or the availability of a significant tax benefit with a short window of opportunity. Sometimes a developing business need creates a new set of tax problems, or pressure exerted by Congress or the Administration puts more heat on some taxpayers while giving others more slack. All these share in creating a unique mix that in turn creates special opportunities and pitfalls in the coming year and beyond. The past year has seen more than its share of these developing issues.

Top Federal Tax Issues for 2017 CPE Course identifies those recent events that have developed into the current "hot" issues of the day. These tax issues have been selected as particularly relevant to tax practice in 2017. They have been selected not only because of their impact on return preparation during the 2017 tax season but also because of the important role they play in developing effective tax strategies for 2017 and beyond. Some issues are outgrowths of several years of developments; others have burst onto the tax scene unexpectedly. Among the latter are issues directly related to the recent economic downturn and tax legislation designed to assist in a recovery. Some have been emphasized in IRS publications and notices; others are just being noticed by the IRS.

This course is designed to help reassure the tax practitioner that he or she is not missing out on advising clients about a hot, new tax opportunity; or that a brewing controversy does not blindside their practice. In addition to issue identification, this course provides the basic information needed for the tax practitioner to implement a plan that addresses the particular opportunities and pitfalls presented by any one of those issues. Among the topics examined in the *Top Federal Tax Issues for 2017 CPE Course* are:

- Compliance Issues for the Global U.S. Business
- Navigating IRS's Redesigned LB&I Division
- PEOs (Professional Employer Organizations)
- Tangible Property Rules Update
- Tax Deadlines: A Changing Landscape
- Penalties and Interest: Rule Changes
- Partnership Audit Rules: Initial Considerations
- Identity Theft: Reaction and Strategies
- Coordinating Multiple Retirement Accounts
- Tax Aspects of Charitable Fundraising

Study Questions. Throughout the course you will find Study Questions to help you test your knowledge, and comments that are vital to understanding a particular strategy or idea. Answers to the Study Questions with feedback on both correct and incorrect responses are provided in a special section beginning at ¶ 10,100.

Index. To assist you in your later reference and research, a detailed topical index has been included for this course.

Final Exam. This course is divided into three Modules. Take your time and review all course Modules. When you feel confident that you thoroughly understand the material, turn to the Final Exam. Complete one, or all, Module Final Exams for continuing professional education credit.

Go to **CCHGroup.com/PrintCPE** to complete your Final Exam online for immediate results and no Express Grading Fee. Your Training History provides convenient storage for your CPE course Certificates. Further information is provided in the CPE Final Exam instructions at ¶ 10,200.

October 2016

PLEDGE TO QUALITY

Thank you for choosing this CCH® Learning Solutions product. We will continue to produce high quality products that challenge your intellect and give you the best option for your Continuing Education requirements. Should you have a concern about this or any other Wolters Kluwer product, please call our Customer Service Department at 1-800-248-3248.

COURSE OBJECTIVES

This course was prepared to provide the participant with an overview of specific tax issues that impact 2016 tax return preparation and tax planning in 2017. These are the issues that "everyone is talking about;" each impacts a significant number of taxpayers in significant ways.

Upon course completion, you will be able to:

- Recognize the differences between the FBAR and FATCA reporting requirements;
- Identify the Action Plan items of the Organisation for Economic Cooperation and Development's BEPS project;
- Recognize LB&I's goals and ideas for reorganizing its structure and revising its examination process;
- Identify recent changes made by LB&I to its structure and operations;
- Recognize the roles of the CPEO and its customers for employment tax withholding, reporting, and payment functions;
- Identify which employees are excluded employees versus covered employees under the CPEO regulations;
- Recognize the *de minimis* expensing rule with updated per item expensing limits for taxpayers without an applicable financial statement;
- Identify what clients need to know about key legislative changes affecting bonus depreciation and other depreciation provisions that go into effect into 2016 and later;
- Recognize which individuals and entities are required to file returns under current laws;
- Identify major revisions made by recent legislation for income tax returns of certain entities;
- Recognize what penalties may be imposed for failure to file accurate information properly and on time;
- Identify the types of penalties applied for failure to file or pay with tax returns;
- Recognize the duty of consistency between the returns filed for partners and their partnerships;
- Identify ways in which adjustments and assessments are implemented for a reviewed tax year;
- Recognize major federal legislation addressing identity theft;

- Identify techniques individuals and businesses can use to minimize threats to their identities;

- Recognize the differences between defined contribution plans and defined benefit plans and identify the major kinds of defined contribution plans;

- Identify the differences between elective deferrals and employer contributions, and the difference between employer matching contributions and "nonelective" contributions;

- Recognize the minimum contributions that trigger filing requirements for charitable contributions; and

- Identify the forms required for timely filing contribution reports to the IRS and associated penalties for failure to substantiate the contributions.

One **complimentary copy** of this course is provided with certain copies of Wolters Kluwer publications. Additional copies of this course may be downloaded from **CCHGroup.com/ PrintCPE** or ordered by calling 1-800-248-3248 (ask for product 10024491-0004).

Contents

MODULE 2: CHANGES IN FILING DEADLINES, AUDITS, AND PENALTIES

5 Tax Deadlines: A Changing Landscape

6 Penalties and Interest: Rule Changes

7 Partnership Audit Rules: Initial Considerations

x

MODULE 1: BUSINESS COMPLIANCE ISSUES FOR 2017—Chapter 1: Compliance Issues for the Global U.S. Business

¶ 101 WELCOME

In their ongoing effort to close the *tax gap,* or the taxable amounts underreported on tax returns, Congress and the Internal Revenue Service (IRS) continue to extend the information reporting requirements for taxpayers and financial institutions domestically and abroad. With the ability to locate and collect monies already owed, Congress can, in effect, increase revenues without having to increase taxes. At the same time, information reporting is extremely useful to the IRS because collecting this data enables the agency to verify a taxpayer's income by matching what is reported by one taxpayer with that provided by another party and then act upon discrepancies. As a result, these matching efforts are likely to expand even further. In keeping with this trend, this chapter examines the reporting requirements for foreign assets and financial interests imposed by the *Foreign Account Tax Compliance Act* (FATCA) and the FinCEN Form 114, *Report of Foreign Bank and Financial Accounts* (FBAR), and discusses how certain taxpayers may decide to use the Offshore Voluntary Disclosure Program (OVDP) developed by the IRS. The chapter also discusses the base erosion and profit shifting (BEPS) project of the Organisation for Economic Cooperation and Development (OECD).

¶ 102 LEARNING OBJECTIVES

Upon completion of this course, you will be able to:

- Recognize the differences between the FBAR and FATCA reporting requirements;
- Recognize the civil and criminal penalties associated with noncompliance with the FATCA and FBAR requirements;
- Identify how the OVDP may be used;
- Recognize the differences between the OVDP and the Streamlined Compliance Process; and
- Identify the Action Plan items of the Organisation for Economic Cooperation and Development's BEPS project.

¶ 103 INTRODUCTION

U.S. persons with foreign financial interests may be subject to various information reporting requirements. A *U.S. person* includes:

- A citizen or resident of the United States;
- A domestic partnership;
- A domestic corporation;
- Any estate (other than a foreign estate); and
- Any trust, if

- A court within the United States is able to exercise primary supervision over the administration of the trust, and

- One or more U.S. persons have the authority to control all substantial decisions of the trust (Code Sec. 7701(a)(30) and Reg. § 1.1471-1T(b)(141)(i)).

COMMENT: The terms of FATCA were codified in Code Secs. 1471 to 1474 and 6038D.

First, under FATCA, U.S. citizens, resident aliens, and certain nonresident aliens must file information returns using Form 8938, *Statement of Specified Foreign Financial Assets,* with their annual income tax returns for any year in which their interests in specified foreign assets exceed the applicable reporting threshold.

Second, a U.S. person with financial interests in or signature authority over foreign financial accounts generally must file FinCEN Form 114, *Report of Foreign Bank and Financial Accounts* (FBAR) if, at any point during the calendar year, the aggregate value of the accounts exceeds the reporting threshold.

These reporting requirements may often overlap, but they apply separately. Thus, a person who satisfies both the FATCA and the FBAR filing requirements must file both Form 8938 and FinCEN Form 114. Filing one of the forms does not satisfy the filing requirement for the other form.

Different policy considerations apply to Form 8938 and FinCEN Form 114. In addition to tax administration, FBAR reporting is also used for law enforcement purposes. These differences are reflected in the different categories of persons required to file each form, the different filing thresholds, and the different assets and accompanying information required on each form.

¶ 104 FATCA REQUIREMENTS

As discussed above, FATCA mandates that for some taxpayers a report of foreign financial assets be made. Accordingly, *specified persons* who hold an interest in a "specified foreign financial asset" during the tax year must attach to their tax returns a Form 8938 to report certain information for each asset if the total value of all such assets exceeds an applicable reporting threshold amount. *Specified person* means a specified individual or a specified domestic entity (§ 1.6038D-1(a)(1)).

This requirement applies to any U.S. citizen and any individual who is resident alien for any part of the tax year. A nonresident alien who makes the election to be treated as a resident alien for purposes of filing a joint return for the tax year must also file Form 8938, as must a nonresident alien who is a bona fide resident of American Samoa or Puerto Rico.

Form 8938 must also be filed by any domestic entity formed or availed for purposes of holding, directly or indirectly, specified foreign financial assets, in the same manner as if the entity were an individual.

COMMENT: On February 22, 2016, the IRS released T.D. 9752 adopting Proposed Reg. § 1.6038D-6 as a final regulation. Under Treas. Reg. § 1.6038D-6 designated specified domestic entities are subject to the reporting requirement. They include certain closely held domestic corporations or partnerships, as well as certain domestic trusts. Reporting by specified domestic entities as provided for in final regulations is required effective after December 31, 2015.

Interests

A specified person has an interest in a specified foreign financial asset if any income, gains, losses, deductions, credits, gross proceeds, or distributions from holding or disposing of the asset are or would be required to be reported, included, or otherwise reflected on the specified person's income tax return. The interest exists even if there are no income, gains, losses, deductions, credits, gross proceeds, or distributions from holding or disposing of the asset included or reflected on the taxpayer's income tax return for that tax year (Treas. Reg. § 1.6038D-2(b)(1)).

> **COMMENT:** Therefore, a specified person must file a Form 8938 despite the fact that none of the specified foreign financial assets that must be reported affects his or her tax liability for the year (Treas. Reg. § 1.6038D-2(a)(8)).

STUDY QUESTION

1. Which of the following is *not* a U.S. person potentially subject to FATCA and/or FBAR requirements?

   a. A foreign estate

   b. A domestic corporation

   c. A domestic trust

   d. A holding company for specified foreign financial assets

Specified Foreign Financial Assets

Specified foreign financial assets include:

- Any financial account maintained by a foreign financial institution; and
- Any of the following assets that is not held in an account maintained by a financial institution

   - Any stock or security issued by a person other than a U.S. person (as defined above),

   - Any financial instrument or contract held for investment that has an issuer or counterparty that is other than a United States person, and

   - Interest in a foreign entity (Treas. Reg. § 1.6038D-3(a), (b)).

Financial accounts. The primary type of specified foreign assets is financial accounts maintained by foreign financial institutions. "Financial account" and "foreign financial institution" are generally defined by reference to the Code Sec. 1471 FATCA rules that require withholding from payments to foreign financial institutions. Thus, a *financial account* is any depository or custodial account maintained by a foreign financial institution, as well as any equity or debt interest in a foreign financial institution (other than interests that are regularly traded on an established securities market) (Treas. Reg. § 1.6038D-1(a)(7), (8)).

A *foreign financial institution* (FFI) is generally any financial institution (other than a U.S. entity) that:

- Accepts deposits in the ordinary course of a banking or similar business;
- Holds financial assets for the account of others as a substantial part of its business; or
- Is engaged (or holds itself out as being engaged) primarily in the business of investing, reinvesting, or trading in securities, partnership interests, commodities, or any interest (including a futures or forward contract or option) in such securities, partnership interests, or commodities (Treas. Reg. § 1.1471-5(d)).

However, for purposes of the FATCA reporting requirements for specified persons, a specified foreign financial asset also includes a financial account maintained by a financial institution organized under the laws of a U.S. territory. As a result, such an account is subject to FATCA unless it is owned by a bona fide resident of the relevant U.S. territory.

FATCA also imposes complex reporting requirements for foreign financial institutions. Under Code Sec. 1471, FFIs are required to report to the IRS certain information about financial accounts held by U.S. taxpayers or by foreign entities in which U.S. taxpayers hold substantial ownership interests. If an FFI fails to meet the FATCA requirements, a U.S. withholding agent must deduct and withhold a tax equal to 30 percent on any "withholdable payment" made to the FFI after June 30, 2014, unless the withholding agent can reasonably rely on documentation that the payment is exempt from withholding. No withholding is required, however, if an FFI enters into an agreement with the IRS to provide the required information. An FFI may also be deemed to meet the requirements of the agreement. These agreements encourage reporting by U.S. taxpayers. If the taxpayers fail to comply with the reporting requirements themselves, the FFIs will provide the required information directly to the IRS, which can then use that information to target the noncompliant taxpayer (Notice 2014-33).

> **COMMENT:** The FATCA rules apply to the foreign financial account itself. The assets held in the account do not have to be separately reported on Form 8938, because their value is included in the determination of the account's maximum value.

> **COMMENT:** Foreign deposit and custodial accounts are reported on Part I of Form 8938.

Other assets. The following items are also specified foreign assets if they are held for investment, even if they are not held in an account maintained by a foreign financial institution:

- Any stock or security issued by a person other than a U.S. person;
- Any financial instrument or contract held for investment that has an issuer or counterparty that is not a U.S. person; and
- Any interest in a foreign entity (Treas. Reg. § 1.6038D-3(b)(1)).

> **COMMENT:** The other assets categories are broad and may sometimes overlap, so a single asset may fall into more than one category. For example, stock issued by a foreign corporation is stock that is issued by a person other than a U.S. person and is also an interest in a foreign entity.

> **COMMENT:** The IRS has stated that an interest in a social security, social insurance, or other similar program of a foreign government is not a specified foreign financial asset.

Examples of assets other than financial accounts that may be considered *other specified foreign financial assets* include, but are not limited to:

- Stock issued by a foreign corporation;
- A capital or profits interest in a foreign partnership;
- A note, bond, debenture, or other form of indebtedness issued by a foreign person;
- An interest in a foreign trust;

- An interest rate swap, currency swap, basis swap, interest rate cap, interest rate floor, commodity swap, equity swap, equity index swap, credit default swap, or similar agreement with a foreign counterparty; and

- Any option or other derivative instrument with respect to any of the items listed as examples in this paragraph or with respect to any currency or commodity that is entered into with a foreign counterparty or issuer (Treas. Reg. § 1.6038D-3(d)).

    COMMENT: Specified foreign financial assets that are not held in deposit and custodial accounts are reported on Part II of Form 8938.

Exceptions. Exceptions to the reporting requirements apply to particular types of foreign financial assets, as well as assets subject to duplicative reporting, assets held by certain types of trusts, and assets held by certain bona fide residents of U.S. possessions.

The following types of assets are not specified foreign financial assets and, therefore, do not have to be reported on Form 8938:

- A financial account (including the assets held in it) that is maintained by a U.S. payer, such as a domestic financial institution. In general, a U.S. payer also includes a domestic branch of a foreign bank or foreign insurance company and a foreign branch or foreign subsidiary of a U.S. financial institution, if subject to the same tax and reporting rules as the U.S. payer;

- A financial account (including the assets held in it) that is maintained by a dealer or trader in securities or commodities, if all of the holdings in the account are subject to the mark-to-market accounting rules for dealers in securities, or a mark-to-market election is made for all of the holdings in the account; and

- Any other financial asset, if the asset is subject to the mark-to-market accounting rules for dealers in securities or commodities or a mark-to-market election is made for the asset (Treas. Reg. § 1.6038D-3(b)).

The rules intend to limit duplicative reporting and provide that specified foreign financial assets do not have to be reported on Form 8938 if they are properly reported on any of the following timely filed forms for the same tax year:

- Form 3520, *Annual Return to Report Transactions with Foreign Trusts and Receipt of Certain Foreign Gifts;*

- Form 5471, *Information Return of U.S. Persons with Respect to Certain Foreign Corporations;*

- Form 8621, *Information Return by a Shareholder of a Passive Foreign Investment Company or Qualified Electing Fund;* and

- Form 8865, *Return of U.S. Persons with Respect to Certain Foreign Partnerships* (Treas. Reg. § 1.6038D-7(a)(1)).

    COMMENT: The specified person's Form 8938 must identify these other form(s) that reported the specified foreign financial asset and report how many of these forms were filed.

    COMMENT: For purposes of determining whether a specified individual satisfies the applicable reporting threshold, specified individuals must include the value of assets reported on duplicative forms, whereas specified domestic entities must exclude the value of such assets as reported to duplicative forms.

If the grantor trust rules treat a specified person as the owner of one of these trusts or a portion of the trust for income tax purposes, the following assets held by trust (or the owned portion) do not have to be reported on the specified person's Form 8938:

- A domestic trust that is a widely held fixed investment trust;
- A domestic trust that is a liquidating trust created under a court order in a Chapter 7 or Chapter 11 bankruptcy; or
- A foreign trust, if
  - The specified person reports the trust on a Form 3520 timely filed with the IRS for the tax year,
  - The trust timely files Form 3520-A, *Annual Information Return of Foreign Trust With a U.S. Owner,* with the IRS, and
  - The specified person's Form 8938 reports the filing of the Form 3520 and Form 3520-A (Treas. Reg. § 1.6038D-7(b)).

Additionally, bona fide residents of U.S. possessions (American Samoa, Guam, the Northern Mariana Islands, Puerto Rico, or the U.S. Virgin Islands) who must file Form 8938 do not have to report the following specified foreign financial assets:

- A financial account maintained by a financial institution organized under the laws of the U.S. possession where the specified person is a bona fide resident;
- A financial account maintained by a branch of a financial institution not organized under the laws of the U.S. possession where the specified person is a bona fide resident, if the branch is subject to the same tax and information reporting requirements that apply to a financial institution organized under the laws of the U.S. possession;
- Stock or securities issued by an entity organized under the laws of the U.S. possession where the specified person is a bona fide resident;
- An interest in an entity organized under the laws of the U.S. possession where the specified person is a bona fide resident; or
- A financial instrument or contract held for investment, provided each issuer or counterparty that is not a U.S. person either is an entity organized under the laws of the U.S. possession where the specified person is a bona fide resident or is a bona fide resident of that U.S. possession (Treas. Reg. § 1.6038D-7(c)).

Nonvested property. A specified person who receives nonvested interests in property in connection with the performance of personal services does not need to report those interests until they are substantially vested. However, if the specified person makes a valid election under Code Sec. 83(b) (Election to Include in Gross Income in Year of Transfer), he or she is considered to have an interest in the property on the date of transfer, giving rise to a reporting obligation under Code Sec. 6038D.

STUDY QUESTION

---

2. Which of the following is *not* a reportable specified foreign financial asset?

  a. A financial account maintained by a financial institution organized under U.S. territorial law

  b. A currency swap with a foreign counterparty

  c. Stock issued by an entity under the laws of Guam owned by a bona fide resident there

  d. Any interest in a foreign entity

Reporting Threshold

The FATCA requirements apply when:

- A specified person is required to file an annual return; and
- The aggregate value of the specified person's specified foreign assets exceeds the applicable threshold.

The applicable reporting thresholds for specified foreign financial assets are shown in Table 1.

Table 1. Reporting Thresholds for Application of FATCA Requirements			
Taxpayer Type	Threshold Amount on Last Day of Year Exceeding	or	Threshold Amount at Any Time During the Year Exceeding
Unmarried (or married filing separately) and living in United States	$ 50,000		$ 75,000
Joint filers living in United States	$100,000		$150,000
Single (or married filing separately) filers living abroad	$200,000		$300,000
Joint filers living abroad	$400,000		$600,000

These thresholds are not adjusted for inflation (Treas. Reg. § 1.6038D-2(a)(1) through (4)).

> **COMMENT:** The statute requires reporting only when a person's specified foreign financial assets exceed the threshold dollar amounts (for example, $50,000 on the last day of the tax year for unmarried taxpayers). However, the IRS can prescribe a higher dollar amount for the reporting threshold, which was done in T.D. 9567, which increased the reporting threshold for specified individuals who are qualified individuals under Code Sec. 911(d).

> **COMMENT:** Specified individual taxpayers generally must include the value of all of their specified foreign financial assets, even if they are also reported on another form; however, a specified domestic entity generally excludes the value of any specific foreign financial assets that have been reported on another form.

Valuation. Once the reporting threshold is triggered, specified persons must report the maximum value during the tax year of each specified foreign financial asset reported on Form 8938. Account assets are generally valued at their fair market value (FMV). Thus, the maximum value of a specified foreign financial asset is generally equal to a reasonable estimate of the asset's highest FMV during the tax year. If this amount is less than zero, such as in the case of a foreign mortgage, the value of the asset is treated as zero for the purposes of determining the aggregate value and the maximum value of the specified person's specified foreign financial assets. All values must be determined and reported in U.S. dollars (Treas. Reg. § 1.6038D-5(b)).

Financial accounts. The value of assets held in a financial account maintained by an FFI is included in determining the value of that financial account. A specified person may rely upon periodic account statements provided at least annually to determine a financial account's maximum value, unless the specified person has actual knowledge or reason to know (based on readily accessible information) that the statements do not reflect a reasonable estimate of the maximum account value during the tax year (Treas. Reg. § 1.6038D-5(d)).

COMMENT: The value of particular assets held in a financial account does not have to be separately reported on Form 8938 because that value is included in the value of the account itself.

Other assets. The maximum value of a specified foreign asset that is not held in a financial account maintained by an FFI is generally equal to the value of the asset as of the last day of the tax year. However, this general rule does not apply to a specified person with actual knowledge or reason to know, based on readily accessible information, that the FMV determined as of the last day of the tax year does not reflect a reasonable estimate of the maximum value of the asset during the year—for example, because there is a reason to know that the asset's value declined significantly during the year (Treas. Reg. § 1.6038D-5(c)(4)).

An interest in a foreign pension or deferred compensation plan is reported if the value of the specified foreign financial assets is greater than the reporting threshold that applies. In general, the value of an interest in the foreign pension plan or deferred compensation plan is the FMV of the taxpayer's beneficial interest in the plan on the last day of the year. However, if the taxpayer does not know or have reason to know, based on readily accessible information, the FMV of his or her beneficial interest in the pension or deferred compensation plan on the last day of the year, the maximum value is the value of the cash and/or other property distributed to the taxpayer during the year. This same value is used in determining whether the reporting threshold has been met (Treas. Reg. § 1.6038D-5(f)(3)).

EXAMPLE: James Chatley, an individual taxpayer, has publicly traded foreign stock not held in a financial account, with a fair market value as of the last day of the tax year of $100,000. However, based on daily price information that is readily available, the 52-week high trading price for the stock results in a maximum value of the stock during the tax year of $150,000. If James satisfies the applicable reporting threshold, he must report the maximum value of the foreign stock as $150,000, based on readily available information of the stock's maximum value during the tax year.

Trusts. If the specified person is a beneficiary of a foreign trust, the maximum value of the specified person's interest in the trust is the sum of the FMV—determined as of the last day of the tax year—of all of the currency or other property distributed from the foreign trust during the tax year to the specified person as a beneficiary, plus the value as of the last day of the tax year of the specified person's right as a beneficiary to receive mandatory distributions from the foreign trust. This amount is also used to determine the aggregate value of the specified person's specified foreign financial assets, if the specified person does not know or have reason to know based on readily accessible information the FMV of his or her interest in a foreign trust during the tax year (Treas. Reg. § 1.6038D-5(f)(2)).

Estates, pension plans, and deferred compensation plans. The maximum value of a specified person's interest in a foreign estate, foreign pension plan, or a foreign deferred compensation plan is the FMV, determined as of the last day of the tax year, of the specified person's beneficial interest in the assets of the estate, pension plan, or deferred compensation plan. If the specified person does not know or have reason to know (based on readily accessible information) that value, then the maximum value to be reported, and the value to be included in determining the aggregate value of the specified foreign financial assets, is the FMV, determined as of the last day of the tax year, of the currency and other property distributed during the tax year to the specified person as a beneficiary or participant. If the specified person received no distributions during the tax year and does not know or have reason to know (based on readily accessible information) the FMV of the interest as of the last day of the tax year, the maximum value of the asset is equal to the amount of currency or property distributed to the beneficiary or participant during the taxable year (i.e., zero if no distributions are made) (Treas. Reg. § 1.6038D-5(f)(3)).

Jointly owned interests. The treatment of jointly owned interests depends on the specified person's relationship to the other owner. If the owners are married to each other and one spouse is not a specified person, each spouse includes the entire value of the jointly owned asset to determine the total value of his or her specified foreign financial assets.

If both owners are spouses who file jointly (and, therefore, file a single Form 8938), the total value of the jointly owned asset is taken into account only once in determining the total value of the couple's specified foreign financial assets. If the spouses also file Form 8814, *Parents' Election to Report Child's Interest and Dividends,* to include a child's unearned income on their own return, they also must include the maximum value of the child's specified foreign financial assets in the calculation of their own specified foreign financial assets (Treas. Reg. § 1.6038D-2(b)(3)).

If both owners are spouses who do not file jointly, each includes one-half of the value of the jointly owned assets in his or her own specified foreign financial assets. A spouse who files Form 8814 to include a child's unearned income on his or her own return must include the maximum value of the child's specified foreign financial assets in his or her own specified foreign financial assets.

If the owners are not married to each other, each owner includes the entire value of the jointly owned asset to determine the total value of his or her specified foreign financial assets.

Foreign currency. As mentioned above, all values must be determined and reported in U.S. dollars. The value of a specified foreign financial asset that is denominated in a foreign currency is first determined in the foreign currency prior to conversion into U.S. dollars (that is, independently of exchange rate fluctuations during the year). The asset's foreign currency value is then converted into U.S. dollars at the tax year-end spot rate for converting the foreign currency into U.S. dollars (that is, the rate to purchase U.S. dollars). The U.S. Treasury Department's Financial Management Service foreign currency exchange rate is used to convert the value of a specified foreign financial asset into U.S. dollars. If no such rate is available, another publicly available foreign currency exchange rate may be used to determine an asset's maximum value, but the use of such rate must be disclosed on Form 8938.

STUDY QUESTION

3. Co-owners of a jointly owned interest should list the entire value of the interest on Form 8938 *unless* they are:

    a. Married filing separately

    b. Owners not married to each other

    c. Co-owners who are a parent and minor child using Form 8814

    d. Married owners when one spouse is not a specified person

Penalties

Failure to disclose. A $10,000 penalty applies to any failure to properly furnish the required information. If the failure is not corrected within 90 days after the IRS mails notice of it to the taxpayer, an additional $10,000 penalty applies for each 30-day period (or portion thereof) in which the failure continues after that 90-day period expires. This additional penalty with respect to any failure is limited to $50,000. Married taxpayers who file a joint return are treated as one taxpayer for purposes of the penalty, and their liability for the penalty is joint and several (Treas. Reg. § 1.6038D-8(a), (b), (c)).

For purposes of assessing the penalty, if an individual with multiple financial assets does not provide sufficient information to determine their aggregate value, the IRS presumes that the aggregate value exceeds the reporting threshold. In other words, the IRS presumes that the individual was required to file Form 8938 and, therefore, is liable for penalties for failing to do so (Treas. Reg. § 1.6038D-8(d)).

The penalty is not imposed on any specified person that can show that the failure is due to reasonable cause and not willful neglect. The determination of whether a failure to disclose a specified foreign financial asset on Form 8938 was due to reasonable cause and not due to willful neglect is made on a case-by-case basis, taking into account all pertinent facts and circumstances. The specified person must make an affirmative showing of all the facts alleged as reasonable cause for the failure to disclose (Treas. Reg. § 1.6038D-8(e)).

Accuracy-related penalty. A 40 percent accuracy-related penalty applies to underpayments attributable to transactions involving undisclosed foreign financial assets. *Undisclosed foreign financial assets* are foreign financial assets that are subject to information reporting under various provisions, but for which the required information was not provided by the taxpayer (Treas. Reg. § 1.6038D-8(f)).

Limitations. Reporting failures can also affect the limitations period for assessments. The statute of limitations on tax assessment does not begin to run until the taxpayer provides the required information. In addition, although the IRS normally has a *maximum* of three years to assess tax, it has a *minimum* of three years to assess tax arising from improperly reported specified foreign financial assets. These rules generally apply to the taxpayer's entire tax liability; however, if the taxpayer has reasonable cause for the reporting failures, these rules apply only to items related to the unreported specified foreign financial assets.

Finally, the normal three-year limitations period for assessments is extended to six years for any substantial omission of gross income in excess of $5,000 that is attributable to a specified foreign financial asset. This extension applies even if the taxpayer's specified foreign financial assets:

- Are properly reported;
- Fall below the reporting threshold; or
- Are included in classes of assets that the IRS has excepted from the reporting requirements.

STUDY QUESTION

4. The IRS statute of limitations for assessments may ***not*** be extended if:
   a. The assets that increase gross income more than $5,000 fall in the classes of excepted assets
   b. The specified foreign financial assets with values of more than $5,000 are properly reported
   c. The omitted income amount in question is less than $5,000
   d. The value of the specified foreign financial assets that increase gross income by more than $5,000 falls below the reporting threshold

¶ 105 FBAR REQUIREMENTS

Under the terms of the FBAR requirements, a U.S. person with financial interests in or signature authority over foreign financial accounts generally must file FinCEN Form 114, *Report of Foreign Bank and Financial Accounts* if, at any point during the calendar year, the aggregate value of the accounts exceeds the reporting threshold of $10,000. FBARs must be electronically filed through the BSA e-filing system. For the 2015 tax year FinCEN Form 114 is due June 30, 2016. Beginning with the 2016 tax year, FinCEN Form 114 is due April 15 (*The Surface Transportation and Veterans Health Care Choice Improvement Act of 2015,* H.R. 3236, P.L. 114-41), and filers are able to seek a six-month extension of the deadline.

Those subject to FBAR reporting are:

- U.S. citizens;
- Resident aliens; and
- Entities created, organized, or formed under U.S. laws, including, but not limited to
  - Domestic corporations,
  - Partnerships,
  - Limited liability companies (LLCs),
  - Trusts, and
  - Estates.

The federal tax treatment of a person or entity does not determine whether an FBAR filing is required.

> **COMMENT:** An entity disregarded for federal tax purposes must still file an FBAR if filing is otherwise required.

> **EXAMPLE:** FBARs are required under Title 31 and not under any provisions of the Internal Revenue Code (Title 26). Thus, a single-member LLC, which is a disregarded entity for U.S. tax purposes, must file an FBAR if one is otherwise required.

Interest

A U.S. person can have a financial interest in a foreign account in three situations.

Owner of record or the holder of legal title. A U.S. person has a financial interest in each bank, securities, or other financial account in a foreign country for which that person is the owner of record or holds legal title, regardless of whether the account is maintained for that person's own benefit or for the benefit of others. If an account is maintained in the name of more than one person, each U.S. person in whose name the account is maintained has a financial interest in that account.

Constructive owner. A U.S. person has a financial interest in each bank, securities, or other financial account in a foreign country if the owner of record or holder of legal title is a person acting on behalf of the U.S. person, such as an attorney, agent, or nominee with respect to the account.

Deemed owner. A U.S. person is deemed to have a financial interest in a bank, securities, or other financial account in a foreign country if the owner of record of holder of legal title is:

- A corporation in which the U.S. person owns, directly or indirectly, more than 50 percent of the voting power or the total value of the shares;
- A partnership in which the U.S. person owns, directly or indirectly, more than 50 percent of the profits or capital interest;
- Any other entity, other than a trust, in which the U.S. person owns, directly or indirectly, more than 50 percent of the voting power, total value of the equity interest or assets, or profits interest;
- A trust, if the U.S. person is the trust grantor and has an ownership interest for U.S. federal tax purposes; or
- A trust, if the U.S. person
  - Has a present beneficial interest in more than 50 percent of the assets, or
  - Receives more than 50 percent of the trust's current income (based on the calendar year).

However, a U.S. person does not have a financial interest in a discretionary trust merely because of the person's status as a discretionary beneficiary. Similarly, a remainder interest in a trust is not a present beneficial interest in the trust.

Signature Authority

Qualification of an individual. An individual has *signature or other authority* over an account if the individual has the authority, alone or in conjunction with another, to control the disposition of money, funds, or other assets held in a financial account by direct communication, written or otherwise, to the person with whom the financial account is maintained. An individual also has signature or other authority over an account if the FFI will act upon a direct communication from that individual regarding the disposition of assets in that account. Additionally, an individual has signature or other authority in conjunction with another if the FFI requires a direct communication from more than one individual regarding the disposition of assets in the account.

Exceptions. Exceptions to the FBAR requirements apply to officers and employees of financial institutions that have a federal functional regulator, certain entities that are publicly traded on a U.S. national securities exchange, and certain entities that are otherwise required to register their equity securities with the Securities and Exchange Commission (SEC). These exceptions apply, however, only when the officer or employee has no financial interest in the reportable account.

The exceptions to the FBAR requirements include:

- Bank officers and employees need not report that they have signature or other authority over a foreign financial account if
  - The account is owned or maintained by the bank,
  - The officer or employee has no financial interest in the account, and
  - The bank is examined by the Office of the Comptroller of the Currency, the Board of Governors of the Federal Reserve System, the Federal Deposit Insurance Corporation, the Office of Thrift Supervision, or the National Credit Union Administration;
- Officers and employees of a financial institution that is registered with and examined by the SEC or Commodity Futures Trading Commission (CFTC) need not report that they have signature or other authority over a foreign financial account if
  - The account is owned or maintained by the financial institution, and
  - The officer or employee has no financial interest in the account;

- Officers and employees of an authorized service provider (ASP) need not report that they have signature or other authority over a foreign financial account if

  - The account is owned or maintained by an investment company that is registered with the SEC, and

  - The officer or employee has no financial interest in the account. An ASP is an SEC-registered entity that provides services to a regulated investment company (RIC). Because mutual funds do not have employees of their own, they can use ASPs, such as investment advisors, to conduct their day-to-day operations. Thus, this exception can apply to persons who do not qualify for the exception for RICs, discussed above, but it is limited to the reportable accounts of RICs that are managed by the ASP;

- Officers and employees of an entity with a class of equity securities (or American depository receipts) listed on any U.S. national securities exchange need not report their signature or other authority over the entity's foreign financial accounts if the officer or employee has no financial interest in the accounts. This exception also applies if the American depository receipts are listed on the designated offshore market. In addition, if the entity is a U.S. entity, the officers and employees of any U.S. subsidiary need not report that they have signature or other authority over a foreign financial account of the subsidiary if

  - The officer or employee has no financial interest in the account, and

  - The U.S. subsidiary is named in a consolidated FBAR filed by the parent; and

- Officers and employees of an entity that has a class of equity securities (or American depository receipts in respect of equity securities) registered under Section 12(g) of the *Securities Exchange Act* need not report their signature or other authority over the entity's foreign financial accounts if the officer or employee has no financial interest in the accounts. This exception applies when corporations must register their stock with the SEC and comply with related reporting requirements because of their size in terms of assets and shareholders (currently more than $10 million in assets and more than 500 shareholders of record).

Accounts

An *account* is a formal relationship with a person, including a financial institution, to provide regular services, dealings, and other financial transactions. The length of the time the service is provided does not affect the fact that a formal account relationship has been established. For example, an escrow arrangement can qualify as an account, even if it exists for only a short period of time. However, an account is not established simply by conducting transactions like wiring money or purchasing a money order.

Bank accounts, securities accounts, and other financial accounts are all reportable accounts. *Bank accounts* include savings deposit, demand deposit, checking, and other accounts maintained with persons engaged in a banking business. This includes time deposits such as certificate of deposit accounts (CDs) that allow individuals to deposit funds with a banking institution and redeem the initial amount (along with interest earned) after a prescribed period of time. *Securities accounts* are accounts with persons engaged in the business of buying, selling, holding, or trading stock or other securities.

Other financial accounts include:

- Accounts with persons in the business of accepting deposits as a financial agency;
- Insurance or annuity policies with cash value;

- Accounts with persons who act as brokers or dealers for futures or options transactions in commodities that are on or subject to the rules of a commodity exchange or association;
- Accounts with mutual funds or similar pooled funds that issue shares that are available to the general public and have a regular net asset value determination and regular redemptions; and
- Other investment funds.

COMMENT: The inclusion of "accounts with persons in the business of accepting deposits as a financial agency" is intended to ensure that deposit accounts and similar arrangements are covered by the reporting requirements, despite international differences in terminology, financial institution operations, and legal frameworks.

COMMENT: When a reportable account is an insurance policy with cash value, the owner of the policy, not the beneficiary, is responsible for filing the FBAR.

COMMENT: A federal district court (***U.S. v. J.C. Hom,*** DC Calif., 2014-1 ustc ¶ 50,307) has held that because foreign poker websites functioned for a U.S. poker player as banks, his online accounts with them were reportable.

Exceptions. Certain accounts are specifically exempted from the reporting requirements. For example, no reporting is required with respect to correspondent accounts that are maintained by banks and used solely for bank-to-bank settlements.

Several other types of accounts are excluded from the reporting requirements based on the governmental status and functions of the entities and agencies involved.

The reporting requirements do not apply to:

- Accounts of an international financial institution that includes the United States as a member;
- Accounts in a U.S. military banking facility or U.S. military finance facility operated by a U.S. financial institution designated by the U.S. government to serve U.S. government installations abroad;
- Accounts of a department or agency of the United States, an Indian tribe, or any state or its political subdivisions, or a wholly owned entity, agency, or instrumentality of any of the foregoing, including
  - An employee retirement or welfare benefit plan of a governmental entity, and
  - A college or university that is an agency of, an instrumentality of, owned by, or operated by a governmental entity; and
- Accounts of an entity that is established under the laws of, and exercises governmental authority on behalf of, the United States, an Indian tribe, any state or its political subdivision, or any intergovernmental compact among states and/or Indian tribes. An entity generally exercises governmental authority only if it has taxing, police, and/or eminent domain powers.

Foreign accounts. A *foreign country* is any area outside the geographical boundaries of the United States. The *United States* for FBAR purposes includes the States, the District of Columbia, all U.S. territories and possessions, and the Indian lands as defined in the *Indian Gaming Regulatory Act.* A *foreign financial account* is a reportable account located outside the United States. For instance, an account with a U.S. bank is a foreign financial account if it is maintained in a branch of the bank that is physically located outside the United States. Conversely, an account with a foreign bank is not a foreign account if it is maintained in a bank branch that is physically located in the United

States. The mere fact that an account may contain holdings or assets of foreign entities does not mean the account is foreign, as long as the account is maintained with a financial institution in the United States.

EXAMPLE: Joshua Bloom, a U.S. citizen, has an account with a securities broker located in New York. He occasionally uses this account to purchase securities of foreign companies. Because Joshua maintains his securities account with a financial institution in the United States, the account is not a foreign account even though it contains foreign securities.

COMMENT: A federal district court (***U.S. v. J.C. Hom,*** DC Calif., 2014-1 ustc ¶ 50,307) has held that digital online accounts with poker websites were located in the foreign countries where the websites that created and managed the accounts were located, not the geographic location of the funds. Thus, it was irrelevant where the poker websites opened their own accounts.

In an omnibus account, a U.S. institution acts as the global custodian for a U.S. person's foreign assets and creates pooled cash and securities accounts in the non-U.S. market to hold assets for multiple investors. The omnibus account is in the name of the global custodian. When the U.S. person has no legal right to the account and cannot directly reach the foreign assets in it, the U.S. person is treated as maintaining an account with a financial institution located in the United States.

An omnibus account with a financial institution located in the United States is not a reportable foreign account if the U.S. person:

- Does not have any legal right to the account; and
- Can access foreign holdings in the account only through the U.S. institution.

COMMENT: A custodial arrangement that permits the U.S. person to have direct access to foreign assets maintained at a foreign institution is a reportable foreign financial account.

Valuation

An account's maximum value is a reasonable approximation of the greatest value of currency or nonmonetary assets in the account during the year. Periodic account statements can establish the maximum value of an account, as long as the statements fairly reflect that value during the calendar year. This includes a statement that provides the account value at the end of the statement period, as long as it is a bona fide statement prepared in the ordinary course of business.

Account value is determined in the currency of the account. Any value stated in foreign currency must be translated into U.S. currency by using the Treasury's Financial Management Service Rate from the last day of the calendar year. If no such rate is available, the FBAR filer must use another verifiable exchange rate and identify its source. If the currency is of a country that uses multiple exchange rates, the filer must use the one that would apply if the currency in the account were converted into U.S. dollars on the last day of the calendar year.

Penalties

The civil penalty for *willfully* failing to file an FBAR may be as high as the greater of $100,000 or 50 percent of the total balance of the foreign account per violation. *Nonwillful* violations that the IRS determines were not due to reasonable cause are subject to a $10,000 penalty per violation.

The criminal penalties are also harsh. For example, a person who fails to file a tax return is subject to a prison term of up to one year and a fine of up to $100,000. Willfully failing to file an FBAR and willfully filing a false FBAR are both violations that are subject to criminal penalties under U.S. tax law.

Possible criminal charges related to tax matters include tax evasion (Code Sec. 7201), filing a false return (Code Sec. 7206(1)), and failure to file an income tax return (Code Sec. 7203). Willfully failing to file an FBAR and willfully filing a false FBAR are both violations that are subject to criminal penalties under 31 U.S.C. § 5322. Additional possible criminal charges include conspiracy to defraud the government with respect to claims (18 U.S.C. § 286) and conspiracy to commit offense or to defraud the United States (18 U.S.C. § 371).

Table 2 summarizes penalties associated with the criminal charges under FBAR requirements.

Table 2. Comparative Prison Terms and Fines for Violating Tax Laws and FBAR Requirements		
Violation	Maximum Prison Term	Maximum Fine
Tax evasion	5 years	$250,000
Filing false return	3 years	$250,000
Failing to file an FBAR	10 years	$500,000
Conspiracy to defraud government for claims	10 years	$250,000
Defrauding government	5 years	$250,000

STUDY QUESTION

5. Which individual violation of the tax reporting laws potentially carries the highest maximum fine?

    a. Tax evasion

    b. Filing a false return

    c. Failing to file an FBAR

    d. Defrauding the government

¶ 106 OFFSHORE VOLUNTARY DISCLOSURE PROGRAM

Taxpayers who have failed to previously to report their taxable income—including failing to disclose their interests in foreign accounts (and failing to file the applicable FBARs)—but who have not been contacted by the IRS may consider filing delinquent or amended income tax returns or otherwise notifying the IRS of the reason for their noncompliance.

Historically, voluntary disclosure programs were put in place by the IRS in order to give those taxpayers who had not been fully compliant a method of coming forward without fear of criminal prosecution. The theory behind the voluntary disclosure programs makes sense, as it would be impossible for the IRS to catch every taxpayer who is noncompliant; the better approach is to entice them to come forward voluntarily. Their incentive, as stated, is no criminal prosecution and perhaps a promise of reduced taxes and related penalties/interest if the noncompliant taxpayer agrees to come forward and file all delinquent returns.

Offshore Voluntary Disclosure Program for 2016

The IRS continues to offer the Offshore Voluntary Disclosure Program (OVDP) in 2016. By way of background, the IRS initially offered the OVDP for the period March 2009 through October 2009. The 2009 OVDP was followed by another OVDP that ran from

February 2011 through September 2011. Finally, the IRS announced an OVDP beginning in June 2012 (2012 OVDP) without a specific end date and subject to change and/or closure. In 2014 the IRS made additional amendments to the OVDP.

The common objective of each OVDP is to encourage taxpayers to report offshore accounts by requiring taxpayers to file amended returns, information returns, and delinquent FBARs related to foreign accounts; and pay tax, interest, and penalties under a specific framework in exchange for relief from criminal prosecution. The IRS has disclosed that since the launch of the first program, more than 54,000 taxpayers have become compliant voluntarily, paying about $8 billion in taxes, interest, and penalties.

Because the purpose of the OVDP is to provide a way for taxpayers who did not report taxable income in the past to come forward voluntarily and resolve their tax matters, a taxpayer who has properly reported all of his or her taxable income but not filed FBARs is not eligible for the OVDP. These taxpayers should consider making a quiet disclosure by filing their FBARs and may follow the delinquent FBAR submission procedures provided by the IRS on its website. The IRS will not impose a penalty for the failure to file the delinquent FBARs if the taxpayer properly reported on U.S. tax returns and paid all tax on the income from the foreign financial accounts (as reported on the delinquent FBARs), and the taxpayer had not previously been contacted regarding an income tax examination or a request for delinquent returns for the years for which the delinquent FBARs are submitted.

Voluntary disclosure is required to be complete, accurate, and truthful. Consequently, in addition to disclosing all items relating to foreign financial accounts, OVDP submissions must correct any previously unreported income from domestic sources; inappropriate deductions or credits claimed; or other incomplete, inaccurate, or untruthful items on the originally filed returns. The offshore penalty structure only resolves liabilities and penalties related to offshore noncompliance. Domestic portions of a voluntary disclosure are subject to examination.

For 2016 the OVDP penalty framework requires participants to:

- Provide all required documents;
- File both amended returns (or original tax returns if delinquent) and FBARs for the past eight years;
- Pay the appropriate tax and interest;
- Pay a 20 percent accuracy-related penalty on such tax;
- Cooperate in the voluntary disclosure process, including
  - Providing information on foreign accounts and assets, institutions, and facilitators, and
  - Assigning agreements to extend the period of time for assessing Title 26 liabilities and FBAR penalties;
- Pay a failure-to-file penalty and/or failure-to-pay penalty, if applicable; and
- Pay—in lieu of all other penalties that may apply to the undisclosed foreign accounts, assets and entities, including FBAR and offshore-related information return penalties and tax liabilities for years prior to the voluntary disclosure period—a miscellaneous Title 26 offshore penalty equal to 27.5 percent (or 50 percent in some circumstances) of the highest aggregate value of OVDP assets as defined (in FAQ 35) during the period covered by the voluntary disclosure.

Under the OVDP, as modified by the June 2014 amendments, the 27.5 percent offshore penalty may be 50 percent contingent upon the bank and the taxpayer's timing. In circumstances when the taxpayer's offshore account(s) are held by a bank that is under investigation by the IRS or the Department of Justice (DOJ) prior to the taxpayer's OVDP application submission, the IRS may be more likely to apply the higher penalty rate.

In fact, the IRS has pointed out that, balanced against the modified OVDP program, the government change will bolster its continued effort to combat the misuse of offshore assets. Working closely with the DOJ, the IRS will continue to investigate FFIs that may have assisted U.S. taxpayers in avoiding their tax filing and payment obligations, whereas, on July 1, 2014, the new information reporting regime resulting from FATCA went into effect, and FFIs began to report to the IRS the foreign accounts held by U.S. persons.

Streamlined procedure. Effective as of September 1, 2012, a special procedure for U.S. citizens living abroad was put into place, known as the *streamlined procedure*. The procedure was launched with the objective of bringing U.S. citizens living overseas into compliance with tax obligations. This procedure was only applicable to U.S. taxpayers living abroad who represent a low risk of tax evasion ($1,500 liability threshold) and who have not filed tax returns since 2009.

In 2014, the IRS made significant changes to the streamlined filing compliance procedures, eliminating the low-risk threshold and $1,500 liability threshold. Going forward, taxpayers residing within (domestic) and outside (foreign) of the U.S. who had not willfully failed to disclose their offshore assets and income were allowed to participate in the streamlined procedures by certifying under penalty of perjury that their previous failures to comply were due to nonwillful conduct.

Under the domestic and foreign streamlined procedure programs, taxpayers who have unreported foreign financial accounts must file information returns for the last three years (and six years of FBARs) and remit payment of income tax and interest for each such tax year.

For eligible taxpayers residing outside the United States and participating in the foreign streamlined program, all penalties are to be waived. For eligible U.S. taxpayers residing in the United States and participating in the domestic streamlined program, the only penalty will be a miscellaneous offshore penalty equal to 5 percent of the foreign financial assets that gave rise to the tax compliance issue.

¶ 107 BEPS PROJECT

The Organisation for Economic Cooperation and Development (OECD) originated in 1960 when 18 European countries plus the United States and Canada joined forces to create an organization dedicated to economic development. Currently, 34 member countries worldwide regularly turn to one another to identify problems, discuss and analyze them, and promote policies to solve them.

The OECD base erosion and profit shifting (BEPS) project came into being on February 12, 2013, when the OECD's first formal report on the subject, "Addressing Base Erosion and Profit Shifting," was published. It was noted in that report that due to imperfect interaction between nations' tax regimes, multinationals had been permitted to legitimately structure their tax affairs using profit-shifting arrangements to pay minimal rates of tax, limiting their exposure to corporate tax rates as high as 30 percent, faced by fiscally immobile businesses in some OECD member states. The report was for all intents and purposes a call for the world's governments to come together and tackle the issue of aggressive corporate tax avoidance once and for all.

In July 2013 the OECD released the BEPS Action Plan, consisting of 15 specific actions designed to give governments the domestic and international mechanisms to effectively close loopholes in the international tax system. They included:

- Action 1: Address the challenges of the digital economy
- Action 2: Neutralize the effects of hybrid mismatch arrangements
- Action 3: Strengthen controlled foreign company rules
- Action 4: Limit base erosion via interest deductions and other financial payments
- Action 5: Counter harmful tax practices more effectively, taking into account transparency and substance
- Action 6: Prevent treaty abuse
- Action 7: Prevent the artificial avoidance of PE status
- Action 8: Assure that transfer pricing outcomes are in line with value creation/ intangibles
- Action 9: Assure that transfer pricing outcomes are in line with value creation/ risks and capital
- Action 10: Assure that transfer pricing outcomes are in line with value creation/ other high-risk transactions
- Action 11: Establish methodologies to collect and analyze data on BEPS and the actions to address it
- Action 12: Require taxpayers to disclose their aggressive tax planning arrangements
- Action 13: Re-examine transfer pricing documentation
- Action 14: Make dispute resolution mechanisms more effective
- Action 15: Develop a multilateral instrument

This then called for the delivery of seven actions by September 2014 and included proposals regarding Action 1, Action 2, Action 5, Action 6, Action 8, Action 13, and Action 15. The September 2014 BEPS "outputs," as the OECD termed these series of reports, were delivered in an interim form and, although agreed to, were not finalized as they may be impacted by some of the decisions to be taken with respect to the 2015 "deliverables," with which they interact. It was intended that the 2014 outputs would be consolidated with the remaining 2015 deliverables to ensure a coherent package, scheduled to be delivered to the G20 Finance Ministers in October 2015, together with a plan for follow-up work and a timetable for their implementation.

The 2015 deliverables included measures regarding Action 3, Action 4, Action 7, Action 9, Action 10, Action 11, Action 12, and Action 14.

In February 2015, OECD and G20 countries agreed on three key elements to enable implementation of the BEPS project, including:

- A mandate to launch negotiations on a multilateral instrument to streamline implementation of tax treaty-related BEPS measures (Action 15);
- An implementation package for country-by-country reporting in 2016 and a related government-to-government exchange mechanism to start in 2017 (Action 13); and
- Criteria to assess whether preferential treatment regimes for intellectual property (patent boxes) are harmful or not (Action 5).

In June 2016 in an effort to boost transparency in international tax and country by country reporting, the OECD has focused on ensuring consistent implementation of the BEPS package, including new transfer pricing reporting standards under Action 13 of the BEPS Action Plan. In that regard, additional guidance was released, including the following:

- Guidance on the application of country by country (CbC) reporting to partnerships;
- Transitional filing options for multinational enterprises (MNEs) that voluntarily file in the parent jurisdiction;
- Guidance on the application of CbC reporting to investment funds; and,
- The impact of exchange rate fluctuations on the agreed EUR 750 million filing threshold for MNE groups.

If the BEPS project is to be successful, the recommendations will have to be implemented in all countries, not just the advanced economies that are members of the OECD. The problem is that many emerging and developing economies lack the resources and technical and administrative capacity to make the necessary changes. So-called toolkits have been developed by the OECD to assist developing economies to implement BEPS action items, in cooperation with other international bodies and regional tax organizations. These toolkits contain reports, guidance, model legislation, "train the trainers" materials, and other tools to support capacity building.

When the OECD announced the ambitious timetables for the BEPS project, many observers must have wondered whether the OECD had bitten off far more than it can chew because it is attempting to rewrite a body of international tax rules built up in incoherent fashion largely from the middle of the 20th century, in less than two years.

> **COMMENT:** The effect of the BEPS project on the U.S. tax revenues and jobs remains to be seen. The Congressional Research Service published a report, "Corporate Tax Base Erosion and Profit Shifting: An Examination of the Data," on the impact of BEPS on U.S. tax revenues. The report notes implications for American corporations even if the United States does not adopt the OECD's recommendations.

Regardless of whether the OECD fails to meet its objectives—it looks on course to complete the project on time—change in international business and taxation is coming one way or another. Indeed, with some governments preempting the final results of the BEPS work, change is already happening.

STUDY QUESTION

6. Which of the following is *not* an action item of the OECD's BEPS project?
   a. Preventing treaty abuse
   b. Making dispute resolution mechanisms more effective
   c. Strengthening controlled foreign company rules
   d. Preventing the permanent establishment status

¶ 108 CONCLUSION

As Congress and the IRS continue to focus on the reporting of income and assets held abroad, taxpayers must carefully examine the different reporting requirements set forth above to determine whether the rules apply to the taxpayers' foreign assets and financial interests and then take the necessary steps to comply in order to avoid the penalties.

FATCA generally requires certain U.S. taxpayers (specified individuals) holding foreign financial assets with an aggregate value exceeding $50,000 to report certain information about those assets on a Form 8938. This form must be attached to the taxpayer's annual tax return. Reporting applies for assets held in taxable years beginning after March 18, 2010. Failure to report foreign financial assets on Form 8938 may result in a penalty of $10,000 (and an additional penalty up to $50,000 for continued failure after IRS notification). Additionally, underpayments of tax attributable to undisclosed foreign financial assets will be subject to an additional substantial understatement penalty of up to 40 percent for certain transactions that should have been reported under the applicable code sections.

In addition to the complying with the FATCA reporting requirements, taxpayers also may be required to file FinCEN Form 114 (FBAR). The FATCA requirements may overlap with and affect the same assets as the FBAR requirements, but they apply separately. The reporting threshold for FBAR is lower than that for FATCA. For FBAR purposes, if at any point during the calendar year the aggregate value of the accounts exceeds $10,000, an FBAR must be filed. Willfully failing to file an FBAR may result in civil penalties as high as the greater of $100,000 or 50 percent of the total balance of the foreign account per violation. Nonwillful violations that the IRS determines were not due to reasonable cause are subject to a $10,000 penalty per violation. Criminal penalties, including fines and jail time, may also apply.

Moreover, taxpayers that were not previously in compliance must examine the options available to them, such as the OVDP, and make a determination regarding coming into compliance. Based on recent changes and continual enforcement efforts, it is clear that both the IRS and Congress will continue to maintain their focus on using these new reporting requirements to locate and collect monies owed by U.S. taxpayers.

Finally, the impact of the BEPS project on international business and taxation remains to be seen. There may be implications for American corporations even if the United States does not adopt the OECD's recommendations.

MODULE 1: BUSINESS COMPLIANCE ISSUES FOR 2017—Chapter 2: Navigating IRS's Redesigned LB&I Division

¶ 201 WELCOME

To improve its effectiveness, the IRS Large Business and International (LB&I) Division has undergone a major reorganization of its structure and operations. At the same time, LB&I has transformed its examination procedures so that its exam function will have a greater impact on compliance. This chapter takes a closer look at these developments.

¶ 202 LEARNING OBJECTIVES

Upon completion of this chapter, you will be able to:

- Recognize LB&I's goals and ideas for reorganizing its structure and revising its examination process;
- Identify recent changes made by LB&I to its structure and operations; and
- Identify important changes made to LB&I's examination function.

¶ 203 INTRODUCTION

The IRS is divided into four divisions that are based on the type of taxpayers each division oversees. Each division is headed by a commissioner. The Large Business and International Division (LB&I) oversees corporations, Subchapter S corporations, partnerships, and other entities with assets greater than $10 million. Originally known as the Large and Mid-Size Business Division (LMSB), LB&I has changed its structure in the past with the goal of improving its effectiveness. LB&I changed its name in October 2010 to reflect its growing emphasis on multinational corporations and international taxation.

LB&I's most recent reorganization began in October 2015, the beginning of fiscal year (FY) 2016 for the IRS and its components. This reorganization finds LB&I seeking to maximize its impact on large businesses as resources tighten. Changes to its examination process, which LB&I announced in February 2016, similarly seek to maximize the division's impact on its constituent businesses in the realm of tax compliance.

¶ 204 CURRENT STATE

The IRS in general and LB&I more specifically are enduring lean times. Congress, with a majority hostile to the agency, has made sharp cuts in the IRS's budget (more than $1 billion since 2010). The IRS's FY 2015 budget was $10.9 billion, its lowest since 2007. The FY 2016 budget would have been just as low, until Congress belatedly appropriated $290 million that it directed to taxpayer service (especially telephone assistance), the detection of refund fraud and identity theft, and improving cybersecurity.

This special Congressional funding targeted areas that the IRS is particularly concerned about. The IRS is looking for mechanisms to maintain its mission in the face of declining resources, smaller budgets, and increasing complexity. This mission now includes combatting tax identity theft, providing comprehensive taxpayer services, and improving cybersecurity. IRS computer systems need upgrading and replacing—newer systems could more effectively deal with computer hacking and taxpayer security—but budget cuts are a problem. Funding under a FY 2017 budget likely will continue to present challenges.

IRS Staffing

As a result of these budget problems, the IRS has fewer employees and fewer resources. The IRS's total staffing level has declined from 100,000 employees in 2010 to 85,000 in 2016. As Congress has restricted new hiring, the IRS workforce has begun to age. Significant percentages of managers and executives are becoming eligible to retire (41 and 61 percent, respectively). It is estimated that the overall workforce eligible to retire will increase from 25 percent in 2016 to 40 percent by 2019. This factor, along with the inability to hire, threatens to create a "brain drain" that will deprive the IRS of the personnel and new blood needed to continue tax operations.

At the enforcement level, the overall number of revenue agents (auditors), revenue officers (collections), and criminal investigators has declined at least 15 percent since 2010. The number of appeals officers, who play an important part in resolving taxpayer disputes with the IRS, is down by 20 percent since 2010.

Upgrades in IRS technology have also slowed. These declines are occurring at the same time that the IRS's responsibilities have broadened (most notably, health care insurance issues under the Affordable Care Act and international tax compliance under the *Foreign Account Tax Compliance Act* (FATCA)) and the number of taxpayers filing returns has increased. In some areas, IRS audit coverage is low and has also declined. Large business audits have declined by 22 percent in the most recent year.

LBI staffing and operations. LB&I's staffing has dropped from 7,500 in 2010 to 5,200 at the beginning of fiscal year 2016, because of employees who have retired or left the agency to move into private sector jobs. The 5,200 positions include 2,800 examiners ("revenue agents") trained in domestic issues and 500 trained in international issues. This distribution fails to reflect the view that international tax issues can generate more revenue than domestic issues.

> **COMMENT:** LB&I's current staffing includes 760 employees in its leadership team, 129 economists, and 237 people in its engineering program.

LB&I has also struggled because its responsibilities cover the largest corporations and enterprises, including multinational businesses that have multiple entities and that engage in some of the most complicated activities. LB&I has stated that "the tax returns that LB&I examines are among the most complex returns the IRS receives." The LB&I Concept of Operations (ConOps) stated that "LB&I is pursuing its mission in an increasingly difficult environment in which its budget and resources are shrinking, tax laws are growing more complex, and taxpayers are continuing to evolve."

Concept of Operations

A ConOps is a document describing the desirable characteristics of an organization's system in the future. It is developed from the viewpoint of an individual who will use that system. A ConOps generally evolves from a concept and describes how a set of capabilities may be used to achieve desired objectives. The ConOps is designed to communicate the system's characteristics to stakeholders. ConOps are widely used by government, business, and other enterprises.

ConOps documents generally include the following:

- A statement of goals and objectives;
- Strategies, tactics, policies, and constraints that affect the system;

- Interactions among stakeholders, including the organization's individuals and structures;
- A clear statement of responsibilities and delegated authorities;
- Specific operational processes for the system; and
- Processes for initiating, developing, maintaining, and revising the system.

IRS concept of operations. The IRS ConOps is a vision for where the IRS should be in five years. The IRS Internal Revenue Manual (IRM), Section 2.15.1, describes the objectives of a ConOps. The IRM provides that IRS organizations will use the business ConOps as a strategic framework to express their Future State Initiative's vision. An organization's ConOps is typically a key driver of changes to any of the six domains of change—organization, location, business process, data, applications, and/or technology. The IRS's ConOps identifies the following themes for the IRS of the future:

- Data-centric operations—continuously improve operations and decision making with universal access to data (both internally and externally sourced) and incorporation of robust data analytics;
- A simplified taxpayer experience—empower taxpayers, improve customer experience, and increase taxpayer satisfaction by providing convenient and accessible compliance knowledge and tools;
- Expanded partnerships with the tax community;
- Compliance risk-focused operations—focus operations on emerging and significant compliance risks, preventing future noncompliance and maintaining flexible business operations;
- Flexible and well-supported workforce; and
- Strategic workload allocation—efficiently match work to appropriate resources through automated systems and filters, incorporating an understanding of workforce capabilities and capacities.

This process incorporates the IRS's Future State Initiative, which aims to prepare the IRS to adapt to the changing needs of taxpayers and the tax community. The focus of the IRS's Future State Initiative is on how to provide taxpayers with the services they need in a way that works for them, including a more complete online experience, with the same level of service as when dealing with a financial institution or a retailer. The idea is that taxpayers would have an account with the IRS where they could log in securely, get information about their account, and interact with the IRS. The approach could free up limited IRS personnel resources and could help IRS act more quickly and effectively on the enforcement side.

> **COMMENT:** The IRS Taxpayer Advocate has criticized the IRS ConOps for viewing the IRS primarily as an enforcement agency, with taxpayer service receiving less emphasis. The advocate notes that 98 percent of all tax revenue collected by the IRS is paid voluntarily and timely; less than 2 percent is collected through enforcement action.

LB&I concept of operations. Consistent with the Future State Initiative, the IRS's four operating divisions are making changes with the goals of improving taxpayer service, better equipping employees, and achieving better compliance outcomes. The LB&I ConOps actually dates back to December 31, 2014, a precursor to the changes being made in 2015 and 2016. The division's ConOps provides that in order for LB&I work to matter more than it does today, the division will need to better identify and prioritize areas of compliance risk to more effectively address taxpayer compliance. The ConOps includes a chart describing the division's overall process. It states that based on information obtained internally and externally, the division aims to analyze risk; move toward an outcome-driven approach that prioritizes risk areas and associated issues; plan, design, and build campaigns; select work; select the best-suited resources (including knowledge management) and provide the right support necessary to execute work; and execute campaigns. The process also includes using continuous feedback to achieve improvement.

Risk identification. Risk identification will not merely be based on information in tax returns, a method that makes it difficult to identify emerging issues and risk areas. Instead, the division will take a more proactive outward-looking approach using data analytics from multiple sources. The division believes that this approach will also improve LB&I's ability to provide earlier guidance and direction on issues to taxpayers.

Campaigns. Campaign design and planning will include centralized work selection, described as an approach for centrally selecting work, including automated filtering and manual classification processes. At the same time, the division will centralize issue selection to decide what issues to address and how to address them. Compliance operations will also continue to include a limited issue examinations program.

> **COMMENT:** LB&I's Office of Compliance Planning and Analytics will be part of this process.

The LB&I ConOps: presents the future of compliance and service for LB&I, and charts a path forward to change the way LB&I is structured; changes the way LB&I selects work; develops better training and career paths and better tools and support; and defines clearly the compliance goals of all LB&I work. LB&I's guiding principles for executing its mission of fair and effective tax administration are:

- Maintain a flexible, well-trained workforce—cultivate an environment of continuous learning to support a flexible workforce with focused training, foundational skill sets, specialized knowledge, and dynamic tools;
- Select better work—use data analytics and examiner feedback to select better work with intended compliance outcomes;
- Use an effective mix of treatment stream options—employ an integrated set of tailored treatment streams to improve flexibility to address current and emerging issues and achieve compliance outcomes; and
- Employ a robust feedback loop—drive continual collection and analysis of data and feedback to enhance ability to focus, plan, and execute work, and promote innovation and feedback-based improvement.

STUDY QUESTION

1. The Future State Initiative of the LB&I Division:
   a. Aims to prepare the IRS to adapt to the changing needs of taxpayers and the tax community
   b. Resulted from increases in LB&I staffing and budget since 2010
   c. Resulted from recent increases in the number of large business audits
   d. Is intended to decentralize campaign design and planning for large organization auditing

LB&I FY 2016 Focus

The LB&I FY 2016 Focus Guide describes LB&I's reorganization, priorities for FY 2016, and some ideas behind the reorganization. The guide, dated January 2016, is presented as a statement from LB&I Commissioner Douglas O'Donnell to LB&I employees. O'Donnell indicates that the strategy for the division's future state is in place and that LB&I will develop new priorities through FY 2016 that support the strategy.

> **COMMENT:** The LB&I FY 2017 focus is expected to continue FY 2016 priorities with fine tuning of processes revised as experience requires and as budget restraints necessitate.

LB&I's future state will move from a model that focused on returns and evaluated their audit potential based upon risk (or that directly assigned returns under the Coordinated Industry Case (CIC) program of continuous audit). The challenge is to determine where to devote LB&I's resources, particularly its personnel, the document states. The new model will use campaigns that target areas of noncompliance, set compliance goals for the targeted areas, and create specific plans to achieve that compliance. LB&I is changing its approach to continuous audit (and is removing the CIC designation), although it will continue to select some large taxpayers for audit. LB&I will use a centralized issue selection approach as it moves toward the future state of using campaigns.

To accomplish this, LB&I will need to adjust processes, share information, and collaborate (internally). It will change its structure to move toward a future state that provides flexibility for the most efficient and effective use of resources. The structure will support LB&I's core guiding principles (described in the paragraph above).

> **COMMENT:** "The new structure reflects one LB&I," the focus guide states.

FY 2016 priorities. The Focus Guide describes LB&I's priorities for FY 2016. These include: structural change; practice areas; knowledge management; examination process improvement; workload selection; campaigns; offshore compliance; and the *Foreign Account Tax Compliance Act* (FATCA), enterprise risk management (ERM), and employee engagement. *Structural change* refers to execution of LB&I's future structure and operations, "to increase efficiency and better serve taxpayers." Workload selection includes ongoing efforts to use centralized classification and workload selection, including a CIC pilot and issue-focused filtering projects.

Employee engagement. The division seeks to encourage an engaged workforce. LB&I collected data and feedback in a 2015 survey on employees' view of their job, manager, and leadership that suggested a need for more engagement. It seeks to increase employee engagement by sharing information through LB&I's Getting It Right Together website, two-way communications, town hall meetings, and other methods.

LB&I knowledge management. LB&I's goals for issue management are to:

- Identify and catalogue the knowledge base necessary to identify and address compliance issues among the population of LB&I filers;
- Develop a comprehensive training strategy for employees throughout their careers;
- Leverage resources more efficiently by identifying skills best suited to accomplish needed tasks and to promote knowledge-sharing and transfer of skills; and
- Continue to pilot processes that better match available resources with identified issues.

LB&I has abandoned its tiered issue approach and continues to move a from taxpayer-focused exams focus to issue-focused examinations. Commentators note that LB&I's evolution toward an issue focus is reflected by LB&I's use of Issue Practice Groups (IPGs) and International Practice Networks (IPNs)—IPGs for domestic issues, IPNs for international issues. IPGs and IPNs are designed to provide examination teams with the technical advice they need, and to foster effective collaboration and the sharing of knowledge and expertise across LB&I and Chief Counsel. LB&I has viewed IPGs and IPNs as a better mechanism for balancing the need for consistency with the recognition that there is no single approach to examining and resolving issues.

> **COMMENT:** Despite their apparent usefulness, LB&I officials have suggested that the use of IPNs and IPGs may change or be eliminated in the reorganization. Another possibility is that IPGs and IPNs will be renamed "practice networks" and continue to be used.

Since December 2014, LB&I has been issuing and using international practice units (IPUs) as an important knowledge management tool that provides information to examiners and other employees. IPUs can be basic educational tools for IRS agents. They discuss a fact pattern and provide a framework for agents to determine whether there are issues to examine. IPUs can run from 10 to 50 pages, sometimes more. According to the IRS, IPUs serve as both job aids and training materials on international issues, providing information on general international tax concepts as well as information about specific types of transactions. The IRS has cautioned that IPUs are not official pronouncements of law and cannot be used, cited, or relied upon officially.

Types of IPUs include process units, transaction units, and concept units. Concept units are general explanations of an area of the tax law. They do not provide instructions for audits, unlike other types of IPUs. Transaction units include an issue and transaction overview, a summary of potential issues, and audit steps. Process units include a process overview, summary of process steps, and other considerations and impacts to be audited.

FATCA and offshore compliance. Offshore compliance and FATCA oversight are priorities in FY 2016. FATCA efforts focus on U.S. taxpayers with bank accounts and investments overseas. LB&I's goals for FATCA include exchanging FATCA information with other countries, participating in multilateral dialogues, analyzing data to identify unreported or underreported income, ensuring compliance by U.S. and foreign financial institutions with reporting and withholding requirements, and mitigating fraudulent and erroneous refund claims.

STUDY QUESTION

---

2. The LB&I Division's new issue management goals:

    a. Are centered on taxpayer-focused exams

    b. Abandon the use of international practice units

    c. Reflect issue-focused examinations using IPGs and IPNs

    d. Downplay the focus on FATCA and international financial accounts

---

¶ 205 PRIOR LB&I STRUCTURE

Formerly, LB&I divided its taxpayers into industry groups that, in its view, shared economic characteristics, geographical locations, and tax issues. The division believed this system would improve managerial efficiency and reduce costs. The industry groups included Communications, Technology & Media (CTM), headquartered in the western United States; Financial Services, located in New York; Heavy Manufacturing & Transportation (HMT), located in the eastern United States; Natural Resources & Construction (NRC), located in the South; Retailers, Food, Pharmaceutical & Healthcare (RFPH), located in the Midwest; and Global High Wealth. Each group had a director located in the headquarters area for that group.

The LB&I commissioner directly managed three positions: the director for Pre-Filing & Technical Guidance (PFTG), the deputy commissioner (International), and the deputy commissioner (Operations). The domestic and international functions within LB&I were under two separate deputy commissioners. Having a deputy commissioner (international) reflected LB&I's emphasis on the importance of international taxation.

¶ 206 NEW STRUCTURE

Top Leadership

Under the new structure, LB&I has a single deputy commissioner, currently Rosemary Sereti, who reports to the LB&I commissioner, Douglas O'Donnell. There no longer is a separate deputy commissioner (International) or deputy commissioner (Operations). This change reflects LB&I's renewed emphasis on a single unified organization, rather than an organization with an emphasis split between domestic and international taxation.

Reporting to the single deputy commissioner are two assistant deputy commissioners (ADCs), one for International and one for Compliance Integration. The latter reflects the reorganization of the compliance function. These two positions are currently held by Theodore Setzer (located in New York) and David Horton (located in Downers Grove, Illinois), respectively. The ADC International will act as the U.S. Competent Authority. The ADC Compliance Integration will oversee compliance campaigns and supervise two important compliance-related operations, the director, Data Solutions, and the director, Compliance Planning and Analytics. These two offices will be crucial to identifying issues to be developed as campaigns, among other functions. The Compliance Planning office will centralize workload selection into one office.

> **COMMENT:** With the highest international position now at the ADC level, LB&I's international function will have input into the handling of cases, but not control. Cases will be under one umbrella. The international function will be more a part of the overall organization.

Another position reporting directly to the deputy commissioner is the director of Program and Business Solutions, who will address technology issues. This office supervises the director, Technology and Program Solutions, and the director, Resource Solutions. These offices will be crucial to the structural reorganization and the changes to the examination process, which will each require reallocations of personnel and other resources to reflect the new way of doing business.

Like the other three Business Operating Divisions, LB&I will continue to have a division counsel in charge of field attorneys who provide advice to the division leadership and to its field operations. It is unclear whether division counsel will need to realign to match the new structure. Previously, there were five area counsel, one for each of the five industry groups. Area counsel could be assigned to one or more practice areas, either subject matter and geographical.

> **COMMENT:** LB&I's senior leadership team includes the commissioner and deputy commissioner, the three officials (the ADCs and the director, Program and Business Solutions) who report to the deputy commissioner, and the directors of the nine practice areas, who also report to the deputy commissioner.

Practice Areas

The old LB&I was divided into industry groups. The new LB&I is organized into nine practice areas (PAs), five based on subject matter and four geographical compliance areas. The practice areas that address subject matter include Pass-Through Entities, Enterprise Activities, Cross-Border Activities, Withholding and International Individual

Compliance, and Treaty and Transfer Pricing. Each PA is led by a director. The fact that three of the five subject matter PAs involve international tax issues reflects the continued importance of international tax issues to LB&I.

> **COMMENT:** Practice area directors will report to the deputy commissioner. The PAs will include specialist groups that may be involved in examinations.

Subject Matter Areas

The subject matter practice areas include the following responsibilities:

- The director, Enterprise Activities, oversees the director, Financial Institutions and Products, and the director, Corporate/Credit. Enterprise Activities will cover banks, insurance companies, RICs, REITS, REMICs, corporate issues and credit, the Affordable Care Act, and penalties;
- The director, Withholding and Individual International Compliance, oversees the director of Field Operations (Foreign Payments Practice), and the director of Field Operations (International Individual Compliance);
- The director of Treaty and Transfer Pricing oversees the director of Field Operations (Transfer Pricing Practice), which includes a team of economists; the director (Treaty Administration), which includes the treaty assistance interpretation team and also oversees the exchange of information and collaboration with the Joint International Tax Shelter Information Center (JITSIC), and the director, Advance Pricing and Mutual Agreement (APMA);
- The Pass-Through Entities PA is organized in a different fashion, with a deputy director, Pass-Through Entities, and a senior advisor. Its responsibilities include the promoter program; and
- The director, Cross Border Activities will oversee two geographical offices, Field Operations East and Field Operations West.

Geographical Practice Areas

The geographical practice areas, each led by a director, are:

- Western Compliance, which includes Field Operations West and Southwest, computer audit specialists;
- Central Compliance, which includes Field Operations North Central and South Central;
- Eastern Compliance, which includes Field Operations Great Lakes and Southeast; and
- Northeastern Compliance, which includes Field Operations North Atlantic and Mid-Atlantic.

The four geographic practice areas include:

- Western Compliance (Alaska, Arizona, California, Colorado, Hawaii, Idaho, Montana, Nevada, New Mexico, Oregon, Utah, Washington, and Wyoming);
- Central Compliance (Arkansas, Iowa, Kansas, Louisiana, Minnesota, Missouri, Nebraska, North Dakota, Oklahoma, South Dakota, and Texas);
- Eastern Compliance (Alabama, Florida, Georgia, Illinois, Indiana, Kentucky, North Carolina, Michigan, Mississippi, Ohio, South Carolina, and Tennessee); and
- Northeastern Compliance (Connecticut, Delaware, Maine, Maryland, Massachusetts, New Hampshire, New Jersey, New York, Pennsylvania, Rhode Island, Vermont, Virginia, West Virginia, and Washington, D.C.).

The four geographic practice areas are also divided into smaller areas where some specialty practice areas will be based. For example, in the Western Compliance area, Utah, Colorado, Arizona, and New Mexico compose the Southwest Subpractice area and this area will house computer audit specialists and the global high-wealth team. Meanwhile, in the Central Compliance area, Minnesota, Iowa, and North and South Dakota comprise the North Central Subpractice area and will house engineering specialists. The tax computations specialists will be housed in a subpractice area of Eastern Compliance.

LB&I Compliance and Examinations

The LB&I reorganization is part of the IRS's "Future State," which is a high-level restructuring initiative across all of the major divisions of the IRS. The changes are intended to increase efficiency and drive meaningful changes in the way the IRS operates by doing more with less.

The new LB&I examination process provides for an organizational approach to conducting examinations, consistent with the IRS's Future State Initiative. From the first contact with the taxpayer through the final stages of issue resolution, the examiners will take a strategic approach to effective tax administration.

The goal of the process is to complete the examination in an efficient and effective manner through the collaborative efforts of both the examination team and the taxpayer working together in the spirit of cooperation, responsiveness, and transparency.

The reorganization moves LB&I from a model where returns are scored based on risk, or directly assigned (the CIC model), to one that focuses on:

- Articulated observed or perceived noncompliance;
- Describing compliance expectations; and,
- Creating specific plans to move the taxpayer toward expected compliance.

The new model is intended to provide flexibility for the most efficient and effective use of resources when employees address compliance risk.

LB&I will change its approach from one of continuous audit with some large taxpayers, while retaining an appropriate audit presence. The new organizational model, five practice areas that represent subject matter and four that represent regions, is intended to improve synergy and increase skill-sharing by aligning professionals with the same or similar areas of focus.

A practice area is a group of employees who focus on one or more areas of expertise. Each practice area will study compliance issues within its area of expertise and suggest campaigns to be included in the compliance plan. A campaign could result in a range of actions from a full-blown audit to a soft letter alerting the taxpayer to LB&I's concerns about an activity the taxpayer has completed or is planning to complete.

LB&I has also established an enterprise risk management (ERM) program to develop an agency-wide approach to risk management. The ERM will continue using a centralized issue selection approach while evolving into the Future State, simultaneously working to identify and understand the risks and foster a culture in which everyone is comfortable identifying and elevating risks and concerns.

The LB&I Risk Governance Board will seek to integrate risk management into LB&I's decision-making processes. The board reviews LB&I enterprise risks and approves the implementation of risk responses. When the board identifies risk with an impact beyond LB&I, it will elevate the risk to the IRS's ERM Office. The board will support LB&I employees to implement and champion risk management.

STUDY QUESTION

3. Which of the following is **_not_** one of the major changes in the LB&I Division structure?

    a. Replacing multiple deputy commissioners with a single one

    b. Eliminating the assistant deputy commissioner positions for international exams and compliance

    c. Dividing the division into practice areas rather than industry groups

    d. Participation in the IRS's Future State to overhaul the examination process

Principles

LB&I will use the Agile Model to build its new examination structure. The Agile Model is an alternative to traditional project management that helps teams respond to unpredictability through incremental, iterative work cadences, known as sprints. LB&I's Agile Model includes the same guiding principles as the LB&I ConOps: a flexible, well-trained workforce; selection of better work; tailored treatments; and integrated feedback loops. Knowledge management, as previously described, is also one of the keys to making the LB&I's Agile Model work.

Issue-Based Approach

LB&I has decided to improve its coverage of taxpayers by focusing on issues, not just on specific taxpayers. Therefore, LB&I will move away from the CIC approach (any potential changes to the compliance assurance process (CAP) have not yet been determined).

An issue-driven examination process will focus the right resources on the right issues. It encourages collaboration within issue teams in which examiners and managers are equally responsible and accountable for the examination and supports knowledge transfer among LB&I employees.

The goals of the issue-based approach are to:

- Improve the audit planning process;
- Reduce examination cycle time;
- Improve currency; and
- Enhance resource usage.

LB&I's examination focus will shift to a centralized issue selection and return selection approach. The centralized issue-development process or "campaign" will focus on how to identify and address compliance risks. Campaign-related actions could include development of training materials, technical positions, and audit aids.

The objective of the issues-based approach is to direct resources to cases with the highest compliance risk. LB&I will use data analytics to identify noncompliance and to develop compliance campaigns to address current and emerging compliance concerns.

The issues-based approach includes the issue-team concept and defines the roles and responsibilities of the issues team members. The issues team and the taxpayer are encouraged to work collaboratively to establish audit steps, agree to an examination timeline, and develop the issues selected for examination.

The issues development model relies on active dialogue and fact sharing and seeks ongoing acknowledgment of facts to ensure accurate tax determinations.

The new process emphasizes the importance of cooperation between the issue team and the taxpayer to define the scope and expectations of the examination. LB&I employees are expected to work transparently and collaboratively with taxpayers to understand the taxpayer's business and share the issues that have been identified.

In addition, taxpayers and their representatives are encouraged to provide LB&I employees with an overview of their activities, operational structure, accounting systems, and global tax organizational chart. To aid in the exchanges of information LB&I is planning to build an information exchange portal

Campaigns

The combined input of LB&I employees and data analysis will be used to identify areas of noncompliance and strategically focus resources to those areas. Campaigns are intended to identify:

- Areas of potential noncompliance;
- Intended compliance outcomes;
- Specific, tailored treatment streams to achieve compliance outcomes;
- The resources needed to execute the tailored treatment streams;
- Training, guidance, mentors, and other support; and
- Feedback from employees so that an approach to an issue can be modified as needed.

The new approach identifies the issue, adds resources, and then resolves the issue. Once LB&I selects a particular issue for audit or other compliance action, it will then select taxpayers. The campaign approach will look at taxpayers of all sizes, instead of focusing on the biggest taxpayers.

A campaign on a particular issue can take an exam approach or compliance approach aiming to change taxpayer behavior by issuing guidance, providing a safe harbor, or devising a program for taxpayers to bring issues to the IRS, such as the Offshore Voluntary Disclosure Program.

Shift to Risk Assessment

The new process shifts from the CIC model with continuous auditing to a risk assessment based on data analytics. The new approach weighs the size of the compliance risk, how often the risk is occurring, where it is occurring, and whether the risk is the result of a promoted scheme.

LB&I defines *risk analysis* as the process of comparing the potential benefits from examining an issue to the resources needed to perform the examination. Once an audit is opened, the new process calls for the audit team to conduct risk analysis regularly during the audit to consider whether the team should continue to pursue a particular issue.

The idea of risk assessment is to address the greatest compliance concerns and focus on major issues that involve the largest dollars of potential noncompliance and need for official guidance. The changes are designed to increase audit coverage and to improve compliance. Thus, a campaign may be the reason a return is chosen for an examination, but the LB&I team must also "risk assess" the return; therefore, the normal issues that team members see can be developed.

Under the old system, LB&I had 100 percent audit coverage of the very largest corporations but barely covered smaller corporations.

In the past, LB&I focused on selecting taxpayers for examinations using various audit triggers. The compliance campaign approach is very different from the previous tiered-issue process. The compliance approach uses a centralized risk management office to look for broad issues to address and then, using both tax returns and public information, looks for companies that are compliance risks.

¶ 207 OLD EXAM PROCESS

Formerly, LB&I divided its taxpayers into industry groups that it viewed as sharing characteristics and geography (the CIC model, with continuous auditing).

The Quality Examination Process (QEP) was a systematic approach for engaging and involving LB&I Division taxpayers in the tax examination process, from the earliest planning stages through resolution of all issues and completion of the case. QEP set the foundation for improved communication between LB&I agents and taxpayers. QEP also supported greater consistency in the exam process.

IRS agents and exam teams retained the authority to determine the issues to be examined and the documentation needed to conduct the exam. Timely, clear, and consistent communication between the team and taxpayer during the process directly influenced the scope of the examination and the depth of the analysis for issues under audit.

LB&I's Quality Examination guidelines, as outlined in the IRS's IRM, provided a framework for effectively managing even the most complex tax examinations. Examinations typically progressed in three distinct phases: planning, execution, and resolution. Effective coordination and timely communication between exam teams and taxpayers were essential to each of these phases.

Initial Planning Meeting

In the previous exam process, the exam team would hold an initial planning meeting with the taxpayer. Discussion topics included, but were not limited to, a review of the preliminary risk analysis; the anticipated exam process for the issues identified, along with timeframes and key milestones; the importance of transparency and openness during the exam process; roles and responsibilities of team members, the taxpayer, and its representatives; and the potential involvement of specialists, technical advisors, and counsel.

During the initial meeting, the team and taxpayer would discuss possible contingencies resulting from new developments during the exam and/or changes to the exam plan. They would review the information document request (IDR) management process; dispute resolution options, such as the Appeals Fast Track Settlement process; LB&I's Rules of Engagement to be used when elevating problems; ground rules for the frequency of meetings and transmission of information; resource availability; and logistics (i.e., building access, exam team work space, telephone and internet access, information/data security, secure messaging, etc.).

During the initial meeting and as needed through subsequent planning meetings, the exam team and taxpayer would discuss prior audit cycle or exam results, materiality thresholds relating to identification and selection of examination issues; other potential compliance issues and required compliance checks; affirmative issues and/or claims the taxpayer was expected to raise; strategies the parties would use for resolving compliance issues; and the use of a midcycle risk analysis, if warranted.

Taxpayer Orientation

During the initial meeting, or as soon as possible thereafter, the taxpayer provided a comprehensive orientation of its business operations to the exam team. The orientation included overviews of the taxpayer's business activities, recordkeeping and financial statement preparation, operational structure, list of key functions, and an organization chart. The taxpayer would explain how it prepared its tax returns, discussed all large or unusual events that occurred in the years under examination, and reviewed significant events and/or changes from prior cycles/years.

Exchange of Additional Transactional and Financial Information

At this stage, the taxpayer would also provide the exam team with relevant business and financial information regarding acquisitions, dispositions, accounting method changes, tax shelters, book-to-tax reconciliations, and all other pertinent information.

Finalizing the Exam Plan

The exam team would use all the information gathered to develop and finalize an examination plan that specified the issues to be examined, timeframes, personnel required, processes to be followed, and respective responsibilities. Representatives for both the IRS and the taxpayer would sign the examination plan, acknowledging their understanding of the plan and commitment to achieving the milestone and timeline dates.

The exam team would consider taxpayer input during the preparation of the exam timeline and target milestone dates (i.e., exam plan completion date, 50 percent risk analysis review, last date for IDRs to be issued, last date for claims to be filed, last date for Forms 5701, *Notice of Proposed Adjustment,* to be issued, turnaround dates for IDRs and Forms 5701, target date for issuance of the Revenue Agent Report (RAR), and more).

Exam teams would encourage the use of appropriate issue resolution strategies (Fast Track, Rules of Engagement, early referrals to Appeals, etc.) while the exams were in progress. A key goal during the resolution phase was to work proactively with the taxpayer to identify and implement issue resolution strategies, based on the facts and circumstances of the taxpayer's case.

Preaudit

The next step in the old LB&I audit process, involved the exam team gathering publicly available information (annual reports, SEC filings, materials from the taxpayer's web site, etc.) and internal IRS data (current transcripts, data on related entities, etc.), and then conducting a preliminary risk analysis to determine whether an examination was warranted.

At its first meeting with the taxpayer, the exam team presented and discussed with taxpayer the "Achieving Quality Tax Examinations through Effective Planning, Execution and Resolution" publication.

Based upon the initial risk analyses and review of preliminary documents (annual statements, tax returns, historical files, etc.), the exam team advised the taxpayer of potential examination areas/issues, and/or business units the team planned to review.

The exam team and taxpayer would discuss the availability and accessibility of personnel assigned to the exam. In addition, the exam team would:

- Notify the taxpayer if significant involvement by technical advisors, Office of Chief Counsel, and/or specialists was anticipated;
- Endeavor to reach agreement with the taxpayer on the facts of an issue or case before extensive involvement of a technical advisor;
- Coordinate as early as possible when assistance from the Office of Chief Counsel was anticipated. Contact with Counsel can be made informally via telephone or e-mail, or formally, such as through a request for a Technical Advice Memorandum (TAM);
- Invite technical advisors and/or Counsel to attend key issue meetings between the taxpayer and the IRS, as needed and appropriate; and
- Employ the use of summonses during the IDR management process when appropriate. Prior to issuance of any summonses, the taxpayer would be given notice and encouraged to provide the requested information via a presummons letter.

The Examination's Scope

During the examination, the exam team would discuss with the taxpayer any new issues identified during the exam that were not included in the original examination plan before any extensive audit work on those issues. The exam team also would discuss with the taxpayer subsequent risk analysis results indicating the scope, depth, and status of the audit.

The exam team considered the use of statistical sampling or alternative testing methods (mutually agreed upon judgment sampling) if the records were voluminous.

The taxpayer would provide preliminary information on issues, in order to narrow the scope of the audit and focus on the most significant issues. The exam team would inform the taxpayer when issues were dropped or the audit's scope was narrowed.

The exam team would also advise the taxpayer whether the examination would be expanded for issues such as tax shelters, listed transactions, or similar issues discovered during the audit. Finally, the exam team would engage the appropriate issue management team and/or technical advisor as early as possible in the development of a tiered issue.

STUDY QUESTION

4. In the old exam system of LB&I, the Quality Examination Process:
    a. Served as an Appeals Office system
    b. Involved taxpayers throughout the examination to improve agent-taxpayer communications
    c. Provided taxpayers with an orientation overview for the exam
    d. Focused on resolving options of the Appeals Fast Track Settlement

¶ 208 THE NEW EXAM PROCESS

The new examination process maintains the emphasis on communication between the taxpayer and the examination team. The new process also recognizes that not all examinations are the same in scope, size, and complexity and allows for suitable adjustments in the exam process.

The new process sets clear expectations for LB&I examiners, taxpayers, and representatives. Examiners are expected to work transparently in a collaborative manner with taxpayers to understand the taxpayer's business and share the issues that have been identified for examination.

In addition, the new process encourages taxpayers and their representatives to work transparently with examiners to provide an overview of business activities, operational structure, accounting systems, and a global tax organizational chart.

> **COMMENT:** The new exam process presumes that both LB&I and taxpayers have an interest in obtaining tax certainty by completing examinations in a fair, efficient, and timely manner.

The examination will still begin with an initial meeting between the exam team and the taxpayer. At this initial meeting, the examination process will be discussed so that the taxpayer and the exam team have a clear understanding of the process and what is expected. This first meeting also establishes expectations for working collaboratively to develop audit steps, timelines, and provision of appropriate personnel to actively assist in the development of the identified issues.

The new process requires both the exam team and the taxpayer to be responsive, cooperative, and transparent. It is expected that both the taxpayer and the exam team will benefit in terms of resource usage and tax certainty when the parties have open and meaningful discussions of the issues throughout the examination process.

> **COMMENT:** LB&I may change performance measures for employees from the number of cases closed to the number of cases opened and the amount of time expended on each case.

LB&I Examination Team

Under the new process, the LB&I examination team will work transparently and cooperatively with the taxpayer to understand the taxpayer's business and will share the issues that the exam team has identified for examination.

The issue team. An issue team is comprised of LB&I employees who will work with taxpayer personnel, who are most knowledgeable about a given issue, to ensure the successful development and management of each issue examined. The size of an issue team will depend upon the complexity of the issue. Each issue team will work with the taxpayer in a transparent manner to develop the examination procedures tailored to the issues selected, in order to establish the relevant facts and ensure that each party's position is fully understood.

Under the LB&I's new examination process, the case manager will have overall responsibility for the case. Each issue will have a designated manager who will collaborate with the case manager. The issue manager will be a manager of one of the technical team members. The issue manager has oversight over the planning, execution, and resolution of the issue. This will include ongoing risk assessment and ensuring coordination with subject matter experts as appropriate. The issue manager will also evaluate the strengths and weaknesses of each side's tax position and seek resolution at the earliest appropriate point.

The exam team will engage the taxpayer in the development of the audit steps and potential timeline appropriate for the issues selected in the examination plan and provide a final copy to the taxpayer. The team will also discuss the IDRs with the taxpayer before issuing them to ensure the requests identify the issue and are properly focused. The exam team will also review the IDR responses and provide feedback to the taxpayer regarding the adequacy of the responses. If complete responses are not received by the agreed date, the exam team will follow the IDR enforcement process to obtain the documents.

The exam team will keep the taxpayer informed of the status of each issue on a regular basis and provide written documentation of all relevant facts, seek taxpayer acknowledgment and, if the issue is not agreed, appropriately document all disputed facts. The exam team will apply the law to the facts in a fair and impartial manner and prepare a well-developed Form 5701 and Form 886-A, *Explanation of Items.*

Taxpayer's Responsibilities

The taxpayer or the taxpayer's representative is responsible for working transparently with the exam team by providing a thorough overview of business activities, operational structure, accounting systems, and a global tax organization chart. For each issue, the taxpayer should identify personnel with sufficient knowledge:

- To provide input during the planning stage;
- To agree to initial audit steps and timelines; and
- To actively assist in the development of the issues selected by the exam team.

The taxpayer will be expected to review and discuss the IDRs with the exam team before the requests are issued to ensure that the IDRs are properly focused and properly identify the issues. The taxpayer will also be expected to work with the exam team to reach a reasonable response date for each IDR.

For each issue identified for examination, the taxpayer will need to provide the requested workpapers and supporting documents. The taxpayer and the exam team will collaborate to arrive at a statement of facts for the unagreed issues and to provide support for any additional or disputed facts.

The taxpayer is also responsible for fostering early resolution of the examination by providing a written legal position for all issues in dispute.

The exam team and the taxpayer will have an issue resolution tool to help resolve issues at the earliest appropriate point in the examination.

Risk Assessment

An initial assessment to determine whether the tax return warrants examination will be completed upon the exam team's receipt of the case. The exam team and the case manager will consult and collaborate with specialist managers and examiners for a comprehensive initial assessment. If the return is not selected for examination, the return will be surveyed.

A return survey is an analysis and evaluation of audit potential and resources that must be completed by the exam team. A return may be surveyed after assignment when the following conditions are met:

- The taxpayer or taxpayer's representative has not be contacted;
- The taxpayer's records have not been inspected; or
- The examiner determined an examination will not result in a material change in the taxpayer's tax liability.

The risk analysis is a process that is based on experience, judgment, and objective investigation. When the team performs the risk analysis, an issue-based approach will be used to identify issues that are material or have significant compliance risk. Moreover, risk analysis is an ongoing process throughout the examination.

The ongoing risk assessment will focus on issues that raise significant compliance challenges. The detail and depth of the risk analysis may vary according to the complexity of the tax return.

A comprehensive risk analysis should:

- Define the scope of the audit;
- Assign the right resources to the issues; and
- Establish a case timeline based on all the issue timelines.

The comprehensive risk analysis will be conducted by the exam team with input from the taxpayer in order to leverage and effectively use resources.

The factors to be considered during the risk analysis process may change as additional facts are developed. Therefore, the exam team will periodically update its analysis. The team will also establish priorities when weighing the potential benefits and the resources needed.

Some of the factors the exam team will consider when conducting the risk analysis include:

- Return information, including related returns. The returns will be reviewed to determine possible large, unusual and questionable amounts. The risk assessment will determine the size and complexity of the case, including any related entities, changes between years and the entities' locations;
- The potential tax adjustment compared with the resources needed;
- Whether additional returns should be examined. For example, income recognition and expense deductions between related parties may require the examination to be expanded to include the related parties' returns. Similarly, the tax treatment and valuation of assets in mergers and acquisitions may require examining the returns of the acquired and acquiring entities;
- Weighing the risks and benefits against the resources required to examine a highly complex issue such as transfer pricing;
- Whether prior cycle issues have been settled or are pending in the Appeals Office. For issues that have been resolved, the exam team will consider the settlement authority. For open issues, the exam team will have ongoing discussions with the taxpayer on the status of the issue before Appeals;
- Items of strategic importance and compliance consideration;
- The financial condition of the entity and other collectability considerations;
- Adjustment potential (whether the return is worth the effort);
- Potential impact on future years;
- Litigation considerations;
- Business risks that may result in material misstatement in financial statements;
- Significant changes in the entity such as large acquisitions, reorganizations, or other unusual events;
- Significant changes in the taxpayer's industry, new products, service changes, or a new line of business;
- Tax haven locations and significant changes in or expansion into different tax jurisdictions;
- Operations in areas with unstable economies;
- The degree of regulation complexity;
- The effective tax rate (ETR) changes and trends in U.S. and worldwide foreign tax credits;
- The taxpayer's systems and controls; and
- Schedule UTP, *Uncertain Tax Positions Statement,* reviewed to identify the highest compliance risks.

When a team performs a risk assessment, the overall tax impact will be considered. For example, the offset of potential adjustments by different issues:

- Whether a foreign tax credit may be reduced or increased by an unrelated issue adjustment;

- The overall tax effect of flow-through adjustments, such as potential dividend adjustments, which may be negligible if the primary partner/member is a government entity owning an 80 percent equity base for which dividends may be exempt; and

- The impact of potential adjustments on prior years (e.g., a research credit adjustment may provide an offsetting adjustment to prior year(s) research credit amounts).

The risk assessment will always determine the materiality of an issue. Materiality is a relative, not an absolute, concept relating to the significance of an amount, transaction, or discrepancy. The assessment of what is material is a matter of professional judgment.

When a team risk assesses a return, information is material if a decision is changed or influenced based on the magnitude of an omission or misstatement of accounting information in light of the surrounding circumstances. The absence of an item may be also material.

In setting materiality thresholds, the exam team should consider both quantitative and qualitative factors. These factors include but are not limited to:

- Dollar value;

- Permanency (given equal dollar value, an item which causes a permanent difference in tax liability is more material than one that reverses in future periods); and

- Timing (before selecting an area for examination that might result in a timing adjustment, consideration should be given to the number of years income is deferred or an expense is accelerated).

Principles of materiality may be outweighed by other factors such as policy or compliance considerations: tax shelters, emerging issues, fraudulent items, or items contrary to public policy.

STUDY QUESTION

---

5. For the new LB&I exam, it is the taxpayer's responsibility to:

    a. Perform the risk analysis

    b. Respond promptly to each Form 5701

    c. Determine the materiality of an amount, transaction, or discrepancy

    d. Generate IDRs for issues to resolve in the exam

Planning the Examination

Planning the examination is crucial for an efficient examination. In order to use resources efficiently, examinations must be effectively planned using an issue-driven strategy, according to the new LB&I structure. A successfully executed examination requires the active engagement of both the exam team and the taxpayer starting in the planning phase and continuing throughout the entire examination process.

The planning phase begins with an assessment of the tax return for examination potential. Once a return has been selected for examination, there are multiple planning considerations the exam team members should address. These factors include:

- Familiarizing themselves with the taxpayer and/or their industry;
- Identifying potential issues requiring a specialist's involvement;
- Pending statute dates; and
- Distributing taxpayer information to those involved with the issue assessment of the return.

A risk analysis will be completed during the planning stage of the examination. This risk analysis should be reviewed throughout the development of each issue being examined. The risk-analysis decision points to consider include:

- Whether the return was part of a controlled group;
- Precontact analysis;
- Issue identification;
- Midcycle risk analysis;
- Ongoing factual development;
- Acknowledgment of the facts; and
- Issue resolution.

The initial planning discussions will lay the groundwork for a mutual exchange of information that will assist both the exam team and the taxpayer in defining and carrying out an issue-driven examination. Depending on the scope of the examination and the type of enterprise, the number and types of meetings may vary.

During the examination, the exam team collaborates internally as well as with the taxpayer. This promotes the development of a well-defined issue-driven examination plan. Such an examination plan can effectively serve as the road map for conducting an examination.

At the conclusion of the planning phase, agreements made with the taxpayer will be jointly reviewed and incorporated into the examination plan.

The plan is intended to be nimble and agile and, when warranted, will be adjusted throughout the examination. Both parties should make a clear commitment of resources needed to achieve the established case and issue timelines.

Internal planning prior to meeting with the taxpayer is essential. Internal planning discussions should be considered for all situations where multiple personnel (team members or consultants) will be involved in the examination. Internal planning among the LB&I examination team members allows for the creation of a unified and consistent preliminary examination plan and will facilitate discussions with the taxpayer. Communication and collaboration between team members, taxpayers, and managers on issues, audit procedures, timelines and other responsibilities will lead to a unified and efficient planning and execution of the examination.

The goals for internal planning include the following:

- Preliminary issue identification;
- Preliminary examination procedures;
- Preliminary identification of LB&I issue team members;
- Preliminary target dates; and
- Communication and administrative items.

Factors such as the organizational complexity of the taxpayer, magnitude or complexity of potential issues, personnel availability, exam team size, time availability, and geographic differences may lead to multiple planning discussions. It is important for the planning discussions to be held in a timely fashion to promote progression and continuity.

Execution Phase

At the conclusion of the planning phase, agreements made with the taxpayer will be jointly reviewed and incorporated into the examination plan. The examination plan will be issue focused and also contain the following: the issues identified, audit steps, timeline(s), and communication agreements.

Issue Development Process

Stages of issue development include: determining the facts, applying the law to those facts, and understanding the various tax implications of the issue. The parties will conduct interactive discussions, using the IDR process to develop the facts.

The exam team will make every effort to resolve any factual differences. If required, Forms 5701 are provided to the taxpayer throughout the examination phase to present the government's legal position. The taxpayer's response to these proposals will allow the exam team to understand the taxpayer's position, which will facilitate issue resolution.

Proper issue development means that all relevant facts are identified and documented, and legal positions are clearly presented. The issue team and the taxpayer should actively discuss their factual differences, legal disputes, and other areas of disagreement. The issue team will make timely use of all available tools to resolve issues at the earliest appropriate point and will consider appropriate issue resolution strategies throughout the examination. During issue development the issue team may consult counsel or other subject matter experts.

A meaningful discussion between the exam team and the taxpayer in advance of issuing an IDR will result in a more effective process. After having an initial discussion on the IDR, secure e-mail and e-fax can be used to efficiently share information.. The issue team and the taxpayer will establish reasonable timeframes with firm response dates. Upon receipt of the taxpayer's IDR response, the issue team will review the response and timely inform the taxpayer whether the response is complete. Incomplete or late responses to the IDR will require the team to initiate standard enforcement procedures.

Unagreed Issues

LB&I issue team members are responsible for documenting all the facts so that they can accurately apply the law. For potentially unagreed issues, the issue team members are expected to seek the taxpayer's acknowledgment on the facts, resolve any factual differences, and/or document factual disputes. The issue manager should ensure that all relevant facts, including additional and/or disputed facts, are appropriately considered before a Form 5701, *Notice of Proposed Adjustment,* is issued. If a case is closed to the Appeals Office and the taxpayer provides relevant new information that requires investigation or additional analysis, the case will be returned to exam team's jurisdiction for reconsideration.

Resolution Phase

The goal of the resolution phase is to reach an agreement on the tax treatment of each issue examined and, if necessary, issue an RAR Form 4549, *Income Tax Examination*

Changes, to the taxpayer. Form 886-A, *Explanation of Items,* is the written explanation of adjustments in all unagreed cases.

Many tools are available to resolve issues. These tools, or strategies, are designed to reduce examination time, save resources, and lessen the burden on both parties. LB&I encourages the use of all appropriate issue resolution strategies but requires that the issue team consider Fast Track Settlement for all unagreed issues.

Fast Track is a mediated effort in which the taxpayer, the issue team, and Appeals Office must agree to participate and agree to a mutual resolution. Other issue resolution strategies may be appropriate depending on the type and timing of the particular issue.

Confirming the facts during the execution phase enables the issue team and the taxpayer to work productively, using appropriate issue resolution strategies.

The taxpayer has the primary responsibility to ensure that all facts and legal arguments are provided during the examination process so that the issue team can adequately consider them. The issue team is responsible for insuring that it documents the facts and arguments, adequately considers them, and presents them objectively to Appeals if it cannot resolve the issue with the taxpayer.

In order to adequately consider both sides of an issue, all cases received in Appeals must have at least 365 days remaining on the statute of limitations. If the taxpayer raises a new issue or submits relevant new information that merits investigation or additional analysis during the Appeals process, the case will be returned to the exam team for reconsideration. If the taxpayer presents a relevant new theory or legal argument during the Appeals process, Appeals will engage the examination team members for their review and comment, but will retain jurisdiction of the case.

The goal of the resolution phase is to resolve tax controversies so that both the taxpayer and the exam team can achieve tax certainty. Both parties must engage in good faith discussions to do so. In many instances, at the conclusion of this phase taxpayers and the exam team will perform a joint critique of the exam process and will recommend improvements. Among the items the parties should address is the future tax treatment of agreed issues to eliminate carryover and recurring adjustments.

Refund Claims

All refund claims should be brought to the attention of the exam team as soon as the taxpayer becomes aware of any potential refund claim. LB&I will only accept informal claims that are provided to the exam team within 30 calendar days of the opening conference because claims filed after the 30-day window create resource challenges. LB&I will not require a formal claim if an issue has been identified for examination, unless IRS published guidance specifically requires formal claims to be filed for an issue (e.g., Notice 2008-39 for research credit claims).

After the 30-day window, claims for refund for issues not identified for examination must be filed using Form 1120X, Form 1040X, or Form 843, as required by Treasury regulations. In limited circumstances exceptions to the formal claims process may be granted by LB&I senior management.

> **COMMENT:** Netting of claims does not preclude the requirement for filing a formal claim for refund.

All claims for refund, formal and informal, must meet the standards of Reg. § 301.6402-2, which provides that a valid claim must:

- Set forth in detail each ground upon which the credit or refund is claimed;
- Present facts sufficient to apprise the IRS of the exact basis for the claim; and
- Contain a written declaration that it is made under penalties of perjury.

LB&I will discuss refund claims not meeting the regulations and provide the taxpayer an opportunity to correct the deficiencies. LB&I will not act on an incomplete or otherwise invalid claim for refund.

Taxpayers will file a formal claim with their IRS service center and should concurrently provide the exam team with a fully documented and factually supported copy of the claim, so that the exam team may make a tax determination of the issues without requiring the use of IDRs. This will allow the exam team to quickly determine whether to accept or examine a claim.

Refund claims will be risk assessed in the same manner as any other audit issue. If an issue on a claim needs to be examined, LB&I and the taxpayer will discuss the potential need for additional resources and extend the statute and examination timeline as necessary.

Exit Strategy

In many instances, at the conclusion of the resolution phase taxpayers and the exam team will perform a joint critique of the exam process and will recommend improvements. Among the items the parties will address is the future tax treatment of agreed issues to eliminate carryover and recurring adjustments.

STUDY QUESTION

6. When issues remain unagreed after the development process, the issue team is required to consider:

    a. Fast Track Settlement

    b. A petition to the Appeals Office

    c. Referral to the Tax Court

    d. Resubmission to the technical team

¶ 209 CONCLUSION

The LB&I Division is changing its focus, its structure, and its operations. It is moving from an emphasis on industry groups and on specific taxpayers to a focus on practice areas, risk analysis, and compliance campaigns. LB&I is centralizing its structure and some decision-making features, such as the identification of risk and the launching of campaigns. Its exam function now operates using issue teams to address issues and work with taxpayers. As it deals with diminishing resources, LB&I believes that these changes will enable it to "work smarter" and to have a greater impact on taxpayers and compliance.

MODULE 1: BUSINESS COMPLIANCE ISSUES FOR 2017—Chapter 3: PEOs (Professional Employer Organizations)

¶ 301 WELCOME

A professional employer organization (PEO) is an organization that enters into an agreement with a client to perform, among other tasks, the federal employment tax withholding, reporting, and payment functions related to workers performing services for the client. Effective for wages for services performed on or after January 1, 2016, a *certified* professional employer organization (CPEO) is treated for federal employment tax purposes as the sole employer of a worksite employee performing services for a customer of the CPEO for remuneration the CPEO paid to the employee. To become a CPEO, a person must apply with the IRS for CPEO treatment and be certified by the IRS as meeting certain requirements. This chapter reviews all of the requirements for attaining and maintaining the CPEO status.

¶ 302 LEARNING OBJECTIVES

Upon completion of this chapter, you will be able to:

- Recognize the roles of the CPEO and its customers for employment tax withholding, reporting, and payment functions;

- Identify which employees are excluded employees versus covered employees under the CPEO regulations; and

- Recognize the process for obtaining and maintaining CPEO certification.

¶ 303 INTRODUCTION

A PEO—also known as an employee leasing company—is an organization that enters into an agreement with a client to perform the federal employment tax withholding, reporting, and payment functions related to workers performing services for the client. A PEO might also perform other functions for the client, such as managing human resources, employee benefits, workers' compensation claims, and unemployment insurance claims. The client typically pays the PEO a fee based on payroll costs plus an additional amount.

The rules for becoming and maintaining status as a certified professional employer organization (CPEO) are detailed, and include rigorous quarterly and annual reporting requirements. The Treasury Department and the IRS view tax compliance of a CPEO applicant or CPEO, and of its responsible individuals, related entities, and precursor entities, as an important factor in determining whether the CPEO applicant's or the CPEO's certification presents a material risk to the IRS's collection of federal employment taxes.

¶ 304 TYPES OF EMPLOYMENT TAXES MANAGED BY PEOS

Worksite

Under common-law rules, an employer-employee relationship generally exists when the person for whom services are performed has the right to control and direct the individual who performs the services, not only as to the result to be accomplished by the work but also as to the details and means by which that result is accomplished. For federal employment tax purposes, this does not mean that the employer must actually direct or control the manner in which the worker performs services, but merely that the employer has the right to do so (Treas. Reg. § 31.3401(c)-1(b)). However, if one person controls the worker's services and another person controls the payment for those services, then the person controlling the payment is usually the employer for federal employment tax purposes (Code Sec. 3401).

An employer is generally liable for paying and withholding various federal employment taxes, including federal income tax withholding from employee wages, *Federal Insurance Contributions Act* (FICA) taxes or *Railroad Retirement Tax Act* (RRTA) taxes, and *Federal Unemployment Tax Act* (FUTA) tax.

Employers must deduct federal income tax from employees' wages and deposit it with the federal government (Code Sec. 3401 et seq.).

FICA taxes are imposed on wages received by employees and wages paid by employers; thus, both the employee and the employer must pay FICA taxes. Employers must withhold the employee's share of FICA taxes from the employee's wages and pay a matching amount on a regular basis (Code Sec. 3101 et seq.; Code Sec. 3111 et seq.). The employee and employer generally each are subject to a 7.65 percent FICA tax rate, consisting of a 6.2 percent rate for old-age, survivors, and disability insurance (OASDI) (i.e., Social Security) and a 1.45 percent rate for hospital insurance (HI) (i.e., Medicare). The Social Security tax rate applies only to wages paid up to the Social Security wage base for the year ($118,500 in 2016). The wage base applies separately to each common-law employer, with exceptions for successor employers and common paymasters, as well as certain motion picture project employers (Code Sec. 3512). There is no limit on wages subject to the Medicare tax.

Further, the employee's portion of the Medicare component of FICA is increased by an additional 0.9 percent for wages in excess of $200,000 ($250,000 in the case of a joint return, $125,000 in the case of a married taxpayer filing separately) (Code Sec. 3101(b)(2); Reg. § 31.3102-4).

RRTA is equivalent to FICA for railroad employers and employees (Code Sec. 3201 et seq.).

FUTA taxes are imposed on employers to fund the federal unemployment insurance program, which works with state unemployment insurance programs to pay benefits to unemployed workers. FUTA imposes a tax on employers:

- Who employed one or more persons in covered employment on at least one day in each of 20 weeks during the current or preceding calendar year; or
- Who paid wages (in covered employment) of at least $1,500 ($20,000 for agricultural labor, $1,000 for household employees) in a calendar quarter in the current or preceding calendar year.

The FUTA tax rate is 6 percent, but the employer is allowed a partial credit against the tax based on its state unemployment insurance tax liability (Code Secs. 3301 and 3302). The FUTA tax applies only to first $7,000 of wages paid to each employee in the calendar year. This FUTA wage base generally applies separately to each common-law employer (Code Sec. 3512).

Successor Employers

Special rules apply to FICA, RRTA, and FUTA taxes when, during a calendar year, one employer (the successor employer) acquires substantially all the assets used in a trade or business of another employer (the predecessor employer) or used in a separate unit of the predecessor employer and, immediately after the acquisition, the successor employer employs, in any of its trades or businesses, an individual who, immediately before the acquisition, had been employed by the predecessor employer in the acquired trade or business. In this situation, wages paid by the predecessor employer are treated as if paid by the successor employer for purposes of applying the applicable annual wage base (and the additional Medicare tax withholding threshold, for Medicare tax purposes) (Code Secs. 3121(a)(1); 3231(e)(2)(C); 3306(b)(1)).

Professional Employer Organizations

Under the typical arrangement, the PEO is the employer or coemployer of the client's employees, and is responsible for paying the employees and for the related federal employment tax compliance. A PEO also may manage human resources, employee benefits, workers' compensation claims, and unemployment insurance claims for the client. The client typically pays the PEO a fee based on payroll costs plus an additional amount. In most cases, however, the employees working in the client's business are the client's common-law employees for federal tax purposes, and so, under general rules, the client is legally responsible for federal employment tax compliance (T.D. 9768, May 4, 2016). Certification of the PEO as a CPEO, however, generally allows it to become solely responsible for the client's employment taxes.

¶ 305 CERTIFIED PROFESSIONAL EMPLOYER ORGANIZATIONS

The *Stephen Beck, Jr., Achieving a Better Life Experience Act of 2014* (ABLE Act), enacted on December 19, 2014, as part of the *Tax Increase Prevention Act of 2014* (P.L. 113-295), added new Code Secs. 3511 and 7705 to address the federal employment tax consequences and certification requirements of a CPEO. These provisions became effective for wages for services performed on or after January 1, 2016. The ABLE Act required the IRS to establish a voluntary program for persons to apply to become certified as a CPEO. The IRS began accepting applications for CPEO certification in July 2016.

Effective for wages for services performed on or after January 1, 2016, a CPEO is treated as the sole employer of a worksite employee performing services for a customer of the CPEO regarding remuneration that the CPEO paid to the employee. However, the exceptions, exclusions, definitions, and other rules that are based on type of employer and that would otherwise apply to the federal employment taxes imposed on the individual's remuneration but for the CPEO rules, still apply to the remuneration (Code Sec. 3511(a)).

A CPEO is a person who timely applies to be treated as a certified professional employer organization under Code Sec. 3511 and has been certified by the IRS as meeting certain requirements for certification (Code Sec. 7705(a)). For the CPEO to qualify as the sole employer of a particular individual, at least 85 percent of the individuals performing services for the CPEO's customer at the worksite where the individual works must be employed under a service contract with the CPEO (Code Sec. 7705(e)(3)).

Solely for purposes of a CPEO's liability for federal employment taxes and its other obligations under the federal employment tax rules, the CPEO is considered the employer of any individual (*other than* a worksite employee or individual with net earnings from self-employment derived from the trade or business of the CPEO's customer) who is performing services covered by a contract meeting the service contract requirements, but only for remuneration that the CPEO paid to the individual. The exceptions, exclusions, definitions, and other rules that are based on type of employer and that would otherwise apply to the federal employment taxes imposed on the individual's remuneration, still apply to the remuneration (Code Sec. 3511(c)).

These exemptions, exclusions, definitions, and other rules are presumed to be based on the customer for whom the covered employee provides services. If a covered employee performs services for more than one customer of the CPEO during the calendar year, the presumption applies separately to remuneration that the CPEO paid to the covered employee for services performed for each customer. If the presumption is rebutted, then the exemptions, exclusions, definitions, and other rules will be based on the person that is the common-law employer of the covered employee (Prop. Reg. § 31.3511-1(b)).

Code Secs. 3511 and 7705 set forth the general provisions for the CPEO program, but are not intended to create any inference for determining who is an employee or employer for federal tax purposes—other than for purposes of the CPEO rules—or for purposes of any other provision of law (Code Sec. 7705(g); ABLE Act, § 206(h)). The IRS is authorized to prescribe necessary or appropriate regulations to carry out the purposes of Code Secs. 3511 and 7705 (Code Secs. 3511(h) and 7705(h)).

The Treasury and IRS have issued proposed regulations that taxpayers can rely on for guidance on a CPEO's federal employment tax liabilities and other obligations under Code Sec. 3511 (Prop. Reg. § § 31.3511-1 and 301.7705-1). They also have released temporary regulations that contain the requirements a person must satisfy in order to become and remain a CPEO (Temp. Reg. § § 301.7705-1T and 301.7705-2T). In addition, the IRS has provided detailed procedures for the application process, and interim guidance that modifies certain requirements (Rev. Proc. 2016-33; Notice 2016-49).

> **COMMENT:** The online application process for becoming a CPEO opened in July 2016.

Treatment of Certain Credits

There is special treatment under the CPEO rules for certain specified federal tax credits:

- Regarding a worksite employee performing services for a customer of a CPEO, the credit applies to the *customer*, not the CPEO.
- In computing the credit, the *customer*, not the CPEO, takes into account wages and federal employment taxes that the CPEO paid regarding the worksite employee if the customer paid the CPEO for the wages and employment taxes; and
- The CPEO must provide both the customer and the IRS with any information that the customer needs to claim the credit (Code Sec. 3511(d); Prop. Reg. § 31.3511-1(e)(1)).

This treatment applies specifically to the following credits:

- The research and experimentation credit under Code Sec. 41;
- The Indian employment credit under Code Sec. 45A;
- The excess employer Social Security tax credit under Code Sec. 45B;

- The orphan drug credit under Code Sec. 45C;
- The small employer health insurance credit under Code Sec. 45R;
- The work opportunity credit under Code Sec. 51;
- The empowerment zone employment credit under Code Sec. 1396; and
- Any other credit designated by the IRS (Code Sec. 3511(d)(2); Prop. Reg. § 31.3511-1(e)(2)).

COMMENT: These credits are typically available to employers based on the amount of wages and federal employment taxes paid by the employer (NPRM REG-127561-15, May 4, 2016).

FUTA Credit. A CPEO is entitled to credits against FUTA tax under Code Sec. 3302 for contributions made by either the CPEO or its customer to a state's unemployment fund for wages paid to a worksite employee (Code Sec. 3302(h)). The CPEO is also entitled to the additional credit allowed under Code Sec. 3303 representing the reduction in the state unemployment contribution that results from the employer's low incidence of unemployment (Code Sec. 3303(a)).

Public Disclosure

The IRS will publicize the name and address of each CPEO and its effective date of certification, as well as the name and address of each person whose certification is suspended or revoked (Code Sec. 7705(f); Temp. Reg. § 301.7705-2T(a)(3), (n)(4)(ii)).

The IRS will publish the list of CPEOs and the effective date of their certification on the IRS website at **www.irs.gov/CPEOs**. The list will be updated by the 15th day of the first month of every calendar quarter, to reflect newly certified CPEOs. An organization will not appear on this list until the IRS has received the organization's proof of bond on Form 14751, *Certified Professional Organization Surety Bond* (Rev. Proc. 2016-33, § 7).

STUDY QUESTION

1. All of the following are roles the IRS assumes for CPEOs *except:*
   - a. Certifying the person as a CPEO
   - b. Giving both the customer and the CPEO information needed to claim specified tax credits
   - c. Publicizing the names and addresses of CPEOs on its website
   - d. Issuing regulations containing requirements for becoming a CPEO

¶ 306 WORKSITE EMPLOYEES

Treatment as a CPEO under Code Sec. 3511 applies to remuneration paid by the CPEO to a worksite employee performing services for a customer of the CPEO. A *worksite employee* is an individual who performs services or a customer of the CPEO under a written contract between the CPEO and the customer that meets certain requirements at a worksite that meets the 85 percent threshold requirements (Code Sec. 7705(e)(1)).

Service Contract Requirements

The CPEO contract between the CPEO and its customer regarding an individual who provides services to the customer:

- Must be in writing; and
- Must provide that the CPEO will

- Assume responsibility for paying wages to the individual performing services for the customer, regardless of whether the CPEO receives adequate payment from the customer for the services,

- Assume responsibility for reporting, withholding, and paying any applicable federal employment taxes on the individual's wages, regardless of whether the CPEO receives adequate payment from the customer for the services,

- Assume responsibility for any employee benefits that the service contract requires the CPEO to provide, regardless of whether the CPEO receives adequate payment from the customer for the benefits,

- Assume responsibility for recruiting, hiring, and firing workers in addition to the customer's responsibility for those tasks,

- Maintain employee records relating to the individual performing services for the customer, and

- Agree to be treated as a CPEO regarding the individual for purposes of Code Sec. 3511 (Code Sec. 7705(e)(2); Prop. Reg. § 301.7705-1(b)(3)).

85 Percent Threshold Requirements

In determining whether an individual is a worksite employee, at least 85 percent of the individuals performing services for the customer at the worksite where the individual works must be employed under a service contract between the CPEO and its customer. In calculating the 85 percent threshold, individuals who are excluded from "highly compensated employee" treatment under Code Sec. 414(q)(5) are not counted. However, a self-employed individual (see below) *is* counted in this calculation if he or she would be treated as a covered employee (see below) but for the exclusion of self-employed individuals from covered employee treatment (Code Sec. 7705(e)(3); Prop. Reg. § 301.7705-1(b)(17)).

The following "excluded employees" are not counted in calculating the 85 percent threshold:

- Employees who have not completed six months of service;
- Employees who normally work less than 17½ hours per week;
- Employees who normally work during not more than six months during any year;
- Employees who have not reached age 21; and
- Employees who are included in a unit of employees covered by a collective bargaining agreement between employee representatives and the employer (except as provided in regulations) (Code Secs. 7705(e)(3); 414(q)(5)).

Who Is a Customer?

A *customer* is generally any person that enters into a CPEO contract with a CPEO. However, a provider of employment-related services that uses its own employer identification number (EIN) for filing federal employment tax returns on behalf of its clients or that used its own EIN immediately before entering into a CPEO contract with the CPEO, is not a customer, even if the provider has entered into a CPEO contract with the CPEO (Prop. Reg. § 301.7705-1(b)(6)). Note that CPEO treatment does not apply if the customer is related to the CPEO (relationships are described later).

What Is a Worksite?

A *worksite* is a physical location where an individual regularly performs services for a customer of a CPEO. If such a location does not exist, then the location from which the customer assigns work to the individual is the worksite. The individual's residence or a teleworksite cannot be a worksite, unless the customer requires the individual to work there. Contiguous locations—i.e., locations whose borders touch each other—are treated as a single physical location, and thus as a single worksite. Noncontiguous locations are generally treated as separate worksites, but a CPEO can treat such locations as a single worksite only if they are reasonably proximate. Two worksites are not reasonably proximate if they are separated by 35 miles or more, or operate in different industries (Prop. Reg. § 301.7705-1(b)(16)).

Who Is a Covered Employee?

A *covered employee* is an individual (but not a self-employed individual) who performs services for the customer and is covered by the service contract between the CPEO and the customer (Prop. Reg. § 301.7705-1(b)(5)). A covered employee is treated as a worksite employee for an entire calendar quarter if he or she qualifies as a worksite employee at any time during that quarter (Prop. Reg. § 301.7705-1(b)(17)(iv)). Whether a covered employee is a worksite employee is determined separately for each worksite where the employee regularly provides services, and for each customer for which the employee is providing services. An individual may be a worksite employee of more than one worksite during a calendar quarter (Prop. Reg. § 301.7705-1(b)(17)(v)).

Who Is a Self-Employed Individual?

A *self-employed individual* is one with net earnings from self-employment (as defined in Code Sec. 1402(a) but without regard to the exceptions stated there) from providing services covered by a CPEO contract, but only with regard to such net earnings. The net earnings may be derived from providing services as a nonemployee to a customer of the CPEO, from the individual's own trade or business as a sole proprietor customer of the CPEO, or as an individual who is a partner in a partnership that is a customer of the CPEO (Prop. Reg. § 301.7705-1(b)(14)). An individual with net earnings from self-employment derived from the customer's trade or business (including a partner in a partnership that is a customer) is not a worksite employee with respect to remuneration paid by a CPEO (Code Sec. 3511(f)). A CPEO has no federal employment tax liability under Code Sec. 3511(a) or (c) for such self-employed individuals (NPRM REG-127561-15, May 4, 2016).

¶ 307 APPLICATION PROCESS FOR CPEO CERTIFICATION

A person must apply to the IRS to be treated as a CPEO under Code Sec. 3511, and must be certified by the IRS as meeting certain requirements (Code Sec. 7705(a); Temp. Reg. § 301.7705-1T(b)(1)).

> **COMPLIANCE NOTE:** The IRS began accepting applications for CPEO certification in July 2016. The program was to have been established no later than six months before the January 1, 2016, effective date of the provision—in other words, before July 1, 2015 (ABLE Act § 206(g)(2)).

General Application Procedures

A person seeking certification as a CPEO must electronically submit a properly completed and executed online application along with any accompanying forms and documentation required for certification. Paper submissions will not be accepted and will be treated as incomplete applications. Documents that must be submitted after the application is submitted and while it is pending also must be submitted electronically unless instructed otherwise. The individual submitting the online application for the applicant must be authorized under Code Sec. 6103(e) to inspect the applicant's federal tax return (Rev. Proc. 2016-33, § 2.01).

If more than one member of a controlled group (within the meaning of Code Sec. 414(b) and (c)) seeks to be certified as a CPEO, each member must submit a separate application; a joint application by group members is not allowed (Rev. Proc. 2016-33, § 2.02).

> **COMPLIANCE NOTE:** The online registration system for CPEO certification is available at **https://services.irs.gov/datamart/login.do**. The sequence for completing an application for certification is:
>
> 1. Individual identity verification—a one-time, online process that allows the IRS to validate the identity of application submitters and "responsible individuals" (defined later);
> 2. Responsible individual personal attestation (RIPA) (discussed below); and
> 3. CPEO application.

Responsible Individuals

RIPA application. Each of the CPEO applicant's responsible individuals must electronically submit a properly completed and executed online RIPA and provide an FD-258, *Fingerprint Card,* at the time and in the manner described in the application instructions. The RIPA is a mandatory prerequisite that gathers information that the IRS will use to perform a suitability check on the individual serving as a responsible individual. Once submitted, the information in the RIPA becomes the applicant's return information, and the IRS may disclose that information to the applicant if disclosure will not impair federal tax administration (Rev. Proc. 2016-33, § 2.01).

> **COMPLIANCE NOTE:** To obtain fingerprint cards and instructions, a requestor must send an email to **sbse.able.cpeo@irs.gov** with "CPEO FINGERPRINT" in the subject line. The IRS will mail them to the requestor. A trained specialist—i.e., police department, sheriff's office—must take the fingerprints. The completed fingerprint cards must be mailed to:
>
> Internal Revenue Service
>
> Submission Processing Center—Austin
>
> 3651 S. IH-35, Stop 6380 AUSC
>
> Attn: CPEOFPC
>
> Austin, TX 78741

The IRS will not accept photocopies of fingerprint cards.

Who is a responsible individual? A responsible individual of a CPEO applicant or a CPEO is any individual who:

- Owns directly or indirectly (and by applying the constructive ownership rules under Code Sec. 1563(e)), at least 33 percent of

  - The total combined voting power of all classes of the corporation's voting stock or of the total value of shares of all classes of its stock, if the applicant or CPEO is a corporation, or

  - The profits interest or capital interest in the partnership, if the applicant or CPEO is a partnership;

- Is a director (i.e., a voting member of the board of directors or equivalent controlling body authorized by state law to make governance decisions on the organization's behalf) or an officer (i.e., president, vice president, secretary, treasurer, etc.) of the applicant or CPEO;

- Serves as chief executive officer, executive director, or president of the applicant or CPEO, or has ultimate responsibility for implementing decisions of the organization's governing body regardless of title (described below);

- Serves as chief operating officer of the applicant or CPEO, or has ultimate responsibility for supervising the organization's management, administration, or operation regardless of title (described below);

- Serves as chief financial officer or treasurer of the applicant or CPEO, or has ultimate responsibility for managing the organization's finances regardless of title (detailed below);

- Is a managing member or general partner of an applicant or CPEO that is a partnership;

- Is the sole proprietor of an applicant or CPEO that is a sole proprietorship;

- Is a responsible individual of a corporation or partnership (as defined by the regulations) if the applicant or CPEO is a disregarded entity owned by the corporation or partnership;

- Is the individual owner if the applicant or CPEO is a disregarded entity owned by the individual; *or*

- Has primary responsibility for the applicant's or CPEO's federal employment tax compliance (Temp. Reg. § 301.7705-1T(b)(13); Notice 2016-49).

An individual with "ultimate responsibility" may include someone not treated as an employee of the organization. If ultimate responsibility resides with multiple individuals who may exercise responsibility together or individually (e.g., copresidents), then each individual is a responsible individual (Temp. Reg. § 301.7705-1T(b)(13)).

Nonrefundable User Fee

The individual who submits the certification application will be automatically directed to pay a $1,000 user fee through **www.pay.gov.** The IRS will not process an application until the user fee is received. Once processing has begun, the user fee will not be returned even if the application is withdrawn or denied (Rev. Proc. 2016-33, § 2.03).

Accompanying Documents

With its online application, a CPEO applicant must submit the items summarized here (Rev. Proc. 2016-33, § § 2.04, 2.05, 2.06; Notice 2016-49):

- A signed letter from a qualified surety, confirming that the surety agrees to issue a bond to the applicant if and when it is certified, in the amount required by the certification requirements and under the terms set out in Form 14751, *Certified Professional Employer Organization Surety Bond;*

- A copy of its annual audited financial statements for the most recently completed fiscal year as of the application submission date (or for the immediately preceding fiscal year if the audit of the most recently completed fiscal year's financial statements is not completed by that date);

- An unmodified opinion of an *independent* CPA that the financial statements are presented fairly and according to generally accepted accounting principles (GAAP);

- A "Note to the Financial Statements" (included in the audited financial statements covered by the opinion) that states that the financial statements reflect positive working capital (or reflect negative working capital, if certain requirements are met), and provides a detailed calculation of the working capital;

- An assertion, signed by a responsible individual under penalties of perjury, that the applicant has withheld and made deposits of all federal employment taxes for which it is liable (but not FUTA tax) for the most recently completed calendar quarter as of the application submission date;

- An examination level attestation from an *independent* CPA stating that the assertion is fairly stated in all material respects; and

- A statement, signed by a responsible individual of the applicant under penalties of perjury, verifying that the applicant has positive working capital (as defined by GAAP) for the most recently completed fiscal quarter, and including a detailed calculation of the working capital, and a copy of the applicant's unaudited financial statements for that quarter if available.

More details on these accompanying documents appear later in this chapter.

Suitability and Tax Compliance Check

In its application, the CPEO applicant must identify its responsible individuals (described earlier) as well as its precursor entities and related entities if applicable (discussed later in this chapter). The IRS will investigate the accuracy of statements and representations made in the application by conducting background checks of the applicant, any related entities or precursor entities, and responsible individuals. This may include checks on tax compliance, criminal background, professional experience, credit history, professional sanctions, and other relevant facts (Rev. Proc. 2016-33, § 3).

By submitting an application, an applicant and its responsible individuals agree to provide any additional information that the IRS may request to facilitate its investigations. The applicant and each responsible individual must take any actions needed to authorize the IRS to conduct background checks and investigate the accuracy of statements and submissions, including waiving confidentiality and privilege in situations where the IRS cannot otherwise obtain information from relevant third parties (such as former employers) due to confidentiality, nondisclosure, or similar agreements. The IRS may deny certification if the applicant or responsible individuals fail to provide such information or take such action (Rev. Proc. 2016-33, § 3).

Complete, Timely Application

A person must submit a complete, accurate, and properly executed CPEO application that provides the information required, in the time and manner set forth in the regulations and any further IRS guidance. Additionally, the applicant's responsible individuals also must submit any information specified in the regulations and IRS guidance (Temp. Reg. § 301.7705-2T(a)(1); Rev. Proc. 2016-33, § 4.02). An applicant will be certified only if the IRS is satisfied that the application and supporting documentation meet the certification requirements so as not to present a material risk to its collection of federal employment taxes (Rev. Proc. 2016-33, § 4.01).

An application is not complete and accurate if it does not contain all of the items required by the certification requirements. Although the IRS generally will request additional information from a CPEO applicant that submitted an incomplete application, it may deny an incomplete application without requesting additional information (Rev. Proc. 2016-33, § 4.02). Even if an application is complete, the IRS may request additional information before approving or denying certification, such as an explanation regarding a potential failure to meet a certification requirement, or a written work history or third-party references to support representations on the applicant's knowledge or experience (Rev. Proc. 2016-33, § 4.03).

Material Changes Affecting Application

Within 30 days of its occurrence, a CPEO applicant must notify the IRS of any change that materially affects the continuing accuracy of any agreement or information that was previously made or provided as a part of its application (Rev. Proc. 2016-33, § 4.04). A material change includes, but is not limited to:

- Any change in the tax compliance, criminal background, or professional license or registration status of the applicant, or any of its precursor entities, related entities, or responsible individuals;

- Any change to the applicant's fiscal year;

- Any change that results in another individual being considered a responsible individual of the applicant, or in another entity being considered a precursor entity or a related entity of the applicant; or

- The discovery of significant errors or new facts relevant to any agreement or information provided as part of the application.

Notice of Approval and Proof of Bond

If the IRS approves an application for certification, it will issue to the CPEO applicant a notice of certification that specifies the effective date of certification and indicates that the effective date is contingent upon timely receipt by the IRS of an acceptable Form 14751 regarding its surety bond (Temp. Reg. § 301.7705-2T(a)(2); Rev. Proc. 2016-33, § 6.01). If the CPEO applicant is a member of a controlled group and other group members are also applying for certification, the IRS will issue a separate notice to each applicant group member that has been approved for certification. The IRS will issue the notice of certification electronically or by mail (Rev. Proc. 2016-33, § 6.01).

A CPEO applicant has 30 days from the date of the notice of certification to submit proof of a surety bond. The applicant must submit a properly completed and executed Form 14751 that is signed by both a qualified surety and the CPEO (or CPEOs, in the case of a controlled group), and is in the required bond amount. If the applicant fails to provide such proof the 30-day period, its certification will not become effective, and the IRS will subsequently send a notice of final denial to the applicant with no opportunity to request review (Rev. Proc. 2016-33, § 6.02).

If an applicant in a controlled group receives a notice of certification after other group members are already certified, the applicant (or other group members) must post a superseding bond, in the form of a properly completed and executed Form 14751, that identifies all CPEOs in the controlled group and reflects the correct bond amount for all CPEOs in the group, including the CPEO applicant. If the applicant fails to submit a superseding bond on Form 14571 within the 30-day period, the applicant's certification will not become effective, and the IRS will subsequently send to the applicant a final notice of denial with no opportunity to request review; this will not affect the status of the other CPEOs in the controlled group (Rev. Proc. 2016-33, § 6.02).

Effective Date of Certification

The effective date of certification will typically be the first day of the first calendar quarter following the date of the certification notice. However, if a CPEO applicant submits a complete and accurate application before October 1, 2016, and is certified, the effective date of its certification will be January 1, 2017, even if the date of its certification notice is after January 1, 2017 (Rev. Proc. 2016-33, § 6.03; Notice 2016-49).

Procedures for Denied Application

If the IRS decides that a CPEO application should be denied because the applicant failed to satisfy any of the certification requirements, it will issue to the applicant a notice of *proposed* denial that:

- Lists the reason(s) for the denial of certification; and
- Advises the applicant of its opportunity to request review of the proposed denial (Temp. Reg. § 301.7705-2T(a)(2); Rev. Proc. 2016-33, § 8.01).

However, if an applicant's failure to comply with a certification requirement is not subject to reasonable factual or legal dispute, the IRS will instead issue a notice of *final* denial, which states the reason(s) for the denial but will not provide an opportunity for review (Rev. Proc. 2016-33, § 8.02).

Failures that are not subject to reasonable factual or legal dispute include (but are not limited to):

- Submitting an incomplete application for certification;
- Failing to respond to an IRS request for additional information needed for a complete application by the date required;
- Submitting a modified CPA opinion of annual audited financial statements (such as a qualified opinion, an adverse opinion, or a disclaimer of opinion);
- Submitting annual audited financial statements (or quarterly statements submitted by an applicant's responsible individual) that reflect negative working capital and failing to meet the exceptions for negative working capital; and
- Failing to provide proof of the bond required within 30 days after the date of the notice of certification.

Review request. To request a review of a notice of proposed denial, the CPEO applicant must submit a written statement of the facts, law, and arguments in support of its position. The applicant must submit the statement to the IRS CPEO program office identified in the notice, within 30 days from the date of the notice. Arguments supporting the applicant's position should focus on the factual information provided by the applicant and its responsible individuals, including whether any information provided with or after the application has changed or was incorrect. The IRS will *not* consider arguments concerning the materiality of information provided or whether certain facts present a material risk to its collection of federal employment taxes (Rev. Proc. 2016-33, § 8.03).

If the applicant does not submit a timely request for review of a notice of proposed denial, the IRS will issue a notice of final denial to the applicant (Rev. Proc. 2016-33, § 8.04).

After a request for review is submitted, the IRS CPEO program office will review the request and the accompanying written statement of supporting arguments. If it determines that the applicant qualifies for certification, the CPEO program office will issue a notice of certification to the applicant. If the CPEO program office maintains its position denying the application, the office will forward the request for review and the case file to the IRS Office of Professional Responsibility (OPR) (Rev. Proc. 2016-33, § 8.05). OPR will apply an abuse of discretion standard to its review and accordingly will issue either a letter notifying the applicant that notice of certification will be issued or a letter of final denial (Rev. Proc. 2016-33, § 8.06).

Before OPR issues its final determination, a CPEO applicant may withdraw its request for review, but only by written request of a responsible individual authorized to correspond with the IRS on the applicant's behalf. Upon receipt of the withdrawal request, the IRS will complete the processing of the application as if no request for review was received (i.e., the IRS will issue a notice of final denial) (Rev. Proc. 2016-33, §8.07).

Withdrawal of application. An application may be withdrawn only on the written request of a responsible individual authorized to correspond with the IRS on the CPEO applicant's behalf. Note that the IRS may retain the withdrawn application, all supporting documents, and any information submitted in connection with the withdrawal request, for use in tax administration (Rev. Proc. 2016-33, §5).

STUDY QUESTION

2. If an applicant for CPEO certification receives a notice of proposed denial:

    a. The applicant must contact the IRS Office of Professional Responsibility if a review of the denial is requested

    b. The applicant may submit a written request for review of the denial within 30 days from the date of the notice

    c. The applicant should withdraw the original application and submit a replacement set of documentation

    d. The applicant may request return of the user fee submitted with the application

¶ 308 CERTIFICATION REQUIREMENTS

To receive and maintain certification, a CPEO applicant or CPEO must do the following (Code Sec. 7705(b); Temp. Reg. §301.7705-2T(b)):

- Demonstrate that it—and its owners, officers, and other persons specified in the regulations—meets requirements established by the IRS, including requirements regarding tax status, background, experience, business location, and annual financial audits (see below);

- Agree to satisfy the bond requirements and the independent financial review requirements (discussed in detail later in this chapter);

- Agree to satisfy reporting obligations imposed by Code Sec. 3511(g) and the IRS (Temp. Reg. §301.7705-2T(m));

- Adopt the accrual method of accounting to compute its taxable income, unless the IRS approves another method (Temp. Reg. §301.7705-2T(l));

- Verify on a periodic basis (to be determined by the IRS) that the organization continues to meet the certification requirements (Temp. Reg. §301.7705-2T(j)); and

- Agree to provide written notice to the IRS of any change that materially affects the continuing accuracy of any agreement or information previously made or provided to the IRS (Temp. Reg. §301.7705-2T(k)).

Any precursor entities, related entities (see below), and responsible individuals (described earlier) of the CPEO applicant or CPEO must meet all requirements that apply to them under the regulations and IRS guidance. The IRS may deny an application, or revoke or suspend a CPEO's certification, if an applicant, a CPEO, or any of these other persons fails to meet a requirement. The IRS will deny an application, or revoke or suspend certification, if the failure to meet a requirement presents a material risk to its collection of federal employment taxes (Temp. Reg. §301.7705-2T(b)).

COMPLIANCE NOTE: Existing CPEOs and their responsible individuals will use the online registration system (**https://services.irs.gov/datamart/login.do**) to periodically verify information previously submitted and meet annual and quarterly program requirements.

What Is a Precursor Entity?

A *precursor entity* is a related entity (see below) of a CPEO applicant that is or was a provider of employment-related services that has either:

- Made a substantial asset transfer to the CPEO applicant during the calendar year in which the applicant applies for certification or any of the three preceding calendar years, or plans to make such a transfer while the application is pending or in the 12-month period following the application date; or

- Ceased operations or dissolved during the calendar year in which the CPEO applicant applied for certification or any of the three preceding calendar years (Temp. Reg. § 301.7705-1T(b)(10)(i)).

Who Is a Provider of Employment-Related Services?

A *provider of employment-related services* is a person that provides employment tax administration, payroll services, or other employment-related compliance services to clients (e.g., collecting, reporting, and paying employment taxes on wages or compensation paid by the person to individuals performing services for the clients). This includes, but is not limited to, a CPEO (Temp. Reg. § 301.7705-1T(b)(11)). A provider of employment-related services is considered a related entity of a CPEO applicant for precursor entity purposes if it is a related entity (see below), or would be a related entity based on the provider's ownership and responsible individuals at the time of its substantial asset transfer, its ceasing of operations, or its dissolution (as applicable), and on the applicant's ownership and responsible individuals at the time of the application (Temp. Reg. § 301.7705-1T(b)(10)(ii)).

What Is a Substantial Asset Transfer?

A *substantial asset transfer* occurs when a person transfers 35 percent or more of the value of its operating assets in one or a series of transactions. Operating assets include both tangible and intangible resources related to conducting the transferor's trade or business, and include but are not limited to intangible assets such as contracts, agreements, receivables, employees, and goodwill (which includes the value of a trade or business based on expected continued customer patronage due to its name, reputation, or any other factors). A service contract (or a service agreement described in Reg. § 31.3504-2(b)(2)) entered into by a provider of employment-related services is treated as transferred from the provider to a CPEO applicant if the applicant reports, withholds, or pays under its EIN any applicable federal employment taxes on the wages of any individuals covered by the contract or agreement, even if the contract or agreement is not formally transferred to the applicant (Temp. Reg. § 301.7705-1T(b)(15)).

Who Is a Related Entity?

A person (an individual or entity) is a *related entity* of a CPEO applicant or a CPEO if:

- The person is a provider of employment-related services, and either of the following is true

  - A majority of the CPEO applicant's or CPEO's directors or officers comprises directors or officers of the provider, or

  - An individual owns 33 percent or more of the stock, voting stock, or capital or profits interest of both the provider and the CPEO applicant or CPEO; *or*

- The person and the CPEO applicant or CPEO are members of the same controlled group as defined by Code Sec. 414(b) and (c) and its regulations, except that "at least 80 percent" in Code Sec. 1563(a) and Reg. § 1.414(c)-2 is replaced by "more than 50 percent" (by "more than 5 percent" if the person is a provider of employment-related services) (Temp. Reg. § 301.7705-1T(b)(12)).

Suitability Requirements

The IRS may deny a CPEO application, or revoke or suspend a CPEO's certification, for the reasons listed below, which affect the CPEO applicant's or CPEO's suitability to perform its professional functions (Temp. Reg. § 301.7705-2T(c)(1)). CPEO status may be rejected for any of the following reasons:

- The CPEO applicant or CPEO, or any of its precursor entities, related entities, or responsible individuals

  - Has failed to pay any applicable federal, state, or local taxes, or failed to timely and accurately file any required federal, state, or local tax or information returns, unless the failure is due to reasonable cause and not willful neglect,

  - Has been charged with or convicted of any criminal offense under federal, state, or local law, or is the subject of an active IRS criminal investigation,

  - Has been sanctioned, or had a license, registration, or accreditation denied, suspended, or revoked, by a court of competent jurisdiction, licensing board, assurance or other professional organization, or federal or state agency, court, body, board, or other authority, for misconduct involving dishonesty, fraud, or breach of trust, or that otherwise bears upon the applicant's or CPEO's suitability to perform its professional functions (this includes criminal or civil penalties for violating state laws that prohibit transferring or acquiring a business solely or primarily to obtain a lower unemployment tax rate or avoid a higher unemployment tax rate),

  - Is listed on any sanctions list compiled by the Treasury Department's Office of Foreign Assets Control (OFAC), including but not limited to the OFAC Consolidated Sanctions List and the OFAC Specially Designated Nationals (SDN) List, or

  - Fails to demonstrate a history of financial responsibility, which the IRS may assess by checking the credit history and other similar indicators;

- The CPEO applicant or CPEO and its responsible individuals fail to demonstrate adequate collective knowledge or experience of

  - Federal or state employment tax reporting, depositing, and withholding requirements,

  - Handling and accounting of payroll, tax payments, and other funds on behalf of others,

  - Effective recordkeeping systems,

  - Retention of qualified personnel and legal advisors as needed, and

  - General business and risk management;

- The CPEO applicant or CPEO, or any of its responsible individuals, gives or participates in giving false or misleading information to the IRS (including by intentionally omitting relevant information), and knows or has reason to know that the information is false or misleading, including but not limited to

  - Facts or other matters contained in testimony, federal tax returns, and financial statements and opinions regarding such statements,

  - Applications for CPEO certification and all accompanying documents,

- Affidavits, declarations, assertions, attestations, statements, and agreements,

- Periodic verifications that the certification requirements continue to be met, and

- Any other information required to be provided by Code Sec. 3511(g), the regulations, or IRS guidance.

Business Entity Requirements

A CPEO must be a business entity described in Reg. § 301.7701-2(a). A sole proprietorship can be a CPEO, and so can a domestic disregarded entity that is wholly owned by a United States person. A trust cannot be a CPEO (Temp. Reg. § 301.7705-2T(c)(2); Notice 2016-49).

Business Location Requirements

A CPEO applicant or CPEO must:

- Be created or organized in the United States or under U.S. or state law;
- Have at least one established, physical U.S. business location where regular operations that constitute a trade or business within the United States (under Code Sec. 864(b)) take place, a significant portion of its CPEO-related functions are carried on, and administrative records are kept;
- Have a majority of its responsible individuals be U.S. citizens or residents; and
- Use only financial institutions described in Code Sec. 265(b)(5) to hold its cash and cash equivalents, receive customer payments, and pay wages and federal employment taxes (Temp. Reg. § 301.7705-2T(d)). Such institutions are subject to state or federal supervision as financial institutions, banks, or trust companies.

   COMPLIANCE NOTE: The physical address of an applicant's principal administrative office or place of business must include the suite, room, or other unit number after the street address. The IRS will reject a CPEO application if a P.O. box or a C/O ("in care of") address is provided. An applicant that is a corporation should not use the address of the registered agent for its state of incorporation.

   EXAMPLE: Employment Experts Corporation is applying for CPEO certification. The corporation's principal office is located in Little Rock, Arkansas, but it is incorporated in Nevada. On its CPEO application, Employment Experts should enter the Little Rock address.

IRS Authorization to Check Background

A CPEO applicant or CPEO, and each of its responsible individuals, must authorize the IRS to investigate the accuracy of statements and submissions (and if needed, waive confidentiality and privilege), and to conduct comprehensive background checks (e.g., checks on tax compliance, criminal background, professional experience, credit history, and professional sanctions). An applicant or CPEO, and any of its responsible individuals, must also provide any additional information the IRS may request to facilitate the background investigations (Temp. Reg. § 301.7705-2T(c)(3); Rev. Proc. 2016-33, § 3). Each responsible individual must also submit fingerprints as prescribed in IRS guidance (Temp. Reg. § 301.7705-2T(c)(3); Rev. Proc. 2016-33, § 2.01). The IRS may deny certification if a CPEO applicant or its responsible individuals fail to provide additional information as requested or to take steps to authorize the IRS to conduct background checks and investigate accuracy of statements and submissions (Rev. Proc. 2016-33, § 3).

Consents to Disclose

A CPEO applicant or CPEO must provide consents for the IRS to disclose confidential tax information to the applicant's or CPEO's customers and to other persons, as necessary to carry out the purposes of the CPEO certification regulations. The information pertains to the applicant's or CPEO's certification and obligations to report, deposit, and pay federal employment taxes as required in IRS guidance (Temp. Reg. § 301.7705-2T(i)).

User Fee

Any user fee charged in connection with the certification program must be an annual fee and cannot be more than $1,000 per year (Code Sec. 7528(b)(4)).

STUDY QUESTION

---

3. Which of the following is *not* a certification requirement for CPEOs?

   a. Authorization for the IRS to investigate the applicant's background, statements, and submissions

   b. Being an individual taxpayer

   c. Adequate knowledge or experience of federal or state employment tax reporting, depositing, and withholding

   d. Consent for the IRS to disclose confidential tax information to the CPEO's customers and other necessary persons

---

¶ 309 BOND REQUIREMENTS

To qualify as a CPEO, an organization must post a bond for the payment of federal employment tax for each bond period—i.e., the period April 1 through March 31 of the following calendar year—in a form acceptable to the IRS and for a prescribed minimum amount (Code Sec. 7705(c)(2); Temp. Reg. § 301.7705-2T(g)(1)).

The bond amount generally must equal at least the *greater* of:

- $50,000; or
- Five percent of the CPEO's federal employment tax liability under Code Sec. 3511 during the calendar year immediately before the start of the bond period, but no more than $1 million (Temp. Reg. § 301.7705-2T(g)(2)).

A CPEO must meet the bond requirements without posting collateral (Temp. Reg. § 301.7705-2T(g)(5)). A surety company that issues a bond to a CPEO must hold a certificate of authority from the IRS as an acceptable surety on federal bonds and meet any other requirements prescribed in IRS guidance (Temp. Reg. § 301.7705-2T(g)(6)).

Requirements for CPEO Applicants

With its application for certification, a CPEO applicant must submit a signed letter from a qualified surety. The surety letter must:

- Confirm that the surety agrees to issue a bond to the applicant if and when it is certified as a CPEO; and
- State that the surety agrees to issue a bond in the required amount and under the terms set forth in Form 14751 (Rev. Proc. 2016-33, § 2.04(1)).

If the applicant is a member of a controlled group of which other members are CPEO applicants or CPEOs, the surety letter must also contain the name and EIN of each applicant and each CPEO that the bond covers or will cover. All CPEO members of a controlled group must be on the same bond in the required amount, applied as if all members (and/or any of their precursor entities, if applicable) were one organization (Rev. Proc. 2016-33, § 2.04(1)).

As mentioned earlier, if the IRS approves the application, the applicant has 30 days from the date the IRS provides notice of certification to submit a properly completed and executed Form 14751, which provides for a bond in the required amount and is signed by both a qualified surety and the CPEO (Rev. Proc. 2016-33, § 2.04(2)). An applicant that is a member of a controlled group with existing CPEOs has 30 days from the notice of certification date to post a *superseding* bond using a properly completed and executed Form 14751, which provides for a bond in the required amount and is signed by both a qualified surety and the CPEOs (Rev. Proc. 2016-33, § 2.04(2)).

Bond Amount in First or Second CPEO Year

If a CPEO has no federal employment tax liability under Code Sec. 3511 for all or a portion of a prior calendar year because it was not certified as a CPEO during that period, the liability that applies to the bond requirement for the entirety or portion of that prior calendar year is the federal employment tax liability of the CPEO—and of any precursor entity that has made a substantial asset transfer to the CPEO—that results from one or more service agreements (as described in Reg. § 31.3504-2(b)(2)). The precursor entity's federal employment tax liability during a prior calendar year applies only to the extent it results from service agreements that have been or are intended to be transferred to the CPEO at the time the bond amount is determined. For these purposes, an entity is considered a precursor entity of a CPEO if it was the CPEO's precursor entity when the CPEO was a CPEO applicant (Temp. Reg. § 301.7705-2T(g)(2)(ii)).

Cancellation of Bond

The bond must provide that the surety can cancel the bond only after it gives written notice of cancellation to the IRS and the CPEO, as prescribed in IRS guidance. The bond also must provide that, if a surety cancels the bond without issuing a superseding bond to the CPEO, the surety will remain liable for all of the CPEO's federal employment tax liability accrued during the total bond period, up to the penal amount of the bond at the time of cancellation. The total bond period starts with the effective date of the first bond issued by the surety to the CPEO in any consecutive series of bonds issued by that surety before the cancellation, and ends with the cancellation. A cancelling surety remains liable for as long as the IRS may assess and collect taxes for the total bond period (Temp. Reg. § 301.7705-2T(g)(3)).

Strengthening Bond

If the CPEO or the IRS subsequently determines during the period for which the bond amount applies that the CPEO's federal employment tax liability for the prior calendar year was higher than the amount reported and paid, and the CPEO makes an adjustment or the IRS makes an assessment reflecting this determination, and if the posted bond was less than $1 million, the CPEO must post a strengthening bond that, together with the initially posted bond, equals a total amount that reflects the adjusted federal employment tax liability, up to $1 million. Alternatively, the CPEO could post a superseding bond in the adjusted amount (Temp. Reg. § 301.7705-2T(g)(4)).

Controlled Group

All CPEO applicants and CPEOs that are members of a controlled group within the meaning of Code Sec. 414(b) and (c) are treated as a single CPEO applicant or CPEO (as the case may be) for purposes of the bond requirement (Code Sec. 7705(c)(4); Temp. Reg. § 301.7705-2T(h)).

¶ 310 INDEPENDENT FINANCIAL REVIEW REQUIREMENTS

To qualify as a CPEO, an organization must meet certain independent financial review requirements (Code Sec. 7705(c)(3)).

A CPEO must provide the following financial information:

- Annual financial statements—by the "audit date" (i.e., the last day of the sixth month after the end of every fiscal year, starting with the first fiscal year that ends after the effective date of certification), the CPEO must prepare and provide to the IRS

  - A copy of its annual audited financial statements for the fiscal year,

  - An opinion of an *independent* certified public accountant (CPA) that those financial statements are presented fairly in accordance with generally accepted accounting principles (GAAP), and

  - A "Note to the Financial Statements" (included in the audited financial statements covered by the opinion) that states that the financial statements reflect positive working capital (or negative working capital, if the CPEO satisfies certain requirements, explained below), and provides a detailed calculation of the working capital (Temp. Reg. § 301.7705-2T(e)(1); Notice 2016-49);

- Quarterly assertions and attestations on CPEO's federal employment tax obligations—by the last day of the second month after the end of every calendar quarter, starting with the first calendar quarter that ends after the effective date of certification, the CPEO must provide the following to the IRS

  - An assertion, signed by a responsible individual under penalties of perjury, stating that the CPEO has withheld and deposited all federal employment taxes (other than FUTA taxes) as required for the calendar quarter,

  - An examination level attestation from an *independent* CPA, stating that the assertion described above is fairly stated in all material respects, and

  - A statement, signed by a responsible individual under penalties of perjury, verifying that the CPEO has positive working capital (as determined under GAAP) at the end of the most recently completed fiscal quarter, as well as any additional financial information specified in IRS guidance (Temp. Reg. § 301.7705-2T(f)(1)).

If a CPEO fails to file the quarterly assertion and attestation for any calendar quarter, the independent financial review requirements will not be met for the period that starts on the attestation due date (Code Sec. 7705(c)(5)).

A CPEO with negative working capital might still meet the annual financial statements requirements and/or the quarterly assertions and attestations requirements if certain exceptions are met (discussed below). Also, certain immaterial failures of the CPEO's federal employment tax responsibilities will not defeat the quarterly assertion requirement (discussed below).

General Requirements for CPEO Applicants

CPEO applicants are subject to similar annual financial statement and quarterly assertion and attestation requirements, as discussed below. There are additional requirements if a CPEO applicant was not operating as a provider of employment-related services for some or all of its most recently completed fiscal year.

Applicant's annual financial statements. Along with its application for certification, a CPEO applicant must submit a copy of its annual audited financial statements for the most recently completed fiscal year as of the date it submits its application (Temp. Reg. § 301.7705-2T(e)(2)(i); Rev. Proc. 2016-33, § 2.05(1), § 2.05(2)). With each financial statement, the applicant must submit:

- An *independent* CPA's opinion that the statement is presented fairly and in accordance with GAAP; and
- A "Note to the Financial Statements" (included in the audited financial statements covered by the opinion) that states that the financial statement reflects positive working capital or, if the requirements are met, reflects negative working capital, and provides a detailed calculation of the working capital (Temp. Reg. § 301.7705-2T(e)(2)(i); Rev. Proc. 2016-33, § 2.05(2); Notice 2016-49).

The CPA's opinion must be unmodified: it cannot be a qualified opinion, an adverse opinion, or a disclaimer of opinion. The opinion must also be accompanied by a written declaration, signed by the CPA, that the CPA is currently qualified as a CPA (Rev. Proc. 2016-33, § 2.05(3); Notice 2016-49).

If an applicant submits its application before the last day of the sixth month after its most recently completed fiscal year, but the audit of its financial statements for that fiscal year has not been completed when it submits its application, the applicant must provide the annual audited financial statements and independent CPA's opinion for the immediately prior fiscal year, if any, and then subsequently provide the financial statements and opinion for the most recently completed fiscal year by the last day of the sixth month after that fiscal year ends (Temp. Reg. § 301.7705-2T(e)(2)(i); Rev. Proc. 2016-33, § 2.05(1)).

> **EXAMPLE:** FinancialServices Corp. applies for CPEO certification on September 1, 2016. FinancialServices' most recently completed fiscal year ended on June 30, 2016, but the corporation's annual audited financial statements for that period are not yet complete at application time. FinancialServices should submit with its application the annual audited financial statements for the fiscal year that ended on June 30, 2015. The corporation then must submit the annual audited financial statements for the fiscal year that ended on June 30, 2016, by no later than December 31, 2016.

Under transition relief, if an applicant is required to submit a copy of its annual audited financial statements and CPA opinion for a fiscal year ending before September 30, 2016, it will not fail to meet the financial statement requirements if it submits with those financial statements:

- A CPA's unmodified opinion that the financial statements are presented fairly in accordance with GAAP; and
- A separate statement, signed by a responsible individual under penalties of perjury, that the financial statements reflect positive working capital for the fiscal year (or, if the requirements are met, reflect negative working capital for the fiscal year), along with a detailed calculation of the working capital (Notice 2016-49).

¶310

For a fiscal year that ends after it submits its application and on or before the effective date of certification (if applicable), the applicant must provide the annual audited financial statements and independent CPA's opinion by the last day of the sixth month after the fiscal year ends, even if the applicant is certified before the IRS has received the audited financial statements (Temp. Reg. § 301.7705-2T(e)(2)(i); Rev. Proc. 2016-33, § 2.05(1)).

Special rules, discussed later, are invoked when an applicant is a controlled group member.

Applicant's quarterly assertions, attestations, and working capital statements. For the most recently completed calendar quarter as of the date of its application for certification, a CPEO applicant must provide:

- An assertion, signed under penalties of perjury by a responsible individual of the applicant, stating that the applicant has withheld and deposited all federal employment taxes for which it is liable for the quarter (FUTA taxes do not need to be included);

- An examination level attestation from an *independent* CPA, stating that the assertion is fairly stated in all material respects and complies with the requirements of the American Institute of Certified Public Accountants' Statements of Standards for Attestation Engagements (including the specific requirements for Examination Reports), and a written declaration, signed by the CPA, that the CPA is currently qualified as a CPA; and

- A statement, signed by a responsible individual under penalties of perjury, verifying that the applicant has positive working capital (as defined by GAAP) for the most recently completed fiscal quarter, along with a detailed calculation of the applicant's working capital, and a copy of the applicant's unaudited financial statements for the most recently completed fiscal quarter (if available) (Temp. Reg. § 301.7705-2T(f)(3)(i); Rev. Proc. 2016-33, § 2.06; Notice 2016-49).

The applicant must continue to provide this documentation for every subsequently completed calendar quarter while its application is pending for some or all of the quarter. The documentation must be provided by the last day of the second month after the end of each subsequent quarter, even if the applicant is certified before this deadline (Temp. Reg. § 301.7705-2T(f)(3)(i); Rev. Proc. 2016-33, § 2.06).

Additional Requirements for "Newly Established" CPEO Applicants

If a CPEO applicant was not operating as a provider of employment-related services for all or part of the most recently completed fiscal year as of the date it submits its application for certification, then in addition to the required items described above, this "newly established" applicant must also provide:

- A copy of the audited financial statements of any precursor entity, if one exists, or of any related entity if it does not have a precursor entity, for the entity's most recently completed fiscal year as of the application date;

- An unmodified opinion of an *independent* CPA that those financial statements are presented fairly and in accordance with GAAP;

- A "Note to the Financial Statements" (included in the audited financial statement covered by the opinion) that states that the financial statements reflect positive working capital or, if the requirements are met, reflect negative working capital (see below), and provides a detailed calculation of the entity's working capital; and

- Any additional information prescribed in IRS guidance (Temp. Reg. § 301.7705-2T(e)(2)(ii); Rev. Proc. 2016-33, § 2.05(5); Notice 2016-49).

¶310

Further, if the applicant was not operating as a provider of employment-related services during all or part of the most recently completed calendar quarter as of its application date or during any calendar quarter that ends while its application is pending, it must provide to the IRS the assertion, examination level attestation, and working capital statement described above for any precursor entity, if applicable (Temp. Reg. § 301.7705-2T(f)(3)(ii); Rev. Proc. 2016-33, § 2.06(4)). This information must be provided by the last day of the second month after the end of each applicable calendar quarter, beginning with the most recently completed calendar quarter as of the application date (or as of the date the entity became a precursor entity while the application was pending), and for all subsequent quarters while the application is pending and the applicant is not operating as a provider of employment-related services for all or any portion of a quarter (Rev. Proc. 2016-33, § 2.06(4)).

Exceptions to Positive Working Capital Requirements

If a CPEO applicant's or CPEO's annual audited financial statements for a *fiscal year* do not reflect positive working capital, it will not fail to meet the positive working capital requirement for its financial statements if:

- The applicant or CPEO has negative working capital for no more than two consecutive fiscal quarters of that fiscal year, as shown by the annual audited financial statements (for the final fiscal quarter in the fiscal year), and the statement, signed by a responsible individual under penalties of perjury, verifying that the applicant or CPEO has positive working capital (as determined under GAAP) at the end of the most recently completed fiscal quarter (for any other fiscal quarter), or, for an applicant, by submitting quarterly unaudited financial statements for those quarters;

- The applicant or CPEO provides to the IRS an explanation describing the reason for the failure, as prescribed in IRS guidance; an applicant also must provide a detailed calculation of the negative working capital; and

- The IRS determines that the failure does not present a material risk to its collection of federal employment taxes (Temp. Reg. § 301.7705-2T(e)(3); Rev. Proc. 2016-33, § 2.05(4); Notice 2016-49).

A CPEO applicant or CPEO with negative working capital at the end of a *fiscal quarter* will not fail to meet the quarterly positive working capital statement requirements if:

- The applicant or CPEO does not have negative working capital at the end of the two fiscal quarters immediately before the fiscal quarter at issue, as shown by the its annual audited financial statements if available, or the statements, signed by a responsible individual under penalties of perjury, verifying that the applicant or CPEO has positive working capital (as determined under GAAP) for those quarters, or, for an applicant, by submitting quarterly unaudited financial statements for those quarters;

- The applicant or CPEO provides the IRS with an explanation describing the reason for its negative working capital, as prescribed in IRS guidance; an applicant must also provide a detailed calculation of its negative working capital, and unaudited financial statements for the quarter, if available; and

- The IRS determines that the negative working capital does not present a material risk to its collection of federal employment taxes (Temp. Reg. § 301.7705-2T(f)(2)(ii); Rev. Proc. 2016-33, § 2.06(3)).

Immaterial Failures to Perform Employment Tax Responsibilities

If the CPA examination level attestation indicates that the CPEO applicant or CPEO has failed to withhold or deposit federal employment taxes in certain immaterial respects, the applicant or CPEO does not fail to meet the quarterly assertion and attestation requirements if:

- The attestation provides a summary of the immaterial failures that were found;
- The attestation states that the failures were immaterial and isolated, and do not reflect a meaningful lapse in complying with federal employment tax withholding and deposit requirements; and
- The IRS determines that these identified failures do not present a material risk to its collection of federal employment taxes (Temp. Reg. § 301.7705-2T(f)(2)(i); Rev. Proc. 2016-33, § 2.06(2)).

Controlled Group

All CPEO applicants and CPEOs that are members of a controlled group within the meaning of Code Sec. 414(b) and (c) are treated as a single CPEO applicant or CPEO for purposes of the financial statement requirements and the quarterly assertion and attestation requirements. However, the positive working capital requirements apply separately to each CPEO applicant or CPEO (Code Sec. 7705(c)(4); Temp. Reg. § 301.7705-2T(h)).

Special rules, described here, apply to the annual financial statement requirements and the quarterly assertion and attestation requirements when a CPEO applicant is a member of a controlled group of which other members are CPEO applicants or CPEOs.

The applicant must submit copies of *combined or consolidated* annual audited financial statements for all CPEO applicants and CPEOs in the controlled group, with an accompanying unmodified independent CPA's opinion that the financial statements are presented fairly and in accordance with GAAP. The financial statements can also include all group members that are not CPEO applicants or CPEOs. The statements must contain the name and EIN of each CPEO applicant and CPEO in the group, as well as those of each member that is not an applicant or CPEO if the statements include such members (Rev. Proc. 2016-33, § 2.05(6); Notice 2016-49).

Although the applicant is *not* required to provide a copy of its separate financial statements as part of its application, if an applicant's financial position is unclear from the group's combined or consolidated financial statements, the IRS may request additional financial information needed to evaluate the applicant's position, such as the individual applicant's annual balance sheet, income statement, and statement of cash flow (Rev. Proc. 2016-33, § 2.05(6)).

The Note to the Financial Statements of the combined or consolidated annual audited financial statements for the controlled group must state that the individual financial statements of each CPEO applicant or CPEO that is a member of the controlled group reflect positive working capital (as defined by GAAP), or reflect negative working capital (if the requirements are met), along with a detailed calculation of each individual CPEO applicant's or CPEO's working capital. The name and EIN of each member that is included in the consolidated audited financial statements can be listed in either the Note to the Financial Statements or in a separate attachment signed by a responsible individual under penalties of perjury. If it is unclear whether the applicant has positive or negative working capital for the last quarter of the fiscal year based on the group's combined or consolidated financial statements, the IRS may request additional financial information on an individual applicant basis (Rev. Proc. 2016-33, § 2.05(6); Notice 2016-49).

The applicant must submit the quarterly assertions and attestations for all CPEO applicants and CPEOs in the group on a controlled group basis, not for the applicant individually. The quarterly assertions and attestations must contain the name and EIN of each CPEO and CPEO applicant in the controlled group. However, the quarterly working capital statement must relate to the applicant alone, and must not be prepared on a combined or consolidated basis with other group members. If it is unclear whether the applicant has positive or negative working capital for the last quarter of the fiscal year based on the group's combined or consolidated financial statements, the IRS may request additional financial information about the individual CPEO applicant (Rev. Proc. 2016-33, § 2.06(5)).

If the IRS denies certification of the applicant because either the annual audited financial statements or the quarterly working capital statement reflects that the applicant has negative working capital and the applicant fails to meet the exception, the status of other CPEO applicants and CPEOs in the group is not affected (Rev. Proc. 2016-33, § 2.05(6), § 2.06(5)).

STUDY QUESTION

4. A CPEO applicant must submit combined or consolidated annual audited financial statements:

    a. When the applicant is a member of a controlled group of which other members are CPEO applicants or CPEOs

    b. In addition to separate financial statements for the controlled group member making the application

    c. If the CPA's opinion of the controlled group's financial statements is modified

    d. If the statements are not in accordance with GAAP

¶ 311 LIMITATIONS ON RELATED CUSTOMERS, SELF-EMPLOYED INDIVIDUALS, AND OTHER CIRCUMSTANCES

The Code Sec. 3511 rules for CPEO treatment do not apply:

- If a customer is related to the CPEO within the meaning of Code Sec. 267(b) or Code Sec. 707(b), but with "10 percent" substituted for "50 percent" in applying those provisions (see below);
- If a customer has commenced a CPEO contract with the CPEO, but the CPEO has not reported the commencement to the IRS as required (reporting requirements are discussed later);
- To any remuneration paid by a CPEO to a self-employed individual;
- To any CPEO contract that a CPEO enters into while its certification has been suspended; or
- To any CPEO whose certification has been revoked or voluntarily terminated (Code Sec. 3511(e); Prop. Reg. § 31.3511-1(f)).

Related Parties

CPEO treatment does not apply if the customer and the CPEO are related to each other in any of the following ways (Code Secs. 3511(e), 267(b), 707(b); Prop. Reg. § 31.3511-1(f)(1)):

- Members of a family—specifically, spouses, brothers or sisters (by whole or half-blood), ancestors (parents, grandparents, etc.), or lineal descendants (children, grandchildren, etc., including legally adopted children);
- An individual and a corporation if more than 10 percent in value of the outstanding stock is owned, directly or indirectly, by or for the individual;
- Two corporations that are members of the same controlled group (see below);
- A grantor and a fiduciary of any trust;
- A fiduciary of a trust and a fiduciary of another trust, if the same person is the grantor of both trusts;
- A fiduciary and a beneficiary of that trust;
- A fiduciary of a trust and a beneficiary of another trust, if the same person is a grantor of both trusts;
- A fiduciary of a trust and a corporation if more than 10 percent in value of the outstanding stock is owned, directly or indirectly, by or for the trust or a grantor of the trust;
- A person and a tax-exempt organization under Code Sec. 501 that is controlled directly or indirectly by the person or, if the person is an individual, by members of the individual's family;
- A corporation and a partnership if the same persons own more than 10 percent in value of the corporation's outstanding stock and more than 10 percent of the capital interest or profits interest in the partnership;
- An S corporation and another S corporation if the same persons own more than 10 percent in value of the outstanding stock of each corporation;
- An S corporation and a C corporation, if the same persons own more than 10 percent in value of the outstanding stock of each corporation;
- A partnership and a person owning, directly or indirectly, more than 10 percent of the capital interest or profits interest in the partnership;
- Two partnerships in which the same persons own, directly or indirectly, more than 10 percent of the capital interests or profits interests; or
- An executor of an estate and a beneficiary of the estate, but not regarding a sale or exchange that satisfies a pecuniary request.

For these purposes, the following are controlled groups of corporations:

- A parent-subsidiary controlled group in which one or more chains of corporations are connected through stock ownership with a common parent corporation, 10 percent or more of the voting power or value of the stock of each corporation in the group other than the parent is owned by one or more corporations in the group, and the common parent owns at least 10 percent of the voting power or value of the stock of one of the other corporations in the group (not counting stock owned directly by other members);
- A brother-sister controlled group in which five or fewer persons (individuals, estates, or trusts) own stock possessing more than 10 percent of the total combined voting power of all classes of stock entitled to vote, or more than 10 percent of the total value of all stock, taking into account the stock ownership of each person only to the extent the person owns stock in each corporation; or
- A "combined group," which consists of three or more corporations, each of which is a member of either a parent-subsidiary controlled group or a brother-sister controlled group, and at least one of which is the common parent of a parent-subsidiary group and also is a member of a brother-sister group.

¶311

¶ 312 SUCCESSOR EMPLOYERS

With regard to the treatment of successor employers for FICA tax, RRTA tax, and FUTA tax purposes, a CPEO entering into a service contract (CPEO contract) with a customer regarding a worksite employee is treated as the successor employer, and the customer is treated as the predecessor employer for the duration of the service contract. If the contract is terminated, the customer is treated as the successor employer, and the CPEO is treated as the predecessor employer (Code Sec. 3511(b); Prop. Reg. § 31.3511-1(d)(1)).

This treatment does not apply if the covered employee is not a worksite employee at any time during that calendar quarter, regardless of whether the covered employee later becomes or had previously been a worksite employee during the term of the contract (Prop. Reg. § 31.3511-1(d)(2)).

¶ 313 SUSPENSION AND REVOCATION OF CPEO STATUS

The IRS can suspend or revoke a CPEO's certification if it determines that the CPEO fails to satisfy:

- The certification requirements, the bond requirements, or the independent financial review requirements discussed earlier;
- The requirements for reporting to the IRS and the customer (see below); or
- Any applicable accounting, reporting, payment, or deposit requirements (Code Sec. 7705(d); Temp. Reg. § 301.7705-2T(n)(1)).

The IRS will suspend or revoke certification if it determines that the failure presents a material risk to its collection of federal employment taxes (Temp. Reg. § 301.7705-2T(n)(1)).

CPEO treatment does not apply to any service contract that the CPEO enters into during its suspension (Temp. Reg. § 301.7705-2T(n)(2)).

If an organization's certification is revoked, it is not a "CPEO" until it reapplies to be certified and is recertified by the IRS. The organization cannot reapply until one year after the effective date of its revocation (Temp. Reg. § 301.7705-2T(n)(3)).

An organization whose certification has been suspended or revoked must notify its customers of the suspension or revocation. Further, the IRS will notify the public of the suspension or revocation, and may also notify the organization's customers individually (Temp. Reg. § 301.7705-2T(n)(4)).

STUDY QUESTION

5. All of the following situations may cause a CPEO's certification to be suspended or revoked *except:*

- **a.** Failure to satisfy the deposit requirements, such as obtaining a strengthening bond
- **b.** Failure to meet positive working capital requirements for a fiscal quarter
- **c.** Failure to obtain an unmodified opinion for its audited financial statements
- **d.** Failure to meet regular reporting requirements

¶ 314 REPORTING REQUIREMENTS

A CPEO that is treated as an employer of a covered employee must meet all federal tax reporting and recordkeeping requirements that apply to employers under Code Secs. 6001–7874 in a manner consistent with treatment as an employer (Prop. Reg. § 31.3511-1(g)(1)). Additionally, a CPEO must *electronically* file any Form 940, *Employer's Annual Federal Unemployment (FUTA) Tax Return,* and Form 941, *Employer's Quarterly Federal Tax Return,* and all required accompanying schedules, as well as any other returns, schedules, or forms and documents required by further IRS guidance (Prop. Reg. § 31.3511-1(g)(2)(i); Temp. Reg. § 301.7705-2T(m)(2)).

Electronic filing is a *condition* of CPEO certification (Prop. Reg. § 31.3511-1(h)(4)). The IRS may waive the electronic filing requirement for undue economic hardship, which is determined principally by how much the cost of filing electronically exceeds the cost of filing on or by other media. A waiver request must be made according to applicable IRS guidance (Prop. Reg. § 31.3511-1(g)(2)(ii)).

> **COMMENT:** The proposed regulations state that a failure to electronically file Forms 940 or 941 (and all required schedules) is not a failure to file under Code Sec. 6651(a)(1) or a failure to make a report under Code Sec. 6652(n) (Prop. Reg. § 31.3511-1(h)(4)). However, a CPEO that fails to file electronically risks having its certification suspended or revoked.

Reporting to IRS

A CPEO must report the following to the IRS, as prescribed in IRS guidance:

- The commencement or termination of any CPEO contract with a customer, or any service agreement with a client, and the customer's or client's name and EIN;
- Along with any Form 940 and Form 941 that it files, all required schedules (including but not limited to the applicable Schedule R or any successor form) containing any information the IRS may require about each customer under a CPEO contract and each client under a service agreement;
- A periodic verification that the CPEO continues to meet the certification requirements;
- Any change that materially affects the continuing accuracy of any agreement or information that the CPEO previously made or provided to the IRS;
- A copy of its audited financial statements, and an opinion of an independent CPA regarding the statements;
- The required quarterly assertions and attestations regarding the CPEO's withholding and depositing of federal employment taxes, and the required quarterly statements that the CPEO has positive working capital;
- Any information the IRS determines is necessary to promote compliance regarding the specified tax credits and the credits against FUTA tax under Code Sec. 3302 (described earlier in this chapter); and
- Any other information the IRS may prescribe in further guidance (Code Sec. 3511(g)(1); Prop. Reg. § 31.3511-1(g)(3)).

Reporting to Customers

A CPEO must meet the following reporting requirements with respect to its customers, as prescribed in IRS guidance:

- Provide each customer with the information necessary to claim the specified tax credits;
- Notify any customer if its CPEO contract has been transferred to another person, or if another person will report, withhold, or pay, under the other person's EIN, federal employment taxes on the wages of any individuals covered by the customer's CPEO contract, and provide the other person's name and EIN;
- Notify each current customer if the CPEO's certification is suspended or revoked; and
- If any covered employees are not or stop being worksite employees because they perform services at a location where the 85 percent threshold is not met, notify the customer that it may also be liable for federal employment taxes imposed on remuneration the CPEO paid to those employees (Code Sec. 3511(g)(2) and (3); Prop. Reg. § 31.3511-1(g)(4)).

Required Provisions in Customer Contracts and Client Agreements

A CPEO contract between a CPEO and a customer, and any service agreement described in Reg. § 31.3504-2(b)(2) between a CPEO and a client, must:

- Contain the name and EIN of the CPEO reporting, withholding, and paying federal employment taxes on remuneration paid to individuals covered by the contract or agreement;
- Require the CPEO to provide the customer with the required notices and other information for customers, just described;
- Describe the information that the CPEO will provide that is necessary for the customer to claim the specified tax credits; and
- Require the CPEO to notify the customer that the customer may also be liable for federal employment taxes on remuneration paid by the CPEO to covered employees if the worksites where they perform services do not meet (or ever cease to meet) the required 85 percent threshold (Prop. Reg. § 31.3511-1(g)(5)).

If a service agreement between a CPEO and a client is not a CPEO contract—which means that the individuals covered by the contract are not covered employees—or if the CPEO rules do not apply to the contract because the related party limitation or other limitations apply, the service agreement or contract must notify the client that the agreement or contract is not covered by Code Sec. 3511 and does not alter the client's federal employment tax liability on remuneration that the CPEO paid to the employees covered by the agreement or contract (Prop. Reg. § 31.3511-1(g)(5)(ii)).

Penalties

A CPEO that is treated as an employer of a covered employee is generally subject to the same penalties and additions to tax that an employer faces for failing to meet its reporting responsibilities (Prop. Reg. § 31.3511-1(h)(1)). These include, but are not limited to, the penalties and additions for:

- Failure to file tax returns or pay tax under Code Sec. 6651;
- Failure to deposit taxes under Code Sec. 6656;
- Failure to collect and pay over tax, or attempting to evade or defeat tax under Code Sec. 6672 (the trust fund recovery penalty);
- Failure to file correct information returns under Code Sec. 6721;
- Failure to furnish correct payee statements under Code Sec. 6722; and
- Failure to comply with other information reporting requirements under Code Sec. 6723.

A CPEO is also subject to a penalty of $50 per report for:

- Failure to timely provide the reports required to be made to the IRS and to customers (as described above);
- Failure to attach Schedule R (or a successor form) to Forms 941 or 940 as required;
- Failure to timely make the various reports required for CPEO certification; and
- Failure to provide necessary information to a large food and beverage establishment customer for tip reporting purposes (Code Sec. 6652(n); Prop. Reg. § 31.3511-1(h)(2) and (3)).

This $50 penalty increases to $100 per report if the failure is due to negligence or intentional disregard of those reporting rules (Code Sec. 6652(n)).

Further, if a CPEO does not include each customer's EIN on the relevant Schedule R, it is subject to the Code Sec. 6723 penalty for failure to comply with other information reporting requirements (Prop. Reg. § 31.3511-1(h)(3)).

STUDY QUESTION

6. A CPEO's reporting to customers includes:

    a. Notification of each customer separately if the CPEO's certification is suspended or revoked

    b. Providing copies of specified tax credit forms the CPEO has prepared

    c. Notification that the client agreement is nullified because one or more covered employees stop being worksite employees

    d. Copies of the CPEO's audited financial statements and CPA opinion

¶ 315 CONCLUSION

For a failure to comply with quarterly or annual reporting requirements, failure to pay applicable federal, state, or local taxes, or failure to file required tax or information returns as required, the price can be steep: denial of CPEO certification, or suspension or revocation of CPEO status.

MODULE 1: BUSINESS COMPLIANCE ISSUES FOR 2017—Chapter 4: Tangible Property Rules Update

¶ 401 WELCOME

Every taxpayer that uses tangible real or personal property in a business needs to understand the tax rules relating to the distinction between a repair and capital expenditure, as well as the depreciation of those capitalized expenditures and depreciable assets that are purchased or produced.

This chapter covers recent developments relating to repair, capitalization, and depreciation as embodied in the final "tangible property regulations." In addition, many significant changes to depreciation provisions, such as bonus depreciation and the Section 179 allowance, were made by the *Protecting Americans from Tax Hikes Act of 2015 (PATH Act)* (P.L. 114-113). Many of these changes have first gone into effect in 2016. This chapter also details these changes.

¶ 402 LEARNING OBJECTIVES

Upon completion of this chapter, you will be able to:

- Recognize the *de minimis* expensing rule with updated per item expensing limits for taxpayers without an applicable financial statement;
- Recognize the operation of the safe harbor for determining the portion of capitalized and currently deducted costs of remodel-refresh projects on retail buildings and restaurants;
- Identify key differences and similarities in the latest automatic accounting method change revenue procedure that governs changes made to comply with the tangible property regulations;
- Identify what clients need to know about key legislative changes affecting bonus depreciation and other depreciation provisions that go into effect into 2016 and later; and
- Identify important changes to the Code Sec. 179 deduction, including deduction limits and changes related to qualified real property.

¶ 403 INTRODUCTION

The final tangible property regulations were issued in 2013 under T.D. 9636 (9/13/2013) and provide rules for distinguishing between a currently deductible repair and a capitalized expenditure (Reg. § § 1.263-1, -2, and -3) (the "repair regulations"). The tangible property regulations also include rules relating to MACRS general asset accounts (Reg. § 1.68(i)-1), multiple asset and item accounts (Reg. § 1.168(i)-7), and dispositions (Reg. § 1.168(i)-8). These regulations were issued in 2014 under T.D. 9689 (8/14/2014). Although taxpayers, other than "small qualifying taxpayers" described in Rev. Proc. 2015-20, should have filed accounting method changes on Form 3115, *Application for Change in Accounting Method,* to comply with the tangible property regulations for tax years beginning on or after January 1, 2014 (the effective date of the tangible property regulations), these changes may continue to be made for any subsequent tax year by taxpayers not under audit by using the automatic accounting method change procedure of Rev. Proc. 2016-29.

Recent developments to the repair regulations discussed in this chapter include an increase in the elective *de minimis* safe harbor per-item expensing limit for 2016 for taxpayers without an applicable financial statement (AFS) from $500 to $2,500, a new remodel-refresh safe harbor that allows certain taxpayers to deduct 75 percent of remodel-refresh costs (Rev. Proc. 2015-56), and the issuance of a new automatic accounting method procedure (Rev. Proc. 2016-29) that now governs changes to comply with the tangible property regulations.

The *Protecting Americans from Tax Hikes Act of 2015* (PATH Act) (P.L. 114-113) extended the expiration date of many depreciation provisions and made other expiring provisions permanent. Significant substantive changes were made to bonus depreciation and the Section 179 expense allowance. These changes are also covered in this chapter.

¶ 404 2016 *DE MINIMIS* SAFE HARBOR LIMIT INCREASED

The tangible property regulations dealing with repairs include a *de minimis* expensing safe harbor that allows taxpayers to annually elect to deduct the cost of materials and supplies and units of property produced or acquired subject to a per-item dollar limit (Reg. § 1.263(a)-1(f)).

The maximum per-item *de minimis* safe harbor dollar limit is increased from $500 to $2,500 for taxpayers without an applicable financial statement (AFS), effective for tax years beginning on or after January 1, 2016 (Notice 2015-82). The maximum $5,000 per-item limit for taxpayers with an AFS is unchanged.

An AFS is defined (Reg. § 1.263(a)-1(f)) as:

- A financial statement required to be filed with the Securities and Exchange Commission (SEC) (the Form 10-K or the *Annual Statement to Shareholders*);
- A certified audited financial statement used for nontax purposes that is accompanied by the report of an independent certified public accountant; or
- A financial statement (other than a tax return) required to be provided to the federal or a state government or any federal or state agency (other than the SEC or the Internal Revenue Service).

  COMMENT: Although taxpayers without an AFS are not required to have a written accounting policy implementing the safe harbor, an unwritten policy employing a $2,500 per-item deduction limit must still be in effect as of the beginning of the 2016 tax year in order for the $2,500 limit to apply for the 2016 tax year. The per-item deduction limit may exceed $2,500, but only items costing $2,500 or less receive safe harbor protection. Similarly, for each tax year beginning after 2016, an unwritten policy with a $2,500 per-item limit must be in effect as of the beginning of that tax in order for the higher limit to apply.

For tax years beginning before January 1, 2016, the IRS will allow a taxpayer without an AFS to qualify under the safe harbor with respect to items not in excess of the $2,500 limit if all other requirements for the safe harbor are satisfied. Consequently, if a taxpayer had a per-item deduction limit in excess of $500 at the beginning of the pre-2016 tax year, items that cost no more than the limit set (but not in excess of $2,500) will receive safe harbor protection. The IRS will not challenge deductions within the $2,500 limit (or a lesser limit set by the taxpayer's policy) in an audit, assuming the taxpayer meets all requirements for the safe harbor. If an audit is currently being conducted solely on such deductions, it will be discontinued.

¶ 405 REMODEL-REFRESH SAFE HARBOR

> **COMMENT:** This section makes occasional reference to "informal IRS guidance." The term refers to informal opinions expressed by IRS representatives during the Capital Recovery and Leasing panel discussion of the American Bar Association's (ABA's) Section of Taxation 2016 Mid-Year meeting held in Los Angeles, California, January 28–30, 2016. These opinions are not binding on the IRS.

The IRS supplemented the tangible property regulations with a safe harbor that allows a taxpayer operating a retail establishment or a restaurant to change to a method of accounting that allows the taxpayer to treat 25 percent of qualified remodel-refresh costs as capital expenditures under Code Sec. 263 and 75 percent of such costs as currently deductible repair and maintenance expenses (Rev. Proc. 2015-56; Rev. Proc. 2016-29, Section 10.10 (Accounting method change #222)). The 25 percent capitalization amount also applies for purposes of the uniform capitalization rules of Code Sec. 263A.

> **COMMENT:** The uniform capitalization rules require the cost of improvements to property to be capitalized. Consequently, it was necessary to coordinate the safe harbor for Code Sec. 263 with the UNICAP rules by specifically limiting the Code Sec. 263A capitalization amount to 25 percent.

Once the accounting method change is filed, all future remodel-refresh safe harbors for all of a taxpayer's qualified buildings in the same trade or business are subject to the safe harbor. A taxpayer would need to file a nonautomatic method change seeking advance consent to switch out of the safe harbor.

The safe harbor does not contain a provision that allows a taxpayer to make the election on a building-by-building basis. Therefore, if the safe harbor is elected, it applies to all qualified buildings used in a taxpayer's trade or business.

> **COMMENT:** The 75 percent allocation to current deductible expenditures is considered by most practitioners as generous when compared to the typical allocation that results when the repair regulations are on applied on an item-by-item basis to remodel-refresh costs.

The 25 percent capitalized portion is generally treated as nonresidential real property depreciable over a 39-year recovery period. However, some or all of capitalized amount may instead be eligible for a 15-year recovery period as qualified leasehold improvement property, qualified retail improvement property, or qualified restaurant property. For example, if the remodel-refresh is made to the internal structure of the building pursuant to the terms of a lease and the building is at least three years old, the capitalized portion may be considered 15-year qualified leasehold improvement property and is also eligible for bonus depreciation.

> **CAUTION:** It is possible that a portion of remodel-refresh costs will not independently qualify for a 15-year recovery period. In that case, IRS spokespersons suggested that the safe-harbor 25 percent capitalized portion must be reasonably allocated between the costs subject to a 39-year recovery period and costs eligible for a 15-year recovery period.

AFS Required

The safe harbor may only be used by taxpayers with an applicable financial statement (AFS). Consequently, the method is not usually available to small business taxpayers who typically operate one or two stores.

An AFS is an audited financial statement or certain other similar statements (Reg. § 1.263(a)-1(f)).

COMMENT: An IRS spokesperson indicated that the IRS limited the safe harbor to taxpayers with an AFS because such taxpayers were in greater need of relief due to large number of remodel-refreshes conducted by these taxpayers. Small business taxpayers, on the other hand, can apply the tangible property regulation guidelines on the occasional remodel-refresh without undue burden.

Although the repair regulations provide several examples dealing with remodel-refresh costs (Reg. § 1.263(a)-3(j)(3), Examples 6, 7, 8), the IRS and retail and restaurant industries realized that application of the repair versus capital expenditure criteria in the regulations to a multiplicity of remodel-refresh projects is unduly complicated. This safe harbor will go a long way in eliminating disputes with the IRS by creating certainty regarding the proper treatment of most of these costs.

Excluded Retailers

Certain retailers may not use the remodel-refresh safe harbor (Sec. 4.01 of Rev. Proc. 2015-56): These excluded retailers include:

- Automotive dealers;
- Other motor vehicle dealers;
- Gas stations;
- Manufactured home dealers; and
- Nonstore retailers.

Excluded Costs

Certain costs paid during a remodel-refresh project are specifically excluded from the safe harbor (Sec. 6.04 of Rev. Proc. 2015-56). Excluded remodel-refresh costs must be deducted or capitalized in accordance with the provisions of the tax code and regulations that are otherwise applicable.

Code Sec. 110 construction allowances. Amounts paid by a lessor to a lessee for making improvements may constitute a qualified lessee construction allowance under Code Sec. 110. Under Code Sec. 110, the construction allowance is excluded from the lessee's taxable income, and the improvements built with the allowance are owned and depreciated by the lessor. Because the treatment of lessee construction allowances is specifically governed by the tax code, the treatment of lessee construction allowances used in a remodel-refresh project are not affected by the safe harbor. The allowance must be capitalized and depreciated by the owner-lessor in accordance with Code Sec. 110.

Section 1245 property. Amounts paid for Section 1245 property during a remodel-refresh are not subject to the safe harbor. Thus, Section 1245 property that would otherwise be treated as a separately depreciable asset must be capitalized and depreciated under the cost segregation rules, usually over a five-year period (Asset Class 57.0 of Rev. Proc. 87-56).

CAUTION: It is common for taxpayers to forgo a cost segregation study and depreciate the entire cost of a building, including Section 1245 components of the building, as 39-year nonresidential real property or 27.5-year residential real property, as applicable. An IRS spokesperson informally indicated that this treatment is technically incorrect but that IRS auditors generally allow or disregard such improper treatment because the treatment favors the government. Now, however, if the remodel-refresh safe harbor applies, the IRS would be disadvantaged if the taxpayer were to treat 75 percent of Section 1245 property costs as currently deductible. Consequently, in the case of taxpayers using the remodel-refresh safe harbor, auditors will not likely overlook the failure to properly categorize property connected with a remodel-refresh as Section 1245 property that is excluded from the safe harbor.

> **COMMENT:** IRS auditors may but are not required to change improper accounting methods that favor the government. The IRS expects that a taxpayer would file the change on its own in this situation.

Code Sec. 179 deductions. Amounts expensed under Code Sec. 179 are also not subject to the safe harbor. For example, remodel-refresh improvements that a taxpayer elects to expense as qualified real property (Code Sec. 179(f)) are not taken into account under the safe harbor. The same rule applies to amounts deducted under Code Sec. 179D (energy efficient commercial building property) and Code Sec. 190 (expenses to remove architectural and transportation barriers).

Temporary closings. Remodel-refresh costs incurred during a temporary closing are not eligible for the safe harbor. A temporary closing is a closing of the qualified building during normal business hours for more than 21 consecutive calendar days.

> **COMMENT:** This rule presumably is designed to prevent particularly extensive remodel-refresh projects from qualifying for the safe harbor.

Remodel-refreshes prior to placing building in service. Remodel-refreshes performed prior to the date that the taxpayer places the building in service are not eligible for the safe harbor. No portion of these costs is repair expenses. The costs are treated as part of the acquisition cost of the building (Reg. § 1.263(a)-2(d)(1)).

Initial buildout for lessee. The costs of an initial buildout of a building for a new lessee do not qualify under the safe harbor.

Interaction with Other Safe Harbors and Elections

The routine maintenance safe harbor (Reg. § 1.263(a)-3(i)), which allows taxpayer to deduct certain routine maintenance costs that might otherwise be capitalized, does not apply to amounts paid or incurred during a remodel-refresh. The routine maintenance safe harbor, however, continues to apply to amounts paid for excluded remodel-refresh costs or amounts not incurred in a remodel-refresh project (Sec. 5.05 of Rev. Proc. 2015-56).

A safe harbor allowed by the tangible property regulations allows *small taxpayers* with average gross receipts of $10 million or less to make an annual election to deduct as a repair expense all repairs and improvements to a building that cost $1 million or less if the total cost of such repairs and improvements does not exceed the lesser of $10,000 or 2 percent of the cost of the building (Reg. § 1.263(a)-3(h)).

The safe harbor for remodel-refreshes states that a qualified taxpayer that uses the remodel-refresh safe harbor may not elect to apply the safe harbor for buildings to amounts paid for repair, maintenance, improvement, or similar activities related to a remodel-refresh project during the tax year (Sec. 5.05 of Rev. Proc. 2015-56).

> **COMMENT:** This language means that the safe harbor for buildings may be elected by a taxpayer using the remodel-refresh safe harbor but that remodel-refresh costs are not taken into account in applying the building safe harbor.

> **COMMENT:** The safe harbor guidance does not explain the interaction of the remodel-refresh safe-harbor with the annual election to capitalize repair expenses if such expenses are capitalized on the taxpayer's books and records (Reg. § 1.263(a)-3(n)). Based on the preceding rules for the routine maintenance safe harbor and safe harbor for small taxpayers, one would expect that the election to follow books would be allowed but disregarded for all costs associated with the remodel-repair project.

Building and Improvements Must Be Placed in General Asset Accounts

In order to apply the safe harbor, the building (if depreciable under MACRS) and improvements capitalized under the safe harbor must be placed in separate MACRS general asset accounts (GAAs) (Sec. 5.02(6) of Rev. Proc. 2015-56).

> **CAUTION:** Only buildings and improvements that are depreciable under MACRS may be placed in a general asset account. The safe harbor, however, also applies to buildings that are not depreciable under MACRS. Additions and improvements made after 1986 to a building, including capitalized remodel-refresh costs, are depreciated under MACRS even if the building is not MACRS property and must be placed in a GAA.

A taxpayer changing to the safe harbor accounting method will need to make a late GAA election for all existing buildings that are eligible for the safe harbor at the time the change in accounting method is filed. The late election is considered an accounting method change. However, it is made as part of the accounting method change to elect the safe harbor (Sec. 11.10(4)(b) of Rev. Proc. 2016-29).

Late GAA elections must also be made for any addition or improvement that was previously made to the building and that is depreciable under MACRS. The late election for additions and improvements must be made whether or not the addition or improvement related to a prior remodel-refresh project (Sec. 5.02(6) (a) (iii) of Rev. Proc. 2016-56).

> **COMMENT:** The remodel-refresh safe harbor makes no specific reference regarding the treatment of future improvements that are made to a building that is subject to the remodel-refresh safe harbor. Nevertheless, it appears that these future improvements, like all past improvements, must be placed in a GAA even if they are unrelated to the remodel-refresh project.

> **COMMENT:** A building placed in a GAA that is later demolished may continue to be depreciated. The property is not subject to the rule (Code Sec. 280B) that requires demolition costs and losses to be capitalized to the basis of the land. Note, however, that a building placed in service and disposed of in the same tax year may not be depreciated or placed in a GAA. However, it is possible that a GAA antiabuse rule could prevent this planning technique in some cases (Reg. § 1.168(i)-(1)).

Revocation of Partial Disposition Elections

Because a building subject to the remodel-refresh safe harbor method must be placed in a GAA, a taxpayer may not make a partial disposition election (Reg. § 1.168(i)-8(d)) to claim retirement losses on building components (such as a replaced original roof) after the building is placed in the GAA (Sec. 5.02(4) of Rev. Proc. 2015-56). The partial disposition election does not apply to assets that are in a GAA. Also, it does not apply assets that are not depreciated under MACRS.

The safe harbor method must be applied on a cutoff basis to a building if a taxpayer previously claimed one or more retirement losses on structural components of the building by making a timely partial disposition election or by filing an accounting method change to make a late partial disposition election *unless* the taxpayer revokes those earlier elections (Sec. 11.10(4)(c) of Rev. Proc. 2016-29). Application of the safe harbor on a cutoff basis means that the taxpayer may not apply the safe harbor method to any remodel-refreshes on that building that took place prior to the year for which the change to the safe harbor method is made.

EXAMPLE: Tillman Inc. operates two retail buildings, A and B. It filed an accounting method change for the 2014 tax year to make a late partial disposition election to claim a retirement loss on building A's original roof, which was disposed of in 2010. No partial disposition election was made for building B. In 2016 Tillman Inc. incurs remodel-refresh expenses for both buildings and files an accounting method change for 2016 to use the safe harbor method. Unless Tillman files a timely accounting method change to revoke the partial disposition election for building A, the safe harbor method will be applied on a cutoff basis for building A (i.e., the safe harbor will not apply to any remodel-refresh costs that occurred prior to the tax year for which an accounting method change to use the remodel-refresh safe harbor is made). The safe harbor is not applied on a cutoff method to building B because no prior partial disposition elections were made. Tillman may, therefore, compute a Code Sec. 481(a) adjustment for prior remodel-refreshes on building B.

The election to revoke a prior partial disposition election is a separate accounting method change that is described in Section 6.20 of Rev. Proc. 2016-29.

COMMENT: A taxpayer may also revoke prior timely elections on an amended return if the limitations period for assessment has not expired. If this route is followed, however, a taxpayer will also need to file amended returns for all tax years subsequent to the partial disposition election year to reflect the depreciation that could have been claimed on the retirement loss during those years (Sec. 5.02(4)(b)(ii)(A) of Rev. Proc. 2015-56).

CAUTION: The IRS has set a deadline for filing an accounting method change to revoke a prior-year partial disposition election to a tax year beginning after December 31, 2013, and ending before December 31, 2016 (6.20(3) of Rev. Proc. 2016-29). The revocation, if timely, may be filed concurrently (i.e., on the same Form 3115) with the change to adopt the remodel-refresh safe harbor method. A taxpayer, however, that waits to file a change of accounting method to use the safe harbor method until the year that a remodel-refresh occurs must file the revocation separately within the deadline period if the remodel-refresh safe harbor method change will be filed for a tax year after the deadline for making the revocation.

EXAMPLE: North Shore Inc., a calendar year corporation, owns a single MACRS building and filed an accounting method change for 2014 to make a late partial disposition election for certain retirements that occurred in earlier tax years. North Shore completes a remodel-refresh in 2017 and files an accounting method change to adopt the safe harbor for the 2017 year. This method change must include a late election to place the building in a GAA and all prior improvements in GAAs. Because North Shore did not file a timely accounting method change to revoke the earlier late disposition election, the safe harbor is applied on a cutoff basis and prior remodel-refreshes are not subject to the safe harbor. Because the building is now in a GAA no future partial disposition elections are allowed.

COMMENT: A taxpayer that wants to apply the safe harbor basis on a cutoff basis may deliberately choose not to revoke prior partial disposition elections.

COMMENT: Originally, the IRS required that an accounting method change to revoke a prior partial disposition election be made for the qualified taxpayer's first or second tax year beginning after December 31, 2013 (Sec. 6.43 of Rev. Proc. 2015-14, as added by Rev. Proc. 2015-56). However, this deadline was extended to any tax year beginning after December 31, 2013, and ending before December 31, 2016 (6.20(3) of Rev. Proc. 2016-29, superseding Rev. Proc. 2015-14). The IRS extension reflects that fact that deadline for revoking elections had already passed for some taxpayers with a short tax year as of the date that the safe harbor was issued, thus unfairly penalizing such taxpayers.

> **COMMENT:** An IRS spokesperson informally indicated that the 75/25 percent deduction-capitalization split was determined by taking into account the denial of the partial disposition election. The 75 percent deduction portion would have been reduced if partial disposition elections had been allowed. Not allowing partial disposition elections was done for the sake of simplification.

STUDY QUESTION

1. Which of the following costs are taken into account in computing the amounts capitalized and deducted under the remodel-refresh safe harbor?

- **a.** Cost of Section 1245 property
- **b.** Cost of Section 1245 property expensed under Code Sec. 179
- **c.** Initial build-out costs of the property for a new lessee
- **d.** Cost of 15-year qualified leasehold improvement property that is not expensed under Code Sec. 179(f) as qualified real property

¶ 406 NEW ACCOUNTING METHOD CHANGE PROCEDURE USED TO APPLY TANGIBLE PROPERTY REGS

All automatic accounting method changes, including those relating to the tangible property regulations, are governed by Rev. Proc. 2016-29, effective for accounting method changes filed on or after May 5, 2016, for a year of change ending on or after September 30, 2015. Rev. Proc. 2016-29, supersedes Rev. Proc. 2015-14.

Repair Regulations

The accounting method change procedures relating to the repair regulation portion of the tangible property regulations (generally, Reg. §§ 1.263(a)-1, -2, and -3), which were previously described in Section 10.11 of Rev. Proc. 2015-14, are now found in Section 11.08 of Rev. Proc. 2016-29. Modifications made to Sec. 10.11 of Rev. Proc. 2015-14 by Rev. Proc. 2015-20, which allowed small business taxpayers to comply with the repair regulations without filing Form 3115, are now incorporated into the text of Section 11.08. The designated accounting number change for each particular method change is the same under both procedures.

Waiver of eligibility limitations extended one year. The most significant substantive change made by Rev. Proc. 2016-29 to the changes for complying with the repair regulations contained in superseded Rev. Proc. 2015-14 is a one-year extension of the waiver of the eligibility limitations of Section 5.01(d) of Rev. Proc. 2015-13 (preventing a taxpayer from filing a Form 3115 under the automatic procedure in its last year of a trade or business) and Section 5.01(f) (preventing a taxpayer from filing the same accounting method change for the same item under the automatic procedure in a five-year period, ending in the year of change) (Section 10.11(2)(a) of Rev. Proc. 2016-29).

Under superseded Rev. Proc. 2015-14, these eligibility limitations did not apply to a change made under Section 10.11 for any tax year beginning before January 1, 2015 (Rev. Proc. 2015-14, Section 10.11(2)(a)). The deadline had been extended one year to tax years beginning before January 1, 2016 (Rev. Proc. 2016-29, Section 11.08(2)). Thus, the same change to comply with the final repair regulations may be filed any number of times for the 2012, 2013, 2014, and 2015 tax years.

> **COMMENT:** For a tax year beginning on or after January 1, 2016, if a taxpayer may not file a change under the automatic procedure because of the eligibility limitations, the taxpayer must file the change using the advance consent procedure of Rev. Proc. 2015-13. Under the advance consent procedure, the taxpayer must receive actual consent from the IRS to make the change and will pay an $8,600 filing fee. Immediate consent to change accounting methods is granted under the automatic procedure unless the IRS advises otherwise and no fee is charged.

Advance consent required if credit claimed. Another significant change adds a rule that prevents a taxpayer from using the automatic method procedure to change from capitalizing and depreciating an asset to deducting its cost as a repair expense if the taxpayer claimed any type of income tax credit on the asset. If a credit was claimed, a taxpayer must file the change using the advance consent procedure. Furthermore, the automatic consent procedure may not be used to change from capitalizing to deducting if the taxpayer is a corporation that made an election under Code Sec. 168(k)(4) to forgo bonus depreciation on the capitalized amount (Sec. 11.08(1)(b) of Rev. Proc. 2016-29).

> **COMMENT:** The IRS was concerned about situations in which a taxpayer changes from capitalizing to expensing an asset and winds up claiming both a credit on the capitalized amount and a repair deduction for the previously capitalized amount (double dipping). In this situation the IRS expects that the taxpayer should compute a Section 481(a) adjustment that recaptures the credit. Previously, this rule requiring use of the advance consent procedure only applied to the rehabilitation credit when a change from an impermissible method to a permissible method of depreciating an asset (Change #7) was made. It now applies to any credit where a Change #7 is made or a change from capitalizing to deducting pursuant to the repair regulations is made under Section 11.08 of Rev. Proc. 2016-29.

> **COMMENT:** Change #7 is one of the most common automatic accounting method changes and is often filed in conjunction with changes under the repair regulations when it is discovered that a taxpayer used an incorrect depreciation period or failed to claim depreciation on an asset.

MACRS Tangible Property Regulations

The final tangible property regulations include regulations under the modified accelerated cost recovery system (MACRS) dealing with general asset accounts (Reg. § 1.168(i)-1), item and multiple asset accounts (Reg. § 1.168(i)-7), and dispositions of assets (Reg. § 1.168(i)-8).

Various accounting method changes to comply with these MACRS regulations, which were effective for tax years beginning on and after January 1, 2014, were previously contained in Sections 6.32 through 6.40 of Rev. Proc. 2015-14, as modified by Rev. Proc. 2015-20. Changes to comply with these MACRS regulations now appear in Sections 6.10 through 6.18 of Rev. Proc. 2016-29, which supersedes Rev. Proc. 2015-14, effective for Form 3115s filed on or after May 5, 2016, for a year of change ending on or after September 30, 2015.

Changes described in Sections 6.27 through 6.31 in Rev. Proc. 2015-14 related to accounting methods that were permitted under the temporary or proposed MACRS tangible property regulations. These changes are obsolete because 2013 was the last tax year in which methods in the temporary and proposed regulations could be applied. Consequently, they are not included in Rev. Proc. 2016-29.

Rev. Proc. 2016-29 also removes the accounting method change allowed by Rev. Proc. 2015-14 to make a late MACRS general asset account election for assets placed in service in tax years beginning before January 1, 2012 (Section 6.32 of Rev. Proc. 2015-14). This election was required to be made no later than a taxpayer's last tax year beginning before January 1, 2014, and is now obsolete.

The accounting method change *to revoke* these late GAA elections (Section 6.34 of Rev. Proc. 2015-14) was retained by Rev. Proc. 2016-29 (Section 6.11) because certain fiscal-year taxpayers, as of the May 5, 2016, issuance date of Rev. Proc. 2016-29, still had time to meet the deadline for filing this change. The deadline requires the late GAA election to be revoked by filing an accounting method change for the taxpayer's last tax year beginning before January 1, 2015.

Eligibility rule extended. An important substantive change made by Rev. Proc. 2016-29 to depreciation method changes under Rev. Proc. 2015-14 extends the waiver of the eligibility rule in Section 5.01(1)(f) of Rev. Proc. 2015-13 by one year to any tax year beginning before January 1, 2016, for the following method changes:

- Section 6.13, relating to depreciation of leasehold improvements under Reg. § 1.167(a)-4;
- Section 6.14, relating to a change from a permissible to another permissible method of accounting for depreciation of MACRS property under Reg. §§ 1.168(i)-1, 1.168(i)-7, and 1.168(i)-8;
- Section 6.15, relating to dispositions of a building or structural component under Reg. § 1.168(i)-8;
- Section 6.16, relating to dispositions of tangible depreciable assets (other than a building or its structural components) under Reg. § 1.168(i)-8; and
- Section 6.17, relating to dispositions of tangible depreciable assets in a general asset account under Reg. § 1.168(i)-1.

As discussed earlier, the eligibility rule in Sec. 5.01(1)(f) prevents a taxpayer from using the automatic consent procedure if the taxpayer has made or requested a change for the same specific item during any of the five tax years ending with the year of change.

> **COMMENT:** The eligibility rule of Sec. 5.01(1)(d) of Rev. Proc. 2015-13, which prevents a taxpayer from using the automatic method change in the last year of a trade or business, does not apply to these accounting method changes regardless of the year of change.

Advance consent required for Change #7 if credit claimed. Another important change prevents a taxpayer from changing from an impermissible method of depreciation to a permissible method (Change #7) described in Section 6.01 if the taxpayer has claimed any type of federal income tax credit on the property for which the change is being made (Section 6.01(1)(c)(xvi)). In the past, this rule only applied if the taxpayer claimed the rehabilitation credit.

STUDY QUESTION

2. Which of the following is correct regarding Rev. Proc. 2016-29, the new revenue procedure governing automatic changes to comply with the repair regulations?

    a. Rev. Proc. 2016-29 applies to Forms 3115 filed on or after May 5, 2016, for tax years ending on or after January 1, 2016

    b. A taxpayer who claims an investment tax credit on depreciable property may not file an automatic change to correct the depreciation period of the property

    c. Waiver of the eligibility limitation that prevents a taxpayer from filing accounting method changes for the same item more than once in a five-year period has been extended to apply to accounting method changes to comply with the tangible property regulations filed in tax years beginning before January 1, 2010

    d. Rev. Proc. 2016-29 includes an accounting method change to make a late GAA election for assets placed in service before January 1, 2012

¶ 407 BONUS DEPRECIATION

The PATH Act made several important changes to bonus depreciation that will affect the preparation of tax returns for 2016 and beyond (Code Sec. 168(k), as amended by the PATH Act).

First and foremost, bonus depreciation, which was scheduled to expire after 2014, was extended to apply to property placed in service through 2019. The 50 percent rate continues to apply to property placed in service in 2015, 2016, and 2017. The rate, however, is reduced to 40 percent for property placed in service in 2018 and to 30 percent for property placed in service in 2019 (Code Sec. 168(k)(6), as added by the PATH Act). Unless extender legislation is again enacted, bonus depreciation will expire after 2019.

> **COMMENT:** To reflect the reduction of the bonus depreciation rates in 2018 and 2019, the $8,000 increase in the otherwise applicable first-year depreciation cap on passenger automobiles on which bonus depreciation is claimed will be reduced to $6,400 for a vehicle placed in service in 2018 and to $4,800 for a vehicle placed in service in 2019 (Code Sec. 168(k)(2)(F), as amended by the PATH Act).

Although bonus depreciation will generally expire after 2019, long production property produced by or for a taxpayer and placed in service in 2020 will continue to qualify for bonus depreciation at the 30 percent rate. The 40 percent rate will apply to long production property placed in service in 2019. The 50 percent rate applies to long production property placed in service before 2019 (Code Sec. 168(k)(6), as added by the PATH Act).

If long production property is placed in service in 2020, the cost attributable to 2020 production *(progress expenditures)* is not eligible for bonus depreciation (Code Sec. 168(k)(2)(B)(ii), as amended by the PATH Act).

Long production property is defined as property that:

- Has a recovery (depreciation) period of at least 10 years or is tangible personal property used in the trade or business of transporting persons or property, such as commercial aircraft;
- Is subject to the uniform capitalization rules of Code Sec. 263A; and
- Has a production period exceeding one year and a cost exceeding $1 million (Code Sec. 168(k)(2)(B)).

Qualified Improvement Property Replaces Qualified Leasehold Improvement Property

Effective for property placed in service on or after January 1, 2016, qualified improvement property qualifies for bonus depreciation. The *qualified improvement property* category replaces the *qualified leasehold improvement property* category of qualifying property.

Qualified improvement property is defined as any improvement to an interior portion of a building that is nonresidential real property if the improvement is placed in service after the date the building was first placed in service (Code Sec. 168(k)(3), as amended by the PATH Act).

> **COMMENT:** The use of the phrase "first placed in service" means that the improvement can qualify if the building was first placed in service by any person. For example, if a taxpayer buys an existing building that was previously placed in service by another person, qualified improvements made by the taxpayer at any time after the taxpayer purchases the building can qualify for bonus depreciation when the improvements are placed in service by the taxpayer.

Qualified improvement property does not include expenditures attributable to the enlargement of a building, any elevator or escalator, or the internal structural framework of the building.

Qualified *leasehold* improvement property (which qualified for bonus depreciation prior to 2016) was defined similarly to qualified improvement property except that the following additional limitations applied:

- The improvement needed to be made pursuant to the terms of a lease by the lessor or lessee (or sublessee) and the lessee (or sublessee) must occupy the building;
- The improvement needed to be placed in service more than three years after the building was first placed in service by any person; and
- Improvements that were structural components benefiting a common area of the building did not qualify (Code Sec. 168(k)(3), prior to amendment by the PATH Act).

> **COMMENT:** Qualified improvement property is defined much more broadly than qualified leasehold improvement property because the improvement does not need to be made pursuant to a lease. Any property that meets the definition of qualified leasehold improvement property will necessarily meet the definition of qualified improvement property and will be eligible for bonus depreciation beginning in 2016.

> **CAUTION:** Qualified improvement property does not qualify for a 15-year recovery period unless the qualified improvement property is:

- 15-year leasehold improvement property;
- 15-year retail improvement property; or
- 15-year restaurant improvement property, as discussed below.

STUDY QUESTION

3. Under the PATH Act, bonus depreciation:

    a. Is permanently extended

    b. Decreases to 40 percent in 2018 and to 30 percent in 2019

    c. May not be claimed after 2018 on long production property

    d. Is unavailable for improvements to interiors of nonresidential property

Specified Plants; Bonus Allowed in Year of Planting or Grafting

Effective for specified plants that are planted or grafted beginning in 2016, a taxpayer may elect to claim a depreciation deduction equal to 50 percent of the adjusted basis of the specified plant in the tax year in which it is planted or grafted in the ordinary course of the taxpayer's farming business as defined in Code Sec. 263A(e)(4) (Code Sec. 168(k)(5), as added by the PATH Act).

A *specified plant* is:

- Any tree or vine that bears fruits or nuts; and
- Any other plant that will have more than one yield of fruits or nuts and that generally has a preproductive period of more than two years from the time of planting or grafting to the time at which the plant begins bearing fruits or nuts.

The deduction reduces the adjusted basis of the specified plant. If an election to claim the 50 percent deduction is made, the regular bonus depreciation deduction may not be claimed when the specified plant is placed in service.

    COMMENT: A depreciable tree, vine, or plant is considered placed in service in the tax year that it first becomes productive, i.e., bears fruit, nuts, etc. in a commercial quantity (Reg. § 1.46-3(d)(2)), flush language). This new provision in effect accelerates the 50 percent bonus depreciation deduction that would otherwise apply in the year that the specified plant became productive to the year of planting or grafting.

    CAUTION: Although a 50 percent deduction may be claimed in the year of planting or grafting, the provision does not accelerate the regular depreciation deductions on the remaining basis to the year of planting or grafting. Accordingly, regular depreciation deductions continue to begin in the placed-in-service year, which is the tax year that the specified plant produces crops.

The specified plant must be planted or grafted in the United States.

The election is made annually. It is only revocable with IRS consent.

If the 50 percent deduction is claimed, neither the 50 percent deduction nor any regular depreciation deductions on the specified plant are subject to alternative minimum tax (AMT) adjustments (i.e., the deductions are claimed in full for AMT purposes).

The 50 percent deduction is not subject to capitalization under the uniform capitalization rules of Code Sec. 263A (Code Sec. 263A(c)(7), as added by the PATH Act).

In the case of a specified plant that is planted or grafted in 2018, the applicable deduction percentage is reduced to 40 percent and, if planted or grafted in 2019, is reduced to 30 percent. This reduction corresponds to the reduction required on property for which the regular bonus depreciation deduction is claimed.

¶407

Coordination with Long-Term Method of Accounting

The PATH Act extended through 2019 the special rule that disregards bonus depreciation for purposes of determining the percentage of completion of a long term contract. Under this rule, the cost of property with an MACRS recovery period of seven years or less that qualifies for bonus depreciation is taken into account as a cost allocated to the contract as if bonus depreciation had not been enacted if the property was placed in service (Code Sec. 460(c)(6)(B)(ii), as amended by the PATH Act):

- In 2010 (2010–2011 in the case of transportation property with a recovery period of seven years or less that is property with a longer production period (LPP) described above); and
- In 2013–2019 (2013–2020 in the case of transportation property that is LPP described above).

STUDY QUESTION

---

4. The PATH Act bonus depreciation deduction for specified plants:

   a. Is claimed in the year the specified plants are planted or grafted

   b. Applies to annual crops such as corn and wheat

   c. Is available for fruit trees planted and raised outside of the United States

   d. Requires a one-time election that applies to all specified plants grown by the same farmer in the year of election and thereafter

---

¶ 408 PERMANENT EXTENSION OF 15-YEAR RECOVERY PERIOD FOR QUALIFIED LEASEHOLD, RETAIL, AND RESTAURANT IMPROVEMENTS

The PATH Act permanently extends the 15-year recovery (depreciation) period under MACRS for:

- Qualified leasehold improvement property;
- Qualified retail improvement property; and
- Qualified restaurant property.

Although the recovery period is only 15 years, the applicable depreciation method is the straight-line method. The half-year or mid-quarter convention applies.

The 15-year recovery periods were scheduled to expire after 2014 but are now permanent. Without the extension, a 39-year recovery period would have applied.

The definition of *qualified leasehold improvement property* that is eligible for bonus depreciation prior to 2016 continues to apply after 2015 for purposes of the 15-year recovery period (Code Sec. 168(e)(6)). This definition is discussed above under the rules for bonus depreciation but generally means an improvement to the internal portion of a building by a lessor or lessee pursuant to the terms of a lease. The leasehold improvement must be made more than three years after the building was placed in service by any person (i.e., not necessarily the lessor or lessee making the improvement).

Qualified retail improvement property is defined the same way as qualified leasehold improvement property except that the improvement must be made to the internal portion of a building used in the retail trade or business of selling tangible personal property to the general public; it does not matter whether the improvement is made under a lease by a lessor or a lessee (Code Sec. 168(e)(8)).

Qualified restaurant property is broadly defined as any improvement to a restaurant and also includes a restaurant building. Improvements to the internal or external structure may qualify. The improvement does not need to be made to a building that has been in service more than three years. The improvement does not need to be made pursuant to a lease (Code Sec. 168(e)(7)).

Bonus depreciation. As discussed earlier, beginning in 2016, qualified improvement property qualifies for bonus depreciation (Code Sec. 168(k)(3), as amended by the PATH Act). A 15-year qualified leasehold improvement property and 15-year qualified retail improvement placed in service in 2016 and later will necessarily qualify for bonus depreciation because qualified leasehold improvement property and retail improvement property are defined in such a way that they will necessarily meet the definition of qualified improvement property.

A 15-year qualified restaurant property that is a restaurant building cannot meet the definition of qualified improvement property and, therefore, cannot qualify for bonus depreciation in 2016 or later. However, an improvement to the interior of a restaurant may qualify for bonus depreciation in 2016 or later if the improvement meets the definition of qualified improvement property. External improvements to a restaurant building qualify for a 15-year recovery period but do not constitute "qualified improvement property" for bonus depreciation purposes.

For property placed in service prior to 2016, bonus depreciation may only be claimed on 15-year qualified retail improvement property and 15-year qualified restaurant property if such property also met the definition of qualified leasehold improvement property under the bonus depreciation rules.

¶ 409 CODE SEC. 179 CHANGES FOR TAX YEARS BEGINNING IN 2016

The PATH Act permanently extended the $500,000 annual cap on the Code Sec. 179 deduction and the $2 million investment limitation.

However, beginning in 2016, the $500,000 annual cap on the Code Sec. 179 deduction and the $2 million investment limitation are adjusted annually for inflation (Code Sec. 179(b)(6), as added by the PATH Act).

For tax years beginning in 2016, the annual cap, as adjusted for inflation, remains at $500,000. The investment limitation, however, is increased from $2 million to $2,010,000 (Rev. Proc. 2016-14).

> **COMMENT:** The investment limitation causes the annual cap to be reduced by the cost of a taxpayer's purchases of Section 179 property during the tax year in excess of the investment limitation amount. Consequently, if a taxpayer purchases more than $2,510,000 of Section 179 property in a tax year beginning in 2016, the $500,000 cap is completely phased out and no amount may be expensed under Section 179 ($2,510,000 – $2,010,000 = $500,000 reduction to the $500,000 cap).

Qualified Real Property

The PATH Act also permanently extended the option to elect to treat the three categories of property with a 15-year recovery period (qualified leasehold improvement, retail improvement, and restaurant property) as Section 179 property. For purposes of Code Sec. 179, these three categories of property are collectively referred to as *qualified real property* (Code Sec. 179(f), as amended by the PATH Act).

In tax years beginning on or after January 1, 2016, the $250,000 limitation on the amount of qualified real property that could be expensed under Code Sec. 179 is eliminated. Consequently, for a tax year beginning in 2016, up to $500,000 of the cost of qualified real property may be applied toward the overall $500,000 limitation that applies to a tax year beginning in 2016.

> **CAUTION:** Any amount of qualified real property that is expensed under Code Sec. 179 is subject to ordinary income recapture under Code Sec. 1245 to the extent of gain upon disposition of the property (Code Sec. 1245(a)(3)(C)). Bonus depreciation claimed on qualified real property is treated as an accelerated depreciation deduction and is subject to recapture under Code Sec. 1250 in an amount equal to the difference between the bonus deduction and straight-line depreciation that could have been claimed on the bonus deduction (Reg. § 1.168(k)-1(f)(3)).

Portable Air Conditioning and Heating Units

In tax years beginning on or after January 1, 2016, the Code Sec. 179 deduction may be claimed on portable air conditioning and heating units (Code Sec. 179(d), as amended by the PATH Act).

> **CAUTION:** Property used in the provision of lodging does not qualify for expensing (Code Sec. 179(d)(1)). Therefore, portable air conditioning and heating units used in a residential rental unit may not be expensed. Hotels and motels that provide lodging on a transient basis are excepted from this rule. Accordingly, portable units used by such hotels and motels may be expensed (Reg. § 1.48-1(h)).

> **COMMENT:** Heating, ventilating, and air conditioning (HVAC) units used to cool and heat a building do not qualify for expensing because HVACS are permanently affixed structural components and, therefore, constitute Section 1250 property. Unless a specific exception applies, such as that for qualified real property, only Section 1245 property may be expensed under Code Sec. 179.

Additional Changes

Effective for tax years beginning on or after January 1, 2015 (one year earlier than the preceding changes), the new law made the following Section 179 provisions permanent:

- Expensing of "off-the-shelf" computer software (Code Sec. 179(d)(1), as amended by the PATH Act);
- Allowing taxpayers to file amended returns without IRS permission to make, revoke, or change a Section 179 election (Code Sec. 179(c)(2), as amended by the PATH Act); and
- The expensing deduction for qualified real property (the $250,000 annual limit is also increased to $500,000 after 2015 as explained above) (Code Sec. 179(f), as amended by the PATH Act)).

STUDY QUESTION

5. Which of the following is *not* a change to the Section 179 deduction made by the PATH Act?

- **a.** Removing the rule that allows a taxpayer to make, change, or revoke a Section 179 expense election on an amended return without IRS consent
- **b.** Indexing the limitations for inflation in future years
- **c.** Permanently allowing Section 179 expensing for off-the-shelf software
- **d.** Allowing expensing of portable air conditioning and heating units as Section 179 property

¶ 410 DEPRECIATION-RELATED CHANGES FOR SPECIAL TAXPAYERS IN 2016

The PATH Act temporarily extended the following targeted depreciation provisions.

Extension of Corporate Election to Claim Accelerated AMT Credit in Lieu of Bonus Depreciation

The PATH Act extends the election for corporations to forgo bonus depreciation and instead claim unused AMT credits for four years to apply to property placed in service through 2019 (2020 for long production property and certain noncommercial aircraft). In tax years beginning in 2016, the election is made annually and the amount of unused credits that may be claimed is no longer subject to an annual limitation of $30 million dollars or 6 percent of unused pre-2006 AMT credits (Code Sec. 168(k)(4), as amended by the PATH Act).

If the election is made, the Code Sec. 53(c) limitation on the amount of unused AMT credits that may be claimed in a tax year continues to be increased by the "bonus depreciation amount" for all assets placed in service during the tax year. The *bonus depreciation amount*, for each asset placed in service in a tax year, as in the past, is equal to 20 percent of the difference between (1) the first year depreciation (including bonus depreciation) that could be claimed on the asset if the bonus is claimed and (2) the first-year depreciation that could be claimed on the asset if bonus depreciation were not claimed.

The "maximum increase amount" limitation on the bonus depreciation amount is removed effective for tax years ending after 2015. Under this limitation, the bonus amount could not exceed the lesser of $30 million or 6 percent of the taxpayer's unused AMT credits attributable to tax years beginning before 2006.

The maximum increase amount is replaced with a new limitation on the bonus depreciation amount (Code Sec. 168(k)(4)(B)(ii), as amended by Act Sec. 143(b)(3) of P.L. 114-113).

Under the new limitation the bonus depreciation amount computed for a tax year may not exceed the lesser of:

- 50 percent of the corporation's minimum tax credit under Code Sec. 53(b) for the corporation's first tax year ending after 2015; or

- The minimum tax credit for the tax year, determined by taking into account only the adjusted net minimum tax (as defined in Code Sec. 53(d)) for tax years ending before January 1, 2016 (determined by treating credits as allowed on a first-in, first-out basis).

> **EXAMPLE:** QPEX, a calendar-year corporation that places property that is 10-year MACRS property costing $100,000 in service in June 2016, elects to forgo bonus depreciation to claim an accelerated AMT credit carryforward. QPEX first computes the bonus depreciation and regular depreciation on the MACRS bonus depreciation property. Bonus depreciation is $50,000 ($100,000 × 50%). Regular depreciation is $5,000 (($100,000 – $50,000 × 10% first-year percentage for 10-year property = $5,000). The $55,000 sum of the bonus depreciation and regular depreciation is reduced to $45,000 by the $10,000 depreciation that could be claimed in 2016 on the property if the bonus depreciation deduction was not claimed ($100,000 × 10% first-year percentage for 10-year property = $10,000). Assume that QPEX's 2016 limitation amount on the bonus depreciation amount is $200,000. The bonus depreciation amount is equal to the lesser of: (1) $9,000 ($45,000 × 20%) or (2) $200,000. Because $9,000 is less than $200,000, the bonus depreciation amount is $9,000. In this situation, QPEX could increase its AMT tax

liability limitation by $9,000 and claim an additional refundable $9,000 AMT credit by forgoing bonus depreciation.

Race Horses

The three-year MACRS recovery period for race horses regardless of age is extended two years to apply to property placed in service before January 1, 2017 (Code Sec. 168(e)(3), as amended by the PATH Act).

Motorsports Entertainment Complexes

The seven-year recovery period for motorsports entertainment complexes is extended two years to apply to property placed in service before January 1, 2017 (Code Sec. 168(i)(15), as amended by the PATH Act).

Election to Expense Film Production Costs Extended to Live Theatrical Productions in 2016

The election to treat the cost of a qualified film or television production as a currently deductible expense was extended by the PATH Act for two years to apply to productions commencing before January 1, 2017. In addition, the election was expanded to apply to live staged productions of a play (with or without music) that commence in 2016 (Code Sec. 181, as amended by the PATH Act). A qualified live theatrical production commences production on the date of the first public performance of the production for a paying audience (Act Sec. 169(d)(3) of the PATH Act).

The election applies regardless of the cost of the film or theatrical production and the first $15 million of production costs are deductible ($20 million if a significant portion of the production costs are incurred in low-income communities and certain financially distressed areas).

Indian Reservation Property: 2016 Election Out of Shortened Recovery Periods

Special shortened recovery periods apply to property located on an Indian reservation. This provision was extended two years by the PATH Act to apply to property placed in service before January 1, 2017 (Code Sec. 168(j), as amended by the PATH Act).

Effective for tax years beginning on or after January 1, 2016, taxpayers are permitted to make an election out of the special depreciation periods for any class of property. For example, an election out could be made for all MACRS five-year property (which is eligible for a shortened three-year recovery period) placed in service during 2016 on an Indian reservation. The election out is irrevocable (Code Sec. 168(j)(8), as added by the PATH Act).

> **COMMENT:** The election will permit taxpayers to use the regular depreciation periods to recover the cost of Indian reservation property in order to claim smaller amounts of depreciation in the earlier tax years of the recovery period. Under current law, a taxpayer wishing to reduce up-front depreciation deductions could also elect the alternative depreciation system (ADS), which is based on the straight-line depreciation method and recovery periods that are generally longer than the regular depreciation periods that would apply if the new election out is made.

> **CAUTION:** There is no AMT adjustment on depreciation deductions claimed using the shortened recovery periods for Indian reservation property. Consequently, an election out could inadvertently trigger an AMT liability.

STUDY QUESTION

6. The PATH ACT extended all of the following for two years (through 2016) *except:*

    a. The election to treat film or television production costs as currently deductible expenses

    b. The corporate election to claim unused AMT credits in lieu of bonus depreciation

    c. The three-year MACRS recovery period for race horses

    d. The seven-year recovery period for motorsports entertainment complexes

¶ 411 CONCLUSION

Although the IRS has provided the foundational rules for distinguishing between repairs and capital expenditures in the final tangible property regulations dealing with repairs and capital expenditures, the future will undoubtedly bring additional modifications and refinements. Practitioners will need to keep pace with new developments in this evolving practice area in order to best serve their clients. This chapter aimed to help in this regard and also in keeping abreast with changes relating to depreciation in general.

CPE NOTE: When you have completed your study and review of chapters 1-4, which comprise Module 1, you may wish to take the Final Exam for this Module. Go to **CCHGroup.com/PrintCPE** to take this Final Exam online.

MODULE 2: CHANGES IN FILING DEADLINES, AUDITS, AND PENALTIES—
Chapter 5: Tax Deadlines: A Changing Landscape

¶ 501 WELCOME

This chapter explores the revisions to filing deadlines made by the *Surface Transportation and Veterans Health Care Choice Act of 2015* (P.L. 114-41) (Surface Transportation Act) and the *Protecting Americans from Tax Hikes Act of 2015* (P.L. 114-113) (PATH Act). This chapter also highlights a temporary extension available to filers of certain forms under the *Patient Protection and Affordable Care Act* (P.L. 111-148) (ACA) along with the temporary suspension of another ACA-related tax, the medical device excise tax.

¶ 502 LEARNING OBJECTIVES

Upon completion of this chapter, you will be able to:

- Recognize which individuals and entities are required to file returns under current laws;
- Identify major revisions made by recent legislation for income tax returns of certain entities;
- Identify how the PATH Act changed filing dates for Forms W-2, W-3, and other forms; and
- Recognize changes to the extension period for filings under the 2015 legislation.

¶ 503 INTRODUCTION

In 2015, Congress made significant revisions to the due dates for filing many important and common returns, including Form 1065, *U.S. Return of Partnership Income;* Form 1120, *U.S. Corporation Income Tax Return;* FinCEN Report 114, *Report of Foreign Bank and Financial Accounts* (known as the FBAR); and more. The revisions also accomplish, at least in part, a long-sought-after goal: to better align return deadlines with the deadlines for information returns, as well as with the workflow of return preparers during the regular filing season and the extended filing season. The change affecting the FBAR, for example, aligns FBAR filings with Form 1040, *U.S. Individual Income Tax Return,* filings. For the most part, the changes apply for the first time in 2017 for 2016 calendar year tax returns.

¶ 504 FILINGS BY ENTITY TYPE

Corporations

Form 1120, *U.S. Corporation Income Tax Return,* is required to be filed annually by domestic corporations to report the income, credits, gains, losses, deductions, and income tax liability of the corporation unless it elects or is required to file a special return. Every corporation subject to income tax must file an income tax return. The return must be made if the corporation was in existence during any part of the tax year and must cover that part of the tax year that the corporation was in existence Corporate income tax returns are usually filed on Form 1120, but specified types of corporations are required to file on specialized forms.

Corporations with assets of $10 million or more on Schedule L of Form 1120 are required to file Form 1120 electronically. The electronic filing requirement does not apply to corporations that file fewer than 250 returns during the calendar year ending with or within its tax year.

To assess whether an organization meets the 250 return prerequisite, returns of all types are aggregated. If a corporation that is required to file electronically fails to do so, the corporation is deemed to have failed to file the return, and an addition to tax may apply. The electronic filing requirement applies to all members of the Form 1120 series of returns, including amended and superseding returns.

> **COMMENT:** All members of a controlled group of corporations, as defined in Code Sec. 1563(a), must file their corporate income tax returns on magnetic media if the aggregate number of returns required to be filed by the controlled group of corporations is at least 250.

> **COMMENT:** In the case of a short year return, an entity is required to file electronically if, during the calendar year that includes the short tax year of the entity, the entity is required to file at least 250 returns of any type, including, for example, income tax returns, returns required under Code Sec. 6033, information returns, excise tax returns, and employment tax returns.

Corporations may generally request waivers of the electronic filing requirement if they cannot meet the requirement due to technology constraints or if compliance with the requirements would result in undue economic hardship to the business. To request a waiver, the corporation must file a written request. If the electronic return cannot be accepted for processing, the corporation must file a paper return by the later of the due date of the return (including extensions) or 10 calendar days after the date the IRS last gives notification that the return has been rejected, provided the first notification was made on or before the due date of the return (including extension) and the last notification was made within 10 calendar days of the first notification. However, the business must contact the IRS for assistance in correcting rejected returns before filing the paper return.

Partnerships

Every domestic partnership must file a partnership return for each tax year. The term *partnership* includes a limited partnership, syndicate, group, pool, joint venture, or other unincorporated organization, through or by which any business, financial operation, or venture is carried on, that is not, within the meaning of IRS regulations under Code Sec. 7701, a corporation, trust, estate, or sole proprietorship. The return currently in use is Form 1065, *U.S. Partnership Return of Income* and includes Schedule K-1, *Partner's Share of Income, Credits, Deductions, Etc.* The partnership return must be filed for the tax year of the partnership regardless of the tax years of the partners. The partnership return must contain the information required by the form and the accompanying instructions.

A *foreign partnership* is a partnership that is not created or organized in the United States or under the law of the United States or of any state. Generally, a foreign partnership that has gross income effectively connected with the conduct of a trade or business within the United States or has gross income derived from sources in the United States must file Form 1065, even if its principal place of business is outside the United States or all its members are foreign persons. A foreign partnership required to file a return generally must report all of its foreign and U.S. source income. A foreign partnership with U.S. source income is not required to file Form 1065 if it qualifies for either of the following two exceptions.

Exception for foreign partnerships with U.S. partners. A return is not required if:

- The partnership had no effectively connected income (ECI) during its tax year;
- The partnership had U.S. source income of $20,000 or less during its tax year;
- Less than 1 percent of any partnership item of income, gain, loss, deduction, or credit was allocable in the aggregate to direct U.S. partners at any time during its tax year; and
- The partnership is not a withholding foreign partnership as defined in Reg. 1.1441-5T(c)(2)(i).

Exception for foreign partnerships with no U.S. partners. A return is not required if:

- The partnership had no ECI during its tax year;
- The partnership had no U.S. partners at any time during its tax year;
- All required Forms 1042 and 1042-S were filed by the partnership or another withholding agent as required by Reg. 1.1461-1(b) and (c) and Reg. 1.1461-1T(b) and (c);
- The tax liability of each partner for amounts reportable under Reg. 1.1461-1(b) and (c) and Reg. 1.1461T(b) and (c) has been fully satisfied by the withholding of tax at the source; and
- The partnership is not a withholding foreign partnership as defined in Reg. 1.1441-5T(c)(2)(i).

COMMENT: Correct information on Schedules K-1 is important because the IRS matches the data to other tax returns to ensure accurate reporting.

COMMENT: A partnership that has no income, deductions, or credits for federal income tax purposes for a tax year is not required to file a partnership return for that year.

Most partnerships are also required to file a balance sheet. This sheet is entered on Form 1065, Schedule L, *Balance Sheets.* Partnerships reporting to the Interstate Commerce Commission or to any national, state, municipal, or other public officer may submit copies of their balance sheets prescribed by those authorities, as of the beginning and end of the tax year, instead of completing Schedule L. However, there must be sufficient information to enable the IRS to reconstruct a balance sheet similar to Schedule L. Schedule L does not have to be completed if:

- The partnership's total receipts for the tax year are less than $250,000;
- The partnership's total assets at the end of the tax year are less than $1; and
- Schedules K-1 are filed with the return and furnished to the partners on or before the due date of the partnership return, including extensions.

A domestic partnership that elects to be excluded from the partnership rules or is deemed to have made the election is not required to file a partnership return. However, when the partnership affirmatively elects not to be subject to the partnership rules, it must timely file a partnership return for the election year, containing the information required under the exclusion election.

The return of a partnership must be filed with the IRS service center described in the relevant IRS revenue procedure, publication, form, or instructions to the form. Partnerships that have more than 100 partners are required to file returns electronically.

¶504

The IRS may waive the electronic filing rules if hardship is shown in a request for waiver. A determination of hardship is based on all of the facts and circumstances. One factor is the reasonableness of the incremental cost to the partnership of complying with the electronic filing requirements. Other factors, such as equipment breakdowns or destruction of magnetic media filing equipment, also may be considered. A request for waiver must be made in accordance with applicable revenue procedures or publications. The waiver must specify the type of partnership return and the period to which it applies.

> **COMMENT:** A partnership has more than 100 partners if, over the course of the partnership's tax year, the partnership had more than 100 partners. This applies regardless of whether a partner was a partner for the entire year or whether the partnership had more than 100 partners on any particular day in the year. However, only those persons having a direct interest in the partnership must be considered partners for purposes of determining the number of partners during the partnership's tax year.

S Corporations

S corporations must file annual returns on Form 1120S, *U.S. Income Tax Return for an S Corporation*, for each tax year that the election to be treated as an S corporation is in effect. Returns for S corporations must be filed no later than the 15th day of the third month after the close of the S corporation's tax year or March 15 for S corporations using the calendar year. The following information must be included on the return:

- Items of gross income and allowable deductions;
- Names and addresses of all persons owning stock in the corporation at any time during the tax year;
- Number of shares of stock owned by each shareholder at all times during the tax year;
- Amount of money and other property distributed during the year by the corporation to each shareholder and the date of each distribution;
- Each shareholder's pro-rata share of each item of the corporation for the tax year; and
- Any other information required by Form 1120S.

S corporations must also provide a statement containing information from Form 1120S to any person who was a shareholder during the tax year covered by the return. The statement must be provided on or before the day the return is filed. Ordinarily, S corporations meet this requirement by giving shareholders Schedule K-1, *Shareholder's Shares of Income, Crediting, Deductions, Etc.,* of Form 1120S.

> **COMMENT:** The deadline for filing Form 1120S may be postponed for persons serving in the Armed Forces of the United States or in support of the Armed Forces in a combat zone, or who are hospitalized as a result of such service. The postponement extends through the period of service, plus the period of continuous qualified hospitalization plus an additional 180 days.

> **COMMENT:** S corporations with less than $250,000 of gross receipts and less than $250,000 in assets do not have to complete Schedules L and M-1 of Form 1120S.

S corporations with assets of $10 million or more must file Form 1120S electronically. The electronic filing requirement applies to S corporations that file at least 250 returns during the calendar year ending with or within its tax year. In determining whether an S corporation has assets of $10 million or more, the value of an organization's assets is determined based on total assets at the end of the tax year. To assess whether an organization meets the 250 return prerequisite, returns of all types are aggregated. The IRS may grant waivers of the e-file requirement in cases of undue hardship. If an organization that is required to e-file fails to do so, the organization is deemed to have failed to file the return and an addition to tax may apply. The IRS will approve or deny requests for a waiver based on each taxpayer's particular facts and circumstances.

If the electronic return cannot be accepted for processing electronically, the taxpayer must file a paper return by the later of the due date of the return (including extensions), or 10 calendar days after the date the IRS last gives notification that the return has been rejected—provided the first transmission was made on or before the due date of the return (including extensions) and the last transmission was made within 10 calendar days of the first notification. However, the taxpayer must contact the IRS for assistance in correcting rejected returns before filing the paper return.

STUDY QUESTION

1. Electronic filing is required for:

    a. A C or S corporation with assets of $10 million or more

    b. A corporation in a controlled group filing 51 or more returns annually

    c. An S corporation that does not issue Schedule K-1 to shareholders

    d. A partnership with fewer than 250 partners

¶ 505 SURFACE TRANSPORTATION ACT

The Surface Transportation Act was signed into law by President Obama on July 31, 2016. The Surface Transportation Act was a temporary extension of federal highway spending put in place while lawmakers debated a multiyear extension of federal highway spending. To help offset the cost of the Surface Transportation Act, lawmakers looked to revising a number of filing due dates for many tax and information returns.

    COMMENT: According to the Congressional Joint Committee on Taxation, the revisions to certain return filing deadlines in the Surface Transportation Act are projected to generate $314 million in revenue over the next 10 years, largely through expected enhanced compliance on the part of taxpayers.

    COMMENT: The revisions in the Surface Transportation Act had been proposed before in Congress but failed to gain traction in prior years. In 2015, lawmakers needed revenue to offset the cost of the temporary highway bill and they turned to revising certain return due dates to raise the necessary revenue.

Filing Deadlines Before the Surface Transportation Act

Due dates for filing income tax returns by individuals, C corporations, S corporations, and partnerships are set forth in the tax code and regulations. Individuals must file their annual income tax return, Form 1040, Form 1040A, or 1040EZ, on or before the 15th day of the fourth month following the close of the tax year (April 15 for calendar year taxpayers) (Code Sec. 6072(a)). C corporations must file their annual Form 1120 on or before the 15th day of the third month following the close of the tax year (March 15 for calendar year taxpayers) (Code Sec. 6072(b)). S corporations also must file their annual Form 1120-S on or before the 15th day of the third month following the close of the tax year (March 15 for calendar year taxpayers) (Reg. § 1.6037-1(b)). Partnerships must file their annual Form 1065 on or before the 15th day of the fourth month following the close of the tax year (April 15 for calendar year taxpayers).

Many automatic filing extension periods are currently set by regulation or other IRS rules and include:

- Five-month extension for partnerships filing Form 1065 (Reg. § 1.6081-2(a));
- Five-month extension for estates and trusts filing Form 1041 (Reg. § 1.6081-6(a));
- Three-and-a-half month extension for employee benefit plans filing Form 5500 (series) (Reg. § 1.6081-11(a));
- Three-month extension for tax-exempt organizations filing Form 990 (series) (Reg. § 1.6081-9(a));
- Three-month extension for tax-exempt organizations filing Form 4720 for certain excise taxes (Reg. § 1.6081-9(a));
- Three-month extension for split-interest trusts filing Form 5227 (Reg. § 1.6081-9(a));
- Three-month extension for coal-mine operators filing Form 6069 (Reg. § 1.6081-9(a));
- Three-month extension for charitable organizations or charitable remainder trusts filing Form 8870 regarding certain transfers (Reg. § 1.6081-9(a));
- Six-month extension for foreign trusts filing Form 3520-A (Reg. § 301.6081-2(a)); and
- Extension obtained by a filer of Form 3520 to report certain foreign transactions with the filers' return (Notice 97-34, 1997-1 CB 422).

C corporations are allowed an automatic three-month extension to file Form 1120 (Code Sec. 6081(b)). However, the IRS has issued regulations extending the automatic extension period for corporations to six months (Reg. § 1.6081-3(a)).

Filing Deadlines Changed by the Surface Transportation Act

The due dates for certain returns have been codified and modified by the Surface Transportation Act.

Corporations. Generally applicable to returns for tax years beginning after December 31, 2015, the Surface Transportation Act revises the due date (without extension) for filing of Form 1120 by C corporations to the 15th day of the fourth month following the close of the tax year (April 15 for calendar year taxpayers) (Code Sec. 6072, as amended). A special rule in the Surface Transportation Act provides that for C corporations with fiscal years ending on June 30, the changes do not begin to apply until returns due for tax years beginning after December 31, 2025 (Act Sec. 2006(a)(3)(B) of the 2015 Surface Transportation Act). As a result, June 30 fiscal-year corporations retain a filing deadline of September 15 until returns for tax years starting in 2026.

Partnerships. The Surface Transportation Act codified the due dates for the filing of Form 1065 by partnerships and the filing of Form 1120-S by S corporations. The Surface Transportation Act also modifies the due date (without extension) for filing of Form 1065. Returns for tax years beginning after December 31, 2015, must be filed on or before the fifteenth day of the third month following the close of the partnership's tax year.

> **COMMENT:** The effect of the Surface Transportation Act is that both Form 1065 and Form 1120-S will be due on or before the 15th day of the third month following the close of the tax year (March 15 for calendar year taxpayers).

COMMENT: As a result of the change in the due date for partnership returns to March 15, partners who are individuals will receive their Schedule K-1, in time to report the information on their Form 1040. Proponents of the change had argued that it will keep many individuals from having to seek a six-month extension to file their Form 1040.

Extensions. The Surface Transportation Act also directs the IRS to modify the relevant regulations regarding automatic filing extensions (using Form 7004 or other extension form) and due dates for tax years beginning after December 31, 2015. The modifications include:

- A maximum six-month extension (currently five months) for partnerships filing Form 1065 (ending on September 15 for calendar year taxpayers);
- A maximum five-and-a-half month extension (currently five months) for trusts filing Form 1041 (ending on September 30 for calendar year taxpayers);
- A maximum three-and-a-half month extension (same as before) for employee benefit plans filing Form 5500 (series) (ending on November 15 for calendar year taxpayers);
- A maximum six-month extension (currently three months) for tax-exempt organizations filing Form 990 (series) (ending on November 15 for calendar year taxpayers);
- A maximum six-month extension (currently three months) for tax-exempt organizations filing Form 4720 beginning on the due date for filing the return (without regard to any extensions);
- A maximum six-month extension (currently three months) for split-interest trusts filing Form 5227 beginning on the due date for filing the return (without regard to any extensions);
- A maximum six-month extension (currently three months) for coal-mine operators filing Form 6069 beginning on the due date for filing the return (without regard to any extensions);
- A maximum six-month extension (currently three months) for charitable organizations or remainder trusts filing Form 8870 beginning on the due date for filing the return (without regard to any extensions);
- A due date equal of the 15th day of the third month after the close of a trust's tax year for trusts filing Form 3520-A (with a maximum six-month extension (same as before)); and
- A due date of April 15 for calendar year filers of Form 3520 with a maximum extension of six months ending on October 15.

COMMENT: Before the Surface Transportation Act, Reg. § 1.6081-5 provided an extension of time up to and including the 15th day of the sixth month following the close of the taxpayer's tax year for the filing of income tax returns and payment of income tax by:

- Certain partnerships and domestic corporations that keep records outside of the United States and Puerto Rico;
- Foreign corporations that maintain an office or place of business within the United States;
- U.S. citizens or residents whose tax homes and abodes, in a real and substantial sense, are outside of the United States and Puerto Rico; and
- U.S. citizens and residents in military or naval service and on permanent, nonpermanent, or short-term duty outside of the United States and Puerto Rico.

COMMENT: The six-month automatic extension currently provided by Reg. § 1.6081-3(a) to C corporations filing Form 1120 is codified (Code Sec. 6081(b)) under the Surface Transportation Act. This change applies to returns for tax years beginning after December 31, 2015. However, a special rule provides that in the case of any calendar year C corporation with a tax year beginning before January 1, 2026, the maximum extension allowed is five months. In the case of a C corporation with a fiscal year ending on June 30 and beginning before January 1, 2026, the maximum extension allowed is seven months (Code Sec. 6081(b)).

COMMENT: The Surface Transportation Act also directed the IRS to modify existing regulations to provide a maximum three-and-a-half month extension for employee benefit plans filing Form 5500 (series) (ending on November 15 for calendar year taxpayers) (Act Sec. 2006(b)(3) of the 2015 Surface Transportation Act). Subsequent legislation, the *Fixing America's Surface Transportation Act of 2015* (FAST Act) (P.L. 114-94), repealed this extension. Repeal is discussed later in this course.

Staggered effective dates. The effective dates of revisions to filing deadlines are staggered under the Surface Transportation Act. Generally, no change in return deadlines takes place before the 2017 filing season for 2016 tax year returns. Amendments to the due dates for returns of partnerships and C corporations generally apply to returns for tax years beginning after December 31, 2015. However, in the case of any C corporation with a tax year ending on June 30, the amendments apply to returns for tax years beginning after December 31, 2025. The amendment codifying the existing six-month automatic extension for C corporation returns is generally applicable to returns for tax years beginning after December 31, 2015. Changes to certain automatic filing extensions and due dates, as also discussed below, do not apply until extensions and filing due dates for tax years beginning after December 31, 2015 (therefore, also generally related to extensions first applicable during the 2017 filing season).

STUDY QUESTION

---

2. The Surface Transportation Act generally lengthens filing extension periods for all of the following *except:*

   a. Trusts filing Form 3520-A

   b. Tax-exempt organizations filing Form 990 or Form 4720

   c. Partnerships filing Form 1065

   d. Charitable organizations or remainder trusts filing Form 8870

¶ 506 FINCEN REPORT 114 (FBAR)

Federal law requires "United States persons" to disclose on FinCEN Report 114, *Report of Foreign Bank and Financial Accounts* (known as the FBAR) any financial interests in, signature authority over, or other authority over foreign financial accounts if the aggregate value of the accounts exceeds $10,000 at any time during the calendar year. The FBAR is not filed with the IRS. The FBAR must be filed directly with the office of Financial Crimes Enforcement Network (FinCEN), which is a bureau of the U.S. Treasury.

EXAMPLE: Joshua Reingeld, a United States person, owns foreign financial accounts 1, 2, and 3 with maximum account values of $1,000, $1,800, and $13,000, respectively. Joshua is required to file an FBAR because the aggregate value of the accounts is above the statutory amount. Joshua must report foreign financial accounts 1, 2, and 3 on the FBAR even though accounts 1 and 2 have maximum account values of less than $10,000.

United States Person

A *United States person* for purposes of the FBAR means any of the following:

- United States citizens (including minor children);
- United States residents;
- Entities, including but not limited to, corporations, partnerships, or limited liability companies created or organized in the United States or under the laws of the United States; and
- Trusts or estates formed under the laws of the United States.

COMMENT: The federal tax treatment of an entity does not determine whether the entity has an FBAR filing requirement. For example, an entity that is disregarded for purposes of the tax code must file an FBAR, if otherwise required to do so. Similarly, a trust for which the trust income, deductions, or credits are taken into account by another person for purposes of the tax code must file an FBAR, if otherwise required to do so.

Financial Account

For FBAR purposes, a *financial account* includes, but is not limited to, a securities, brokerage, savings, demand, checking, deposit, time deposit, or other account maintained with a financial institution (or other person performing the services of a financial institution). A financial account also includes a commodity futures or options account, an insurance policy with a cash value (such as a whole life insurance policy), an annuity policy with a cash value, and shares in a mutual fund or similar pooled fund (for example, a fund that is available to the general public with a regular net asset value determination and regular redemptions).

Foreign Financial Account

For purposes of the FBAR, a *foreign financial account* is a financial account located outside of the United States. For example, an account maintained with a branch of a United States bank that is physically located outside of the United States is a foreign financial account. An account maintained with a branch of a foreign bank that is physically located in the United States is not a foreign financial account.

A United States person has a financial interest in a foreign financial account for which:

- The United States person is the owner of record or holder of legal title, regardless of whether the account is maintained for the benefit of the United States person or for the benefit of another person; or
- The owner of record or holder of legal title is one of the following

  - An agent, nominee, attorney, or a person acting in some other capacity on behalf of the United States person with respect to the account,

  - A corporation in which the United States person owns directly or indirectly: (1) more than 50 percent of the total value of shares of stock or (2) more than 50 percent of the voting power of all shares of stock,

¶506

- A partnership in which the United States person owns directly or indirectly: (1) an interest in more than 50 percent of the partnership's profits (e.g., distributive share of partnership income taking into account any special allocation agreement) or (2) an interest in more than 50 percent of the partnership capital,

- A trust of which the United States person: (1) is the trust grantor and (2) has an ownership interest in the trust for United States federal tax purposes,

- A trust in which the United States person has a greater than 50 percent present beneficial interest in the assets or income of the trust for the calendar years, or

- Any other entity in which the United States person owns directly or indirectly more than 50 percent of the voting power, total value of equity interest or assets, or interest in profits.

COMMENT: Correspondent or "nostro" accounts (maintained by banks and used solely for bank-to-bank settlements) are not required to be reported. A foreign financial account of any governmental entity is not required to be reported by any person. A foreign financial account of any international financial institution (if the United States government is a member) is not required to be reported by any person.

COMMENT: An owner or beneficiary of an individual retirement account (IRA) is not required to report a foreign financial account held in the IRA. A participant in or beneficiary of a retirement plan described in Code Sec. 401(a), 403(a), or 403(b) is not required to report a foreign financial account held by or on behalf of the retirement plan.

Signature Authority

Signature authority is the authority of an individual (alone or in conjunction with another individual) to control the disposition of assets held in a foreign financial account by direct communication (whether in writing or otherwise) to the bank or other financial institution that maintains the financial account.

Individuals who have signature authority over, but no financial interest in, a foreign financial account are not required to report the account in the following situations:

- An officer or employee of a bank that is examined by the Office of the Comptroller of the Currency, the Board of Governors of the Federal Reserve System, the Federal Deposit Insurance Corporation, the Office of Thrift Supervision, or the National Credit Union Administration is not required to report signature authority over a foreign financial account owned or maintained by the bank;

- An officer or employee of a financial institution that is registered with and examined by the Securities and Exchange Commission (SEC) or Commodity Futures Trading Commission is not required to report signature authority over a foreign financial account owned or maintained by the financial institution;

- An officer or employee of an authorized service provider is not required to report signature authority over a foreign financial account that is owned or maintained by an investment company that is registered with the SEC. An *authorized service provider* is an entity that is registered with and examined by the SEC and provides services to an investment company registered under the *Investment Company Act of 1940;*

- An officer or employee of an entity that has a class of equity securities listed (or American depository receipts listed) on any U.S. national securities exchange is not required to report signature authority over a foreign financial account of such entity;

- An officer or employee of a U.S. subsidiary is not required to report signature authority over a foreign financial account of the subsidiary if its U.S. parent has a class of equity securities listed on any U.S. national securities exchange and the subsidiary is included in a consolidated FBAR report of the U.S. parent; and

- An officer or employee of an entity that has a class of equity securities registered (or American depository receipts in respect of equity securities registered) under Section 12(g) of the *Securities Exchange Act* is not required to report signature authority over a foreign financial account of such entity.

FBAR Filing Deadline Before the Surface Transportation Act

Before the Surface Transportation Act, the FBAR had to be received by the Treasury Department for each calendar year on or before June 30 of the succeeding year. The FBAR must be filed electronically.

FBAR Filing Deadline After the Surface Transportation Act

Under the Surface Transportation Act, the due date for filers of the FBAR is changed to April 15. The IRS is also given authority to modify regulations to provide for a maximum extension of six months ending on October 15. Further, the Surface Transportation Act directs that the IRS must provide for an extension based on rules similar to those found under Reg. § 1.6081-5 that addresses foreign-based property and taxpayers. The change affecting the FBAR is applicable for tax years beginning after December 31, 2015. As a result, the first FBARs under the new timetable will cover the 2016 year, for which the filing deadline will be April 15, 2017. The Surface Transportation Act also provides that any penalty for failure to timely request or file an extension may be waived for taxpayers required to file the FBAR for the first time. The Surface Transportation Act made no change to the requirement that the FBAR be filed electronically.

> **COMMENT:** The *Foreign Account Tax Compliance Act* (FATCA) imposed a new reporting requirement in addition to the FBAR. Certain U.S. taxpayers holding specified foreign financial assets with an aggregate value exceeding $50,000 must report information about those assets on Form 8938, *Statement of Specified Foreign Financial Assets.* Form 8938, unlike the FBAR, is attached to the taxpayer's annual federal income tax return. The Surface Transportation Act made no changes to the filing deadline for Form 8938.

> **COMMENT:** In 2015, FinCEN received a record number of FBARs: 1,163,229.

STUDY QUESTION

3. The Surface Transportation Act changed the filing deadline for FBAR for tax year 2016 to:

    a. April 15, 2017, without extensions

    b. June 30, 2017, including an extension

    c. September 30, 2017, without extensions

    d. December 31, 2017, including an extension

¶ 507 FORM W-2, *WAGE AND TAX STATEMENT*

Employers are required to furnish two copies (three or more copies for employees required to file a state, city, or local income tax return) of the Form W-2, *Wage and Tax Statement,* to each employee for whom during the previous calendar year the employer:

- Withheld income tax or Social Security tax (FICA);
- Would have withheld income tax but for the fact that the employee claimed more than one withholding allowance;
- Paid total compensation, including wages not subject to withholding, of $600 or more; or
- Paid any amount for services if the employer is engaged in a trade or business.

The employee must retain Form W-2 as a record for tax purposes. A duplicate copy of Form W-2 must be attached to the employee's income tax return.

> **COMMENT:** Anyone required to file Form W-2 must file Form W-3, *Transmittal of Wage and Tax Statement,* to transmit Copy A of Form W-2.

> **COMMENT:** Under the combined annual wage reporting (CAWR) system, the Social Security Administration (SSA) and the IRS have an agreement, in the form of a Memorandum of Understanding (MOU), to share wage data and to resolve, or reconcile, the differences in the wages reported to them. Employers submit Forms W-2 (listing Social Security wages earned by individual employees) and W-3 (providing an aggregate summary of wages paid and taxes withheld) directly to the SSA. After it records the wage information from Forms W-2 and W-3 in its individual Social Security wage account records, the SSA forwards the information to the IRS.

The SSA copy of Form W-2, accompanied by Form W-3, is filed on or before the last day of February (March 31 if filed electronically) following the calendar year for which it is made.

Changes Under the PATH Act

The PATH Act modifies the due date for filing information on wages reported on Form W-2.

Under the PATH Act, these returns no longer qualify for the extended due date of March 31 for filing electronically. The due date is accelerated to January 31, effective for returns and statements beginning after December 18, 2015.

> **COMMENT:** The accelerated filing date for Forms W-2 and W-3 matches the due date for providing wage statements to employees and written statements to payees receiving nonemployee compensation.

> **COMMENT:** Since the time for filing Forms W-2 and W-3 and any returns reporting nonemployee compensation has been accelerated the IRS should have the information it needs from the SSA about an individual's combined earnings before a credit or refund of an overpayment based on the additional child tax credit or earned income tax credit (EITC) has to be made.

> **COMMENT:** The PATH Act also authorizes employers to use an "identifying number" for each employee rather than an employee's Social Security number on Form W-2.

¶ 508 INFORMATION RETURNS FOR TRANSACTIONS WITH OTHER PERSONS

Every person engaged in a trade or business who makes payments aggregating $600 or more in any tax year to a single payee in the course of the payor's trade or business must file a return reporting these payments. Returns for payments of $600 or more made in the course of a trade or business can be filed on any appropriate form of the

Form 1099 series, though Form 1099-MISC, *Miscellaneous Income,* is generally used. The information to be reported on Form 1099-MISC includes:

- The names, addresses, and identification numbers of the payer and the payee;
- Amounts paid as all types of rents;
- Gross royalty payments of $10 or more;
- A publisher to a literary agent or author or by a literary agent to an author;
- Taxable prizes and awards that are not for services rendered;
- Other types of income;
- Certain payments received by a broker;
- Amounts of backup withholding;
- Payments by insurers to health care providers;
- Amounts paid as nonemployee compensation;
- Crop insurance proceeds;
- Interest subsidy payments;
- State information;
- Excess golden parachute payments; and
- Attorney fees of $600 or more paid in the course of a trade or business.

Changes Under the PATH Act

Prior to the PATH Act, the due date for filing Form 1099-MISC was generally by the last day of February for paper forms and by March 31 if filing electronically. Under the PATH Act, for Forms 1099-MISC related to calendar year 2016 and after, the due date for filing Forms 1099-MISC that report nonemployee compensation in box 7 is January 31.

STUDY QUESTION

4. Changes to the filing deadlines for Forms W-2, W-3, and 1099-MISC have been accelerated for 2016 and thereafter to:

  a. January 1
  b. January 31
  c. February 28 (or 29)
  d. March 15

¶ 509 EARNED INCOME TAX CREDIT

Qualified individuals may claim the EITC on their Form 1040, Form 1040A, or Form 1040EZ. The amount of the EITC varies depending upon the taxpayer's earned income and whether the taxpayer has one, two, more than two, or no qualifying children. When a taxpayer files a return claiming a refundable credit, the IRS often is not in possession of information needed to confirm the taxpayer's eligibility for the credit.

In 2015, the maximum EITC was as follows:

- $6,242 for taxpayers with more than two qualifying children;
- $5,548 for taxpayers with two qualifying children;
- $3,359 for taxpayers with one qualifying child; and
- $503 for taxpayers with no qualifying children.

The credit amount began to phase out at an income level of:

- $23,630 for joint filers with children;
- $18,110 for other taxpayers with children;
- $13,750 for joint filers with no children; and
- $8,240 for other taxpayers with no qualifying children.

The phaseout percentages were as follow:

- 15.98 percent for taxpayers with one qualifying child;
- 21.06 percent for two or more qualifying children; and
- 7.65 percent for no qualifying children.

The PATH Act generally requires that no credit or refund for an overpayment for a tax year will be made to a taxpayer before the 15th day of the second month following the close of that tax year, if the taxpayer claimed the EITC on the tax return. The provision in the PATH Act pertaining to the payment of certain refunds applies to credits or refunds made after December 31, 2016.

> **COMMENT:** Individual taxpayers are generally calendar year taxpayers,. Thus, for most taxpayers who claim the EITC, this rule would apply such that a refund of tax would not be made to the taxpayer prior to February 15 of the year following the calendar year to which the taxes relate.

> **COMMENT:** The PATH Act also generally requires that no credit or refund for an overpayment for a tax year will be made to a taxpayer before the 15th day of the second month following the close of that tax year, if the taxpayer claimed the additional child tax credit (ACTC) on the tax return.

¶ 510 FORM 5500, ANNUAL RETURN/REPORT OF EMPLOYEE BENEFIT PLAN

Any administrator or sponsor of an employee benefit plan subject to ERISA must file information about each plan every year on Form 5500, *Annual Return/Report of Employee Benefit Plan.* Form 5500 asks for general plan information and must be accompanied by relevant schedules, including audited financial statements for larger plans. The schedules require actuarial information, information regarding direct filing entity requirements, financial information, and information about separated participants who are eligible to receive benefits under the plan at a later date.

> **COMMENT:** Filing Form 5500 using the EFAST2 filing system of the U.S. Department of Labor (DOL) is mandatory. A plan sponsor must still keep a signed paper copy in the plan's records.

Form 5500 is the primary source for information for the federal government and the private sector regarding the operation, funding, assets and investments of private pension plans. The IRS, the DOL, and the Pension Benefit Guaranty Corporation (PBGC) use Form 5500 to collect information for their various roles in regulating and monitoring of private pension plans. The DOL enforces ERISA's reporting and disclosure provisions and fiduciary responsibility standards. The IRS similarly uses Form 5500 to examine plan financial transactions and to target plans for examination. The PBGC uses Form 5500 to monitor both single-employer and multiemployer defined benefit pension plan activities, focusing upon assets, liabilities, number of participants, and funding level. The PBGC also uses Form 5500 for participant notice and PBGC insurance premium compliance. The SSA is also a recipient of Form 5500 information, and it uses the data to notify those participants or their survivors who apply for Social Security that they may be entitled to benefits from one or more private pension plans.

Form 5500 is due by the last day of the seventh month following the close of the plan year. The DOL and IRS rules allow the due date to be automatically extended by 2½ months if a request for extension is filed. In the case of a plan that uses the calendar year as the plan year, the extended due date for Form 5500 is October 15. Under the Surface Transportation Act, in the case of returns for taxable years beginning after December 31, 2015, the IRS was directed to provide that the maximum extension for the returns of employee benefit plans filing Form 5500 would be an automatic 3½ month period ending on November 15 for calendar year plans. However, the FAST Act repealed this provision for an automatic 3½ month extension of the due date for filing Form 5500. As a result, the extended due date for Form 5500 is determined under DOL and IRS rules as if the Surface Transportation Act had never been passed.

STUDY QUESTION

5. The FAST Act changed filing requirements for Form 5500 by:

   a. Repealing the Surface Transportation Act provisions for a 3½ month filing extension

   b. Lengthening the filing extension to six months or December 31

   c. Requiring only multiemployer plans to file Form 5500 annually

   d. Eliminating the requirement for the plan sponsor to maintain paper copies of Form 5500

¶ 511 AFFORDABLE CARE ACT REPORTING TEMPORARY EXTENSION

In late 2015, the IRS announced in Notice 2016-4 a temporary extension of filing deadlines for certain 2015 information returns under the *Patient Protection and Affordable Care Act* (ACA). The extension affected Code Sec. 6055 reporting by insurers, self-insuring employers, and other providers of minimum essential coverage (MEC) and Code Sec. 6056 reporting by applicable large employers (ALEs).

Reporting

Under Code Sec. 6055, health insurance issuers, self-insuring employers, government agencies, and other providers of MEC file with the IRS and provide to covered individuals annual information returns and statements about the coverage. Code Sec. 6056 generally requires ALEs to file with the IRS and provide covered individuals annual information returns and statements relating to the health insurance that the employer offers, or does not offer, to its full-time employees.

Forms

The IRS developed new forms for Code Sec. 6055 reporting and Code Sec. 6056 reporting. The forms are:

- Form 1095-B, *Health Coverage;*
- Form 1094-B, *Transmittal of Health Coverage Information Returns;*
- Form 1095-C, *Employer-Provided Health Insurance Offer and Coverage;* and
- Form 1094-C, *Transmittal of Employer-Provided Health Insurance Offer and Coverage Information Returns.*

> **COMMENT:** Another ACA-related information return is not used by employers or insurers. Form 1095-A, *Health Insurance Marketplace Statement,* is used by the ACA Health Insurance Marketplace to report insurance coverage to individuals who obtain health insurance through the marketplace. Form 1095-A also is furnished by the marketplace to individuals to allow them to take the Code Sec. 36B premium assistance tax credit.

Notice 2016-4. In Notice 2016-4, the IRS explained that it was extending the due date for providing to individuals the 2015 Form 1095-B and/or the 2015 Form 1095-C from February 1, 2016, to March 31, 2016. Notice 2016-4 also extended the due date for filing with the IRS the 2015 Form 1094-B, the 2015 Form 1095-B, the 2015 Form 1094-C, and the 2015 Form 1095-C, from February 29, 2016, to May 31, 2016, if not filing electronically, and from March 31, 2016, to June 30, 2016, if filing electronically.

Late filings. In late June 2016 the IRS announced on its website that it was aware that some electronic filers were still in the process of completing their 2015 tax year filings of these ACA-related returns. The IRS also announced that its ACA Information Returns (AIR) system would remain up and running after the June 30, 2016, deadline. The IRS instructed filers who were not able to submit all required ACA information returns by the June 30, 2016 deadline to complete the filing of their returns after the deadline. The IRS also advised that if any submissions had been rejected by the AIR system, filers would have 60 days from the date of rejection to submit a replacement and have the rejected submission treated as timely filed. Filers who received "accepted with errors" messages, were to continue to submit corrections after June 30, 2016, the IRS added.

Penalties. Although penalties may be imposed for failure to timely file required returns, the IRS explained on its website that filers of Forms 1094-B, 1095-B, 1094-C, and 1095-C that missed the June 30, 2016, due date would not generally be assessed late filing penalties if the reporting entity made legitimate efforts to register with the AIR system and to file its information returns, and the entity continues to make such efforts and completes the process as soon as possible. Filers that are assessed penalties may still meet the criteria for a reasonable cause waiver from the penalties, the IRS added.

> **COMMENT:** The IRS instructed paper filers that missed the May 31, 2016, paper filing deadline for 2015 ACA information returns to complete the filing of paper returns as soon as possible.

2016 Forms Filed in 2017. Notice 2016-4 did not affect the filing of 2016 Forms 1094-B, 1095-B, 1095-C, and Form 1095-C in 2017. At the time this course was prepared, 2016 Forms 1095-B and 1095-C were scheduled to be due to employees by February 1, 2017. If filing on paper, 2016 Forms 1094-B, 1095-B, 1094-C, and 1095-C are scheduled to be filed with the IRS by February 28, 2017. If filing electronically, 2016 Forms 1094-B, 1095-B, 1094-C, and 1095-C are scheduled to be filed with the IRS by March 31, 2017.

Medical Device Excise Tax Suspended Temporarily

Effective for sales after December 31, 2012, the ACA imposes a tax equal to 2.3 percent of the sale price on the sale of any taxable medical device by the manufacturer, producer, or importer of such device. The medical device tax is a manufacturers' excise tax, and as a result, the manufacturer or importer of a taxable medical device is responsible for filing Form 720, *Quarterly Federal Excise Tax Return,* and paying the tax. Generally, a taxable medical device is any device, as defined in Sec. 201(h) of the *Federal Food, Drug, and Cosmetic Act.* IRS regulations further define a medical device as one that is listed by the Food and Drug Administration (FDA) under Section 510(j) of the *Federal Food, Drug, and Cosmetic Act.*

The medical device excise tax does not apply to eyeglasses, contact lenses, hearing aids, or any other medical device determined by the IRS to be of a type that is generally purchased by the general public at retail for individual use. This is known as the *retail exemption*. Generally, a device qualifies for the retail exemption if:

- It is regularly available for purchase and use by individual consumers who are not medical professionals; and
- The design of the device demonstrates that it is not primarily intended for use in a medical institution or office or by a medical professional.

The *Consolidated Appropriations Act, 2016* (part of the PATH Act) (P.L. 114-113) suspended the medical device excise tax for a period of two years. The suspension is effective for sales on or after January 1, 2016, and before January 1, 2018. Manufacturers, producers, or importers of certain medical devices are still responsible for paying the tax on sales made after 2012 and before January 1, 2016. Barring further action by Congress, the medical device tax will commence on sales beginning on January 1, 2018.

STUDY QUESTION

6. The filing deadline for employers filing Form 1095-C, *Employer-Provided Health Insurance Offer and Coverage,* was extended by the IRS in Notice 2016-4 for 2015 health plan coverage to:

- **a.** March 31, 2016, if filed on paper with the IRS
- **b.** April 15, 2016, to employees
- **c.** June 30, 2016, if filed electronically with the IRS
- **d.** April 15 filings to the IRS and distribution to employees

¶ 512 CONCLUSION

The revised return filing deadlines in the Surface Transportation Act and the PATH Act affect many types of taxpayers, including individuals, small businesses, partnerships, and corporations. Because the changes are so expansive, Congress provided for staggered effective dates for the revisions to filing deadlines. Although both the Surface Transportation Act and the PATH Act were passed by Congress and signed into law by President Obama in 2015, the provisions affecting filing deadlines did not take effect immediately. Taxpayers, return preparers, and other stakeholders have had some lead time to prepare for the changes, although time is now going short as the 2017 filing season approaches. As highlighted in this course, many of the changes better align return deadlines with the deadlines for information returns, as well as with the workflow of return preparers during the regular filing season and the extended filing season.

MODULE 2: CHANGES IN FILING DEADLINES, AUDITS, AND PENALTIES— Chapter 6: Penalties and Interest: Rule Changes

¶ 601 WELCOME

The Internal Revenue Code (IRC or the tax code) abounds with specific provisions covering a wide range of taxpayer and tax return preparer conduct. Some are relatively simple and some are mind-numbingly complex. The primary purpose of penalties is to encourage voluntary compliance with the rules imposed by the tax code. This chapter examines penalties relating to both informational returns and income tax returns, exploring the types of erroneous information provided to the IRS that have civil consequences.

¶ 602 LEARNING OBJECTIVES

Upon completion of this chapter, you will be able to:

- Recognize what penalties may be imposed for failure to file accurate information properly and on time;
- Identify the types of penalties applied for failure to file or pay with tax returns;
- Recognize the types of intentional fraud; and
- Identify situations in which interest is imposed on tax not paid.

¶ 603 INTRODUCTION

The need for increased compliance and new revenue sources has caused Congress to increase the number of penalties, especially for filing information returns, and the monetary amounts per penalty, including making several subject to inflation adjustment. Professional tax return preparers must be aware of potential penalties, their scope, and the effects on taxpayer conduct to properly address the pitfalls and make clients aware of the financial consequences of violation of the tax code's rules and regulations.

¶ 604 INFORMATION RETURN PENALTIES

The IRS uses third-party information reporting to increase voluntary compliance and improve collections. The term "information return" means any statement, form, or return as described in Reg. § 301.6721-1(g) and Code Sec. 6724(d)(1). Code Secs. 6721, 6722, and 6723 contain the provisions for application of information return penalties. Under Code Sec. 6721, penalties may be assessed for failure to file correct information returns by the due date. Similar penalties under Code Sec. 6722 are exacted for failure to furnish correct payee statements. Code Sec. 6723 fills in with penalties for failure to comply with "other information reporting requirements." Code Sec. 6724 provides that the Code Secs. 6721, 6722, and 6723 penalties shall not be imposed if the failure is due to reasonable cause.

Failure to File an Information Return

The penalty for failure to file a correct return is imposed on any "person," including a corporation, that fails to file, or fails to include all required information, or includes incorrect information, on an information return (Code Sec. 6721(a) and (b); Reg. § 301.6721-1(a)(1).) Information returns or statements that are subject to the failure to file rules are provided in Code Sec. 6724(d)(1). The applicable returns must be filed with the Internal Revenue Service, or in some cases, the Social Security Administration, on or before the required filing date. The required filing date is the date prescribed for filing an information return, including any filing extension.

The total amount of each penalty that may be imposed for a calendar year is subject to a maximum limit. The annual maximum limit is reduced for small businesses. A *small business* is defined as a business whose average annual gross receipts for the three most recent tax years before the current year are $5 million or less. Beginning with returns required to be filed after December 31, 2014, the penalty and maximum dollar amounts are subject to inflation adjustment.

It should be noted that a failure to timely file an information return or a failure to provide correct information on an information return includes a failure to use the correct format. For example, the penalty may apply if incomplete or incorrect information is given, or if the taxpayer files on paper when electronic filing was required, or if the taxpayer fails to file machine-readable paper forms. The penalty applies also to any failure to file electronically, when required, but is imposed only if the taxpayer is filing 250 or more information returns (100 information returns in the case of a partnership having more than 100 partners).

Tiers of penalties. When proper filing requirements are not met, the taxpayer is subject to a penalty that varies based on the length of time it takes to correct the failure. This three-tier penalty structure serves as an incentive to correct any errors as soon as possible. Using the parameters provided in Code Sec. 6721, in 2016, as adjusted for inflation, if a correct information return or statement:

- Is filed after the prescribed filing date but on or before the date that is 30 days after the prescribed filing date, the amount of the penalty for returns required to be filed after December 31, 2015, is an inflation-adjusted $50 per return (remaining at $50 for 2016) (i.e., the tier 1 penalty), with a maximum penalty of an inflation-adjusted $500,000 per calendar year ($532,000 for 2016, except an inflation-adjusted $175,000 per calendar year for small businesses ($186,000 for 2016); or

- Is filed after the date that is after 30 days after the prescribed filing date but on or before August 1 of the calendar year in which the required filing date occurs, the amount of the penalty for returns required to be filed after December 31, 2015, is an inflation-adjusted $100 (remaining at $100 per return in 2016) (i.e., tier 2 penalty), with a maximum penalty of an inflation-adjusted $1.5 million per calendar year (for 2016, $1,596,500) ($532,000 for small businesses in 2016, up from an unadjusted $500,000) $100 per return (i.e., the tier 2 penalty), with a maximum penalty of $1,596,500 per calendar year ($532,000 for small businesses); or

- Is not filed on or before August 1 of any year, the amount of the penalty for returns to be required to be filed after December 31, 2015, is an inflation-adjusted $250 ($260 per return in 2016) (i.e., tier 3 penalty), with a maximum penalty of an inflation-adjusted $3 million per calendar year (for 2016, $3,193,000) ($1,064,000 for small businesses, up from an unadjusted $1 million base amount) (*Trade Preferences Extension Act of 2015* (P.L. 114-235); Rev. Proc. 2015-53).

Safe harbor exception. A *de minimis* exception to the failure to file penalty is available for a limited number of information returns that are originally filed without all of the required information or with incorrect information that are corrected on or before August 1. These corrected returns will be treated as having been filed with all of the required correct information. This exception does not apply to information returns that are not due on February 28 or March 15.

The number of information returns that may qualify for this exception for any calendar year is limited to the greater of 10 returns or 0.5 percent of the total number of information returns that are required to be filed by the taxpayer during the calendar year. If the failure to file is due to reasonable cause and not to willful neglect, the return is not considered in determining the number of qualifying returns for purposes of the *de minimis* exception. However, returns required to be filed for the year that are not due on February 28 or March 15 are included in this calculation even though they do not qualify for the *de minimis* exception. In the event that the number of returns corrected on or before August 1 exceeds the number of returns to which the *de minimis* exception applies, the exception applies to those returns that will give the filer the greatest reduction in the penalty amount.

If an error or omission on an information return is inconsequential, a penalty is not assessed on the filer. An inconsequential error or omission refers to any failure that does not prevent or hinder the IRS from processing the return, from correlating the information required to be shown on the return with the information shown on the payee's tax return, or from otherwise putting the return to its intended use. However, errors and omissions related to a taxpayer identification number (TIN), the payee's surname, or any monetary amounts are never inconsequential.

Intentional disregard. Any failure to file correct information returns due to intentional disregard of the requirements negates the filer's eligibility for the penalty reduction for subsequent correction, the *de minimis* failure exception, or the lower limitations based on gross receipts of $5 million or less. The term *intentional disregard* refers to a knowing or willful failure to timely file an information return or furnish the correct information on an information return. This determination is based on the facts and circumstances of each case, which generally include but are not limited to whether:

- The failure is part of a pattern of conduct of repeatedly failing to file timely or repeatedly failing to include correct information;

- The correction was promptly made upon discovery of the failure;

- The filer corrects a failure within 30 days after the date of any written request from the IRS to file or to correct the error; and

- The amount of the information reporting penalties is less than the cost of complying with the requirement to file a timely and correct information return.

The *Creating Small Business Jobs Act of 2010* (P.L. 111-240) increased the intentional disregard penalty for information returns and made the penalty amounts subject to adjustments for inflation. The penalty for each intentional disregard of filing an information return for returns required to be filed after December 31, 2015, in 2016, as adjusted for inflation, is the greater of $530 per return or:

- 10 percent of the aggregate amount of the items required to be reported correctly other than a return of a broker, a return reporting direct sales, a return relating to mortgage interest, a business currency transaction report, a return relating to foreclosures and abandonments of security, a return relating to sales or exchanges of partnership interests, or a return relating to dispositions of donated property;

- 5 percent of the aggregate amount of the items required to be reported correctly in the case of a return required to be filed by a broker, a return relating to sales or exchanges of partnership interests, or a return relating to dispositions of donated property;

- The greater of $26,600 or the amount of cash received in the transaction, up to a maximum of $106,000 in the case of a business currency transaction report (cash receipts of more than $10,000) required with respect to any transaction or related transactions; or

- 10 percent of the value of the benefit of any contract with respect to which information is required to be included on the return in the case of a return required to be filed under Code Sec. 6050V (Rev. Proc. 2015-53).

The maximum penalty limitation of $1.5 million ($3 million for returns required to be filed after December 31, 2015) is not applied to failures due to intentional disregard of the reporting requirements. Likewise, the intentional disregard penalty is not taken into account in determining the maximum limitation (or reduced limitation, if applicable) for any other penalties.

Failure to Furnish/File Correct Payee Statement

In addition to filing information returns detailing all wages, various types of income, and some deductions for the tax year, individuals, trades, and businesses are required to furnish copies of the returns or other statements to the taxpayers. These copies are referred to as *payee statements*. Any failure to furnish a payee statement on time to the proper person, and any failure to include all of the information required to be shown on a payee statement, or the inclusion of incorrect information, is subject to a penalty under Code Sec. 6722. A failure to include correct information encompasses a failure to include the information required by applicable information reporting statutes or by any administrative pronouncement issued thereunder, such as regulations, revenue rulings, revenue procedures, or information reporting forms or form instructions.

The penalty structure is similar to the three-tier penalty structure found under Code Sec. 6721, as discussed previously. Inflation adjustments will be made to the per statement and yearly maximum penalty amounts annually. As with information returns, the penalty amounts for payee statements are dependent upon the timely correction of the failures. If the correction is made:

- Within 30 days after the original due date for statements required to be filed after December 31, 2015, the amount of the penalty is $50 per statement, with a yearly maximum penalty amount of $532,000 ($186,000 for small businesses); or

- Within a period that runs from 31 days after the due date up to August 1 of the calendar year in which the statement was required to be filed for statements required to be filed after December 31, 2015, the amount of the penalty is $100 per statement, with a maximum yearly penalty amount of $1,596,500 ($532,000 for small businesses); or

- After August 1 of the calendar year prescribed for furnishing these statements required to after December 31, 2015, the penalty is $260 per statement, with a maximum yearly penalty amount of $3,193,000 ($1,064,000 for small businesses) (Rev. Proc. 2015-53).

Small businesses are those with gross receipts of not more than $5 million.

No more than one penalty is imposed on a single payee statement even if there is more than one failure for that statement. However, when imposing the penalty, composite payee statements are treated as separate statements.

Safe harbor exceptions. An inconsequential error or omission on a payee statement refers to any failure that cannot reasonably be expected to prevent or hinder the payee from timely receiving correct information and reporting it on the applicable return or otherwise putting the statement to its intended use. However, the following errors and omissions are never inconsequential:

- An incorrect dollar amount;
- An incorrect payee address;
- Using an inappropriate form for the information provided, such as an unacceptable substitute for an official form of the IRS; and
- Using a statement mailing for interest, dividends, patronage dividends, or royalties.

There is a *de minimis* penalty exception that parallels the relief offered for information returns; i.e., the relief is limited to the greater of 10 payee statements with failures, or one-half of 1 percent of total payee statements required to be filed for the calendar year.

Intentional disregard. Any failure due to intentional disregard of the Code Sec. 6722 requirements to furnish a payee statement is assessed per failure penalty for statements required to be filed. For a definition of intentional disregard, see the previous discussion on failure to file information return. The penalty for intentional disregard is not reduced for corrections, and neither the *de minimis* exception nor the small business exception reduces the maximum penalty available.

The penalty amount for a failure due to intentional disregard for statement required to be filed after December 31, 2015, in 2016, as inflation adjusted, is equal to the greater of $530 or:

- 10 percent of the aggregate amount of the items required to be reported correctly for payee statements other than those related to a brokered transaction, a direct sale, mortgage interest, foreclosures and abandonments of security, sales or exchanges of partnership interests, or dispositions of donated property; or
- 5 percent of the aggregate amount of the items required to be reported correctly for payee statements related to a brokered transaction, a sale or exchange of a partnership interest, or a disposition of donated property.

The maximum penalty limitation of $3,193,000 ($1,064,000 for small businesses) is not applied to failures due to the intentional disregard penalty under Code Sec. 6722(e)(2) nor taken into account in determining the maximum limitation (or reduced limitation, if applicable) for any other penalties (Rev. Proc. 2015-53).

Failure to Comply with Other Information Reporting Requirements

Under Code Sec. 6723, Failure to Comply with Other Information Reporting Requirements, a penalty of $50 is imposed for each failure to timely comply with specified information reporting requirements or for each failure to include correct information. For failures to comply with more than one specified information reporting requirement or multiple instances of failures to comply with any of these requirements, multiple penalties are imposed. If the information filed is both late and incomplete or inaccurate, however, the noncompliant actions are treated as a single failure, and only one penalty is assessed.

Specified information reporting requirements that are covered under Code Sec. 6723 include:

- Partnership notification when an exchange of a partnership interest occurs;
- Furnishing TINs for inclusion on any return, statement, or other document (other than an information return or payee statement); on furnishing the TIN to another person; on furnishing the TIN of another person; or on furnishing the TIN of a tax return preparer;
- Furnishing a TIN to another person, or including another person's TIN on a return when one deducts alimony or separate maintenance payments;
- Furnishing a TIN to claim a dependency exemption on an income tax return; and
- Furnishing the payor's and recipient's TIN with respect to certain seller-provided financing.

The total penalty imposed on any person for all failures to comply with the Code Sec. 6723 reporting requirements during one calendar year cannot exceed $100,000.

STUDY QUESTION

---

1. An inconsequential error on a payee statement includes one that:
    a. Involves underreporting monetary amounts of $100 or less
    b. Allows the payee to put the statement to its intended use
    c. Fails to apply existing revenue procedures to the statement
    d. Involves the payee's surname

¶ 605 INCOME TAX RETURN PENALTIES

Most duties imposed under the tax code are enforced by penalties, variously referred to as *penalties, additions to tax,* or *additional amounts.* Penalties are imposed for failing to file a return, failing to pay tax, failing to report information to the IRS or to others, failing to pay over tax collected from others, understating tax liability, and other failings.

Failure to File Penalty for Returns Other Than Informational Returns

A taxpayer who fails to file a tax return when it is due is subject to a penalty of 5 percent of the tax due for each month or part of a month that the return is not filed, up to a maximum penalty of 25 percent, unless it is shown that the failure to file was due to reasonable cause and not willful neglect. This penalty is known as the failure to file (FTF), or delinquency penalty. The FTF penalty applies only if there is an underpayment of tax. The delinquency penalty applies to income, gift, estate and most excise tax returns, but not information returns.

The minimum penalty for failure to file an income tax return within 60 days of its due date, including extensions, is the lesser of $135 or the amount of tax owed with the return.

For a fraudulent failure to file, the delinquency penalty is raised to 15 percent per month up to a maximum of 75 percent of the amount of tax owed.

Late return defined. When a return, payment, or request for extension of time to file is postmarked/time stamped on or before the due date—including due dates extended by virtue of the regular due date falling on a Saturday, Sunday, or legal holiday—it is considered timely filed without regard to the date it is received by the IRS. A tax return is considered late when a taxpayer fails to file it on or before the prescribed due date, taking into consideration all permitted extensions, and then the period of delinquency begins. The taxpayer has the burden of proving that any request for an extension was timely filed with the IRS. A timely filed *request* for an extension is not a timely filed *return;* therefore, the request does not in and of itself avoid incurring the late filing penalty.

The period of delinquency runs from the day after the due date of the return, as set forth in Code Sec. 6072, until the date the return is actually received by the IRS. The FTF penalty is imposed for each month or part of a month in which the delinquency continues. In determining the number of months that the penalty is imposed, the due date of the return determines when months begin and end. Each month subject to the penalty ends on the day of the month that corresponds with the day of the month of the latest return due date as determined above. Each new month subject to the penalty shall begin the next day, with the following exceptions:

- When the day of the month of the due date is the last day of the month, each new month subject to penalty shall begin on the first day of the following month; and

- For February, if the day of the month of the due date does not exist in February (i.e., if the day of the month is the 30th or the 31th), the new month subject to penalty shall begin on the first day of March. Because the penalty cannot exceed 25 percent, it is not charged for more than 5 months.

Reasonable cause. Reasonable cause relief is generally granted when the taxpayer exercises ordinary business care and prudence in determining tax obligations, but is unable to comply with those obligations. In deciding whether the taxpayer exercised ordinary business care and prudence, consideration is given to all the facts and circumstances of the taxpayer's financial situation, including the amount of the taxpayer's expenditures and investments in speculative or illiquid assets in light of income and other assets. A taxpayer is considered to have exercised ordinary business care and prudence if the taxpayer made reasonable efforts to conserve sufficient assets in marketable form to satisfy tax liabilities and, nevertheless, was unable to pay all or a portion of the tax when it became due.

Willful neglect. Willful neglect for failing to file a timely return has been interpreted by the courts as a conscious, intentional failure or reckless indifference. A conscious or intentional failure exists when the taxpayer is aware of the duty to file the return by the due date but fails to file the return under circumstances that do not justify the failure. Reckless indifference is established when the taxpayer is aware of the duty to file on time but disregards a known or obvious risk that the return might not be filed by the due date.

Penalty amount. The delinquency penalty is imposed on the net amount of tax due. This amount is the correct tax liability minus any tax payments made on or before the due date of the return and any credits that may be claimed on the return. The penalty is based on the taxpayer's correct tax liability, not on the amount of tax actually shown on the return. Thus, it applies to the tax shown on the taxpayer's original return, as well as any additional tax later found due on the return.

Failure to Pay Penalty

The basic failure-to-pay (FTP) penalty applies if a taxpayer files, either on time or late, a return acknowledging a tax liability but fails to pay the tax admittedly owed. If the IRS prepares a return for a nonfiler, the amount of the penalty is calculated in the same manner as if the taxpayer filed a late return.

¶605

The FTP penalty equals 0.5 percent of the amount of the tax if the failure extends no longer than a month, with an additional 0.5 percent per month (or fraction of a month) up to a maximum of 25 percent. In the case of the failure to pay tax shown on the return, the penalty is imposed on the amount shown on the return less amounts that have been withheld, estimated tax payments, partial payments, and other applicable credits.

The FTP penalty, whether of an amount shown on the return or an amount required to be shown, increases from 0.5 percent to 1 percent per month after the IRS issues a notice of intention to levy under Code Sec. 6331(d) or notice and demand for immediate payment under Code Sec. 6331(a) (relating to jeopardy assessments). The penalties are coordinated with the taxpayer's bankruptcy proceeding, the failure-to-file penalties, and the penalties for fraudulent filing.

Reasonable cause. The late payment penalty does not apply if the taxpayer shows that the failure to pay is due to reasonable cause and not to willful neglect. Whether the failure to pay is due to reasonable cause is determined as of the due date of the tax. Thus, if a taxpayer's failure to pay on the due date is not attributable to reasonable cause, subsequent events preventing payment at a later date do not affect the imposition of the penalty. However, evidence regarding events after the return's due date can be relevant to rebut a taxpayer's claim that the failure to pay was due to reasonable cause.

Generally, the taxpayer must pay the tax due before the IRS will abate a FTP penalty for reasonable cause. The penalty continues to accrue until the tax is paid. The taxpayer may have reasonable cause for some months, but not for others, and the IRS cannot make a correct determination until after the tax is paid.

Overlapping penalties. Frequently, a taxpayer who fails to file a timely return also fails to pay the tax shown due. In those situations, the taxpayer is subject to both the FTF penalty and the penalty for failing to pay a tax shown due on the return (FTP penalty). For any month in which both penalties apply, the amount of the FTF penalty is reduced by the amount of the FTP penalty (0.5 percent per month). Thus, the total penalty for any one return for any one month or partial month generally may not exceed 5 percent of the tax liability (15 percent for a fraudulent failure to file).

STUDY QUESTION

2. The period of delinquency, as set forth under Code Sec. 6072, for a late income return subject to a failure to file penalty:

   a. Begins on the date the IRS receives the return

   b. Applies whether or not any tax is due with the return

   c. Runs from the day after the return's due date until the IRS actually receives the return

   d. Applies to information returns, gift tax returns, and estate tax returns

¶ 606 INCOME TAX RETURN PENALTIES: OTHER TYPES

Frivolous Returns and Submissions

In addition to other penalties that may be imposed, there is a $5,000 penalty for filing a frivolous return or submission under Code Sec. 6702. The penalty for frivolous submissions and returns covers:

- Persons;
- Any frivolous federal tax return (and not just income tax returns); and
- Certain submissions to the IRS that are not tax returns.

The IRS maintains an annual list of common frivolous arguments made by individuals and groups that oppose compliance with federal tax laws, as well as the legal responses to refute the claims on **www.irs.gov** ("The Truth About Frivolous Arguments").

The penalty for frivolous federal tax returns is imposed when an individual files what purports to be a tax return but:

- The filing does not contain information on which the substantial correctness of the self-assessment may be judged; or
- The filing contains information indicating on its face that the self-assessment is substantially incorrect; *and*
- The filing is based on a position that the IRS has identified as frivolous; *or*
- The filing reflects a desire to delay or impede the administration of the federal tax laws.

An additional penalty of $5,000 is imposed on any person that submits a specified frivolous submission. A specified frivolous submission is a specified submission that either:

- Is based on a position that the IRS has identified as frivolous in its prescribed frivolous positions list; or
- Reflects a desire to delay or impede the administration of federal tax laws.

A *specified submission* is a request for a hearing after the IRS files a notice of lien or the taxpayer receives a prelevy Collection Due Process (CDP) Hearing Notice, and an application relating to an installment agreement, a compromise, or a taxpayer assistance order.

The frivolous return penalty is assessed in addition to any other penalty provided by law, and the IRS has the burden of proof in any related proceeding. The penalty is not imposed on a taxpayer that withdraws a submission within 30 days after receiving notice from the IRS that it is a specified frivolous submission. Additionally, at its discretion the IRS is authorized to reduce the penalties in order to promote compliance with and administration of the federal tax laws.

Accuracy-Related Penalties for Taxpayers

Prior to 1986, there were separate penalties in the tax code for negligence, substantial understatement of tax, and overvaluation. The *Tax Reform Act of 1986* (TRA) (P.L. 99–514) combined, expanded, and integrated those provisions in the Code Sec. 6662 accuracy-related penalty.

The accuracy-related penalty is imposed on a tax underpayment that is attributable to the following noncompliant taxpayer conduct:

- Negligence or disregard for rules and regulations;
- A substantial understatement;
- A valuation misstatement;
- An overstatement of pension liabilities;
- A substantial estate or gift tax understatement;
- Gross misstatements;
- Tax benefits claimed by reason of a transaction lacking economic substance; or
- An undisclosed foreign financial asset understatement.

¶606

Generally, the penalties are equal to 20 percent of the tax underpayment; however, this amount increases to 40 percent for;

- Undisclosed foreign financial asset understatements;
- Gross valuation misstatements;
- Substantial pension liability overstatements;
- Substantial estate and gift tax understatements; and
- Underpayments attributable to nondisclosed noneconomic substance transactions.

Foreign financial asset understatements. In addition to general income tax reporting requirements, a U.S. person with financial interests in or signature authority over foreign financial accounts may be subject to reporting on FinCEN Form 114, *Report of Foreign Bank and Financial Accounts* (FBAR) if, at any point during the calendar year, the aggregate value of the accounts exceeds the reporting threshold of $10,000. The civil penalty for failing to file an FBAR may be as high as the greater of $100,000 or 50 percent of the total balance of the foreign account per willful violation ($10,000 penalty for nonwillful violations). FBAR reporting is beyond the scope of this chapter.

Coordination. The accuracy-related penalties are coordinated with each other and with the civil fraud penalty (discussed later). There are ordering rules that determine the penalty amount when both the accuracy-related penalty and the civil fraud penalty apply, or when different rates are mandated. The penalty is not imposed on a taxpayer with reasonable cause for the underpayment who acted in good faith.

COMMENT: Code Sec. 6694, Understatement Of Taxpayer's Liability by Tax Return Preparer, and Code Sec. 6695, Other Assessable Penalties with Respect to the Preparation of Tax Returns for Other Persons, are beyond the scope of this chapter. They may be imposed in addition to any penalty paid by the taxpayer.

Negligence or Disregard for the Rules and Regulations

Negligence includes the "failure to make a reasonable attempt to comply" and "careless, reckless, or intentional disregard" of the rules and regulations. Reg. §1.6662-3 states that "negligence is strongly indicated by a failure to report income from an information return; a failure to investigate credits, exemptions, or deductions that would seem to a reasonable person 'too good to be true;' and a failure to treat a partnership or S corporation item consistently with the relevant partnership or S corporation return."

Any failure to keep adequate books and records or to properly substantiate items reported on a return is also considered negligence, along with:

- Unreported or understated income;
- Significantly overstated deductions or credits;
- Careless, improper, or exaggerated deductions;
- Misrepresentation or miscategorization of deductions in a manner that conceals their true nature;
- Unexplainable items;
- Issuance of a negligence penalty by a cooperative state program and/or state report (only in conjunction with other evidence);
- Substantial errors on an issue that has been adjusted in a prior year; and
- Incorrect or incomplete information provided to the return preparer.

Reasonable basis exception. A return position that has a reasonable basis is not attributable to negligence. Reasonable basis is a relatively high standard of tax reporting; that is, significantly higher than not frivolous or not patently improper. The reasonable basis standard is not satisfied by a return position that is merely arguable or that is merely a colorable claim. The reasonable basis standard is generally satisfied by a return position that is reasonably based on one of the authorities that can be used as substantial authority to avoid the substantial understatement penalty, even if the position does not satisfy the substantial authority standard. Thus, a taxpayer with substantial authority sufficient to avoid the understatement penalty also has reasonable basis sufficient to avoid the negligence penalty.

The reasonable basis exception is unique to the negligence penalty. However, all of the accuracy-related penalties are subject to an exception if the taxpayer acts with reasonable cause and good faith. Consequently, a return position that does not satisfy the reasonable basis exception to the negligence penalty may nevertheless qualify for relief under the reasonable cause and good faith exception to the accuracy-related penalties.

Adequate disclosure exception. The negligence component of the accuracy-related penalty is not imposed on any portion of an underpayment that is attributable to a position contrary to a rule or regulation if the position is adequately disclosed. A position that is contrary to a regulation must also represent a good faith challenge to the regulation. This disclosure exception does not apply if the position does not have a reasonable basis, or if the taxpayer fails to keep adequate books and records or to substantiate the item properly.

Disregard of the rules or regulations includes any careless, reckless, or intentional disregard of the rules or regulations. Rules or regulations include the provisions of the tax code, temporary or final regulations issued under the tax code, and revenue rulings or notices, other than notices of proposed rulemaking, issued by the IRS and published in the Internal Revenue Bulletin. These definitions also state:

- A disregard of the rules or regulations is *careless* if the taxpayer does not exercise reasonable diligence to determine the correctness of a return position that is contrary to the rules or regulations;

- A disregard is *reckless* if the taxpayer makes little or no effort to determine whether a rule or regulation exists, under circumstances that demonstrate a substantial deviation from the conduct that a reasonable person would observe; and

- A disregard is *intentional* if the taxpayer knows of the rule or regulation that is disregarded.

However, a taxpayer who takes a position contrary to a revenue ruling (other than with respect to a reportable transaction) has not disregarded the ruling if the contrary position has a realistic possibility of being sustained on its merits. An item or position that is not contrary to a regulation must be disclosed on Form 8275, *Disclosure Statement.* A position that is contrary to a regulation must be disclosed on Form 8275-R, *Regulation Disclosure Statement.* In addition, the statutory or regulatory provision or ruling in question must be adequately identified on the Form 8275 or Form 8275-R. 75 No other type of disclosure is adequate.

Substantial Understatement of Income Tax

The accuracy-related penalty applies only to the amount of the *underpayment,* not the entire amount of the *understatement.* An *understatement* of tax is defined as the excess of the taxpayer's actual tax liability over the amount shown on the return. An understatement that exceeds the applicable statutory minimum is considered a substantial understatement. A *substantial understatement* refers to an understatement that exceeds:

- The greater of 10 percent of the tax required to be shown or $5,000 for individuals; or
- The lesser of 10 percent of the tax required to be shown (or if greater, $10,000), or $10 million for corporations.

The understatement amount is increased by the aggregate amount of the tax-payer's reportable transaction understatements in order to make this determination. However, the substantial understatement penalty is not applicable to any amount that is subject to the Code Sec. 6662A accuracy-related penalty for reportable transaction understatements. Generally, an understatement is reduced to the extent that either:

- The position generating the understatement is supported by substantial authority; or
- The relevant facts affecting the item's tax treatment are disclosed by the taxpayer on the return, and there is a reasonable basis for the tax treatment of the disclosed item.

Substantial Valuation Misstatements

A 20 percent accuracy-related penalty is imposed on the portion of an underpayment that is caused by a substantial valuation misstatement, if the underpayment exceeds the statutory dollar thresholds. For purposes of the accuracy-related penalty, a substantial valuation misstatement occurs when:

- The value or adjusted basis of property claimed on a return is overstated by 150 percent or more of the correct value or basis (for gross valuation misstatements, 200 and 400 percent, respectively);
- Transactions are entered into by persons owned or controlled directly or indirectly by the same interests, and the amount claimed for property or its use or for remuneration for services, is 200 percent or more (or 50 percent or less) than the amount determined to be correct (for gross valuation misstatements, 400 percent and 25 percent, respectively); or
- The net Code Sec. 482 transfer price adjustment exceeds the lesser of $5 million or 10 percent of the taxpayer's gross receipts (for gross valuation misstatements, $20 million and 20 percent, respectively).

A *gross* valuation misstatement arises in the same three situations as a *substantial* valuation misstatement, but the thresholds are increased as noted above. The accuracy-related penalty is increased to 40 percent for gross valuation misstatements. The penalty is imposed on the portion of the understatement attributable to a substantial or gross misstatement only if the aggregate of all portions of the underpayment attributable to the misstatement exceeds a certain dollar amount. Generally, for corporations other than S corporations, this amount is $10,000; for other entities, the amount is decreased to $5,000. There is no disclosure exception available for the valuation misstatement penalty; however, a reasonable cause exception does apply, except for gross valuation misstatements of charitable deduction property.

Overstatement of Pension Liabilities

An employer must make certain assumptions involving estimates of future economic conditions and events when the employer calculates the funding requirements for a defined benefit plan. These assumptions can significantly affect the estimates of plan costs and deduction limits on employer contributions. When the actuarial determination of liabilities taken into account in computing the employer's deduction for contributions to a defined benefit pension plan exceeds the correct liability, an overstatement of pension liabilities occurs.

The corresponding penalty for an underpayment attributable to an overstatement of pension liabilities varies depending on the extent of the overstatement. If the actuarial determination of pension liabilities is at least 200 percent but less than 400 percent of the amount determined to be correct, a substantial overstatement of pension liabilities exists; if 400 percent or greater, a gross overstatement of pension liabilities exists. The penalty amounts are imposed on the underpayment attributable to the overstatement at the rate of 20 percent and 40 percent for substantial and gross overstatements of pension liabilities. A *de minimis* exception applies if the underpayment attributable to the overstatement of pension liabilities is less than or equal to $1,000.

There is an exception for any portion of an underpayment that is based on reasonable cause if the taxpayer acted in good faith with respect to that portion. Reliance by an employer on an actuary or other professional as to the proper amount of the pension plan contribution deduction is, however, not a reasonable basis or good faith claim.

Substantial Estate or Gift Tax Understatements

A penalty similar to the substantial understatement of income tax applies to substantial estate or gift tax valuation understatements. A substantial valuation understatement exists if the value of any property claimed on an estate or gift tax return is 65 percent or less of the correct valuation amount, but not 40 percent or less, of the amount determined to be correct. In such cases, the penalty amount is 20 percent of the portion of the underpayment that is attributable to the understatement.

A gross understatement exists when the values for property claimed on an estate or gift tax return are decreased to 40 percent or less of the amount determined to be correct. In the event of a gross estate or gift tax valuation understatement, a 40 percent penalty is imposed on the portion of the underpayment that is attributable to the valuation understatement.

If the underpayment attributable to the understatement of valuation or with respect to the estate of the decedent is not more than $5,000 for the tax period, the penalty does not apply. However, even for underpayments of less than $5,000, the IRS may assess the accuracy-related penalty if the underpayment is the result of negligence or disregard of rules or regulations. In addition, when a person prepares an appraisal that results in a substantial or gross valuation misstatement or understatement, a civil penalty may be imposed. Comparable to the other accuracy-related penalties, there are reasonable basis and good faith exceptions for estate and gift tax underpayments attributable to a valuation understatement.

Inconsistent Estate Basis Reporting Penalty

An accuracy-related penalty will be imposed for inconsistent estate basis reporting under Code Sec. 6662(b)(8). *Inconsistent estate basis reporting* is defined as claiming basis on a return that exceeds the basis of property as determined under Code Sec. 1014(f). The penalty will apply to property described in proposed regulations to Code Sec. 1014 that has been acquired from a decedent or by reason of the death of the decedent whose return required by Code Sec. 6018 is filed after July 31, 2015. A detailed discussion of the consistent basis reporting requirements as required for estate and income tax purposes is beyond the scope of this chapter.

Transactions Lacking Economic Substance

A penalty of 20 percent is imposed on underpayments attributable to any disallowance of claimed tax benefits due to a transaction lacking economic substance, as defined in Code Sec. 7701(o), or by the failure to meet the requirements of any similar rule of law. Under the economic substance doctrine, a transaction has economic substance only if:

- The transaction changes the taxpayer's economic position in a meaningful way; and
- The taxpayer has a substantial purpose for entering into the transaction.

These requirements must be met without regard to any federal income tax benefits derived from the transaction.

For underpayments attributable to a nondisclosed noneconomic substance transaction, the penalty is increased to 40 percent. A nondisclosed noneconomic substance transaction is any portion of a Code Sec. 6662(b)(6) transaction with respect to which the relevant facts affecting the tax treatment are not adequately disclosed in the return or in a statement attached to the return. This determination is generally based on the return as originally filed or as amended by the taxpayer prior to contact by the IRS. Therefore, amendments or supplements to a tax return are not taken into account in determining whether a position has been disclosed if they are filed after an audit contact or other specified inquiry takes place.

Although Code Sec. 6662(b)(6) transactions are technically covered by the penalty, the IRS issued a directive that limits the imposition of penalties due to the application of any other "similar rule of law" or judicial doctrine (e.g., step transaction doctrine, substance over form, or sham transaction) until further guidance is issued.

Foreign Financial Asset Understatements

A 40 percent accuracy-related penalty is imposed for underpayment of tax that is attributable to an undisclosed foreign financial asset understatement. An undisclosed foreign financial asset understatement is the portion of the understatement that is attributable to any transaction involving an undisclosed foreign financial asset. An undisclosed foreign financial asset for any tax year is any asset that is subject to information reporting for that year under certain rules, but for which the required information is not provided by the taxpayer. The undisclosed foreign financial asset rules:

- Generally require every U.S. person (a citizen or resident of the United States, a domestic corporation, domestic partnership, or an estate or trust, other than a foreign estate or trust) that owns a controlling interest in a foreign business entity to furnish certain information about the entity and its subsidiaries;
- Require property transfers by U.S. persons to foreign corporations in corporate reorganizations or distributions and certain transfers to foreign partnerships be reported to the IRS;
- Generally require individuals holding interests in specified foreign financial assets to attach to their income tax returns, for tax years beginning after March 18, 2010, certain information with respect to each asset if the aggregate value of all the assets exceeds $50,000;
- Require a U.S. person who is a 10 percent (or greater) partner in a foreign partnership to report changes to his or her ownership interest in the partnership; and
- Generally require reporting with respect to foreign trusts with a U.S. grantor and foreign trusts that distribute money or property to a U.S. person.

¶606

Thus, if a taxpayer is required to disclose amounts held in a foreign financial account but fails to do so, any underpayment of tax related to the transaction that gave rise to the income would be subject to the 40 percent penalty, as would any underpayment related to interest, dividends, or other returns accrued on such undisclosed amounts. The 40 percent penalty for undisclosed foreign financial asset understatement is subject to the same defenses that are otherwise available for the accuracy-related penalties.

STUDY QUESTION

3. The percentage of penalties imposed on income tax returns generally jumps from 20 percent to 40 percent of underpayments that are:

    a. Inconsequential understatements

    b. Gross understatements

    c. Substantial understatements

    d. Reasonable basis understatements

¶ 607 CIVIL FRAUD

The civil fraud penalty is imposed for an intentional attempt to evade or otherwise prevent the collection of taxes. The fraud penalty applies only when a return is filed. Fraud most commonly consists of the omission of income, but other types of conduct evidencing fraud, often referred to as badges of fraud, may qualify, including:

- Claiming false deductions;
- Falsely characterizing ordinary income as capital gain income;
- Reporting fictitious transactions;
- Claiming false tax credits;
- Claiming excess withholding tax;
- Claiming false marital status; or
- Claiming false exemptions.

Some of the main defenses to fraud are that the underpayment was caused by inadvertence or negligence or by an honest mistake, the taxpayer relied in good faith on the opinion of a tax professional, and that there is an honest difference of opinion as to the taxpayer's tax liability. The absence of specific badges of fraud—or the presence of badges of honesty—may be evidence that the taxpayer lacked fraudulent intent. The Tax Court has observed that if a previous bad record tends to sustain a fraud charge, a good record tends to refute a fraud charge.

Because direct evidence of a taxpayer's fraudulent intent is hard to obtain, the IRS and the courts often look at circumstantial evidence. Some indicators of fraud include filing false returns, creating false documents, maintaining a double set of books, concealing assets, destroying records, consistently understating tax on returns, and failing to cooperate with the IRS. The taxpayer's knowledge of the tax laws is also an important factor in determining whether fraud is indicated. On a joint tax return, a spouse is not liable for the fraud penalty unless it is established that part of the underpayment is due to the spouse's fraudulent behavior.

A civil fraud penalty is assessed and collected in the same manner as the underlying tax on which it is imposed. Therefore, when the penalty is imposed on income, gift, or estate taxes, the deficiency procedures apply. Although the Fifth Amendment privilege can be invoked by the taxpayer to avoid testifying in a civil fraud case, a second notice of deficiency may be issued to impose the fraud penalty. If a taxpayer is convicted of tax evasion, he or she is collaterally estopped from contesting the civil fraud penalty. However, the taxpayer is not estopped if convicted for filing a false return. There is no time limit for collecting a deficiency with respect to a fraudulent return. Neither taxes for which a fraudulent return is made nor the fraud penalty can be discharged in a bankruptcy proceeding.

The civil fraud penalty is imposed in addition to any other penalties that are imposed against the taxpayer. However, the accuracy-related penalty is not assessed on any portion of an underpayment to which the civil fraud penalty applies. A separate penalty is imposed in the case of a fraudulent failure to file a return (described later).

The amount of the fraud penalty is 75 percent of the underpayment attributable to the fraud. The underpayment is computed by deducting from the taxpayer's correct tax liability the sum of the amount of tax shown on the taxpayer's return and any amounts not shown on the return that were previously assessed or collected. Any rebates made are added to the amount of the underpayment. The portion of the underpayment attributable to fraud is computed by calculating the underpayment that would result if all items on the return except the items attributable to fraud were correctly reported.

> **NOTE:** Generally, imposition of the criminal fraud penalty does not preclude civil prosecution, and vice versa. Although taxpayers have repeatedly argued that a previous criminal conviction for fraud prohibits imposition of a civil fraud penalty on the same action, courts not only permit such proceedings but estop the taxpayer from denying the conduct that formed the basis of the prior criminal conviction.

Fraudulent Failure to File

There is a separate penalty for a fraudulent failure to file. The IRS has the burden of proving that the failure to file is fraudulent. Generally, the possible outcomes in each case are dependent upon sustaining the burden of proof; however, any alternative determinations made in the notice of deficiency are taken into account. For example, if the IRS:

- Does not sustain its burden on the fraud element but makes an alternative determination in the notice of deficiency that the taxpayer is liable for the basic failure to file penalty, then the court considers the basic penalty and the attendant burden is on the taxpayer;
- Does not sustain its burden on the fraud element and fails to make an alternative determination in the notice, but asserts in its answer or other pleading that the taxpayer is liable for the basic penalty, then the court considers the basic penalty, but the burden is on the IRS;
- Does not sustain its burden on the fraud element and fails to make either an alternative determination in the notice or to assert the basic penalty in its pleadings, the court cannot consider the penalty and the taxpayer is not liable for any failure to file penalty.

For a fraudulent failure to file a return, the penalty is 15 percent of the tax liability for each month or partial month that the return is late, up to a maximum of five months, or 75 percent.

STUDY QUESTION

4. Which of the following claims is *not* a badge of fraud?

    a. Claiming that ordinary income is capital gain income

    b. Claiming income without evidence on a Form W-2 or Form 1099 that it was earned

    c. Claiming false tax credits

    d. Claiming false deductions

¶ 608 MISCELLANEOUS PENALTY PROVISIONS

Underpayment of Estimated Tax (Individuals)

A penalty is imposed on the underpayment of estimated tax by an individual and most trusts and estates. It generally consists of an addition to tax equal to the applicable underpayment rate of interest that accrues on the underpayment for the period of the underpayment (Code Sec. 6654(a)). In determining the addition to tax for an underpayment of individual estimated tax, the federal short-term rate that applies during the third month following the tax year of the underpayment will also apply during the first 15 days of the fourth month following such tax year (Code Sec. 6621(b)(2)(B); Reg. § 301.6621-1). Changes in the interest rate apply to amounts of underpayments outstanding on the date of change or arising thereafter.

The IRS is also authorized to waive the penalty for underpayment of estimated tax of an individual if the underpayment is due to casualty, disaster, or other unusual circumstances, and the imposition of the penalty would be against equity and good conscience. The penalty may also be waived for an individual who retired after having attained age 62, or who became disabled, in the tax year for which the estimated payment was due or in the preceding tax year and the underpayment was due to reasonable cause and not to willful neglect.

The amount of an underpayment of estimated tax and the amount of the resulting penalty is computed on Form 2210, *Underpayment of Estimated Tax by Individuals, Estates, and Trusts,* and attached to the individual's income tax return; farmers and fishermen use Form 2210-F, *Underpayment of Estimated Tax by Farmers and Fishermen.* If Form 2210 is not completed and attached to the individual's return, the IRS will compute the penalty for the taxpayer. When the IRS computes the penalty, however, it will investigate any reason why the penalty should be waived.

Bad Checks

A specific penalty is imposed for remitting a bad check or money order to the IRS in payment of any amount receivable under the tax code. The penalty for providing the IRS with a bad check or money order is expanded to apply to any instrument of payment for any amount by a commercially acceptable means (including check, money orders, credit cards, debit cards, or charge cards). The penalty applies to payments of any amount due under the tax code, including electronic payments that are not duly paid, or paid and subsequently charged back to the Secretary of Treasury.

Generally, the penalty is equal to 2 percent of the payment amount. If the amount remitted is less than $1,250, however, the penalty equals the lesser of $25 or the payment amount. The penalty does not apply if the IRS is satisfied that the person tendered the payment instrument in good faith and with reasonable cause to believe that it would be duly paid. The penalty is collected, upon notice and demand, in the same manner as tax.

Erroneous Claims of Refunds or Credits

For the filing of an erroneous claim for refund or credit, a penalty equal to 20 percent of the excessive amount of an erroneous refund or credit claim is assessed. The penalty does not apply:

- If the taxpayer has a reasonable basis for the erroneous claim;
- If the erroneous claim relates to the earned income credit; or
- To any portion of the excessive amount that is subject to the accuracy-related penalty or the civil fraud penalty.

An understatement arising from an erroneous refund or credit claim is subject to a 20 percent penalty, just as an underpayment is subject to the 20 percent accuracy-related penalty. For purposes of this penalty, a transaction entered into that has any excessive amount attributable to a transaction lacking economic substance is not treated as having a reasonable basis.

Early Retirement Plan Distribution

Any taxpayer who receives an early or nonexempted distribution from a qualified retirement plan is subject to an increase in income tax in an amount equal to 10 percent of the early distribution. The tax on an early distribution is most commonly assessed when such distribution is made prior to the recipient attaining the age of 59½. The increased tax is referred to as a tax on early distributions, whether the distribution is early or nonexempted. The 10 percent penalty is in addition to any regular income tax owed on the distribution. The plan administrator is not required to withhold the amount of the additional income tax on such a distribution.

Although distributions from deferred compensation plans of governmental and tax-exempt employers are not directly subject to the increased tax, an early distribution from the eligible deferred compensation plan of a governmental employer that includes amounts accumulated in a qualified retirement plan and rolled over to the governmental plan is subject to the increased tax.

Disclosure of Return Information by Return Preparers

A return preparer who uses return information for any purpose other than to prepare a return or who makes an unauthorized disclosure of return information is subject to a $250 penalty for each disclosure, up to a maximum of $10,000. If the action is undertaken knowingly or recklessly, the preparer may be subject to criminal penalties or a fine of up to $1,000, or up to a year in jail, or both, together with the cost of prosecution. A taxpayer may bring a civil action for damages against the U.S. government if an IRS employee offers the taxpayer's representative favorable tax treatment in exchange for information about the taxpayer.

Disclosure of Return Information by Third Parties/Government Employees

A taxpayer may bring a damage action against a person who knowingly or negligently makes an unauthorized disclosure or inspection of any return or return information of the taxpayer. Returns and tax return information are confidential and may not be disclosed to federal or state agencies or employees except as provided in Code Sec. 6103. A *return* is defined as any tax return, information return, declaration of estimated tax, or claim for refund filed under the Internal Revenue Code. Return information includes: the taxpayer's identity; the nature, source or amount of income, payments, receipts, deductions, net worth, tax liability, deficiencies, closing (and similar) agreements; and information regarding the actual or possible investigation of a return. All officers and employees of the United States, of any state, and of any local child support enforcement agency are prohibited from disclosing tax returns and return information. The prohibition also applies to most other persons who have had access to returns or return information by virtue of permitted disclosures of such returns or information under Code Sec. 6103.

¶ 609 CRIMINAL PENALTIES

Criminal penalties, i.e., felony charges, may be incurred when the taxpayer:

- Willfully fails to make a return, keep records, supply required information, or pay any tax or estimated tax;
- Willfully attempts in any manner to evade or defeat the tax; or
- Willfully fails to collect and pay over the tax.

In addition to the felony charges listed, misdemeanor charges can be brought for:

- Making fraudulent statements to employees;
- Filing a fraudulent withholding certificate; or
- Failing to obey a summons.

It should be noted that the criminal penalties are in addition to the civil penalties. A good faith misunderstanding of the law or a good faith belief that one is not violating the law negates, however, the willfulness element of a tax evasion charge. A detailed discussion of criminal charges and defenses is beyond the scope of this chapter.

STUDY QUESTION

---

5. The 20 percent penalty for filing an erroneous refund or credit claim for tax liabilities is applicable if:

    a. The excessive amount is subject to the accuracy-related penalty

    b. The taxpayer presents a reasonable basis for the erroneous claim

    c. The taxpayer's claim is related to the earned income tax credit

    d. The understatement arises from a transaction lacking economic substance

---

¶ 610 INTEREST

Imposition of Interest

Interest is imposed if the amount of any tax is not paid on or before the last day prescribed for its payment. Interest is charged because the IRS does not have use of the taxpayer's money for any period in which the tax is unpaid or underpaid. Assuming that the underlying tax has been properly assessed, interest can be assessed by the IRS without issuing a notice of deficiency at any time during the period in which the underlying tax is collectible. Generally, any tax must be collected within the 10-year period following assessment; however, interest not previously assessed may be assessed at any time during the 10-year collection period.

Determining Payment Dates

Payment of tax is usually due when the return is due. If the taxpayer elects to have the IRS compute the income tax, however, the tax is due 30 days after the IRS mails a notice to the taxpayer of the amount due. If the due date of a return falls on a Saturday, Sunday, or legal holiday, thereby extending the time for paying the tax to the next day that is not a Saturday, Sunday, or legal holiday, interest nevertheless runs from the original due date if the tax is not timely paid.

There are several situations in which interest on underpayments is not assessed:

- For a failure to pay estimated tax by individuals and corporations, although underpayments of estimated tax are subject to an addition to tax measured by the interest rate on underpayments of tax; or
- For an employer's failure to pay unemployment tax; or
- For a railroad's failure to pay the railroad unemployment repayment tax; or
- On adjustments to taxes made to compensate for underpayments of Social Security tax, railroad retirement tax, or wage withholding.

Generally, interest runs from the original due date for the tax to the date payment is received and accrues during periods for which an extension has been granted. The running of interest and penalties is suspended, however, if the IRS fails to notify an individual taxpayer of the liability. An IRS notice of interest due from a taxpayer must include a detailed computation of the interest payment, as well as the tax code section that authorizes the collection of the interest sought.

However, if a tax liability for one tax year is satisfied through credit of an overpayment from a subsequent year, interest runs on the liability:

- From the due date of the return for the earlier year to the due date of the return for the subsequent year if that return is filed timely or filed during an extension period; or
- To the actual date of filing if the return is delinquent.

In a similar vein, if any part of an underpayment is satisfied by credit of an overpayment (from another year or from a different type of tax), interest does not accrue on the portion of the underpayment so satisfied for any period that interest would have been allowed on the overpayment if it were refunded instead of credited. This rule does not apply if a net interest of zero applies.

For taxes that are payable by stamp, such as certain excise taxes, or in other situations without a prescribed last date for payment, interest starts running from the date the liability for the tax arises, as long as that date is not later than the date that the IRS issues a notice and demand for the tax. The last date for payment of the accumulated earnings tax is the due date of the income tax return for that year.

A taxpayer can stop the running of interest by fully paying a proposed deficiency before it is assessed. This can be accomplished by making an advance remittance or deposit of tax before an assessment takes place. A taxpayer may designate how this advance remittance is to be allocated. Interest on unpaid taxes also stops running when a bankruptcy proceeding is commenced.

Determining Applicable Interest Rate

Generally, the underpayment rate applies to underpayments of tax and to penalties, additional tax, and erroneous refunds. However, the underpayment rate is applied to interest underpayments in certain transactions including, but not limited to:

- A gain on property transferred to a trust at less than fair market value;
- A failure by an individual to pay estimated tax;
- A failure by a corporation to pay estimated tax;
- A net increase in a taxpayer's nonqualified, nonrecourse financing on Code Sec. 38 property;

- Tax benefits resulting from late retirement of certain boilers; and
- A failure to turn over property subject to levy.

Underpayments. The interest rate payable on underpayments is set at 3 percent over the federal short-term rate for most taxpayers. Interest on underpayments is compounded daily, except in the case of an underpayment of estimated tax.

Abatement of interest. Although delay by the IRS in settling a case does not stop the running of interest, the IRS, at its discretion, can abate the assessment of all or part of any interest on:

- A deficiency partially or wholly attributable to any unreasonable error or delay by an IRS officer or employee in performing a ministerial or managerial act; or
- A payment of any tax subject to deficiency procedures to the extent that any delay in payment is attributable to late performance of a ministerial act by an IRS officer or employee.

A "ministerial act" is a nondiscretionary procedural act that occurs during the processing of a case after all conferences and reviews have taken place. The following illustrate delays caused by a ministerial act:

- A delay in transferring an audit from one district office to another; or
- A delay in issuing a notice of deficiency once all agreed and unagreed issues have been identified and all other prerequisites for issuing the notice have been met.

It is just as important to know those delays that are not caused by ministerial acts, including:

- A delay in the start of an examination or a delay in work on a case in progress due to other IRS priorities;
- A delay in resolving an audit allegedly caused because the IRS agent was sent to a training class, assessed an improperly large deficiency, then launched and subsequently dropped a civil fraud investigation; or
- The passage of a considerable amount of time in the litigation phase of a tax shelter dispute.

A "managerial act" is an administrative act that occurs during the processing of the taxpayer's case involving the temporary or permanent loss of records or the exercise of judgment or the management of personnel.

The IRS does not have the authority to abate interest on employment taxes under Code Sec. 6404(e)(1) because employment taxes are not included in the definition of a deficiency nor are they subject to the deficiency procedures. In the event that any significant aspect of the error or delay is caused by the taxpayer, interest cannot be abated. Such error or delay, however, is not attributable to the taxpayer solely because he or she consented to an extension of the statute of limitations.

Although abatement is at the discretion of the IRS, taxpayers may seek relief in the Tax Court on the basis that the IRS abused its discretion. If the court finds that such abuse occurred, the taxpayer is sometimes described as being entitled to abatement.

A taxpayer can also request an abatement of interest by filing Form 843, *Claim for Refund and Request for Abatement,* with the IRS Center where the tax return was filed. The words "Request for Abatement of Interest Under Section 6404(e)" should be written across the top of the form. A separate Form 843 should be filed for each tax year or each different type of tax, except that a single Form 843 can be used if the interest to be abated for different tax years or for different types of taxes were caused by error or delay in performing a single ministerial or managerial act.

STUDY QUESTION

6. Which of the following is a managerial act that may abate imposition of an interest assessment by the IRS?

    a. A delay in issuing a notice of deficiency after prerequisites for issuance have been met

    b. A delay in work on a case in progress because of different IRS case priorities

    c. Personnel management issues at the IRS during processing of the case

    d. A delay in transferring the taxpayer's audit materials from one IRS district office to another

¶ 611 CONCLUSION

This chapter is intended to broaden knowledge of multiple different penalties that may be imposed on taxpayers. It is key in a successful practice to be able to advise and caution taxpayers regarding the tax positions they may wish to take and the consequences of not meeting all tax filing obligations. A working knowledge of penalties will also enable a practitioner to ensure that should a letter from the IRS be received by a client, the practitioner will be in a position to confidently address the issues to minimize the financial consequences to the client.

MODULE 2: CHANGES IN FILING DEADLINES, AUDITS, AND PENALTIES— Chapter 7: Partnership Audit Rules: Initial Considerations

¶ 701 WELCOME

The most significant change in partnership audit rules since the enactment of the *Tax Equity and Fiscal Responsibility Act of 1982* (P.L. 97-248) (TEFRA) is the *Bipartisan Budget Act of 2015* (P.L. 114-74) (BBA), enacted on November 2, 2015. The new law repeals the TEFRA audit rules and the reporting and audit procedures for electing large partnerships. The new rules enacted by the BBA, effective for partnership years beginning after December 31, 2017, are contained in new or amended Code Secs. 6221 through 6241. Nevertheless, a partnership may elect to apply the new audit rules to any return of the partnership filed for partnership tax years beginning after November 2, 2015, and before January 1, 2018. The new rules focus the audit, as well as the collection of any adjustment, at the partnership level (Code Sec. 6221(a)), place the burden of the tax on partners in the adjustment year rather than the year under audit, replace the tax matters partner with a partnership representative (Code Sec. 6223), and make changes regarding who is subject to and who can elect out of the new rules. They affect far beyond currently electing large partnerships (ELPs) under the TEFRA rules.

¶ 702 LEARNING OBJECTIVES

Upon completion of this chapter, you will be able to:

- Identify situations in which partnerships may elect to opt out of the Code Sec. 6221 audit rules;
- Recognize the duty of consistency between the returns filed for partners and their partnerships;
- Identify the manner in which the new audit rules will apply to partnerships; and
- Identify ways in which adjustments and assessments are implemented for a reviewed tax year.

¶ 703 INTRODUCTION

The post-2017 partnership audit rules are generally contained in Code Secs. 6221 through 6241, added or amended by the BBA. But note that these new rules are contained in provisions that carry the same tax code section numbers as the pre-2018 TEFRA rules.

> **NOTE:** Keep in mind that the code sections discussed in this chapter refer to the post-2017 provisions, unless otherwise stated.

A partnership may elect—as opposed to being required—to apply the new audit rules to any return of the partnership filed for partnership tax years beginning after November 2, 2015, and before January 1, 2018. Under amended Code Sec. 6221(b), a partnership with 100 or fewer qualifying partners may also opt out of the new audit rules for tax years after 2017, in which case the partnership and partners would be audited under the general rules that apply to individual taxpayers.

Although there is some time to prepare, partnerships will want to start thinking now about how to revise their partnership agreements and partnership structures going forward, and prospective partners will want to be much more careful about exposure to past partnership activities.

> **COMMENT:** The IRS will now need to develop regulations to reflect repeal of the TEFRA rules. Lawmakers provided for a delayed effective date. The BBA's delayed effective date applicable to returns filed for partnership tax years beginning after 2017 should provide an opportunity for stakeholders to amend the new partnership rules as the impact of the new regime is examined more thoroughly. The provisions were essentially taken from H.R. 2821, sponsored by Rep. James Renacci (R-Ohio), who had planned to hold several additional hearings on refine the bill before any floor action. Among the additional tweaks suggested by certain parties have been application of the rules to multitiered partnerships and consideration of foreign and tax-exempt partners, as well as to changes in partnership allocations and membership from year to year.

> **COMMENT:** The *Fixing America's Surface Transportation Act* (July 31, 2015) (Surface Transportation Act) codified the due dates for the filing of Form 1065, *U.S. Return of Partnership Income and Schedule K-1s, Partner's Share of Income* by partnerships and the filing of Form 1120S by S corporations. The Surface Transportation Act also modifies the due date (without extension) for filing of Form 1065 by partnerships. Returns for tax years beginning after December 31, 2015, must be filed on or before the fifteenth day of the third month following the close of the partnership's tax year (March 15 for calendar-year partnerships), a change from the prior filing deadline of on or before the fifteenth day of the fourth month following the close of the partnership's tax year (April 15 for calendar year partnerships).

¶704 ADJUSTMENTS AT PARTNERSHIP LEVEL IN ADJUSTMENT YEAR

Under the new audit rules of amended Code Sec. 6221(a), for a particular year of the partnership (the *reviewed year*), the IRS will examine the partnership's items of income, gain, loss, deduction, or credit, and any partners' distributive shares of the items, at the partnership level. Any adjustments will be taken into account by the partnership and not by the individual partners in the year that the audit or any judicial review is completed (the "adjustment year") and will be collected from the partnership, not the individual partners (Code Secs. 6232(a) and 6233(b)(2)). Any adjustment will include any tax attributable to the adjustment that is assessed and collected, and any related penalty, addition to tax, or additional amount.

Background

Under the TEFRA audit rules, once the audit was completed and any resulting adjustments were determined, the IRS had to recalculate the tax liability of each partner in the partnership for the particular audit year. The IRS had complained that such a workflow was an inefficient use when applying its limited audit resources to partnerships, which have changed in scope dramatically since the TEFRA rules were introduced in 1982.

> **COMMENT:** Partnerships are among the fastest growing type of business entity. According to the IRS, the number of partnerships has grown at an average annual rate of 3.9 percent since 2003.

¶ 705 ELECTION TO OPT OUT

An eligible partnership may elect to opt out of the partnership-level audit rules (Code Sec. 6221(b)). To be eligible to elect out, the partnership must have 100 or fewer partners. A *qualifying partner* for this purpose is a partner for whom the partnership is required under Code Sec. 6031(b)(1)(B) to furnish a Schedule K-1 (Form 1065) for the tax year. In addition, each partner of the partnership must be:

- An individual;
- A C corporation or foreign entity that would be treated as a C corporation if it were a domestic entity;
- An S corporation; or
- The estate of a deceased partner (Code Sec. 6221(b)(1)(C)).

Thus, the election to opt out is not available to a tiered partnership—that is, any partnership having a partner that is classified as a partnership for federal tax purposes.

The election to opt out must be made with a timely filed return and include a disclosure of the name and taxpayer identification number (TIN) of each partner (Code Sec. 6221(b)(1)(D)). The IRS may provide alternative identification methods for any foreign partners (Code Sec. 6221(b)(2)(B)). The electing partnership must notify each partner of the election in a manner that the IRS will prescribe (Code Sec. 6221(b)(1)(E))). Once the election is made, the partnership and partners will be audited under the general rules that apply to individual taxpayers.

If any partner is an S corporation, the partnership may elect out only if, in addition to the partner disclosures discussed above, it also discloses the name and TIN of each shareholder of the S corporation for the tax year of the S corporation ending with or within the partnership tax year for which the partnership is electing to opt out of the audit rules (Code Sec. 6221(b)(2)(A)). Each shareholder of the S corporation is counted as a partner for purposes of qualifying to elect out (Code Sec. 6221(b)(2)(A)). The new Code Sec. 6221(b)(2)(C) states that the IRS may provide similar rules by regulation or other guidance for any partners not described in Code Sec. 6221(b)(1)(C).

> **COMMENT:** A partnership with 10 or fewer qualified partners must make an affirmative election to opt out of the new audit rules. Under the old rules, a small partnership was not subject to the TEFRA audit regime unless the small partnership made an affirmative election to opt in to the audit rules.

> **CAUTION:** Information returns required to be provided by the partnership to its partners (i.e., Schedule K-1) generally may not be amended after the due date of the partnership's returns except when the partnership makes an election to apply the audit adjustment rules at the partner level, and not at the partnership level (Code Sec. 6031(b), as amended by P.L. 114-74 and P.L. 114-113, generally applicable to returns filed for partnership tax years beginning after December 31, 2017).

¶ 706 DUTY OF CONSISTENCY BETWEEN RETURNS

Under the new rules that apply to partnership returns filed for partnership tax years beginning after December 31, 2017, partnerships and their partners will be audited at the partnership level (Code Secs. 6221 through 6241). Under these new rules, on the partner's return, a partner generally must treat an item of income, gain, loss, deduction, or credit attributable to a partnership in a manner consistent with the treatment of that item on the partnership return (Code Sec. 6222(a)). Any underpayment of tax attributable to a partner's failure to comply with the consistency requirement is treated as if the underpayment were due to a mathematical or clerical error on the partner's return (Code Sec. 6222(b)). As a result, the IRS can immediately assess any additional tax against the partner without issuing a notice of deficiency, and the partner has no right to petition the Tax Court for a redetermination of the deficiency (Code Sec. 6213(b)). In addition, a petition for abatement, which would generally be allowed under Code Sec. 6213(b)(2), may not be filed for any assessment of an underpayment caused by a partner's failure to consistently report a partnership item (Code Sec. 6222(b)).

The duty of consistency does not apply, and a partner will not be immediately assessed an additional tax for the partner's failure to comply with the consistency requirement for any item, if:

- The partnership has filed a return, but the partner's treatment on the partner's return is (or may be) inconsistent with the partnership's treatment of the item on the partnership return, or the partnership has not filed a return; and
- The partner files with the IRS a notification identifying the inconsistency (Code Sec. 6222(c)).

A partner will be considered to have complied with the notification requirement if the partner:

- Proves that the treatment of the item in question on the partner's return is consistent with the treatment of the item on the statement furnished to the partner by the partnership; and
- Elects to have these rules apply (Code Sec. 6222(c)(2)).

Any final decision reached by the IRS regarding an inconsistent position in a proceeding to which the partnership is not a party is not binding on the partnership (Code Sec. 6222(d)). In the event that a partner is found to have disregarded the rules involving the duty of consistency between returns, the accuracy-related and fraud penalties (Code Secs. 6662 through 6664) may apply (Code Sec. 6222(e)).

> **COMMENT:** As a result, the IRS can immediately assess any additional tax against the partner without issuing a notice of deficiency (Code Sec 6222(b)). The partner has no right to petition the Tax Court for a redetermination of the deficiency. In addition, a petition for abatement, which would generally be allowed under Code Sec. 6213(b)(2), may not be filed for any assessment of an underpayment caused by a partner's failure to consistently report a partnership item.

STUDY QUESTION

1. If a partner underpays tax because the partner fails to comply with the consistency requirement of Code Sec. 6222:

- **a.** The IRS can assess the additional tax against the partner
- **b.** The IRS issues a notice of deficiency
- **c.** The partner may petition the Tax Court to redetermine the amount of the underpayment
- **d.** The partner may file a petition for abatement of an assessment for the underpayment

¶ 707 PARTNERS BOUND BY PARTNERSHIP ACTIONS

Under current law, there are three regimes for auditing partnerships. But under the changes enacted as part of the *Bipartisan Budget Act of 2015*, there will be one set of rules under which audits occur only at the partnership level (for returns filed for partnership tax years beginning after 2017), with an option to elect out of these new rules for certain smaller partnerships. In this new audit regime, all partnerships must designate a partner (or other person) with a substantial presence in the United States to be the *partnership representative*—the person who will have the sole authority to act on behalf of the partnership for purposes of the new partnership audit rules (Code Sec. 6223(a)).

Partnership Representative

Unlike a *tax matters partner* under the TEFRA rules, a partnership representative does not have to be one of the partners. And if the partnership fails to select a partnership representative, the IRS may appoint any person to perform that role. There is currently no limitation on the IRS' authority to designate a person as a partnership representative.

The partnership and all of its partners will be bound by actions taken by the partnership representative and by any final decision in a proceeding brought under the audit rules (Code Sec 6223(b)). All notices of proceedings and adjustments under Code Sec. 6231(a), as added by the BBA, must be mailed to the partnership and the partnership representative—a bifurcated notice requirement that may be especially significant when the partnership representative is not one of the partners.

By empowering a single partnership representative (who need not even be a partner) to bind all partners during a partnership audit, this provision effectively eliminates:

- Any right of partners to opt out of the partnership-level proceeding; and
- Any statutory right of the partners to participate in the partnership examination.

Partners wanting a voice in litigation and settlement decisions related to partnership examinations will need to include those rights in the partnership agreement.

Consistency of Returns

Because the partnership audits will occur at the entity level (barring the election to opt out), Code Sec. 6222 as added by the BBA requires each partner's return to be consistent with the partnership's return. That is, a partner must generally treat on the partner's return a partnership item of income, gain, loss, deduction, or credit attributable to a partnership in a manner consistent with the treatment of that item on the partnership return. In addition, upon completion of an audit, if any tax adjustments are determined, the additional tax, interest, and penalties will be collected from the partnership—resulting in the current partners being responsible for the adjustments caused by actions taken by prior-year partners.

Transition Rules

To date, there are no transition rules addressing when examination issues affect a partnership over a period of years subject to both TEFRA audit rules and these new rules. Further guidance in this area is likely.

¶ 708 DEFINITIONS AND SPECIAL RULES

Code Sec. 6241, as added by the BBA, provides definitions and special rules for the new partnership audit regime contained in Code Sec. 6221 through Code Sec. 6235. The new regime is generally applicable to returns filed for partnership tax years beginning after December 31, 2017. The definitions and special rules are discussed here.

Code Sec. 6241(1): Partnership

A *partnership* is any partnership required to file a return under Code Sec. 6031(a).

Code Sec. 6241(2): Partnership Adjustment

A *partnership adjustment* is an adjustment to the amount of an item of income, gain, loss, deduction, or credit of a partnership, or any partner's distributive share of those items.

Code Sec. 6241(3): Return Due Date

The *return due date* for a tax year is the date prescribed for filing the partnership return for each tax year, determined without regard to extensions.

Code Sec. 6241(4): Payments Nondeductible

An income tax payment required to be made under the new audit rules is not allowed as a deduction.

Code Sec. 6241(5): Partnerships with a Principal Place of Business Outside of the United States

For purposes of the judicial review procedures under Code Sec. 6234, a partnership with a principal place of business outside of the United States is treated as having a principal place of business in the District of Columbia.

Code Sec. 6241(6): Partnerships in Cases Under Title 11 of the Bankruptcy Code

In a Title 11 bankruptcy case, the statute of limitations for making a partnership adjustment, or for the assessment or collection of any imputed underpayment under Code Sec. 6501 or Code Sec. 6502, is suspended. The suspension is for the period during which the IRS is prohibited by reason of the bankruptcy from making the adjustment, assessment or collection, *plus* 60 days for an adjustment or assessment, and six months for collection.

The 90-day limitations period for filing a petition with a court for the judicial review of a partnership adjustment is suspended during the period that the partnership is prohibited by reason of the bankruptcy case from filing the petition under Code Sec. 6234, plus 60 days.

Code Sec. 6241(7): Treatment When Partnership Relationship Ceases to Exist

If a partnership ceases to exist before a partnership adjustment takes effect, the adjustment is taken into account by the former partners of the partnership under regulations issued by the IRS.

Code Sec. 6241(8): Extension to Entities Filing Partnership Returns

If it is determined that an entity is not a partnership (or that there is no entity) for a tax year that a partnership return is filed, the partnership audit rules may be extended, as provided in regulations, to the entity and its items, and to persons holding an interest in the entity.

STUDY QUESTION

2. Required income tax payments under Code Sec. 6241 audit rules are:
    a. Deductible only by U.S. partners for partnerships located outside of the United States
    b. Not allowed as deductions
    c. Deductible only at the partnership level
    d. Limited to partnership adjustments

¶ 709 PARTNERSHIP REPRESENTATIVE

As mentioned above, all partnerships must designate a partner (or other person) with a substantial presence in the United States as the partnership representative—the person who will have the sole authority to act on behalf of the partnership for purposes of the new partnership audit rules (Code Sec. 6223). If the partnership does not designate a partnership representative, the IRS may select any person to perform that function. The partnership and all of its partners will be bound by actions taken by the partnership representative selected by the IRS, and by any final decision in a proceeding brought under the audit rules.

The partnership representative replaces the tax matters partner (TMP) under TEFRA in the role of liaison with the IRS during an audit or in litigation.

¶ 710 ADJUSTMENTS AND UNDERPAYMENTS, GENERALLY

Effective generally for returns filed for partnership tax years beginning after December 31, 2017, if the IRS adjusts any item of a partnership's income, gain, loss, deduction, or credit, or partners' distributive shares of such items, the partnership is required to pay any imputed underpayment with respect to the adjustment in the adjustment year. Any partnership adjustment that does not result in an imputed underpayment (that is, an adjustment that results in an overpayment) is taken into account by the partnership in the adjustment year as either:

- A reduction in nonseparately stated income or an increase in nonseparately stated loss (whichever is appropriate) under Code Sec. 702(a)(8); or

- In the case of an item of credit, as a separately stated item (Code Sec. 6225(a)).

No deduction is permitted for any payment required to be made by a partnership under the audit rules, including the payment of any imputed underpayment (Code Sec. 6241(4)).

For this purpose, an *adjustment year* is:

- In the case of an adjustment pursuant to the decision of a court in a proceeding brought under Code Sec. 6234, the partnership tax year in which such decision becomes final;

- In the case of an administrative adjustment request under Code Sec. 6227, the partnership tax year in which such administrative adjustment request is made; or

- In any other case, the partnership tax year in which a notice of the final partnership adjustment is mailed under Code Sec. 6231 (Code Sec. 6225(d)(2)).

For purposes of the audit rules, a *partnership adjustment* means any adjustment in the amount of any item of income, gain, loss, deduction, or credit of the partnership in the current tax year, or any partner's distributive share of such items (Code Sec. 6241(2)). If a partnership ceases to exist before a partnership adjustment takes effect, then the adjustment is taken into account by the former partners of the partnership under regulations prescribed by the IRS (Code Sec. 6241(7)). The effect of the adjustment occurring at the partnership level means that any additional tax liability from the adjustment falls on the current partners in the partnership unless the partnership ceases to exist. However, the current partners are not subject to joint and several liability for any liability determined at the partnership level.

Determination of Imputed Underpayments

Effective generally for returns filed for partnership tax years beginning after December 31, 2017, any imputed underpayment with respect to any partnership adjustment for any reviewed year (i.e., the partnership tax year to which the item being adjusted relates) is generally determined by:

- Netting all adjustments of items of income, gain, loss, or deduction, and multiplying the net amount by the highest rate of tax in effect for the reviewed year under Code Sec. 1 (income tax) or Code Sec. 11 (alternative minimum tax);
- Treating any net increase or decrease in loss under the preceding item as a corresponding decrease or increase, respectively, in income; and
- Taking into account any adjustments to items of credit as an increase or decrease in the amount determined under the first item above) (Code Sec. 6225(b)(1)).

If any adjustment reallocates the distributive share of any item from one partner to another, that adjustment is taken into account for purposes of determining the imputed underpayment by disregarding:

- Any decrease in any item of income or gain; and
- Any increase in any item of deduction, loss, or credit (Code Sec. 6225(b)(2)).

Modification of Imputed Underpayments

Effective generally for returns filed for partnership tax years beginning after December 31, 2017, under Code Sec. 6225 the IRS is authorized to establish procedures under which the imputed payment may be modified.

In particular, under Code Sec. 6225 the procedures will provide that if one or more partners file amended returns for the reviewed year in which all partnership adjustments are taken into account and pay any resulting tax due with the amended return, then the imputed underpayment amount is determined without regard to the portion of the adjustments already taken into account. However, if any adjustment reallocates a distributive share of an item from one partner to another, the adjustment is disregarded in determining the imputed underpayment only if all affected partners file amended returns.

In addition, the Code Sec. 6225 procedures will provide for determining the imputed underpayment without regard to the portion that the partnership demonstrates is allocable to a partner that is a tax-exempt entity, as defined in Code Sec. 168(h)(2).

The procedures also will provide for taking into account a tax rate lower than that used to determine the imputed underpayment under Code Sec. 6225(b)(1)(A) with respect to any portion of the imputed underpayment that the partnership demonstrates is allocable to a partner that is:

- A C corporation; or
- In the case of a capital gain or qualified dividend, an individual (for this purpose, an S corporation is treated as an individual).

The lower rate cannot be less than the highest rate in effect with respect to the income and taxpayer described in either item.

The portion of the imputed underpayment to which the lower rate applies with respect to a partner is determined by reference to the partner's distributive share of items to which the imputed underpayment relates. However, if the imputed underpayment is attributable to the adjustment of more than one item, and any partner's distributive share of these items is not the same with respect to all of the items, then the portion of the imputed underpayment to which the lower rate applies with respect to a partner is determined by reference to the amount that would have been the partner's distributive share of net gain or loss if the partnership had sold all of its assets at their fair market value as of the close of the partnership's reviewed year (Code Sec. 6225(c)(4)(B)).

In the case of a publicly traded partnership as defined under Code Sec. 469(k)(2), IRS procedures will provide that the imputed underpayment may be determined without regard to the portion of the underpayment attributable to specified passive activity losses allocable to a specific partner (Code Sec. 6225(c)(5)). The specified loss is decreased and the partnership takes the decrease into account in the adjustment year with respect to the specified partner. For this purpose, a *specified passive activity* loss is the lesser of:

- The passive activity loss of the specified partner which is separately determined with respect to that partner's tax year in which or with which the reviewed year of the partnership ends; or

- The passive activity loss determined with respect to the specified partner's tax year in which or with which the adjustment year of the partnership ends (Code Sec. 6225(c)(5)(B).

A *specified partner* is a person who:

- Is an individual, estate, trust, closely held C corporation, or personal service corporation; and

- Has a specified passive activity loss with respect to the publicly traded partnership.

The specified person must continuously meet these requirements for the tax year in which the partnership review years end through the tax year in which the partnership adjustment year ends.

Under Code Sec. 6225(c)(6), the IRS is authorized to provide for additional procedures to modify imputed underpayment amounts on the basis of other factors that the IRS determines are necessary or appropriate.

Anything required to be submitted for purposes of obtaining a modification of an imputed underpayment must be submitted to the IRS no later than the close of the 270-day period beginning on the date on which the notice of a proposed partnership adjustment is mailed under Code Sec. 6231, unless the period is extended with the IRS's consent (Code Sec. 6225(c)(7)). Any modification of the imputed underpayment amount under these rules can be made only upon the IRS's approval (Code Sec. 6225(c)(8)).

Alternative to Payment of Imputed Underpayment by Partnerships

A partnership can make an election within 45 days of the date of the notice of final partnership adjustment to not apply the adjustment rules at the partnership level under Code Sec. 6225 (added by the BBA), but rather at the partner level. The election must be made in the manner prescribed by the IRS. The partnership must furnish to each partner of the partnership for the reviewed year (i.e., the partnership tax year to which the item being adjusted relates) and to the IRS a statement of the partner's share of any adjustment to income, gain, loss, deduction, or credit (as determined in the notice of final partnership adjustment). Once made, the election is revocable only with the IRS's consent (Code Sec. 6226(a)). Under the BBA, Code Sec. 6226 applies generally to elections with respect to returns filed for partnership tax years beginning after December 31, 2017.

Adjustments taken into account by partners. If the election is made, each partner's income tax for the tax year that includes the date the statement was furnished to the partners and the IRS must be increased by the aggregate adjustment amounts for that year (Code Sec 6226(b)(1)). The adjustment amounts are:

- For a tax year of a partner that includes the end of the reviewed year, the amount by which the partner's income tax would increase if the partner's share of the partnership's imputed underpayment were taken into account, plus
- For any tax year after the tax year described above and before the tax year that includes the date the statement was furnished, the amount by which the income tax would increase as a result of the adjustment to tax attributes, described below (Code Sec. 6226(b)(2)).

Any tax attribute that would have been affected if the adjustments were taken into account for the tax year of a partner that includes the end of the reviewed year must be appropriately adjusted as follows:

- For a tax year referred to in the second item above, such tax attributes must be appropriately adjusted for purposes of applying the item above; and
- For any subsequent tax year, such tax attributes must be appropriately adjusted (Code Sec. 6226(b)(3)).

Penalties and interest. Regardless of the election to apply the adjustments at the individual partner level rather than the partnership level, any penalties, additions to tax, or other amounts are determined at the partnership level. In turn, the partners of the partnership for the reviewed year are liable for any such penalty, addition to tax, or additional amount (Code Sec. 6226(c)(1)).

However, interest on an imputed underpayment with respect to which the election is made is determined:

- At the partner level;
- From the due date of the return for the tax year to which the increase is attributable (determined by taking into account any increases attributable to a change in tax attributes for a tax year under Code Sec. 6226(b)(2) (added by the BBA); and
- At the federal short-term rate, plus five percentage points (Code Sec. 6226(c)(2)).

A partnership may file a petition for judicial review of a readjustment under Code Sec. 6234 (added by the PATH Act).

STUDY QUESTION

3. If a partnership elects the alternative payment of imputed underpayments:

    a. Penalties and interest are nonetheless determined at the partnership level

    b. The election must be made before the date of the notice of final partnership adjustment

    c. The tax attributes for subsequent tax years' returns are unaffected

    d. The election is irrevocable

Administrative Adjustment Requests

The BBA states that a partnership can voluntarily file an administrative adjustment request (AAR) with respect to partnership items for any partnership tax year.

AAR requirements. Under the BBA, a partnership can voluntarily file an AAR of one or more items of income, gain, loss, deduction, or credit of the partnership, for any partnership tax year. Code Sec. 6227 generally applies to requests with respect to returns filed for partnership tax years beginning after December 31, 2017.

Any administrative adjustment will be determined and taken into account for the partnership tax year in which the administrative adjustment request is made either:

- By the partnership under rules similar to the Code Sec. 6225 procedures for adjustments at the partnership level due to imputed underpayments; or
- By the partnership and partners under rules similar to the Code Sec. 6226 alternative procedures for adjustments at the partner level.

Under the BBA, some of the imputed underpayment rules will not apply for purposes of the AAR determination, including:

- The procedures for modifying the imputed underpayment amount for partners filing amended returns for the review year;
- The 270-day period for submitting documents for a modification of the imputed underpayment amount; and
- The requirement that the IRS approve the modification of an imputed underpayment amount.

If the alternative procedures are applied, the substitution of the interest rate of five percentage points for three percentage points in Code Sec. 6226(c)(2)(C) will not apply under the BBA. If an adjustment does not result in an imputed underpayment, rules similar to the alternative procedures under Code Sec. 6226 will apply.

The BBA added Code Sec. 6231(a), which requires the IRS to mail notice of any administrative proceedings and adjustments to the partnership and partnership representative.

Period of limitations for AAR requests. An AAR must be filed within a certain period. Specifically, the request must be filed within three years of the later of:

- The date on which the partnership return for the partnership's tax year is filed; or
- The last day for filing the partnership return for that year (determined without regard to extensions).

The request may not, however, be filed after the IRS files a notice of administrative proceeding under Code Sec. 6231, as added by the BBA. Code Sec. 6227 generally applies to requests with respect to returns filed for partnership tax years beginning after December 31, 2017.

Notice to Partnership of Proceedings and Adjustments

The BBA requires the IRS to mail to the partnership and the partnership representative:

- Notice of any administrative proceeding initiated at the partnership level with respect to an adjustment of any item of income, gain, loss, deduction, or credit for a partnership tax year, or any partner's distributive share;
- Notice of any proposed partnership adjustment resulting from the proceeding; and

- Notice of any final partnership adjustment (but not earlier than 270 days after the date on which the notice of proposed partnership adjustment is mailed (Code Sec. 6231(a)).

These notices may be mailed to the last known address of the partnership representative or the partnership. This holds true even if the partnership has terminated its existence. Under the BBA, the notice requirements apply to any proceeding with respect to an administrative adjustment request filed by a partnership under Code Sec. 6227.

If the partnership has filed a petition for judicial review of an adjustment under Code Sec. 6234 (as added by the BBA), no further notices of a final partnership adjustment may be mailed to the partnership without a showing of fraud, malfeasance, or a misrepresentation of material fact (Code Sec. 6231(b)). The IRS, with the consent of the partnership, may rescind any notice of a partnership adjustment. In that case, the notice will not be treated as a notice of partnership adjustment for purposes of the audit rules, and the partnership will have no right to petition for judicial review of the adjustment (Code Sec. 6231(c)).

Assessment, Collection, and Payment Rules

Under the BBA, any imputed underpayment with respect to any partnership adjustment for any reviewed year, as provided under Code Sec. 6225, will be treated for assessment and collection purposes as if it were a tax imposed. Normal assessment and collection proceedings will be followed, except in the case of an imputed underpayment resulting from an AAR under Code Sec. 6227 (added by the BBA), in which case the underpayment must be paid when the request is filed.

No assessment of a deficiency may be made before the close of the 90th day after the day on which a notice of final partnership adjustment was mailed. Further, if the partnership petitioned for judicial review of an adjustment under Code Sec. 6234, no assessment of a deficiency may be made regarding a notice of final partnership adjustment until the decision of the court has become final. Any violation of these restrictions under Code Sec. 6232(c) may be enjoined by the proper court, including the Tax Court. However, the Tax Court will not have jurisdiction to enjoin in the absence of a petition for judicial review under Code Sec. 6234, and then only with respect of the adjustments subject to the petition.

Under Code Sec. 6232(d)(2), the partnership may waive these restrictions on the making of any adjustment. If no proceeding for judicial review of an adjustment is begun during the 90-day period after the date of the notice of final partnership adjustment, the amount for which the partnership is liable cannot be larger than the amount determined in accordance with the notice (Code Sec. 6232(e)).

If the partnership is notified that a mathematical or clerical error results in an adjustment to an item, the assessment restrictions will not apply and, instead, rules similar to those under Code Sec. 6213(b) will apply. This includes any adjustments resulting from a lack of consistency under Code Sec. 6222(a) (as added by the BBA) in the case of a partner who is a partner of another partnership, except that the abatement of the assessment of those mathematical or clerical errors under Code Sec. 6213(b)(2) will not be allowed.

Interest and Penalty Determinations

Interest and penalties for a partnership adjustment for a reviewed year are imposed at the partnership level except where Code Sec. 6226(c) makes partners liable for interest on an imputed underpayment for which an election under Code Sec. 6226 is in effect (Code Sec. 6233(a)).

Interest on reviewed year adjustments is computed for the period beginning on the day after the return due date for the reviewed year and ending on the return due date for the adjustment year (Code Sec. 6233(a)(2)). Any penalty or addition of tax applicable to reviewed year adjustments will be determined at the partnership level as if the partnership were an individual and the imputed underpayment were an actual underpayment for the reviewed year (Code Sec. 6233(a)(3)).

For any failure to pay an imputed underpayment by the due date for the return of the adjustment year, interest is imposed by treating the imputed underpayment as an underpayment of tax, and failure to pay penalties under Code Sec. 6651(a)(2) will apply (Code Sec. 6233(b)). The return due date with respect to the tax year is the date prescribed for filing the partnership return for that tax year, without regard to extensions.

STUDY QUESTION

4. The IRS mails all of the following documents to the partnership and partnership representative *except*:

- **a.** An administrative adjustment request
- **b.** Notice of administrative proceeding
- **c.** Notice of proposed partnership adjustment
- **d.** Notice of final partnership adjustment

Judicial Review of Partnership Adjustments

A partnership that receives a notice of final partnership adjustment may file a petition for readjustment within 90 days after the notice is mailed. The petition may be filed with the Tax Court, the U.S. District Court for the district in which the partnership's place of business is located, or the Court of Federal Claims (Code Sec. 6234(a)), added by the BBA and amended by the PATH Act).

A readjustment petition may be filed with the U.S. District Court or the Court of Federal Claims only if the partnership filing the petition deposits the amount of imputed underpayment with the IRS on or before the date the petition is filed. The court may by order provide that the jurisdictional requirements are satisfied where there has been a good faith attempt to satisfy them. Any shortfall of the amount required to be deposited must be timely corrected. The amount deposited will not be treated as a payment of tax (Code Sec. 6234(b)).

Any court properly petitioned has jurisdiction to determine all items of income, gain, loss, deduction, or credit of the partnership for the partnership tax year to which the notice of final partnership adjustment relates. The court also has jurisdiction to determine the proper allocation of these items among the partners and the applicability of any penalty, addition to tax, or additional amount for which the partnership may be liable (Code Sec. 6234(c)).

Any determination of any court is treated as a final judgment, but is reviewable. The date of any determination will be treated as the date of the court's order entering the decision (Code Sec. 6234(d)).

If an action is dismissed other than by reason of a rescission under Code Sec. 6231(c), the decision of the court dismissing the action will be considered as its decision that the notice of final partnership adjustment is correct. An appropriate order will be entered in the court records (Code Sec, 6234(e)).

Limitations Period on Making Adjustments

Generally, no adjustment for any partnership tax year may be made after the later of:

- The date that is three years after the latest of

  - the date the partnership filed its return for the tax year,

  - the due date of the return, or

  - the date on which the partnership filed an administrative adjustment request;

- In the case of a modification of an imputed underpayment, the date that is 270 days (plus any agreed-to extensions) after the date on which everything required to be submitted to the IRS is submitted; or

- In the case of any notice of proposed partnership adjustment, the date that is 330 days after the date of that notice (plus any agreed-to extensions) (Code Sec. 6235(a), as added by the BBA and amended by the PATH Act).

Under new Code Sec. 6235(b), the statute of limitations may be extended by agreement by the IRS and the partnership. The limitation period is extended to six years in the case of a substantial omission of income. An adjustment may be made at any time in the case of a false return or when no return was filed. A substitute return executed by the IRS under Code Sec. 6020(b) on behalf of the partnership is not treated as a return filed by the partnership (Code Sec. 6235(c)).

The running of the period of limitations is suspended for the period during which a petition for judicial review may be brought, plus one additional year (Code Sec. 6235(d)). The running of the period is also suspended for partnerships for which the IRS is prohibited from making adjustments due to bankruptcy proceedings, plus an additional 60 days for adjustment and assessment, and six months for collection (Code Sec. 6241(6)).

STUDY QUESTION

---

5. A readjustment petition may be filed:

    a. With the Tax Court, U.S. District Court, or Court of Federal Claims

    b. Without an option to review the court's final judgment

    c. Within 30 days of the mailing of the notice of final partnership adjustment

    d. After the partners determine the proper allocation of items in the adjustment

---

¶711 ISSUES RAISED BY THE NEW YORK STATE BAR ASSOCIATION

In May 2016, the Tax Section of the New York State Bar Association (NYSBA) issued its report on the Partnership Audit Rules of the *Bipartisan Budget Act of 2015*. This section of the chapter briefly summarizes some of the new audit regime's potential problems and unresolved issues as identified by the NYSBA. Many of these issues have also been raised by other stakeholders. In addition, the NYSBA's proposal to treat Code Sec. 6225—which provides for partnership adjustments for imputed underpayments—as a withholding tax mechanism is summarized below. Although the points discussed below reflect the views expressed by the NYSBA, they may serve as a fair measure of the kinds of issues the IRS will grapple with in crafting future regulations.

Problems of Overcollection or Undercollection

Under the BBA, if a partnership audit determines that the partnership should have reported additional income or gain (or fewer credits) on its Form 1065 and the Schedule K-1s it issued to its partners, the audited partnership is required to pay to the IRS an imputed underpayment. The *imputed underpayment* is basically an approximation of how much tax would have been paid if that additional income or gain were taxed at the partner level at the highest possible rate under the tax code for the year under audit. This is the main method set out in the BBA for the collection of the additional taxes resulting from a partnership audit.

The fact that computation of imputed underpayments does not account for the interaction of partnership level adjustments with the individual partners' other tax attributes could lead to significant overcollection or undercollection. In connection with this, the NYSBA expresses concern about the possibility for manipulation and even abuse by taxpayers.

Netting Issue: Adjustments That Move Allocations from One Partner to Another

A netting issue arises when an audit results in the reallocation of an item of income from one partner to another. Code Sec. 6225(b)(2) provides that in that case, the imputed underpayment is computed by taking into account only the increased income or decreased deduction and by ignoring the decreased income or increased deduction. The NYSBA believes that this outcome is unfair and has the potential to result in permanent double taxation.

Decreases in Taxes Not Taken into Account

Code Sec. 6226 requires the reviewed year partners to include in their adjustment year taxes the additional taxes they would owe for the reviewed year and all years between the reviewed year and the adjustment year. But under the statutory formula, for each of those years, the partner can take into account the impact on the taxes due in that year only if it results in an increase in the taxes due by the partner, not a decrease. The NYSBA says that this can lead to significant permanent double taxation.

NYSBA's Withholding Tax Approach

The NYSBA believes that Code Sec. 6225 should be treated as a withholding tax mechanism, similar to the regime that currently exists under Code Sec. 1446 with respect to effectively connected taxable income of a partnership that is allocable to foreign partners. Under this approach, says the NYSBA, the payment by the partnership would ensure that the IRS collected an initial amount that approximates the total tax due. After the IRS has collected this initial amount, each partner would then properly take into account its share of the audit adjustments along with a credit for the corresponding amount of initial taxes paid by the partnership and "settle up" with the IRS by paying any additional taxes due or claiming a refund of any amount overpaid.

This approach, says the NYSBA, resolves a problem the association sees with a possible reading of Code Sec. 6225(a) under which Code Sec. 6225(a) is a final payment by the partnership, and no basis adjustments should be made. The result would be that, when Code Sec. 6225(a) applies, the final partnership adjustment (FPA) items are taxed twice.

Instead, the NYSBA advocates interpreting the Code Sec. 6225(a) payment as a collection mechanism only. That is, although the partnership pays the tax, it is essentially acting as an agent for the partners with respect to the tax they owe as a result of the FPA. Under this approach, the reviewed year partners take into account the FPA adjustments and receive a credit for the imputed underpayment paid by the partnership.

STUDY QUESTION

6. Which of the following is **not** to be considered an advisable method under the BBA to compute and meet the liabilities of a final partnership adjustment (FPA)?

    a. Payment of the full imputed underpayment

    b. Use of the Code Sec. 6225 payment mechanism

    c. Having partners amend their own tax returns for the review year to include the payment

    d. Electing to push out the adjustment to reviewed year partners under Code Sec. 6226

¶ 712 CONCLUSION

The new partnership audit regime came as a response to the growing complexity of partnership structures, frequently involving multiple tiers of partnerships. With this increasing complexity as well as the use of partnerships in general, the old TEFRA rules have become difficult for the IRS to apply, resulting in a very low audit rate for partnerships. The new partnership audit rules, however, were inserted into the BBA before committee hearings were complete and before the legislative language was finalized. As the report of the New York State Bar Association suggests, the rush to passage will likely need to be followed by implementing regulations that address a number of crucial issues. Meanwhile, existing partnerships and those being formed need to consider how the new partnership audit liabilities and election rules should be reflected in their current partnership agreements.

CPE NOTE: When you have completed your study and review of chapters 5-7, which comprise Module 2, you may wish to take the Final Exam for this Module. Go to **CCHGroup.com/PrintCPE** to take this Final Exam online.

MODULE 3: NEW CHALLENGES FACING INDIVIDUALS AND TAX-EXEMPT ENTITIES— Chapter 8: Identity Theft: Reaction and Strategies

¶ 801 WELCOME

Identity theft is a particular kind of fraudulent misrepresentation, involving the unauthorized use of another's personal identification information that is most often accompanied by larceny. Until recently, the judicial focus was on the fraud committed and was unaffected by whether or not a person's identification information had been used in the fraud. It was not until the end of the 20th century that federal and state governments enacted laws to levy separate and additional penalties for fraud committed using stolen identity information. In many instances, the commission of fraud is no longer required, because states have criminalized the unauthorized possession, purchase, sale, or distribution of personally identifiable information (PII).

Tax identify theft affects return preparers as well as their individual and business clients. The problem has become epidemic in recent years to the point that the IRS issued Publication 4557, *Safeguarding Taxpayer Data,* that preparers can use to create a client data security plan, and a data theft plan to enact if the practitioners experience a data loss. The IRS has noted: "Tax preparers play a critical role in assisting clients, both individuals and businesses, who are victims of tax-related identity theft." This chapter examines how practitioners can adopt best practices to protect clients' tax information and to advise clients on preventing tax identity theft.

¶ 802 LEARNING OBJECTIVES

Upon completion of this chapter, you will be able to:

- Recognize major federal legislation addressing identity theft;
- Identify techniques individuals and businesses can use to minimize threats to their identities; and
- Identify steps to address identity theft once it is discovered.

¶ 803 INTRODUCTION

The volume and magnitude of identity theft incidents have grown to an alarming extent. According to the Bureau of Justice Statistics, more than 17.6 million Americans—about 7 percent of U.S. residents age 16 or older—were victims of identity theft in 2014, a crime that cost them roughly $15.4 billion. Tax-related identity theft crimes have also risen dramatically. The Treasury Inspector General for Tax Administration (TIGTA) reports that 2,416,773 taxpayers were affected by identity theft in 2013, nearly double the number of victims in 2012 (1,219,208), nearly quadruple the number in 2011 (641,052), and nearly 10 times the number in 2010 (270,518). Final statistics for 2014 and 2015 are yet to be tallied, but preliminary data reveals a continuation of the trend, with some leveling off as the IRS and other government agencies, as well as financial institutions, hurry to put safeguards into place. Tax identity theft most commonly occurs when an individual uses another taxpayer's Social Security number (SSN) to commit "refund-related" identity theft by filing a false tax return and obtaining a fraudulent refund or "employment-related" identity theft by obtaining a job and leaving the unpaid income tax bill incurred from the job on the victim's account.

¶ 804 ADDRESSING THE PROBLEM OF IDENTITY THEFT

Federal Identity Theft Statutes

In the fall of 1998, Congress passed the *Identity Theft and Assumption Deterrence Act* (ITADA), which criminalized identity theft and established penalties of up to 15 years imprisonment and a $250,000 fine. For federal criminal purposes, the statute defines the act of *identity theft* as:

> To knowingly transfer or use, without lawful authority, a means of identification of another person with the intent to commit, or to aid or abet, any unlawful activity that constitutes a violation of federal law, or that constitutes a felony under any applicable state or local law.

The unlawful activity attendant to the unauthorized misuse of another's identification information often includes violations of federal antifraud laws. The ITADA specifically criminalized the following acts of identity theft:

- Producing false identification;
- Transferring identification that has been stolen or produced unlawfully;
- Possessing five or more pieces of false identification;
- Possessing five are more pieces of false identification with the intent to give them to someone else;
- Assessing a false identification document with the intent to defraud the United States;
- Possessing an identification document that was known to be stolen;
- Processing an identification document that looks official but was not provided from an authorized source; or
- Manufacturing, owning, or transferring a machine or device that can be used to produce false identification.

ITADA designated the Federal Trade Commission (FTC) to coordinate efforts by law enforcement agencies across the nation to track down and prosecute identity thieves. Currently, the FTC's Consumer Sentinel Network provides more than 70 federal agencies and offices, as well as nearly 650 state and local agencies with access to millions of consumer complaints regarding identity theft and other instances of fraud.

In 2003, Congress passed the *Fair and Accurate Credit Transactions Act* (FACTA). FACTA amended 15 U.S. Code § 1681a to define the term *identity theft* as "a fraud committed or attempted using the identifying information of another person without authority."

In addition, FACTA amended the *Fair Credit Reporting Act* (FCRA) to provide expanded protection for victims of identity theft. The FCRA, as amended by FACTA, requires credit reporting agencies and creditors to help victims recover from identity theft by allowing consumers to:

- Place fraud alerts on their credit files if they are or believe they may become victims of identity theft;
- Dispute inaccurate information; and
- Receive a free credit report once per year from each of the three credit reporting agencies—Equifax, Experian, and TransUnion. Additionally, the law requires credit reporting agencies and creditors to investigate identity theft claims and correct relevant information.

FACTA also requires financial institutions (and some creditors) to establish programs designed to address identity theft (the "Red Flag Rule"). *Red flags* are suspicious patterns or practices, or specific activities that indicate the possibility of identity theft. To comply with the Red Flag Rule, an identity theft prevention program must:

- Include reasonable policies and procedures to identify the red flags of identity theft that may occur in day-to-day operations;

- Be designed to detect the red flags identified;

- Spell out appropriate actions for resolving detected red flags; and

- Detail how to keep the program current to reflect new threats.

In 2004, the *Identity Theft Penalty Enhancement Act* was signed by President George Bush. This act established enhanced penalties for "aggravated" identity theft, which consists of using another's identity to commit felony crimes, including immigration violations, theft of another's Social Security benefits, and acts of domestic terrorism.

In 2008, the *Identity Theft Enforcement and Restitution Act* became law. This act amended federal law regarding orders of restitution to clarify that the amount of restitution in an identity theft case may include the value of the victim's time that was spent remediating the actual or intended harm of the identity theft. In addition, this act removed the prior jurisdictional restriction regarding computer intrusion crimes that had permitted the federal district courts to hear only those cases where state lines had been crossed in the commission of the crime.

In April 2016 the Senate referred the Tax Return Identity Theft Protection Act of 2016 (S. 2766) to a congressional committee. The bill would further strengthen penalties for tax return identity thieves, enhance sentences for crimes against vulnerable individuals, and clarify the "state of mind" proof requirement in identity theft prosecutions.

State Identity Theft Statutes

Today, every state plus the District of Columbia has a statute that criminalizes identity theft, although there is some variation among the approaches. By example, 29 states address restitution for victims of identity theft crimes, and 5 states have provisions that provide for the forfeiture of any property received or used in connection with an identity theft crime. Many states have heightened penalties if the victim is a senior citizen or disabled person, which may be increased if the identity thief served as the victim's caretaker. New Jersey even imposes a fine of up to $5,000 against any creditor that denies or attempts to reduce credit to a victim of identity theft.

Tax Preparer Penalties for Client Information Disclosure

In addition to penalties for identity theft, Code Secs. 6713 and 7216 provide for monetary and criminal penalties on unauthorized disclosures or use of taxpayer information by a person engaged in the business of preparing or providing services in connection with tax return preparation.

Under Code Sec. 7216, a convicted preparer may be fined $1,000 and be imprisoned for one year for any knowing or reckless disclosure or use of tax return data. The Code Sec. 6713 civil penalty of $250 per person applies for disclosure or use of return data that is not knowing or reckless. To avoid liability, preparers must obtain the taxpayer's written consent before allowing a disclosure.

EXAMPLE: Local City Bank is a tax return preparer and e-file provider under Code Sec. 7216. Its employee, Liam O'Donnell, solicits tax return information from Emily Dermott to prepare her return, but Meghan Smith uses the information to prepare the return. Meghan's secretary, Brenda Nelson, types Emily's tax information into the return preparation software, and an administrative assistant, Ron Black, uses the bank's computer to e-file the return. All of the employees—Liam, Meghan, Brenda, and Ron—are considered tax return preparers for purposes of Code Sec. 7216.

States similarly impose civil and/or criminal penalties against certified public accountants (CPAs) and other tax preparers who fail to properly protect their clients' personal information.

Public Outreach Campaign to Educate Taxpayers on Identity Theft

On November 19, 2015, IRS Commissioner John Koskinen announced a new public outreach campaign to fight identity theft. The "Taxes. Security. Together." campaign is designed to raise public awareness that even routine actions on the Internet and personal devices can affect the safety of the public's personal and financial data. The commissioner stressed that the IRS and tax industry efforts alone, despite being substantial, were not enough to protect taxpayers from the growing crime of identity theft. He appealed to members of the general public to actively protect their personal and financial data from identity thieves. To aid the general public, the IRS began to release weekly tax tips on protecting data. The IRS also updated or created several publications for taxpayers and tax professionals and posted informational videos on YouTube. Information is also shared online across IRS.gov, state websites, and platforms used by the tax software industry and many others in the private-sector tax community. The commissioner highlighted Publication 4524, "Taxes. Security. Together." in particular. The publication lists the basic steps an individual should take to maintain security on electronic devices and identify phishing and malware schemes. Follow-up continued by the IRS during the 2016 filing season and beyond as press releases and similar warnings advised taxpayers and tax practitioners to protect their data while the IRS becomes more "tech savvy" in identifying and preventing ID theft related to tax information.

¶ 805 IRS 2016 SECURITY SUMMIT AND 2017 INITIATIVES TO COMBAT IDENTITY THEFT

The IRS held its annual Security Summit on June 28, 2016, in Washington, D.C., to review the IRS's 2016 successes and finalize its 2017 initiatives. The Security Summit, which is composed of representatives from the IRS, state agencies and the private-sector tax industry, first met in 2015 seeking to counter increasingly sophisticated criminals that were amassing massive amounts of stolen data and using more elaborate schemes in an effort to defeat efforts to identify fraudulent returns.

IRS Commissioner John Koskinen noted the summit's accomplishments had a real and substantial impact on curbing stolen identity refund fraud. "This unique collaboration between the private sector, the states, and the IRS has provided new defenses and protections for taxpayers and the tax system," he said. "We have made significant progress in this effort over the last year, but much more work remains. The summit group will expand our efforts in the coming year, and we will work hard to take new steps to combat the rapidly evolving identity theft and refund fraud schemes."

For 2017, the summit's priorities remain focused on enhanced authentication procedures, improved information sharing, heightened cybersecurity, and greater public education and outreach. 2017 initiatives include:

- Expanding a W-2 Verification Code test to cover approximately 50 million forms. Selected forms contain a 16-digit code that taxpayers and tax preparers enter when prompted by software. The code helps validate not only the taxpayer's identity but also the information on the form. This pilot is among the most visible Security Summit action for 2017.

- Identifying additional data elements from tax returns that will help improve authentication of the taxpayer and identify possible identity theft scams and sharing data elements from corporate tax returns.

- Launching the Identity Theft Tax Refund Fraud Information Sharing & Analysis Center (IDTTRF-ISAC). This will serve as the early warning system for partners who collect and analyze tax-related identity theft schemes.

- Expanding the Security Summit's "Taxes. Security. Together." awareness campaign to tax return preparers to ensure they have the information they need to protect themselves from cyberattacks and to safeguard taxpayer data.

- Creating a process for financial institutions to identify questionable state tax refunds and return them to states for validation. Twenty-three states have signed on so far.

Finally, to ensure that the Summit's work will be ongoing, effective July 1, the Summit has been working under the auspices of the Electronic Tax Administration Advisory Council (ETAAC.) The ETAAC charter was expanded to include the prevention of identity theft to allow the change.

STUDY QUESTION

1. Under the *Identity Theft Penalty Enhancement Act,* all of the following are considered "aggravated" identity theft *except:*

    a. Acts of domestic terrorism

    b. Production of false identification

    c. Theft of an individual's Social Security benefits

    d. Use of an individual's identity to violate immigration rules

¶ 806 ENFORCEMENT DEVELOPMENTS

Stolen Identity Refund Fraud

The IRS has fought aggressively against refund fraud, which includes identity theft. Statistics show, for example, that in calendar year 2015, through November, the IRS rejected or suspended the processing of 4.8 million suspicious returns. So far, the IRS stopped 1.4 million confirmed identity theft returns, totaling $8 billion. Additionally, through November it stopped $2.9 billion worth of refunds in other types of fraud. That's a total of $10.9 billion in confirmed fraudulent refunds protected.

The IRS estimated that during each filing season of 2013 and 2014, for example, more than 5 million tax returns were filed using stolen identities, claiming approximately $30 billion in refunds. The IRS was able to stop or recover more than $24 billion of that total, or approximately 81 percent of the fraudulent claims. The collaboration between the IRS, the Department of Justice, Tax Division (DOJ-Tax) and United States Attorney's Offices have contributed to this success. Statistics for the 2015 and 2016 filing seasons reflect a trend that may have begun to reverse itself with respect to the type of refund fraud that has been evident, but not necessarily with respect to other identity theft fraud contributing to tax refund fraud overall.

DOJ-Tax Directive 144 specifically focuses on identity theft in the context of fraudulent tax refunds and provides for a streamlined investigation and prosecution process. Directive 144 also addresses stolen identity refund fraud (SIRF), in which a perpetrator typically electronically files a false return using the taxpayer's name early in the tax filing season so that the IRS receives the false SIRF return before the actual taxpayer has filed a return. The SIRF perpetrator arranges to have the refund electronically transferred to a debit card or delivered to an address where the refund is stolen out of the mail.

DOJ-Tax established an advisory board of experienced prosecutors to develop and implement uniform national policies for fighting SIRF crimes. By example, the division works closely with the IRS to quickly share information obtained from SIRF investigations and prosecutions, which the IRS can use to make it more difficult for the schemes to be successful by blocking the false refund claims.

> **COMMENT:** Criminals steal PII from taxpayers to generate fraudulent tax returns early in tax season. The Federal Bureau of Investigation (FBI) reports that many SIRF victims and their tax practitioners do not realize that criminals have targeted them until their legitimate tax returns are filed and refunds rejected by the IRS.

> **CAUTION:** Identity thieves may hamper efforts to file the final returns of recently deceased taxpayers as well by filing false individual or estate tax returns to steal refunds, or even assume the deceaseds' identity, a crime called *ghosting*. Those responsible for the deceased's finances should notify the credit reporting agencies, banks, brokerage houses, insurance companies, credit card account issuers, the Social Security Administration (SSA), and motor vehicle offices, by sending them copies of the death certificate. Financial and military records should be secured.

Validation Efforts

The IRS has partnered since mid-2015 with representatives of tax preparation and software firms, payroll and tax financial product processors, and state tax administrators on a collaborative effort to combat identity theft and refund fraud. The new measures include steps to validate taxpayer and tax return information at the time of filing. These steps include:

- Reviewing the transmission of the tax return, including the improper and or repetitive use of internet protocol numbers, the internet "address" from which the return is originating;
- Reviewing computer device identification data tied to the return's origin;
- Reviewing the time it takes to complete a tax return, so computer mechanized fraud can be detected; and
- Capturing metadata in the computer transaction that will allow review for identity theft fraud.

Starting in July 2016, the IRS, state tax agencies, and the tax preparation community continued collaborative efforts in warning tax preparers of the increasing menace of cybercriminals. They did so specifically by launching the "Protect Your Clients; Protect Yourself" campaign to raise awareness among tax professionals on their responsibilities and the common sense steps they could take to protect their clients from identity theft and to protect their businesses (IR-2016-96).

Recognizing the risk to tax preparers, this new effort was an expansion of the Security Summit's 2015 "Taxes. Security. Together." campaign aimed at increasing public awareness for using security software, creating stronger passwords and avoiding phishing emails. "The tax community handles large volumes of sensitive personal and financial information. We need every tax professional to stay on top of security to protect taxpayers as well as their businesses," said IRS Commissioner John Koskinen.

Because of the sensitive client data held by tax professionals, cybercriminals increasingly are targeting the tax preparation community, using a variety of tactics ranging from remote computer takeovers to phishing scams. Putting safeguards to protect taxpayer data would help prevent fraud and identity theft, and enhance customer confidence and trust. The IRS has also released a fact sheet that urges preparers to follow the security recommendations found in Publication 4557, "Safeguarding Taxpayer Data."

Congress Weighs In

Despite IRS efforts to contain ID theft, some in Congress want more protections. For example, Senate Finance Committee Chairman Orrin G. Hatch (R-Utah), on July 12, 2016, introduced a bill intended to protect taxpayers, the Stolen Identity Refund Fraud Prevention Bill (Sen. 3157). The bill would implement guidelines for the IRS in handling stolen identity refund fraud cases and would increase the criminal penalty for misappropriating taxpayer identity in connection with tax fraud. The bill also requires a biannual report from the IRS on the current status of taxpayer stolen identity refund fraud, including details as to detection, prevention, and enforcement activities undertaken by the IRS. "Protecting taxpayers from bad actors looking to use their identities for fraudulent purposes and enhancing overall taxpayer protections has been a priority of the committee," Hatch said in a statement. "By identifying problems plaguing taxpayers and advancing smart legislation to address those issues head on, the American people are seeing real, bipartisan results from this Congress," he added.

Income Tax Relief

The IRS issued Announcement 2015-22, which clarified that individuals who receive identity protection services because their personal information may have been compromised in a data breach need not include in gross income the value of the identity protection services provided by an organization that experienced the data breach. In Announcement 2016-2, the IRS extended this exclusion benefit to include identity protection services provided to employees or other individuals before a data breach occurs. The new guidance, however, did not apply to cash received in lieu of identity protection services, nor to proceeds received under an identity theft insurance policy; the treatment of insurance recoveries is governed by existing law.

Recent Prosecutions

On March 21, 2016, the IRS released the Top 10 Identity Theft Prosecutions for Fiscal Year 2015. These prosecutions are part of the wide-ranging strategy to combat refund fraud and assist taxpayers through detection, prevention and resolving identity theft cases in a timely manner. In fiscal year 2015, the IRS initiated 776 identity theft investigations, which resulted in 774 sentencings through Criminal Investigation enforcement efforts. The courts continue to impose significant jail time with the average months to serve in FY 2015 at 38 months—the longest sentencing being more than 27 years. The following are several of the top identity theft case headlines issued over the course of the last 18 months by the Justice Department:

- Tampa tax fraudster and wife sentenced in massive identity theft tax fraud scheme (sentenced to 324 months and 138 months in prison, respectively); five years of supervised release (3 years for the wife); and $1,820,759 forfeited in a money judgment);
- Nine defendants sentenced in $24 million stolen identity tax refund fraud ring (ringleader sentenced to 180 months in prison, ordered to forfeit $5,811,406);
- Florida man sentenced for stolen ID theft scheme, obstruction of justice. Ringleader and conspirators sentenced in large-scale stolen identity refund fraud scheme (ringleader sentenced to 84 months in prison, three years of supervised release, and ordered to pay $5,643,695; and
- Four Georgia residents sentenced for filing more than 1,100 fraudulent tax returns (ringleader sentenced to 84 months in prison and ordered to pay $1,107,802).

STUDY QUESTION

2. The Department of Justice-Tax Directive 144 focuses on which type of identity theft?
   - **a.** Social Security number theft
   - **b.** Employment-related identity theft
   - **c.** Stolen identity refund fraud
   - **d.** Ghosting

¶ 807 BEST PRACTICES FOR PREVENTING IDENTITY THEFT

There are simple and worthwhile precautions that individuals can take to minimize the vulnerability of personally identifiable information (PII). And should identity theft prove inevitable, even despite best practices, following tips such as reviewing monthly bank statements, obtaining a credit report at least once a year, etc., will allow an individual to notice fraudulent activity when it begins, which is key to a swift response that will contain the extent of the fraud and minimize the damage. Unfortunately, many individuals fall victim to tax refund fraud as a direct result of having their identity stolen, especially Social Security information.

Figure 1 is a checklist the practitioner can provide to clients to aid in protecting their tax and personally identifiable data records.

Figure 1. Some Best Practices for Protecting Personally Identifiable Information

How to Protect Important Information

❑ Secure personal information in the home and workplace. Shred documents that contain personally identifiable information, such as bank and credit card statements.

❑ Protect personal computers using firewalls, antivirus software, and updated security patches (as they are released). Antivirus software can detect spyware and malware that are loaded (or attempting to be loaded) onto a computer in order to compromise security and access information. For best practices regarding Internet fraud prevention, see **www.onguardonline.gov.**

❑ Secure wireless networks.

❑ Create strong passwords and frequently change them. A 2015 Identity Theft survey released by MasterCard found that 46 percent of respondents rarely or never change their passwords for online financial accounts, and 44 percent of respondents use the same password across multiple online platforms.

❑ According to guidance from Google, a strong password is:

○ Unique to each account;
○ Eight characters at a minimum (the longer the password is, the harder it is to guess);
○ A mix of capital and lowercase letters, numbers, and symbols, none of which repeat in any pattern;
○ Not consisting of a word or phrase; and
○ Not based on publicly available personal information (e.g., phone number).

❑ Double-check a website's URL before entering any personal information. For example, confirm that a page that appears to be a government website is followed by .gov. Do not be misled by official-looking logos.

❑ Do not close a browser before logging out of a website.

❑ Encrypt and password-protect sensitive documents.

❑ Check for a "lock" icon on the status bar of the Internet browser. This indicator means information should be safe when it is transmitted.

❑ Set online account settings that send an e-mail or text message if someone attempts to log on to an account from an unrecognized computer or change a password.

❑ Put passwords on all credit card and bank accounts. This provides an additional level of security before an individual can engage in a transaction. When the account holder visits a branch in person, it is advised to write the password down and provide it to the teller, when requested, so that it cannot be overheard.

❑ Destroy expired cards. Some newer credit cards contain metal and cannot be shredded—use the return envelope provided with a replacement card to mail the expired card to the issuer for destruction.

❑ Consider identity theft detection services. Commonly used services include Lifelock, IdentityForce, Identity Guard, and TrustedID.

❑ Do not store passwords on shared computers.

❑ Set up password recovery options and keep them up-to-date. If possible, choose to add a phone number to an account profile in order to receive a code to reset the password via text message.

❑ Look for "https:" (Hypertext Transfer Protocol Secure) at the beginning of any web address used to conduct financial transactions. An https connection, as opposed to just http, verifies the identity of a website or web service for a connecting client, and encrypts nearly all information sent between the website or service and the user.

❑ Only disseminate personally identifiable information, such as a Social Security number when necessary. Ordinarily, businesses and service providers will allow customers to withhold their SSN out of confidentiality concerns.

❑ Check credit reports from the three major credit reporting agencies (Equifax, Experian, and TransUnion) at least every 12 months. A free annual credit report from each agency is available from the jointly operated site AnnualCreditReport.com. A paper copy request form is also available from: Annual Credit Report Request Service, P.O. Box 105, 281 Atlanta, GA 30348-5281. A fourth credit reporting agency, Innovis, also offers consumers one free copy of the Innovis Credit Report every 12 months,

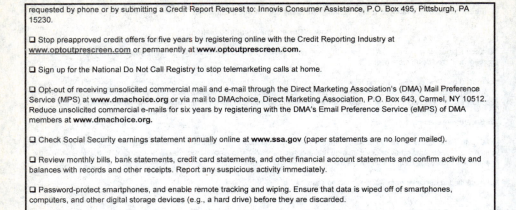

requested by phone or by submitting a Credit Report Request to: Innovis Consumer Assistance, P.O. Box 495, Pittsburgh, PA 15230.

❑ Stop preapproved credit offers for five years by registering online with the Credit Reporting Industry at www.optoutprescreen.com or permanently at **www.optoutprescreen.com.**

❑ Sign up for the National Do Not Call Registry to stop telemarketing calls at home.

❑ Opt-out of receiving unsolicited commercial mail and e-mail through the Direct Marketing Association's (DMA) Mail Preference Service (MPS) at **www.dmachoice.org** or via mail to DMAchoice, Direct Marketing Association, P.O. Box 643, Carmel, NY 10512. Reduce unsolicited commercial e-mails for six years by registering with the DMA's Email Preference Service (eMPS) of DMA members at **www.dmachoice.org.**

❑ Check Social Security earnings statement annually online at **www.ssa.gov** (paper statements are no longer mailed).

❑ Review monthly bills, bank statements, credit card statements, and other financial account statements and confirm activity and balances with records and other receipts. Report any suspicious activity immediately.

❑ Password-protect smartphones, and enable remote tracking and wiping. Ensure that data is wiped off of smartphones, computers, and other digital storage devices (e.g., a hard drive) before they are discarded.

❑ Stay on the lookout for potential scams. There has been an explosion in the number of phishing and pretexting enterprises attempting to trick individuals into revealing personally identifiable information.

The FTC explains *phishing* as the attempt on the internet (using e-mail, texting, or pop-up messages) to impersonate a business to trick the individual to provide personal information. The commission's Consumer Information page (**https://www.consumer.ftc.gov/articles/0003—phishing**) provides examples of phishing messages and also lists the most recent scams by date and topic.

A healthy dose of suspicion can go a long way in helping individuals avoid falling prey to these scams. For instance, often times a scammer will send a message that seems urgent and threatens consequences for missing some fast-approaching deadline. Another red flag is an e-mail that contains grammatical /spelling errors. Taxpayers should not be fooled merely because an e-mail has an official-looking logo.

Preventing Tax Identity Theft

Tax identity theft poses special concerns for business as well as individual taxpayers. A 2013 TIGTA report entitled "Stolen and Falsely Obtained Employer Identification Numbers Are Used to Report False Income and Withholding" (2013-40-120) explained the scope of the problem: millions of tax returns were rejected because invalid EINs were used to report income and withholding. Stolen EINs hampered the efforts of the IRS to verify income and withholding amounts from W-2 forms submitted by employers and employees. Criminals can use business EINs to create fake salaries reported to state agencies as well as the IRS to get refunds to nonexistent workers. As a result, unsuspecting companies receive tax deficiency notifications for payroll taxes.

A 2015 TIGTA report entitled "Processes Are Being Established to Detect Business Identity Theft; However, Additional Actions Can Help Improve Detection" (2015-40-082) stressed that continued efforts are needed to develop and implement systemic processes to detect and prevent business identity theft. TIGTA's analysis of business returns filed during the 2014 processing year identified that 233 tax returns were filed using a known suspicious EIN. Of these, 97 claimed refunds totaling over $2.5 million. TIGTA also determined that processing filters could be developed to identify returns containing certain characteristics that could indicate potential identity theft cases. Thus, business returns containing these characteristics could be identified before any refunds were issued. TIGTA also found that state information sharing agreements do not address business identity theft. Finally, TIGTA also identified that actions are needed to better promote awareness of business identity theft. TIGTA recommended that the IRS:

- Establish procedures to identify business returns containing certain characteristics that could indicate potential identity theft cases;

- Evaluate the potential for expanding information sharing agreements to include the sharing of suspicious or potentially fraudulent business tax return filings; and

- Continue to develop and offer additional outreach materials that directly inform businesses about business identity theft. The IRS agreed with the recommendations.

Businesses can mitigate the risks of tax identity theft by:

- Updating business filings upon any change in contact information as well as annually verifying the accuracy of their Secretary of State information;

- Regularly monitoring their business account activity and contact information with the IRS;

- Conducting an identity theft action plan assessment and developing a communication strategy to use in case of stolen tax and financial information; and

- Following IRS and FTC guidance for protecting tax and financial information of customers and clients.

Practitioners can complement business clients' efforts by routinely truncating SSNs in regular correspondence, keeping the practice's firewalls and antivirus software current, checking the AICPA's website (**aicpa.org/tax**) for tax identity theft tools members can use, and remaining current about steps a practice can take to respond to tax identity theft of their clients' information.

Figure 2. Client Prevention of Tax Identity Theft

Tips for Preventing Tax Identity Theft

❏ File income tax returns early.

❏ Join the IRS's Identity Protection PIN (IP PIN) trial program (currently open only to residents of Florida, Georgia, and the District of Columbia).

❏ No one from the IRS will call a taxpayer without first sending a letter.

❏ No one from the IRS will contact a taxpayer by e-mail or social media. Any e-mail scam from an individual claiming to be from the IRS should be forwarded to **phishing@irs.gov.**

❏ No one from the IRS will contact a taxpayer to request personal or financial information.

❏ No one who is actually from the IRS will threaten a taxpayer with arrest or deportation for failing to pay immediately.

An *identity protection personal identification number* (IP PIN) is a six-digit number assigned to help prevent the misuse of SSN information on fraudulent federal income tax returns. Once provided, an IP PIN must be used to confirm a taxpayer's identity on federal tax returns. In order to obtain an IP PIN, a taxpayer must verify his or her identity online, at **https://www.irs.gov/Individuals/Get-An-Identity-Protection-PIN**. If the taxpayer meets the eligibility requirements, an IP PIN is generated online. Once a taxpayer elects to participate in the IP PIN program, there is no ability to subsequently "opt-out" of the program. An updated IP PIN is provided to the taxpayer via postal mail each December.

The IRS on July 19, 2016, announced that it had restored access to its online IP PIN system. The restoration came with claims that it has returned with stronger authentication requirements for taxpayers. The IP PIN retrieval tool had been pulled offline in March 2016 after finding that people engaged in tax refund fraud had obtained taxpayer

IP PINs. At the time, the IRS stated that, through the end of February 2016, it had stopped 800 fraudulent returns that used IP PINs.

The return of the "Get an IP PIN" tool is said to employ the use of a multifactor authentication process that will help prevent automated attacks. The system requires that taxpayers go through a more rigorous process to set up use of the tool through the IRS's Secure Access portal, the same process used for the relaunched Get Transcript Online tool, which debuted on June 7, 2016.

The Secure Access process requires that taxpayers have immediate access to an email address, account information from a credit card or other loan types and a text-enabled mobile phone. Taxpayers are to review the online IRS Fact Sheet for Get Transcript Online (FS-2016-20), regarding the information the Secure Access e-authentication process requires, as well as the steps outlined in how to register under the new authentication process.

The IRS reports that identity thieves have been contacting taxpayers and requesting financial information in order to send refunds. These calls and other IRS impersonation schemes should be reported to the TIGTA by phone or online at **https:// www.treasury.gov/tigta/contact_report_scam.shtml**. Also, any scams should be reported to the National Fraud Information Center by phone or at **www.fraud.org** by completing the form available online at: **https://secure.nclforms.org/nficweb/ nfic.htm**.

STUDY QUESTION

3. All of the following are clues that a scammer is soliciting PII *except:*
   a. A source that uses the https protocol
   b. A message that threatens consequences for missing a deadline
   c. An e-mail that contains grammatical or spelling errors
   d. An organization that previously indicated it would not request PII via e-mail or text message.

Preventing Other Types of Identity Theft

Figure 3 provides tips practitioners can provide to clients for preventing identity theft of all kinds, as well as other information-related scams.

Figure 3. Prevention of General Identity Theft

Tips for Preventing Identity Theft

❑ Do not post personal information on the internet.

❑ Do not carry documents with PII (i.e., a Social Security card, passport, or list with account passwords) unless it is necessary.

❑ For outgoing mail, use a U.S. Post Office, use a collection box, or give the letter directly to a letter carrier; do not leave outgoing mail in an unsecured mailbox or sticking out of a mailbox.

❑ For incoming mail, use a locking mailbox, secure mail slot, or a P.O. box for delivery.

❑ Arrange to have mail held at the post office while away. Requests to have mail held can be made online at: **https://holdmail.usps.com/holdmail**.

❑ Never sign blank checks or leave an empty space on a check where an additional amount can be added.

❑ Have new checks delivered to a bank or post office box, as opposed to a residential address.

❑ Limit vulnerability by setting up a separate checking account to fund online brokerage (e.g., E-Trade) and payment accounts (e.g., PayPal) instead of linking them to a primary bank account.

❑ Make sure no one is looking over your shoulder at ATMs ("shoulder surfers").

❑ Obtain and use the reader-blocking products such as the Washington State Identity Theft Alliance's Card Protection Wallet Sleeve, which is printable online as **http://identitytheftnetwork.org/Toolkit/OUTREACH/TemplateWalletCard.pdf**.

❑ Do not use a cell phone or e-mail to provide personal information.

❑ Share knowledge regarding identity theft issues with others.

The National Identity Theft Victims Assistance Network (NITVAN) provides a toolkit for victim advocates, attorneys, law enforcement officers, and others involved in assisting victims online from **http://identitytheftnetwork.org/toolkit**.

¶ 808 IDENTITY THEFT INDICATORS AND RESPONSES

People are generally familiar with the multitude of signs of nontax related identity theft, including unfamiliar credit card charges, unexpected cards arriving, letters regarding unfamiliar purchases, overdrawn bank accounts, unauthorized loans, credit denials for no apparent reason, account statements not arriving as expected, and collection calls on behalf of businesses with whom the victim has never had prior contact.

However, individuals may be less familiar with the signs of tax identity theft.

Top Indicators of Tax-Related Identity Theft

Many private for-profit organizations and attorney specialists exist to provide "taxpayer advocate services," such as case reviewer and settlement reviews and consultations. However, the IRS includes the independent office of the Taxpayer Advocate Service (TAS) to counsel taxpayers on their rights and remedies generally. The TAS continues to monitor the degree of success of IRS tax identity theft prevention programs. The service also advises taxpayers on how to conduct a refund trace for stolen refunds.

The TAS states that the most common indicators that an individual is a victim of tax-related identity theft are:

- A taxpayer attempts to file a return electronically, but the IRS rejects the return stating that another return with the taxpayer's SSN has already been filed;

- A taxpayer receives an IRS notice indicating that wages were received from an establishment at which the taxpayer never worked;

- A taxpayer receives a letter from the IRS indicating that

- A return has already been filed, when the taxpayer has not yet filed a return, or

- Multiple returns have been filed; and

- A taxpayer receives a balance due notice, refund offset notice, or collection actions taken against the taxpayer regarding a year for which no return was filed nor refund received.

STUDY QUESTION

4. The Taxpayer Advocate Service:

    a. Issues automatic refunds upon proof that a taxpayer is a victim of tax identity fraud

    b. Is the IRS division that rejects returns from victims of tax identity theft

    c. Provides services independently to help taxpayers resolve tax and identity theft issues

    d. Is an audit appeals office

Steps to Take When Identity Theft Is Suspected

Once an individual learns that his or her PII has been compromised, there are certain steps that one can immediately take in order to prevent, or at least contain, fraudulent misuse.

File a report with the FTC. The FTC maintains an Identity Theft Data Clearinghouse, the nation's repository for identity theft complaints. The FTC systems house over a million ID theft complaints, providing information and coordinating resources among more than 2,000 law enforcement agencies to facilitate the investigations and prosecution of identity theft.

An individual need not wait until fraudulent activity has occurred—a complaint may be filed with the FTC as soon as there has been:

- An attempted identity theft: an individual notices someone trying to use his or her personal information;

- A data breach: an individual's PII was exposed in a company's data breach; or

- A lost wallet or purse.

File a report with the local police department. The victim should go to the local police office with:

- A copy of the FTC Form 14039, *Identity Theft Affidavit*

- A government-issued ID with a photo

- Proof of address (mortgage statement, rental agreement, or utilities bill)

- Any other proof of the theft (bills, IRS notices, etc.)

- FTC's Memo to Law Enforcement, available online at **http://www.consumer.ftc.gov/articles/pdf-0088-ftc-memo-law-enforcement.pdf**. Most police departments are instructed (or required, depending on state law) to take a report when an individual reasonably believes that he or she is a victim of identity theft even though jurisdiction for prosecution may lie elsewhere.

The victim should retain a copy of the police report (or at least the report/case number).

¶808

File Form 14039, *Identity Theft Affidavit,* **with the IRS.** Although IRS Form 14039 is titled *Identity Theft Affidavit,* it may be filed and submitted as soon as an individual has experienced an event involving personally identifiable information that "may at some future time affect" the individual's federal tax records. An individual may submit Form 14039 if:

- The taxpayer is the victim of nonfederal tax related identity theft (e.g., the misuse of PII to obtain credit); or
- No identity theft has yet occurred, but the individual has experienced an event that may result in identity theft (i.e., stolen purse, lost wallet, home robbery).

The form can be submitted by mail to: Internal Revenue Service, P.O. Box 9039, Andover, MA 01810-0939, or by fax. By filing the form, a taxpayer may be selected to receive an IP PIN.

Contact the IRS Identity Protection Specialized Unit. Even before tax records are affected by identity theft, an individual who is at risk due to a lost or stolen purse or wallet, questionable credit card activity, or credit report, should contact the IRS Identity Protection Specialized Unit.

Immediately replace lost or stolen government identification (i.e., passport and driver's license). Contact the Department of Motor Vehicles if the fraud involved a driver's license. Contact the U.S. Passport Office if the fraud involved a passport. See **www.travel.state.gov/passport**.

Immediately replace or cancel lost or stolen credit, debit, and charge cards. Cardholders should keep records of the cards' numbers. The cards' issuers should be notified immediately. Cardholders should freeze or close the accounts at issue so that charges may only be approved with the individual's authorization.

Immediately change logins, passwords, and PINs for compromised accounts. Banks and credit unions should be notified of the theft as well in case thieves try to empty accounts.

Obtain a current credit report. Individuals may request a free credit report each year online at **annualcreditreport**.com. A credit report allows an individual to identify (and obtain contact information for) any businesses where fraudulent accounts have been opened or credit extended.

Notify the fraud department for cell phone services, utilities, or other businesses where accounts may have been compromised. An individual can get records from these sources regarding the identity theft. Section 609(e) of the FCRA requires businesses to provide identity theft victims (as well as designated law enforcement agencies/officers) with copies of all business records relating to any suspected fraudulent activity/transactions. The items that must be disclosed include relevant applications, contracts, receipts, and transaction documents. The FTC provides a sample letter for obtaining business records relating to identity theft, available online at: **https://www.identitytheft.gov/sample-letters/request-records-related-identity-theft.html**.

Challenge liability for any unauthorized transactions. The FTC provides sample dispute letters for both an existing account (available online at: **https://www.identitytheft.gov/sample-letters/identity-theft-dispute-charges-existing-account.html**) and a fraudulently opened new account (available online at **https://www.identitytheft.gov/sample-letters/identity-theft-dispute-new-account.html**).

Ask the business to send a letter confirming that:

- The fraudulent account does not belong to the victim;
- The victim is not liable for the account charges; and
- The charges have been removed from the victim's credit report.

Be aware of FCRA rights. FCRA § 605B7 requires that all businesses that provide information to credit reporting agencies must not submit or provide information that a consumer has identified resulted from identity theft. Further, FCRA § 623(a)(6) requires a business that has furnished inaccurate information to notify each of the credit reporting agencies and provide the correct information. Most importantly, FCRA § 615(f) provides that, when a furnisher of information is notified that a debt is the result of identity theft, the furnisher may not sell, transfer, or place the debt in collection. The FTC provides a sample letter that an individual may use to respond if contacted by a debt collector regarding a debt created by identity fraud, available online at **https://www.identitytheft.gov/sample-letters/identity-theft-debt-collector.html**.

Accept free credit monitoring. If a company or agency's data breach has compromised PII, individuals affected will ordinarily be offered, and should accept, free credit monitoring.

There is no federal or state law that requires a business that compromises customer PII to provide free credit monitoring (although some states, such as California, require those companies that choose to offer credit monitoring to provide it at no cost, for a period of at least 12 months). However, according to an Experian Cybersecurity Survey, only a third of consumers who received notification of compromised account information signed up for a period of free credit monitoring. Charles E. Giblin, Special Agent in Charge of Criminal Investigations and Internal Security for New Jersey's Department of the Treasury, advises victims that "in cases where a business or service provider offers credit protection because a breach of their proprietary system(s), victims should take immediate advantage of the service."

Contact the credit reporting agencies and have a fraud alert added to the credit report. A fraud alert is free and lasts for 90 days. It requires lenders and other creditors to take additional steps to verify an individual's identity prior to establishing any new accounts in the individual's name, or issuing an additional card or increasing the credit limit on an existing account. For Equifax, Experian, and TransUnion, a fraud alert may be placed with any one of the three credit reporting agencies, and that agency will notify the other two to place alerts. In addition, Innovis offers its own separate Fraud alert service, also for 90 days. Individuals should remember that Innovis does not share fraud alerts with the other three credit reporting agencies, so that a fraud alert with Innovis would be in addition, not instead of, a fraud alert with the three major credit reporting agencies.

Send a copy of the completed Identity Theft Report to the credit reporting agencies. As described later, this report combining the FTC *Identity Theft Affidavit* and a police report should be submitted to the agencies. Victims may request that each agency block any fraudulent transactions from appearing on a credit report. FCRA § 605B requires credit reporting agencies to honor consumer requests to remove fraudulent information from a credit report ("blocking") that resulted from an alleged identity theft, within four business days after receipt of a request. The request must include:

- Appropriate proof of the identity of the consumer;
- A copy of an identity theft report;
- The identification of such information by the consumer; and
- A statement by the consumer that the information is not information relating to any transaction by the consumer.

The FTC provides a sample letter online at: **https://www.identitytheft.gov/ sample-letters/identity-theft-credit-bureau.html**.

Consider using an extended fraud alert. An extended fraud alert can last as long as seven years. An extended fraud alert may be requested by submitting a request along with a copy of the victim's Identity Theft Report, and proof of both identity and current address.

Consider a security freeze. A security freeze prevents all third parties, such as credit lenders or other companies, from accessing an individual's credit report without his or her consent.

Dispute unauthorized credit card charges. The FTC provides a sample letter online, available at **https://www.identitytheft.gov/sample-letters/dispute-credit-card-charges.html**. However, the FTC guidance first recommends contacting the company via telephone, or by using the contact information below, in an effort to get unauthorized charges reversed. Identity theft victims are encouraged to contact their card providers as early as possible after noticing suspicious activity, both to reverse any unauthorized charges and to prevent any further misuse.

Dispute unauthorized ATM/debit card transactions. The FTC provides a sample letter available at **https://www.identitytheft.gov/sample-letters/dispute-debit-card-transactions.html**. However, as with disputed credit card transactions, the FTC guidance first recommends contacting the bank via telephone or online in an effort to get unauthorized debits reversed. Identity theft victims are encouraged to contact their financial institution as early as possible after noticing suspicious activity, both to reverse any debits, and to prevent any further misuse.

Contact the U.S. Secret Service. The Secret Service is the primary federal agency tasked with investigating identity theft/fraud and its related activities under 18 U.S.C. § 1028. The Secret Service records criminal complaints, assists victims in contacting other relevant investigative and consumer protection agencies and works with other federal, state, and local law enforcement and reporting agencies to identify perpetrators. The following identity theft crimes are among those investigated by the Secret Service: credit card/access device fraud (skimming); check fraud; bank fraud; false identification fraud; passport/visa fraud; and identity theft.

Contact the U.S. Trustee Program (USTP) if a fraudulent bankruptcy case was filed. Individuals can report suspected bankruptcy fraud to the USTP's Bankruptcy Fraud group. A report should contain specific factual information and supporting documentation, and must detail:

- The name and address of the person or business being reported;
- The name of the bankruptcy case, case number, and the location where the case was filed;
- Any identifying information regarding the individual or the business;
- A brief description of the alleged fraud (including when fraud occurred and was discovered);
- The type of asset that was concealed and its estimated dollar value (or the amount of any unreported income, undervalued asset, or other omitted asset or claim); and
- The name, address, telephone number, and e-mail address of complainant (not required, but recommended).

The request can be submitted via e-mail to: **USTP.Bankruptcy.Fraud@usdoj.gov** or by mail to: Executive Office for U.S. Trustees, Office of Criminal Enforcement 441 G Street, NW, Suite 6150, Washington, DC 20530.

¶808

Contact the Social Security Administration (SSA). Individuals whose SSN information is stolen/misused should contact the SSA Fraud Hotline by phone or by mail at: SSA Fraud Hotline, P.O. Box 17768, Baltimore, MD 21235.

> **CAUTION:** The SSA's policy is that it will only issue a new SSN to a victim of identity theft who continues to be disadvantaged by using the original number. To request a new SSN, an individual must:
>
> - Apply in person at a Social Security office;
> - Complete Form SS-5, *Social Security Administration Application for a Social Security Card,* available online at: **http://www.ssa.gov/forms/ss-5.pdf**;
> - Provide a statement explaining the reasons for needing a new number (including evidence of ongoing problems because of the misuse);
> - Provide current, credible, third-party evidence documenting the reasons for needing a new number; and
> - Provide original documents establishing citizenship or work-authorized legal status, age, and identity.

If a criminal victim, obtain a "certificate of clearance." If an individual's identity was used to commit a crime, the individual should contact the court where the arrest or conviction occurred. The victim will be required to provide proof of identity and a completed Identity Theft Report, and may then request that the court grant a "certificate of clearance" that declares the victim innocent of the crime committed. This can be provided in response to any inquiries about the conviction. The victim should request the assistance of the local district attorney to provide court records and help clear the victim's name. The victim should also check his or her state resources for victims of criminal identity theft. For example, California adds victims of criminal identity theft to the state's Identity Theft Registry (see **https://oag.ca.gov/idtheft/facts/how-to-registry**) and issues victims a Certificate of Identity Theft that may be presented to law enforcement.

Contact the U.S. Postal Inspection Service (USPIS). If the USPS was used to facilitate a fraud, such as: theft of mail or fraudulently changing a mailing address on a credit card or bank account, the victim should file a Complaint for Identity Theft via the U.S. Mail, available online at: **http://ehome.uspis.gov/mailtheft/idtheft.aspx**. Victims can also contact the U.S. Postal Mail Fraud Center by phone.

STUDY QUESTION

5. To prevent all third parties from accessing his or her credit report without consent, an individual uses a(n) _____ on the report.

    a. Fraud alert

    b. Extended fraud alert

    c. Security freeze

    d. Identity Theft Affidavit

Responses Specific to Tax Identity Theft

There are additional steps that a victim of tax-related identity theft should take in order to correct the individual's tax account and prevent further misuse.

Complete an FTC Identity Theft Affidavit. The form is available online at: **https://www.consumer.ftc.gov/articles/pdf-0094-identity-theft-affidavit.pdf**.

Bring the completed FTC Identity Theft Affidavit to the local police department and file a police report. In addition to the FTC Identity Theft Affidavit, bring:

- A government-issued ID with a photo for verification of identification;
- Proof of address (e.g., a utility bill);
- Any documentary proof of the theft or fraud; and
- FTC's Memo to Law Enforcement, available online at **http://www.consumer.ftc.gov/articles/pdf-0088-ftc-memo-law-enforcement.pdf**. Most police departments are instructed (or required, depending on state law) to take a report when an individual reasonably believes that he or she is a victim of identity theft even though jurisdiction for prosecution may lie elsewhere. Retain a copy of the law enforcement report (or at least the report/case number).

File an online complaint with the FBI's Internet Crime Complaint Center (IC3) at www.ic3.gov. The IC3 gives victims of cybercrime a convenient and easy-to-use reporting mechanism that alerts authorities of suspected criminal or civil violations. IC3 sends every complaint to one or more law enforcement or regulatory agencies—international, federal, state, or local—with jurisdiction.

Create an Identity Theft Report. Combine the FTC Identity Theft Affidavit with the police report.

File IRS Form 14039, *Identity Theft Affidavit.* Select the box that states "I am a victim of identity theft *and* it is affecting my federal tax records." The form can be submitted by mail to: Internal Revenue Service, P.O. Box 9039, Andover, MA 01810-0939, or by fax to (855) 807-5720.

Contact the IRS Identity Protection Specialized Unit by phone.

Verify one's identity if an IRS Letter 5071C is received. Recipients' identity may have been compromised. They must verify their identities by calling the number on the letter, or by using the IRS's online Identity Verification tool, available online at **https://idverify.irs.gov**.

Request an IP PIN. If an IRS Letter CP01A or CPO1F is received, the taxpayer has been identified as a possible identity theft victim and may request an IP PIN to further protect the taxpayer's account from tax-related identity theft.

An IP PIN is a six-digit number assigned to help prevent the misuse of SSN information on fraudulent federal income tax returns. Once provided, an IP PIN must be used to confirm a taxpayer's identity on federal tax returns. In order to obtain an IP PIN, a taxpayer must verify his or her identity online at **https://www.irs.gov/Individuals/Get-An-Identity-Protection-PIN**. If the taxpayer meets the eligibility requirements, an IP PIN is generated online. Once a taxpayer elects to participate in the IP PIN program, there is no ability to subsequently "opt out" of the program. An updated IP PIN is provided to the taxpayer via postal mail each December.

The IRS on July 19, 2016, announced that it had restored access to its online identity protection personal identification number (IP PIN). The restoration comes with claims that it has returned with stronger authentication requirements for taxpayers.

The IP PIN retrieval tool was pulled offline in March 2016 after finding that people engaged in tax refund fraud had obtained taxpayer IP PINs. At the time, the IRS stated that, through the end of February 2016, it had stopped 800 fraudulent returns that used IP PINs.

The return of the "Get an IP PIN" tool is said to see the use of a multifactor authentication process that will help prevent automated attacks. The system requires that taxpayers go through a more rigorous process to set up use of the tool through the IRS's Secure Access portal, the same process used for the relaunched Get Transcript Online tool that debuted on June 7.

The Secure Access process requires that taxpayers have immediate access to an e-mail address, account information from a credit card or other loan types and a text-enabled mobile phone. Taxpayers are to review the online IRS Fact Sheet for Get Transcript Online (FS-2016-20); regarding the information the Secure Access e-authentication process requires, as well as the steps outlined in how to register under the new authentication process.

Immediately respond to any IRS notice or letter, and provide a copy of the taxpayer's Identity Theft Report with each communication. If an identity thief has already filed using the taxpayer's SSN, the taxpayer will not be able to electronically file, and must instead submit a paper copy of the tax return to the IRS office where the taxpayer ordinarily files returns, along with:

- IRS Form 14039;
- Identity Theft Report; and
- A photocopy of a document that verifies the individual's identity.

If the IRS informs the taxpayer that he or she did not report all income, and the extra income is attributable to fraud, respond to the letter as soon as possible, in the manner set forth in the notice, providing the documentation listed above.

Consider reaching out to the Taxpayer Advocate Service (TAS) for assistance. TAS handled nearly 58,000 tax-related identity theft cases in 2013, which represented more than 20 percent of its total caseload.

Consider reaching out to a member of Congress and initiating a Congressional Inquiry. A Congressional Inquiry is an inquiry that is made by a Member of Congress to the IRS concerning a constituent's tax account-related issue. A form of constituent service, the Congressional Inquiry process permits members of Congress to access otherwise confidential tax information as the designee of a constituent taxpayer pursuant to the Congressional Affairs Program (CAP). To initiate the Congressional Inquiry process, a taxpayer must contact a member of Congress and provide the member's office with a written disclosure authorization that satisfies the requirements of the *Privacy Act of 1974*. This document can take the form of:

- A traditional power of attorney (POA);
- A Form 8821, *Tax Information Authorization*;
- A Congressional Authorization Form; or
- A taxpayer's informal letter of designation.

However, in order to be valid, the authorization must:

- Name the member of Congress to be designated;
- Include the taxpayer's SSN;
- Identify the tax years at issue; and
- Contain a description of the problem.

The taxpayer must also provide the member of Congress with a copy of Form 14039 and should include the Identity Theft Report as well. The CAP designates governmental liaisons at the IRS that include a local taxpayer advocate through the TAS.

Assume that federal tax-related identity theft is accompanied by state tax-related identity theft, and vice versa. Victims should contact authorities for both.

Obtain an "identity theft passport" if the state offers the program. Eleven states—Arkansas, Delaware, Iowa, Maryland, Mississippi, Montana, Nevada, New Mexico, Ohio, Oklahoma, and Virginia—have created identity theft passport programs to help protect victims from continuing identity theft.

An identity theft passport is a document designed to provide identity theft victims another form of identification that can be presented to creditors or other businesses, and can be presented to law enforcement to prevent a wrongful arrest if a thief uses another's PII during the commission of a crime.

Always include a copy of the completed Identity Theft Report with any communications.

STUDY QUESTION

6. If an individual receives a tax deficiency notice or report of unrelated income, he or she should respond using all of the following paper documents *except:*

    a. A photocopied document that verifies his or her identity

    b. Congressional Affairs Program report

    c. IRS Form 14039, *Identity Theft Affidavit*

    d. Identity Theft Report

¶ 809 CONCLUSION

The IRS, state tax administrators, and the tax industry are making great progress in detecting and resolving identity-theft issues, expanding and strengthening protections against identity theft, and providing victim assistance. However, more improvements are needed as identity theft continues to rise. Individuals must also be vigilant and take the necessary steps to protect themselves from becoming victims of identity theft.

MODULE 3: NEW CHALLENGES FACING INDIVIDUALS AND TAX-EXEMPT ENTITIES— Chapter 9: Coordinating Multiple Retirement Accounts

¶ 901 WELCOME

As individuals progress in their careers and move from employer to employer, they often accumulate multiple retirement plans and accounts. Multiple plans and accounts add both complexity and opportunity for individual taxpayers. This course will examine the wide variety of plans and accounts available, and the contribution limits that apply. It will look at the recently liberalized rules regarding the distribution and rollover of basis in the multiplan and account context. Finally, it will examine required minimum distributions and how multiple plans can affect the requirement.

¶ 902 LEARNING OBJECTIVES

Upon completion of this chapter, you will be able to:

- Recognize the differences between defined contribution plans and defined benefit plans and identify the major kinds of defined contribution plans;
- Identify the differences between elective deferrals and employer contributions, and the difference between employer matching contributions and "nonelective" contributions;
- Recognize the differences between traditional and Roth IRAs and the types of IRAs used in employer plans;
- Identify how elective deferral limits and catch-up limits apply to individual taxpayers and employers; and
- Identify features of plan rollovers and required minimum distributions.

¶ 903 INTRODUCTION

Retirement plans fall broadly into two categories: employer plans and individual retirement accounts (IRAs). Some simplified employer plans are hybrids, using IRAs. Employer plans are popular because employers deduct contributions currently, even though the tax on benefits to employees is deferred. IRAs are personal accounts generally set up by the owner.

¶ 904 TYPES OF PLANS

Employer Plans

The two broad categories of employer plans are defined benefit plans and defined contribution plans. Employers may offer both kinds of plans.

Defined benefit plans. Defined benefit plans are traditional pension plans with fixed monthly payments to retirees and their spouses for the rest of their lives. The monthly payments are generally based on an employee's length of service and compensation amount near retirement. Employers must provide sufficient funding to ensure that the plan is financially sound, with sufficient assets to satisfy these future obligations.

Defined contribution plans. Defined contribution plans let employers and employees decide an amount to contribute, up to annual limits imposed under the tax code. A contribution amount is generally expressed as a percentage of the employee's compensation. Depending on the plan, the amount of a yearly contribution can be fixed over time or determined on a yearly basis.

Profit-sharing plans. Profit-sharing plans allow employers to decide each year whether and how much to contribute.

EXAMPLE: The Flexible Company has a profit-sharing plan. It has a so-so year for revenue in 2015 and decides to contribute 2 percent of compensation to its employees' accounts for that year. It has a good year in 2016 and contributes 6 percent. In 2017, it has a terrible year and contributes nothing.

COMMENT: Note that an employer is not technically required to have any "profit" in order to contribute to a profit-sharing plan. These plans are popular for employers whose business is cyclical.

Money purchase plans. An employer with a money purchase plan must pay a fixed amount each year into its employees' individual accounts. These sums are invested, and at retirement the employee has the opportunity to buy a retirement annuity that will provide fixed payments to the employee and spouse for the rest of their lives.

EXAMPLE: The Yearly Company has a money purchase plan requiring Yearly to contribute 5 percent of compensation each year to its employees' accounts. The plan provides individual accounts for each employee, and the dollar value of the accounts grows over time. At retirement, the employee can use money in his or her account to purchase a lifetime retirement annuity, or to roll over the amount into an IRA.

COMMENT: Defined contribution plans can also allow for employee contributions through elective deferrals of compensation.

Elective deferral arrangements. Elective deferral arrangements allow participating employees to elect whether and how much to take out of their paycheck to contribute to an account set up for that employee. Historically, these arrangements were add-on features to traditional defined benefit employer pension plans and were viewed more as a "bell and whistle" than an actual plan. However, employers have generally moved away from traditional pension plans, leaving the elective deferral plans as the most important plan for many employees.

Examples of elective deferral plans include:

- Qualified cash or deferral arrangement (401(k)) plans;
- Tax-sheltered annuity (403(b)) plans for educational organization employees;
- Eligible deferred compensation (457(b)) plans for local government and tax-exempt organization employees (generally employees of schools, hospitals, churches, and charities); and
- SIMPLE IRA or 401(k) plans (allowing salary reduction contributions, subject to lower limits).

Deferrals are deducted by the employer currently but excluded from the employee's income until distributed, generally at retirement. Employers are allowed to offer designated Roth versions of these plans under which deferrals are included in the employee's income and not taxed when distributed.

COMMENT: Profit-sharing plans and money purchase plans are often coupled with a 401(k) cash or deferral arrangement. Employer contributions are deposited into each employee's 401(k) account. This gives employees a great deal of control over their retirement assets after ceasing service (i.e., retiring or terminating employment) with the employer even if they are too young to retire. They may roll over these assets into a personal IRA or another employer plan if that plan so permits.

Employer contributions. Employer contributions are amounts directly paid into an employee's plan by the employer. These can come in several forms:

- Matching contributions to employee deferral plans;
- "Nonelective" contributions to defined contribution plans; and
- Funding for defined benefit plans.

Matching contributions. Employers that offer elective deferral plans may make matching employer contributions. For example, an employer might offer to match an employee's elective deferral up to 2 percent of the employer's compensation. Although employer matching contributions are made to elective deferral accounts, they are subject to the employer contribution limit rather than the deferral limit.

> **COMMENT:** Matching features are popular because the IRS offers simplified procedures to employers in exchange for the match. Note that by electing to defer a certain amount, an employee is in effect also electing matching contributions.

Nonelective employer contributions. Nonelective employer contributions are contributions an employer makes to a defined contribution plan that are independent of any employee election deferral. Depending on the type of plan, an employer may decide whether and how much to contribute on an annual basis, or the employer might be locked into a fixed contribution amount each year. For example, profit-sharing plans provide maximum discretion for an employer in deciding whether and how much to contribute each year (technically, as already mentioned, actual profits are not even necessary). In contrast, money purchase plans provide a fixed schedule of contributions, regardless of the employer's profitability.

Defined benefit plan contributions. Employers must fund their traditional defined benefit plans sufficiently to satisfy promised future pension benefits. To the extent the employer has control, it is over what benefits to promise rather than how much to contribute. Determining funding levels is the job of pension plan actuaries.

Individual Retirement Accounts

IRAs provide tax benefits similar to employer plans. IRA assets are always accessible by the owner (though early withdrawals may be subject to additional tax).

> **COMMENT:** By law, employees generally do not have access to employer plan assets if they are still working for the employer (this rule is called the rule against "in-service distributions").

Any individual who earns compensation can generally make an IRA contribution. There are two kinds of IRAs: traditional and Roth.

Traditional IRAs. The contributions to a traditional IRA are fully deductible unless the individual is an active participant in an employer plan, in which case the deduction might be limited or unavailable even though the contribution is permitted. The amount grows tax free in the account. Distributions are taxed as ordinary income upon distribution, generally at retirement. Nondeductible contributions on which taxes were paid are treated as basis and not taxed upon distribution.

Roth IRAs. Roth IRAs are similar to traditional IRAs in that assets grow tax free, but otherwise they are the mirror image in tax terms. Contributions are not deductible, but distributions are tax free. If certain distribution rules are not followed (generally, that the Roth IRA be in existence for at least five years and the owner be at least age 59 ½,

¶904

disabled, or deceased), asset growth is taxable. High-income taxpayers are precluded from making contributions, but they may roll over sums from traditional IRAs into Roths.

Uses of IRAs. IRAs are typically used both as a retirement savings device and as a repository for employer plan lump-sum distributions that an individual accumulates over the course of a career. Lump-sum distributions typically occur when an individual leaves an employer, at which time the individual can take a distribution from any 401(k) or similar plan. Employers may also cash out an individual's vested benefit in a traditional pension plan. These distributions would be taxable if not rolled over into an IRA.

> **COMMENT:** Note that employer plan accounts sometimes contain amounts that were contributed on an after-tax basis, and these amounts are not included in income when distributed.

Basis. IRAs can have basis that is not taxable upon distribution. The basis can arise from nondeductible contributions (generally, contributions by individuals who are active participants in an employer retirement plan) or from rollovers of after-tax contributions to an employer plan.

If an individual has an IRA with both taxable amounts and basis, any distribution will contain a pro-rata portion of basis. The taxable portion must be reported on Form 8606, *Nondeductible IRAs*.

> **EXAMPLE:** Jack Schwartz has a single traditional IRA with a balance of $20,000, which includes $300 in basis as of the end of 2015. In 2016, Jack makes no contributions but takes a $5,000 distribution from the IRA. The distribution consists of a nontaxable return of basis in the amount of $75, and a taxable amount of $4,925.

STUDY QUESTION

1. All of the following are types of employer contributions to employees' retirement plans *except:*

  a. Elective deferral arrangements

  b. Money purchase plans

  c. Defined benefit plans

  d. Profit-sharing plans

Employer Plans Using IRAs

There are three kinds of easy-to-administer employer plans that require the employer to set up an IRA for each plan participant:

- Simplified employee plans (SEPs);
- Savings incentive match plans for employees (SIMPLE) IRA plans; and
- Salary reduction simplified employee pension (SARSEP) plans.

Because these are IRAs, the assets are available to participants even if they are still working for the employer sponsor (though early distributions may be subject to early withdrawal additional tax of 10 percent). The balance of an employee's IRA is added to the employee's other IRA balances for purposes of determining required minimum distributions (RMDs), generally once the employee reaches age 70½.

SEP plans. SEP plans are strictly employer contribution plans. Elective deferrals and catch-up contributions are not permitted. Employers can contribute up to 25 percent of each participant's compensation with an annual statutory maximum of $53,000 for 2016. Employers have complete discretion each year whether to contribute 0 percent or 25 percent.

> **COMMENT:** A key advantage of a SEP plan is that it can be set up and contributions made for a tax year as late as the due date (including extensions) for the employer's tax return for that year.

Employers using SEP plans can have other plans as well. Self-employed individuals may set up a SEP plan for their self-employed income even if they participate in their employer's retirement plan. Partners can set up a SEP plan at the partnership level, but they cannot set up separate SEP plans for each partner.

Participants may make their normal IRA contributions and catch-up contributions to their SEP-IRA.

SIMPLE IRA plans. These plans can be used only by small employers (an employer with no more than 100 employees who received at least $5,000 of compensation from the employer for the preceding year). Employers can choose either to match employee elective deferrals up to 3 percent of compensation or to contribute 2 percent annually whether the employee elects to defer anything or not. They allow employees to elect to defer up to a statutory limit of $12,500 for 2016 and an additional $3,000 in catch-up contributions for participants who are age 50 or older. If an employee makes an early withdrawal (generally, before age 59½), and the withdrawal is within two years of participation, the additional tax is 25 percent.

An employer can contribute to a SIMPLE plan only if that is the employer's only plan for the year of contribution. Exceptions are made for employers with union employees who have a separate plan if they are excluded from the SIMPLE plan, and there is a two-year grace period if the business is acquired or sold and the SIMPLE plan only applies to the business's separate employees.

Unlike SEP plans, an employer cannot set up a SIMPLE plan retroactively. It must do so before the effective date. Generally, for an employer setting up a SIMPLE plan for the first time, the effective date can be anywhere between January 1 and October 1, unless the business does not come into existence until after October 1.

> **COMMENT:** SIMPLE 401(k)s are also available and have the same contribution limits.

SARSEP plans. SARSEP plans are an early version of a simplified plan. They could not be set up after 1996, but existing plans have been grandfathered and can take on new participants. For 2016 participants can elect up to defer a statutory amount of $18,000, and participants age 50 or older can make catch-up contributions of up to $6,000. Employers may contribute up to 100 percent of an employee's compensation with a maximum of $53,000 for 2016. Matching contributions are not allowed.

STUDY QUESTION

2. A major difference between a SIMPLE IRA plan and a SARSEP plan offered by an employer is:

    a. The SIMPLE plan has a higher maximum elective deferral

    b. The maximum an employer can contribute is generally higher for a SARSEP plan

    c. The employer cannot make matching contributions for a SEP plan but may for a SARSEP account

    d. Employee salary deferrals are allowed for the SIMPLE IRA but not for a SARSEP

¶ 905 CONTRIBUTION LIMITS

Annual Deferral Limits

An annual deferral limit applies to each employee. The limit is the lesser of 100 percent of compensation, or an inflation adjusted amount set by the tax code. In 2016, the limit is $18,000 for 401(k) plans, 403(b) plans, and SARSEP plans, and $12,500 for salary deferrals under a SIMPLE IRA plan. For employees with more than one plan, these amounts are aggregated for all these plans. A separate $18,000 annual limit for 2016 applies to 457(b) plans. So-called catch-up payments are added to that limit.

    COMMENT: Plans are free to set lower maximum amounts. A plan limit is typically expressed as a uniform maximum percentage of each employee's compensation (e.g., 10 percent of compensation). Plans sometimes have to reduce the deferral limit for a plan year for highly compensated employees in order to meet nondiscrimination requirements.

    EXAMPLE: Beth Robinson is age 43 and defers $2,500 in to her company's 401(k) plan in 2016. She quits and goes to work for an unrelated employer and participates in her new employer's 401(k) plan immediately. The maximum she may defer in 2016 to her new employer's plan is $15,500 (her $18,000 individual limit $2,500 that she has already deferred to her former employer's 401(k)). The amount she can defer to both plans cannot exceed her individual limit for that year.

    EXAMPLE: Tony Fiorini is age 32 and makes a salary deferral election that will result in a deferral of $12,500 through his company's SIMPLE IRA plan in 2016. He is also self-employed and has his own individual 401(k). He may defer up to $5,500 to his 401(k) in 2016, without exceeding his deferral limit.

    EXAMPLE: Janice Steinberg is age 48 years old and works for a school as an administrator and participates both in the school's 403(b) plan and its 457(b) plan. For 2016, she defers $18,000 to her 403(b) plan. Because the annual deferral limit applies separately to 457(b) plans, she may also defer up to $18,000 to her 457(b) plan for a total deferral of $36,000.

    COMMENT: Individuals who have a choice of deferral plans should ordinarily prioritize their deferral amounts to plans to take advantage of any employer matches.

    EXAMPLE: Jackson Collins is age 39 and works two jobs with unrelated employers in 2016, each of which offers a 401(k) plan. Jackson wants to defer the maximum $18,000 annual limit. At Allsilver Corp., his first employer, the company 401(k) plan has a 3 percent match, and the second employer, Allbronze Corp., offers a plan that has no match. Jackson makes $50,000 per year at Allsilver, 3 percent of which is $1,500 so he allocates $1,500 of his $18,000 to the Allsilver's plan. He splits the remaining $16,500 of his $18,000 annual deferral limit between the two plans based on their respective fees and the investment options.

The 100 percent of compensation limit applies to contributions to each *plan* rather than to a participant's total *compensation.*

EXAMPLE: Charles Devaro is age 45 and participates in a 401(k) plan with Nuteo Co. and a SIMPLE IRA plan with an unrelated employer, Tresian Corp. Charles earns $10,000 in compensation in 2016 from Neuteo and another $10,000 from Tresian. Charles cannot defer more than $10,000 to either plan (for example, $12,000 to the 401(k) plan and $8,000 to the SIMPLE IRA plan) because deferrals to each employer's plan cannot exceed 100 percent of the participant's compensation from that employer.

Catch-up Contributions

Employers can allow participants who will be age 50 or older by the end of the tax year to make catch-up contributions. An annual limit of $6,000 in 2016 applies to 401(k), 403(b), and 457(b) state and local government plans, and an annual limit of $3,000 applies to SIMPLE-IRA and SIMPLE 401(k) plans. IRA owners may also make catch-up contributions of up to $1,000 in their traditional or Roth IRAs.

COMMENT: Employers are not required to allow catch-up contributions, so a participant must check with the plan before making the contribution.

In the multiple plan context, even if an individual is enrolled in two plans that do not allow catch-up contributions, the expanded deferral limit can be used because it expands the participant's overall deferral limit from $18,000 to $24,000.

EXAMPLE: Mort Silvers is age 49 in 2015, a year in which the maximum deferral amount is $18,000. He works two jobs for unrelated employers, one of which has a 401(k) plan and the other of which has a 403(b) plan. Both plans allow deferrals up to $18,000, but neither plan has a catch-up feature. He defers $10,000 into his 401(k) plan and $8,000 into his 403(b) plan in 2015, for a total of $18,000, the personal limit for 2015. In 2016 he turns age 50, becoming eligible for up to $6,000 in catch-up contributions for a total personal deferral limit of $24,000. Mort splits the additional $6,000 between the two plans, and defers $13,000 into the 401(k) plan and $11,000 into the 403(b) plan. This is permissible because his deferrals do not exceed the maximum deferrals permitted by each plan, and they do not exceed his personal limit of $24,000.

COMMENT: Catch-up contributions have a privileged status. First, the maximum a highly compensated employee may defer might be lowered from the $18,000 amount due to failure on the part of the plan to satisfy nondiscrimination requirements, but that would not affect the $6,000 catch-up amount. Second, elective deferrals are also limited by another of other general retirement plan limits (see below), but those limits do not apply to catch-up contributions.

Excess Deferrals

If a participant's total deferrals exceed the limit for a year, the participant must tell the plan administrator and ask that the excess deferral be paid out. The plan should pay the participant that amount by April 15 of the following year, in which case the employee's withdrawn amount is not reported again as part of the employee's gross income for the previous year. Any income earned on the withdrawal is reported as gross income for the tax year in which it is withdrawn.

If the employee does not take out the excess deferral by April 15, the excess, though taxable in the year of deferral, is not included in the employee's cost basis in figuring the taxable amount of any eventual benefits or distributions under the plan. In effect, an excess deferral left in the plan is taxed twice—once when contributed and again when distributed.

Special Catch-up Rules for 403(b) and 457(b) Plans

A 403(b) plan participant may be eligible for a separate 15-year catch-up of up to $3,000 if the plan so provides. For participants who use both types of catch-ups, contributions above the participant's annual limit are considered to have been made first under the 15-year catch-up.

However, any 457(b) plan may feature a "last 3-year catch-up," which allows the participant to defer in the 3 years before reaching the plan's normal retirement age:

- Twice the annual 457(b) limit (in 2016, $18,000 × 2 = $36,000); or
- The annual 457(b) limit, plus amounts allowed in prior years that the participant did not contribute.

If a governmental 457(b) allows *both* the age-50 catch-up and the 3-year catch-up, the participant can use the one that allows a larger deferral but not both.

> **EXAMPLE:** Tisha Martin is 29 and participates in a 457(b) and in a 403(b) plan in 2016. Each plan allows the maximum deferrals for 2016. Tisha may defer $18,000 to each plan in 2016.

> **EXAMPLE:** Lawrence Blumenthal is age 50 in 2016. He participates in a state and local government 457(b) plan, and in a 403(b) plan. He may defer $24,000 to each plan if both plans allow age-50 catch-ups ($18,000 plus $6,000 catch-up).

> **EXAMPLE:** Anna Halverston is age 50 in 2016, and is in a nongovernmental 457(b) plan and a 403(b) plan. She may defer $24,000 to the 403(b) plan and $18,000 to the 457(b) plan.

> **EXAMPLE:** Drew Witherston is age 50 in 2016, and is in his educational institution's 403(b) annuity plan and a 457(b) government plan that has a 3-year catch up. He may defer $24,000 to the 403(b) plan, and $36,000 to the 457(b) plan ($18,000 × 2).

Annual Addition Limit

The annual addition limit applies to defined contribution plans. The limit is the lesser of an inflation adjusted statutory amount ($53,000 in 2016) and 100 percent of compensation. The limit applies to the total of employer and employee contributions including:

- Employee elective deferrals;
- Employer matching contributions; and
- Nonelective employer contributions (including contributions to profit sharing, and money purchase plans).

In contrast to the annual elective deferral limit or the catch-up limit that apply to each individual, the annual addition limit applies to each employer and all of its plans. The notable exception is catch-up contributions, which are not subject to the annual addition limit.

> **COMMENT:** SEP plans have a different limit, which is the lesser of 25 percent of compensation and $53,000 (for 2016).

> **EXAMPLE:** Amos Radison, age 40, participates in his employer's profit-sharing plan. He earned $20,000 in compensation for 2016. His employer may contribute up to the lesser of 100 percent of $20,000 or $53,000, which is $20,000. In fact, his employer contributes 10 percent of his compensation, which is $2,000.

> **EXAMPLE:** Use the same facts as above, except Amos earned $200,000 in compensation in 2016. His employer may contribute up to the lesser of $200,000 or

$53,000, which is $53,000. In fact, his employer contributes 10 percent of his compensation, which is $20,000.

Note that there is a limit on how much compensation can be taken into account when the employer calculates its contributions. That limit is $265,000 for 2016.

> **EXAMPLE:** Assume the same facts as previously, except Amos earned $300,000 in 2016. His employer may contribute up to the lesser of $265,000 or $53,000. In fact, his employer contributes 10 percent of compensation Amos earned, which is $26,500 because of the compensation cap.

The $265,000 limit on how much compensation can be taken into account does not apply for calculating elective deferrals.

> **EXAMPLE:** Assume the same facts as previously, except Amos is electing to defer compensation under his employer's 401(k) plan rather than receiving an employer contribution. Amos elects to defer 6 percent of his compensation, which is calculated on the basis of his $300,000 in compensation, or $18,000.

Multiple plans sponsored by the same employer or affiliated group of employers are treated as one plan for purposes of applying the annual addition limit. The limit applies separately for plans provided by unrelated employers.

> **EXAMPLE:** Shirley Warren, age 40, is an employee of Mass Central Company and is enrolled in its money purchase 401(k) plan. She has $18,000 in compensation for 2016, and her annual addition limit is the lesser of $18,000 and $53,000, which is $18,000. Mass Central contributes 10 percent of her compensation ($1,800) to her money purchase plan. Although the general limit for elective deferrals in 2016 is $18,000, Shirley can elect to defer no more than $16,200 to her Mass Central 401(k) without exceeding the annual addition limit.

> **EXAMPLE:** Assume the same facts as above, except Shirley also works for Connecticut Realty Company, which is unrelated to Mass Central. She participates in Connecticut Realty's 401(k) plan, and Shirley may elect to defer up to $1,800 without exceeding her annual deferral limit of $18,000.

Employer Deduction Limits

The deduction for contributions to a defined contribution plan (profit-sharing plan or money purchase pension plan) cannot be more than 25 percent of the compensation paid (or accrued) during the year to eligible employees participating in the plan. The following rules apply:

- Elective deferrals are not subject to this limit, so they are always deductible as long as they are within the elective deferral limit;
- When the employer or employee calculates the amount of compensation paid, elective deferrals are included; and
- The maximum compensation that can be taken into account for each employee is $265,000 in 2016.

> **EXAMPLE:** Melano Company has a profit-sharing/401(k) plan. Its total compensation (including $100,000 in elective 401(k) employee contributions) paid or accrued to participants for the employer's 2016 tax year is $1 million. Melano can deduct up to 25 percent of that amount, or $250,000, in contributions to the plan participants for 2016. Note that the $100,000 elective deferral amount is not counted toward the deduction maximum and hence can be deducted even if Melano makes nonelective contributions of $250,000 to the plan.

A special rule applies in determining the maximum deductible amount for contributions by self-employed individuals (including sole proprietors, and working partners in a partnership or limited liability company) on behalf of themselves. Under this rule, compensation for plan contribution purposes is determined by using an IRS retirement plan contribution deduction worksheet, which in effect limits the deduction to 20 percent of earned income. Earned income is net profit minus self-employment tax.

In addition to the deduction limit discussed here, an employer cannot deduct amounts contributed in excess of the annual addition limit. In the context of self-employed individuals, that means that the individual may not deduct more than $53,000 for 2016 and that the amount of compensation used to calculate the limit may exceed $265,000. These amounts are included in the IRS self-employed deduction worksheet for retirement contributions.

Note that elective deferrals are treated as ordinary compensation for deduction purposes and so they expand the employer's retirement contribution deduction limit (25 percent of compensation or 20 percent of earned income), while not using up the limit. However, they still count toward the annual addition limit.

EXAMPLE: Gerry Ginsburg, age 40, is a sole proprietor. She has profit-sharing and solo 401(k) plan funded by her earnings from the business. She has $100,000 in earned income in 2016. Under the deduction limit rules, she can deduct up to a $20,000 contribution to her profit-sharing plan (20 percent of $100,000). The retirement contribution deduction limit does not apply to elective deferrals, and therefore Gerry can elect to defer the full $18,000 allowed in 2016 for a total of $38,000. This is below the annual addition limit of $53,000 for 2016, so she can deduct the full amount.

EXAMPLE: Consider the same facts as above, except Gerry has $200,000 in earned income from her sole proprietorship. Under the retirement contribution deduction limit, she can deduct up to a $40,000 (20 percent of $200,000) contribution to her profit-sharing plan, and up to $18,000 in elective deferrals for a total of $58,000. However, this amount exceeds the annual addition limit of $53,000 for 2016, and therefore she can only contribute and deduct $53,000. Gerry decides to make the $40,000 contribution, and she elects to defer $13,000 in earned income.

EXAMPLE: Assume the same facts, except Gerry has $300,000 in earned income. Because of the limit on compensation that can be taken into account for purposes of employer contributions, her income is treated as $265,000 for purposes of the deduction limit. That means she can contribute and deduct up to $53,000 (20 percent of $265,000), which is the same as the $53,000 annual addition limit. Note that she cannot contribute and deduct more, so Gerry cannot make an elective deferrals under her solo plan.

EXAMPLE: Use the same facts, except Gerry is also an employee at the unrelated Progressive Software Company, and is enrolled in Progressive's profit-sharing and 401(k) plan. If Progressive contributes to its profit-sharing plan in 2016, the contribution will not in any way affect Gerry's ability to contribute the maximum to her own plan. In addition, because Gerry did not elect to defer any earned income in her solo 401(k), she is free to elect to defer her full $18,000 annual deferral limit to the Progressive 401(k).

EXAMPLE: Assume the same facts as above, except Gerry is age 52 and is eligible to make catch-up contributions. She may contribute an additional $6,000 of elective deferrals for 2016. Her catch-up contribution could be split between the plans in any proportion she chooses. Her maximum contribution to her profit-sharing/solo 401(k) plan would remain $53,000 even if she contributed the full $6,000 catch-up contribution to this plan.

IRA Contributions

The maximum contribution is $5,500 for 2016. The maximum is bumped up by $1,000 for individuals ages 50 and up. An individual must have taxable compensation at least in the amount of the contribution.

> **EXAMPLE:** Janice's income for 2016 consists of $50,000 in dividends and $1,000 in wages. Janice may contribute up to $1,000 (her earned as opposed to unearned income) to an IRA for 2016.

Spousal IRAs. IRAs belong to individual owners and are taxable to the owner's Social Security number. For married taxpayers, each spouse can contribute the respective maximum amounts each year to his or her separate IRA. Taxable compensation, for these purposes, is combined for married joint filers so that a spouse without taxable compensation may still make a contribution.

> **EXAMPLE:** Maurice and Linda Silvers are married. They are 30 years old. In 2016, Linda earns $11,000 in wages. Maurice has no compensation in 2016. Each may contribute the full amount of $5,500 to their IRAs because Linda's compensation may be counted toward Maurice's contribution limit.

Deductible contributions. Contributions to a traditional IRA are generally deductible. Contributions grow tax-free until withdrawn. Upon withdrawal, the contributions and all earnings are taxed at ordinary rates.

Nondeductible contributions. Taxpayers may choose to make nondeductible contributions, or they might have no other option for contributing because the deduction is limited. In particular, the ability of an active participant in an employer plan to take an IRA deduction is phased out for those whose adjusted gross income (AGI) exceeds $61,000 if single, and $98,000 if filing jointly. Nondeductible contributions, whether made by choice or because the taxpayer is an active participant whose income exceeds the threshold, are treated as basis, and those contributions are not taxed when withdrawn. Earnings grow tax-free but are taxed upon distribution

Roth IRAs. Historically, the value of Roth accounts was limited for higher-income taxpayers because of AGI limits on Roth contributions and conversions. These days, however, the limits only apply for regular contributions, not rollovers. That means traditional IRAs can be converted at will, subject to the taxpayer's tolerance for recognizing the rollover amount as current ordinary income.

> **COMPLIANCE POINTER:** For 2016, the ability to make regular Roth IRA contributions begins to phase out starting at an adjusted gross income of $184,000 for joint filers, and at $117,000 for single filers. Note that active participation in an employer plan does *not* affect the ability to make a Roth IRA contribution.

> **COMMENT:** Some taxpayers who are not eligible to make contributions to Roth IRAs because their modified AGI exceeds the limit for such contributions have indirectly made contributions to a Roth IRA by making nondeductible contributions to a traditional IRA and then converting the traditional IRA to a Roth IRA. The Obama Administration, in its FY 2017 budget, proposes that the Roth conversion be effective only to the extent a distribution of those amounts would be includible in income if they were not rolled over.

STUDY QUESTION

3. If an individual participates in both a 403(b) tax-sheltered annuity plan for educational organization employees and a 457(b) deferred compensation plan for government/exempt organization employees:

    a. The individual is ineligible for any 15-year or last 3-year catch-up contribution

    b. He or she may defer $18,000 to each account for a total of $36,000 for 2016

    c. He or she can elect to make catch-up contributions using both the age-related and 3-year 457(b) rules

    d. The individual age 50 or older can use the 3-year catch-up to defer a total of $24,000 between the two plans for 2016

¶ 906 ROLLOVERS

General Rules

The following are the basic considerations and rules that a taxpayer should understand with respect to rollovers:

- Only certain distributions are eligible to be rolled over;
- Not all kinds of plans can accept rollover distributions from every other kind of plan, and the transferor plan and transferee plan must match in that respect;
- Though generally tax-free, rollovers from traditional accounts to Roth accounts generate current tax; and
- There are two kinds of rollovers—those involving distributions directly to the taxpayer and those that do not, and several rules apply to rollovers that involve actual distributions.

Plans eligible for rollovers include:

- IRAs, including simplified employee pension (SEP) IRAs and savings incentive match plans for employees (SIMPLE) IRAs;
- Qualified pension plans (which include 401(k), profit-sharing, money purchase, and defined benefit plans);
- Qualified annuity plans;
- Tax sheltered annuity plans (403(b) plans); and
- State or local government deferred compensation plans (457(b) plans).

Eligible plans include traditional plans and accounts, as well as designated Roth 401(k), 403(b), governmental 457(b) accounts, and Roth IRAs. They do not include nongovernmental 457(b) plans sponsored by tax-exempt organizations.

Rollovers come in two varieties:

- Rollovers that involve a distribution to the taxpayer in the form of a check payable to the taxpayer and subsequent deposit within 60 days by the taxpayer to the receiving plan; and
- Trustee-to-trustee transfers in which the trustee or administrator of the transferor plan or account issues a check payable to the transferee plan for the benefit of the taxpayer.

A rollover with a distribution to the taxpayer results in the money being under the complete control of the taxpayer for up to 60 days. Trustee-to-trustee rollovers never place the money in the control of the taxpayer (though the taxpayer is typically tasked with forwarding the check to the transferee plan). The rules differ somewhat depending on which form the rollover takes.

Rollover distributions (as opposed to trustee-to-trustee distributions) from a non-Roth employer plan are subject to income tax withholding at a rate of 20 percent even if they are going to be rolled over and thus exempt from tax. Withholding can cause a serious cash flow problem for the taxpayer.

> **EXAMPLE:** Michael Wetherton is entitled to a distribution of $100,000 from his employer's plan. If he takes a rollover distribution, he will receive only $80,000 and the remaining $20,000 will be withheld as income tax. If he only rolls over the $80,000, he will owe tax on the $20,000 withheld. Accordingly, if Michael does not have access to $20,000, he will have to borrow the sum to make up the difference for his rollover if he is to avoid tax. His solution, if available, is a trustee-to-trustee transfer.

Traditional-to-traditional plan rollovers. Rollovers may be made from any traditional (i.e., non-Roth) account or plan to any other traditional account or plan (assuming the plan accepts such rollovers).

Special rules apply for rollovers to SIMPLE IRA plans. A rollover cannot be made:

- Prior to December 18, 2015, to a SIMPLE IRA unless it is from another SIMPLE IRA; and
- From a SIMPLE IRA to a non-SIMPLE IRA for at least two years from the initial participation date.

For contributions made after December 18, 2015, SIMPLE IRA owners may, after expiration of the initial two-year period, roll over amounts from a non-SIMPLE plan into their SIMPLE IRA. Plans from which rollovers can be made include traditional IRAs, SEP plans, qualified plans (including 401(k) plans), employer plans funded through an annuity contract, tax-sheltered 403(b) annuity plans, and 457(b) eligible deferred compensation plans of state or local governments.

Rollovers to Roth IRAs. Rollovers can be made to a Roth IRA from virtually any kind of plan, including Roth and traditional IRAs, SEP and SIMPLE IRAs, qualified plans (including 401(k) plans), 403(b) plans, and 457(b) governmental plans. Rollovers from traditional to Roth plans result in current taxation.

Rollovers from Roth IRAs. Rollovers from a Roth IRA can only be made to another Roth IRA.

Rollovers to designated Roth accounts. Rollovers can be made only from another designated Roth account under a different plan, or by means of an in-plan rollover from a traditional qualified plan, including a 401(k), 403(b), and governmental 457(b) plan.

Rollovers from designated Roth accounts. Rollovers can be made from a designated Roth account to a Roth IRA or other designated Roth account.

> **COMMENT:** Employer plans must generally allow rollovers for eligible distributions to IRAs or other eligible plans, but they are not required to accept them. Plan provisions will control and need to be checked.

Rollovers: Once-in-12-months rule for IRAs. An IRA owner is allowed to roll over an IRA distribution once every 12 months. This ban does not apply to employer plans, and it does not apply to trustee-to-trustee IRA rollovers. It only applies to distributions to IRA owners that the owner recontributes to a different IRA within 60 days.

Historically, the IRS applied the once-in-12-months rule generously by applying it on an IRA-by-IRA basis, rather than on a taxpayer-by-taxpayer basis. Accordingly, a taxpayer with multiple IRAs could roll over amounts from each IRA during the course of a 12-month period, as long as the taxpayer only did it once per existing IRA.

Starting for distributions in 2015, the once-in-12-months rule applies on a taxpayer-by-taxpayer basis. Accordingly, if a taxpayer has multiple IRAs, a rollover from one prevents the taxpayer from rolling over again within 12-months from any of the taxpayer's other IRAs as well. This ban applies to all of an individual's IRAs, including traditional, Roth, SIMPLE, and SEP IRAs. Under a transition rule for 2014 distributions, distributions rolled over to another (or the same) IRA in 2014 will not prevent a 2015 distribution from being rolled over provided the 2015 distribution is from a different IRA involved in the 2014 rollover.

EXAMPLE: Joyce Kowalczyk has two IRA accounts: one with Chase Bank and the other with March Investments. On January 1, 2014, she receives a rollover distribution from her Chase IRA. She completes the rollover by February 28 by depositing the distribution into a newly created third IRA with August Securities. Joyce may not make another rollover distribution from either her Chase IRA or her August Securities IRA until January 1, 2015. She may, however, roll over amounts from March Investments account during 2014.

EXAMPLE: Assume the same facts as above, except Joyce takes the distribution on December 31, 2014. Joyce may not make another rollover distribution from either Chase or August until December 31, 2015. She may, however, roll over amounts from March Investments account during 2015.

EXAMPLE: Use the same facts, except that Joyce takes the distribution from August on January 1, 2015. She may not make another rollover until January 1, 2016. This ban includes all of her IRAs.

COMMENT: Historically, individuals with multiple IRAs could have free access to a portion of their total IRA funds throughout the year by making a series of rollovers and by using the full 60-day window for each. Starting in 2015, individuals can no longer rotate rollovers and are limited to no more than one 60-day period per year.

COMMENT: The opportunity for abuse is absent in the case of trustee-to-trustee transfers because the money never lands in the hands of the individual taxpayer. Accordingly, the once-in-12-months rule does not apply to trustee-to-trustee transfers.

PRACTICE POINTER: Married spouses are each counted as individual IRA owners or plan participants for retirement account purposes, so a married couple as a unit can roll over twice within a 12-month period as long as they roll over from IRAs that belong to each of them rather than to only one of them. However, when the rollovers are overlapping, it might draw the attention of the IRS if it appears the couple is merely trying to lengthen the 60-day window.

STUDY QUESTION

4. Rollovers *cannot* be:

   a. Made from a SIMPLE IRA to a non-SIMPLE IRA for at least two years after an individual's initial participation

   b. Made tax free from one Roth IRA to another in a trustee-to-trustee rollover

   c. Made using IRA distributions from two spouses' accounts within 12 months

   d. Made from a non-Roth plan to a Roth IRA

Rollovers: Distribution of Basis

Nontaxable basis can arise from after-tax contributions to an employee plan or nondeductible contributions to a traditional account. Distribution of basis is not taxed. If a distribution is rolled over, the portion (percentage) of the distribution that represents basis will be treated as basis in the recipient plan or IRA.

Distributions from IRAs. If an individual has both nondeductible contributions (basis), and earnings or deductible contributions in the same IRA, each distribution contains a pro-rata portion of basis.

> **NOTE:** Distributions of basis from an IRA cannot be allocated.

> **EXAMPLE:** Wilma Washington has one traditional IRA, with a balance of $100,000, of which $20,000 is basis. In 2016, she makes no new contributions. She opens a new traditional IRA and a new Roth IRA. She distributes $80,000 to the new traditional IRA and $20,000 to the new Roth IRA. Her distribution to the new traditional IRA includes $16,000 of basis, and her distribution to the new Roth IRA includes $4,000 in basis.

If an IRA owner has more than one IRA, and at least one IRA has basis, then any distribution from any of the owner's IRAs will include a pro-rata share of basis in all of the owner's IRAs.

> **EXAMPLE:** Walter Semanchek has two traditional IRAs: a Janus investment and a Fidelity account. Each has a balance of $100,000. The Janus account has $20,000 in basis resulting from nondeductible contributions, and the Fidelity account has none. That means that 10 percent of any distribution from either IRA will be treated as basis. If Walter rolls over $10,000 from Fidelity to a newly created IRA with Vanguard, $1,000 of the rollover amount will be treated as basis.

Distribution of basis from employer plans. A plan participant's employer plans are not aggregated the way an owner's IRAs are. However, distributions of less than the entire balance of the account include a pro-rata share of the basis in the account. There is an ordering rule that the taxable amount representing pretax contributions and earnings comes out first.

> **EXAMPLE:** Gena Columbo has a 401(k) plan through her employer. Her balance is $200,000, $20,000 of which is basis. She terminates employment and takes a partial distribution of $100,000. Her distribution includes $10,000 in basis.

Because of the ordering rule, it is possible for a plan participant to allocate the basis in a situation involving multiple destinations. Historically, employee plan participants who wanted to allocate basis had to take an actual distribution, and then recontribute the amounts to an IRA or different employer plan within 60 days. By taking an actual distribution, however, the participant was subject to 20 percent withholding which meant the participant had to temporarily come up with the withholding amount in cash in order to roll over the entire amount.

A direct rollover from an employee plan would avoid the withholding problem, but until recently the IRS did not specifically permit allocation of basis in the contest of direct rollovers. For distributions on or after January 1, 2015, it does.

> **EXAMPLE:** Charlie Halverston participates in a qualified plan that does not contain a designated Roth account. His $250,000 account balance consists of $200,000 of pretax amounts and $50,000 of after-tax amounts so his account has a basis of $50,000. Charlie separates from service and is entitled to, and requests, a distribution of $100,000. The pretax amount is $80,000 ($100,000 × $200,000 ÷ $250,000). Charlie specifies that $70,000 is to be directly rolled over to the qualified plan maintained by his new employer and that $30,000 is to be paid to Charlie

himself. Because the pretax amount exceeds the amount directly rolled over, the amount directly rolled over to the new plan consists entirely of pretax amounts. The amount paid to Charlie (prior to application of withholding) consists of $10,000 in pretax amounts and $20,000 in after-tax (basis) amounts. Prior to the 60th day after the distribution, Charlie chooses to roll over $12,000 to an IRA. Because the amount rolled over in the 60-day rollover exceeds the remaining pretax amounts, the amount rolled over to the IRA consists of $10,000 of pretax amounts and $2,000 of after-tax amounts.

EXAMPLE: Assume the same facts as above, except that Charlie transfers $82,000 in direct rollovers: $50,000 to the new qualified plan and $32,000 to an IRA. The remaining $18,000 is paid to Charlie. The new qualified plan separately accounts for after-tax contributions. Because the amount rolled over exceeds the pretax amount, the direct rollovers consist of $80,000 in pretax amounts and $2,000 in after-tax (basis) amounts. Charlie may allocate the pretax amounts between the new qualified plan and the IRA prior to the time the direct rollovers are made.

EXAMPLE: Use the same facts as the first example, except assume that the new qualified plan does not separately account for after-tax contributions. In this case, the $2,000 after-tax basis portion cannot be rolled over to the new qualified plan. Thus, the entire $50,000 rolled over to the plan must consist of pretax amounts. The $32,000 rolled over to the IRA consists of $30,000 of pretax amounts and $2,000 of after-tax basis amounts.

EXAMPLE: Assume the same facts as in the first example, except that Charlie makes a direct rollover of $80,000 to a traditional IRA and $20,000 to a Roth IRA. He may allocate the $80,000 that consists entirely of pretax amounts to the traditional IRA so that the $20,000 rolled over to the Roth IRA consists entirely of after-tax amounts.

Note that a plan participant may not simply take a distribution of basis, and leave the rest.

EXAMPLE: Reggy Hastings has a 401(k) with a balance of $100,000, $20,000 of which is basis. He wants to roll over only the $20,000 in basis. If he rolls over only $20,000, however, $4,000 of the $20,000 distribution will be basis.

Rollovers from designated Roth employer accounts can only be made to a Roth IRA or a different designated employer Roth account.

STUDY QUESTION

5. Nontaxable basis in an IRA is created whenever:

    a. A distribution from a single account in an existing plan is rolled over

    b. The rollover is trustee-to-trustee

    c. The participant makes nondeductible contributions to a traditional IRA

    d. The individual's account is subject to 20 percent withholding

¶ 907 REQUIRED MINIMUM DISTRIBUTIONS

General Rules

Starting for the calendar year an individual turns age 70½, an individual who has a traditional IRA (including a SIMPLE IRA and SEP IRA) must begin to take RMDs. The required beginning date for the first year is April 1 of the following calendar year, but after that each annual distribution must be taken by December 31.

EXAMPLE: Burt Weinbahn turns 70½ in 2016. He has until April 1, 2017, to take his first RMD. He then must take his second RMD by December 31, 2017. After that, he must withdraw his RMD by December 31 of each year, through the year he dies. If he has not already done so, his heirs will have to take the last RMD in the year of Burt's death.

COMMENT: There's something to be said about taking the first RMD by December 31 in the year the owner turns age 70½ rather than the following year. That way, the owner will not be pushed up into a higher tax bracket due to taking two RMDs in the same tax year.

The amount of the required minimum distribution is the account balance at the end of the previous year divided by the owner's life expectancy, as determined using the IRS's "Uniform Lifetime Table." A separate table is used if the sole beneficiary is the owner's spouse who is 10 or more years younger than the owner.

An individual's year-end account balance on which RMDs are calculated includes all of the individual's traditional IRA balances added together. Distributions may come out of any one of them, or any combination of them, but the total amount is based on all of them.

EXAMPLE: Jason Connelly, age 71 in 2016, has two traditional IRA accounts, one with a $50,000 balance and one with a $100,000 balance as of December 31, 2015. Jason's RMD for 2016 for his IRAs is based on an account balance of $150,000. If his RMD for 2016 is $10,000, the amount can be taken from either one of the accounts or a combination of both.

Employer plans. The rules are similar for employer defined contribution plans, including profit-sharing, 401(k), 403(b), and 457(b) plans, except that if the individual is still working at age 70½, the required beginning date is postponed until the April 1 after the year of retirement. An individual's employer plans are not aggregated the way an individual's IRAs are, with the exception 403(b) tax-sheltered annuity accounts. An individual may total the RMDs for all of the individual's 403(b) accounts and then take RMDs from any one (or more) of them.

COMMENT: Roth IRAs are not subject to RMDs during the employee's life, but designated Roth 401(k)s, 403(b)s, and 457(b) plans are. It makes a lot of sense to roll over designated Roth accounts to a Roth IRA at the first opportunity (usually upon terminating employment).

The problem with RMDs. Required minimum distributions are designed to ensure that tax-favored retirement plans and accounts are used as intended, i.e., to support workers in retirement, as opposed to passing assets on to the next generation. True, they will add to the tax burden of retirees, but many seniors will be in a lower tax bracket during retirement due to the lack of employment wages and the light taxation of Social Security.

One common problem is that individuals may outlive their retirement savings because they had to accept high distribution amounts in the early part of their retirement. Most individuals do not have the resources to save adequately for retirement, and RMDs make that problem worse.

The problem for wealthier retirees who do not need the cash is that these distributions drive up their gross income unnecessarily each year, and that income that is taxed at ordinary rates. The surplus distributed sums will then reside in taxable investments and potentially generate more unneeded income.

Required Minimum Distributions Not Applied to Roth IRAs

Although no tax is due on distributions from Roth accounts, Roth account holders continue to benefit from the accumulation of tax-free earnings as long as the funds are not withdrawn. Whereas designated Roth accounts held in a 401(k) or other employer-sponsored plans are subject to the RMD rules during the account holder's life, no RMD is required during the life of the Roth IRA holder. (The RMD rules do apply, however, to any Roth account after the death of the holder.)

> **COMMENT:** The Obama Administration, in its FY 2017 budget, has proposed that the same RMD rules apply to Roth IRAs "to support the purpose of the accounts in providing resources for retirement." In addition, the administration reasons that such a rule would close the current loophole that permits Roth accounts within an employer-sponsored plan to be rolled over into Roth IRAs, which currently have no RMD requirement.

Overall, however, the best strategy for avoiding required minimum distributions is to have as much of a retiree's retirement portfolio as possible in Roth IRAs because Roth IRAs are not subject to RMDs for the life of the owner. Taxpayers are free to roll over sums from their traditional IRAs and employer plan accounts as long as the individuals pay tax upon conversions of formerly nontaxed amounts.

> **COMMENT:** Roth contributions are expensive because they offer no tax deduction, and rollovers from traditional IRAs to Roth IRAs are expensive because they are taxed in the year of the rollover at ordinary rates. But funding a Roth is probably worth it for the well-off who will probably be facing the same marginal rates after retirement as before. And the younger the taxpayer, the greater the benefit from a Roth IRA's eventual tax-free distribution.

Required Minimum Distributions: Qualified Charitable Distributions

A fairly beneficial strategy to avoid some of the problems with RMDs is to make qualified charitable distributions to one's favorite charity. These distributions are not taxed to the individual, and they count toward taking RMDs.

> **COMMENT:** Qualified charitable distributions are not eligible for claiming a charitable contribution deduction.

A qualified charitable distribution can be made from traditional or Roth IRAs, but it makes far more sense to take the distribution from a traditional IRA because it is subject to the RMD requirement, and the amount is otherwise a fully taxable distribution. Note that distributions from an ongoing SEP or SIMPLE IRAs do not qualify for this treatment.

> **COMMENT:** The qualified charitable distribution rule was originally enacted as a temporary provision, subject to periodic (and sometimes awkwardly late) extensions by Congress. It has since been made permanent.

An individual making a qualified charitable distribution may exclude up to $100,000 in gross income for the year of distribution. Thus, if an IRA owner maintains multiple IRAs in a tax year, and qualified charitable distributions are made from more than one of these IRAs, the maximum total amount that may be excluded for that year by the IRA owner is $100,000. For married individuals filing a joint return, the limit is $100,000 per individual IRA owner. Although the maximum cap is $100,000, any taxpayer who makes any lesser charitable contribution regularly to any charity can use the amount toward meeting the RMD.

> **EXAMPLE:** Jimmy O'Brien is a taxpayer who gives a total of $2,500 each year to his local church. He can benefit from a direct $2,500 distribution to the church:

his adjusted gross income, which may determine other deductions, is reduced, the exclusion does not depend upon itemizing deductions, and Jimmy may reduce his RMD by that $2,500 amount.

The distribution must be made on or after the date the individual beneficiary of the IRA has reached the age of 70½. Another requirement is that the distribution be made directly by the IRA trustee to an eligible organization.

Required Minimum Distributions: Qualified Longevity Annuity Contracts

In 2014, the IRS introduced a new retirement plan vehicle with which an individual may allocate up to 25 percent of the individual's retirement plan savings to providing lifetime payments beginning no later than age 85. This vehicle is called a *qualified longevity annuity contract* (QLAC). A QLAC may be purchased within a 401(k) plan, 403(b) plan, governmental 457(b) plan, or traditional IRA.

Required minimum distribution relief. Funds allocated to the purchase of a QLAC are not counted for purposes of RMDs until age 85 when payments begin to be made.

> **COMMENT:** The IRS created the QLAC to address the problem of retirees outliving their savings. It helps reduce the RMD burden on retirement savings by temporarily removing assets from the account balances used to determine the amount of required minimum distributions. Because it is an annuity that pays a monthly amount for life to the individual and the individual's beneficiary, it addresses the problem of outliving assets.

QLACs as annuities. Annuity contracts can provide either an immediate or a future stream of income. An annuity such as a QLAC that provides a future stream of income usually provides interest or dividends as well and in that sense doubles as a very conservative investment. Generally, savings annuities that are annuitized at a later date are less expensive than immediate annuities and that is true of QLACs.

Annuities are often sold with features, but QLACs are basic annuities. If the annuitant or the beneficiary does not live until the start date, there is no payout, and the annuity company keeps the premiums. If, however, the annuitant or the annuitant's beneficiary lives until age 120, the company keeps paying each month.

> **COMMENT:** Basic annuities are similar to life insurance and generally provided by the same companies. The main difference between the vehicles is that life insurance is a bet (called a premium) with the insurance company that the owner will die young, whereas annuities are a bet that the owner will die old.

The premiums paid for the QLAC cannot exceed the lesser of $125,000 or 25 percent of the participant's account balance on the date of the payment.

STUDY QUESTION

---

6. A preferable tax strategy is to make qualified charitable distributions from:

    a. An ongoing SEP plan

    b. An ongoing SIMPLE plan

    c. A traditional IRA

    d. A Roth IRA

¶ 908 CONCLUSION

Individuals with multiple retirement plans and accounts must pay particular attention to how the various contribution limits apply across plans and heed the basis allocation rules when taking and rolling over distributions. Multiple plans and accounts provide flexibility when the owner must deal with required minimum distributions.

MODULE 3: NEW CHALLENGES FACING INDIVIDUALS AND TAX-EXEMPT ENTITIES— Chapter 10: Tax Aspects of Charitable Fundraising

¶ 1001 WELCOME

Fundraising is the lifeblood of most charitable organizations. Nonprofit organizations are continually looking for new revenue sources to fund their charitable activities. The tax rules that organizations must follow are numerous and complex.

Most nonprofits have turned to various fundraising activities, which not only lead to opportunities and benefits for the organization, but also introduce complexities that need to be followed. For example, if a charitable organization holds a fundraising event, the organization must provide acknowledgments for all donations received. Further, the donor must have documentation to receive a deduction on his or her tax return. Special rules apply to donations of cars, intellectual property, or benefit (e.g., a dinner or gift) received in return for the donations. Certain fundraising activities, such as advertising in an organization's publication, having gaming at a charity event, or providing travel tours, can lead to a tax on unrelated business income or, worse, revocation of the organization's exempt status.

This chapter explores ways to navigate these federal rules, comply with the reporting requirements, and keep the organization tax-exempt.

¶ 1002 LEARNING OBJECTIVES

Upon completion of this chapter, you will be able to:

- Recognize the minimum contributions that trigger filing requirements for charitable contributions;
- Identify the forms required for timely filing contribution reports to the IRS and associated penalties for failure to substantiate the contributions;
- Recognize ways in which an organization can lose its tax-exempt status; and
- Identify ways in which a tax-exempt organization's revenue is considered unrelated business taxable income.

¶ 1003 INTRODUCTION

The income tax charitable contribution deduction is available to corporations and to individuals who itemize deductions on Schedule A, Form 1040. Any taxpayer who claims a charitable contribution deduction must be prepared to prove that contributions were actually made in the amounts claimed on the taxpayer's tax return. Over the years, the area of charitable contributions has presented many opportunities for tax avoidance and evasion. A great many court decisions have simply addressed the question of whether donations were made and in what amount.

A contemporaneous written acknowledgment (CWA) from the charitable donee is required for a contribution of $250 or more. If donations are made through payroll deductions, each paycheck is a separate payment. Disclosure requirements also apply to donees who provide donors with property or services in exchange for contributions in excess of $75. Also, donors of charitable contributions of cash, checks, or other monetary gifts must retain certain records of the gift, regardless of the amount (Code Sec. 170(f)(17)). There is relief from the requirements for goods and services of insubstantial value.

General recordkeeping requirements may be enhanced by more specific substantiation requirements. For example, a donor is required to maintain reliable written records to establish the value of donated property (money contributions, noncash contributions, property donations greater than $5,000, and donations of cars, boats, and planes). A canceled check is not adequate proof of a charitable contribution of $250 or more.

If the value of a contributed item, or group of items, exceeds $5,000, the donor is required to obtain an appraisal from a qualified appraiser. However, under Code Sec. 170(e)(3), appraisal requirements are less stringent for corporate contributions of inventory for the care of the ill, the needy, or infants.

A donor must file a tax return and itemize deductions to claim a charitable contribution deduction. In addition, IRS Form 8283, *Noncash Charitable Contribution,* must be filed when contributed property exceeds $500 in value. However, C corporations that are not closely held corporations or personal service corporations need not file Form 8283 for any tax year when the corporation's contributions total $5,000 or less. A charitable donee may be required to file Form 8282, *Donee Information Return,* if donated property is disposed of within two years after it is donated.

Penalties are imposed on taxpayers who falsely claim a charitable contribution deduction or who overstate the value of charitable contributions. In addition, charitable donees are subject to a penalty if they fail to comply with the disclosure requirements of Code Sec. 6115 or the *quid pro quo* statement as required by Code Sec. 6115. A *quid pro quo* contribution is a payment that is part contribution and part payment for goods or services received.

¶ 1004 SUBSTANTIATION AND DISCLOSURE REQUIREMENTS

General Rules

Rigorous substantiation and disclosure requirements apply to contributions received that fall into one of the two following categories:

- Contributions of $250 or more; and
- *Quid pro quo* contributions in excess of $75.

These substantiation requirements apply *in addition to* existing recordkeeping requirements for charitable contributions. For example, a donor is still required to maintain reliable written records to establish the value of donated property.

Cash contributions. Donors of charitable contributions of cash, checks, or other monetary gifts must retain certain records of the gift, regardless of the amount. Specifically, the donor must maintain either:

- A bank record; or
- A receipt, letter, or other written communication from the donee indicating the name of the donee organization, the date the contribution was made, and the amount of the contribution.

If these records are not kept for each donation made, then no deduction is allowed for the charitable contribution (Code Sec. 170(f)(17)). This provision more closely aligns the substantiation rules for cash contributions with the substantiation rules for contributing other forms of property to charitable organizations.

PLANNING POINTER: Donating via text message, which has been a popular and convenient way to make charitable donations, will not provide a receipt from the donee organization. However, the IRS may provide specific relief (see IR-2010-12) or accept a cell phone bill that reflects the donation.

CAUTION: A text message campaign may create problems under state charitable solicitation laws.

COMMENT: An IRS spokesperson confirmed to Wolters Kluwer that the substantiation requirement under Code Sec. 170(f)(17) is an either/or proposition: either a bank record or the specified written substantiation will do.

Contributions of $250 or more. A donor will not be allowed to deduct a charitable contribution of $250 or more unless the gift is acknowledged by the charitable donee in writing (Code Sec. 170(f)(8)(A); Reg. § 1.170A-13(f)).

Written acknowledgment. The CWA is required to include:

- The name of the organization;
- The amount of cash and a description, but not the value, of any property contributed;
- Whether the donee organization provided any goods or services in consideration for property contributed; and
- A description and good-faith estimate of the value of any goods or services provided to the taxpayer in exchange for a contribution.

If the goods and services provided in exchange consist solely of intangible religious benefits, a statement is needed to that effect (Reg. § 1.170A-13(f)(2)).

The CWA is not required to list either the donor's Social Security number or tax identification number.

There are no IRS forms for the acknowledgment. Letters, postcards, or computer-generated forms with the proper information are acceptable. An organization can provide either a paper copy of the CWA to the donor, or provide the acknowledgment electronically, such as by an e-mail addressed to the donor (preamble to T.D. 8690).

Contemporaneous requirement. The donor must obtain a CWA from the donee organization. A *contemporaneous acknowledgment* is one that the donor has obtained by the time that the donor's income tax return for the year of the contribution is actually filed or the due date, whichever is earlier (Code Sec. 170(f)(8)(C); Reg. § 1.170A-13(f)(3)). Consequently, a taxpayer may not file an amended income tax return to claim a charitable contribution deduction if the taxpayer obtained the written acknowledgment for the contribution after timely filing the original return (preamble to T.D. 8690).

EXAMPLE: Joanne Redgrave makes a contribution of $300 to her church. In return for the contribution, she is admitted to a memorial service in the church. The written acknowledgment that Joanne requires in order to deduct her contribution should state that she received only intangible religious benefits in return for her contribution. It need not describe the intangible religious benefit or provide an estimate of its value.

It is the donor's responsibility to request substantiation from the charity.

Some corporations have programs under which they "match" charitable contributions made by their employees. A letter sent by the charitable organization to the corporation that notifies the corporation of the employee's gift and thanks the corporation in advance for the gift that it expects to receive is not considered a contemporaneous written acknowledgment (preamble to T.D. 8690).

Separate payments not aggregated. Separate contributions of less than $250 each are not aggregated to determine whether a donor has reached the $250 threshold in a tax year. A donee organization that receives more than one $250 contribution from a donor in a tax year may use a single written acknowledgment to substantiate the multiple contributions (Reg. § 1.170A-13(f)(1)).

Charity's Form 990 cannot serve as acknowledgment. The IRS Office of the Chief Counsel has determined that a taxpayer could not satisfy the contemporaneous written acknowledgment requirement of a contribution to a charity by reference to the charity's Form 990, *Return of Organization Exempt From Taxation* (Chief Counsel Advice 201120022). The chief counsel explained that the IRS has not identified Form 990 or any other form for charities that would serve to satisfy the requirement for a contemporaneous written acknowledgment.

In this situation, the taxpayer failed to obtain a contemporaneous written acknowledgment from the charity for his contribution. The taxpayer sought to satisfy the contemporary written acknowledgment requirement by identifying the contribution in the charity's Form 990.

The *Omnibus Budget Reconciliation Act of 1993* provided that charities do not have to substantiate donations if, under regulations, they report directly to the IRS the information required in a contemporaneous written acknowledgment. However, the chief counsel found that the IRS has not issued regulations nor identified any forms for charities to use for this purpose. Consequently, a taxpayer cannot satisfy the contemporaneous written acknowledgment requirement by reference to Form 990, or any other form, the chief counsel concluded.

Donations of Motor Vehicles, Boats, and Airplanes

A charitable deduction under Code Sec. 170(a) is denied to any taxpayer that fails to obtain a CWA for any "qualified vehicle" donation if the claimed value of the vehicle exceeds $500 (Code Sec. 170(f)(12)(A)).

> **COMMENT:** Much of the past abuse involved taxpayers equating "Blue Book" value with fair market value (FMV).

> **COMMENT:** Once the claimed value of the vehicle donation exceeds $500, these substantiation requirements supplant the substantiation requirements of Code Sec. 170(f)(8), which apply to contributions with claimed values of $250 or more.

For this purpose, a qualified vehicle includes any:

- Motor vehicle that is manufactured primarily for use on public streets, roads, or highways;
- Boat; or
- Airplane (Code Sec. 170(f)(12)(E)).

The term "qualified vehicle" does not include any inventory property.

> **CAUTION:** The substantiation provision bifurcates the tax treatment based on whether the donee organization merely sells the donated vehicle or uses the vehicle in support of its exempt purposes.

If the donee organization sells the qualified vehicle without any significant intervening use or material improvement, the maximum deduction the taxpayer will be allowed under Code Sec. 170(a) will be equal to the gross proceeds received by the donee organization from the sale of that qualified vehicle (Code Sec. 170(f)(12)(A)(ii)).

Significant intervening use depends on the nature, extent, frequency, and duration of the use. *Incidental use* does not rise to the level of significant intervening use. *Material improvement* contemplates major repair or improvement to the vehicle. Routine mainte- nance, minor repairs, such as removing dents and scratches, and cleaning are not material improvements. The rules also prevent an end-run around the sale price rule by a donor's contributing cash to have significant repairs made to enable an inflated FMV rather than sales price to be deducted.

> **COMMENT:** The Conference Report to the *American Jobs Creation Act of 2004* (P.L. 108-357) gives an example of significant intervening use. An organiza- tion delivering meals that uses a car for 10,000 miles would likely be considered significant, but the use of the vehicle for one week or several hundred miles would generally not be significant.

A taxpayer's deduction is also not limited to gross proceeds if the charity sells the vehicle to a needy individual at a price significantly below FMV or gives the vehicle to a needy individual. The sale or gift must be made to help a poor and distressed or underprivileged individual in need of transportation. However, the charity must actually transfer the vehicle to the needy person to have this rule apply. The organization cannot sell the vehicle and give the proceeds of the sale to the needy individual (Notice 2005-44).

The IRS has accused some charities of trying to use an incorrect interpretation of law to circumvent the rules to stop abuses in vehicle donations (IR-2005-145). The charities have been claiming that a vehicle sold at auction is sold to a needy individual for below FMV when the vehicle will (or "may" in some cases) someday be transferred to a needy individual. As a result, taxpayers are told to calculate FMV themselves rather than use the depressed auction price at which the vehicle is sold.

> **COMMENT:** Regardless of whether a needy individual eventually uses the vehicle, the IRS warned that a sale at auction sets the FMV. The charity's gross proceeds from the auction must be used in taking the charitable deduction.

> **PLANNING POINTER:** The deduction limitations on vehicles (as well as boats and planes) add a level of uncertainty to tax planning because taxpayers will not know the value of their donation until they learn what the charity does with it. The charity could sell the vehicle, use it in its charitable work, fix it up and then sell it, or sell or give it to a needy person. Each scenario affects the value of the donation differently.

> **EXAMPLE:** Alice McCaffrey decides to donate her old car to a local charity. She looks up the vehicle's Blue Book value and, based on its condition, believes her car is worth $1,800. Alice donates her vehicle to the charity on October 1, 2016. On December 1, 2016, the charity sells her vehicle for $900. Under the rules in effect prior to the *American Jobs Creation Act of 2004,* Alice would have claimed a $1,800 deduction. In 2016 Alice's deduction is limited to the gross proceeds received by the charity from the sale of her vehicle: $900.

> **EXAMPLE:** A charity delivers meals to needy individuals. Anna Marie Donello donates her old truck to the charity. The charity uses Anna Marie's truck to deliver meals to needy individuals daily for 12 months. This use is significant and substantially furthers a regularly conducted activity of the charity. It is a significant intervening use. Anna Marie's deduction is the FMV of her vehicle.

A taxpayer is required to submit the acknowledgment with the taxpayer's return that includes the deduction (Code Sec. 170(f)(12)(A)(i)). In addition, the donee organi- zation is also required to provide the IRS with a copy of the acknowledgment (Code Sec. 170(f)(12)(D)). The IRS is authorized to issue regulations as necessary to exempt donee organizations from two limitations in situations when sales of the qualified vehicles are in direct furtherance of the organization's charitable purpose. The limitations from which a donee organization could be exempted include:

- The limitation on the donor's deduction not exceeding the gross proceeds that the organization receives from selling the qualified vehicle; and
- When the organization retains the vehicle, the requirement of certification that the vehicle will not be transferred in exchange for money, property, or services prior to completion of the intended use or improvement.

COMMENT: The IRS has released two publications addressing the donation of a motor vehicle to charitable organizations: IRS Pub. 4302, "A Charity's Guide to Car Donations," and IRS Pub. 4303, "A Donor's Guide to Car Donations." The publications aim to educate donors and charities about the rules for donating cars and consequences for breaking those rules. IRS Pub. 4303 puts donors on notice that FMV and not Blue Book value will determine the size of the deduction. "A used car guide may be a good starting point . . . but you should exercise caution. The IRS will only allow a deduction for the FMV of the car, which may be substantially less than the Blue Book value."

COMMENT: A donor should document all of the factors used in calculating FMV, such as condition, mileage, marketability, and comparable sales. Maintenance records, verifiable photographs, vehicle inspection receipts, and the like can help in the inevitable negotiations. The IRS has emphasized that the burden of proving value is entirely on the donor.

Acknowledgment. To be considered contemporaneous, the written acknowledgment must be provided to the donor by the donee organization within 30 days of:

- The contribution of the qualified vehicle; or
- The date of sale of the qualified vehicle by the donee organization if it sells the vehicle without any significant intervening use or material improvement.

The acknowledgment must contain the name and taxpayer identification number of the donor and the vehicle identification (or similar) number (Code Sec. 170(f)(12)(B)). For a car, the vehicle identification number is 17 alphanumeric characters in length. For a boat, the hull identification number is 12 characters in length and is usually located on the starboard transom. For an airplane, the aircraft identification number is 6 alphanumeric characters in length and is located on the tail of a U.S. aircraft.

The acknowledgment must also include:

- If the donee organization sells the qualified vehicle without any significant intervening use or material improvement

  - A certification that the vehicle was sold in an arm's-length transaction between unrelated parties,

  - The gross proceeds of the sale, and

  - A statement that the deductible amount may not exceed the gross proceeds;

or

- If the donee organization retains the qualified vehicle for its usage

  - A certification stating the intended use of the vehicle or any material improvement intended for the vehicle, and the intended duration of such use, and

  - A certification that the vehicle will not be transferred in exchange for money, property, or services prior to completion of the intended use or improvement.

The acknowledgment is required to state whether the donee organization provided any goods or services in consideration of the vehicle. Additionally, the acknowledgment must include a description and good faith estimate of the value of any such goods or services. If the goods or services consist solely of intangible religious benefits, that information should also be included in the acknowledgment. *Intangible religious benefits* include any intangible religious benefit provided by an organization organized exclusively for religious purposes and that generally are not sold in commercial transactions outside the donative context (Code Sec. 170(f)(8)(B)).

If the taxpayer receives a written acknowledgment after filing a tax return for the year of donation, the taxpayer may claim the deduction by filing an amended return after receiving a written acknowledgment from the charity (IR-2005-149).

> **EXAMPLE:** On December 31, 2015, Donelle Washington contributes a Toyota Camry, a qualified vehicle, to Ossent, an organization that is described in Code Sec. 170(c). On January 15, 2016, Ossent sells the qualified vehicle in an arm's-length transaction to an unrelated party without any significant intervening use or material improvement by Ossent. On February 14, 2016, Ossent provides Donelle an acknowledgment that meets the requirements of a CWA under Code Sec. 170(f)(12). Donelle properly claims the deduction allowable under Code Sec. 170(f)(12) in tax year 2015 by attaching the acknowledgment to Form 1040, *Individual Income Tax Return,* that D files by April 15, 2016. To meet its reporting requirements under Code Sec. 170(f)(12)(D), Ossent must report the information contained in the acknowledgment on Copy A of Form 1098-C and file the report with the IRS by February 28, 2017. If Ossent files electronically, the report is due on March 31, 2017.

Form. A donee organization may use Form 1098-C, *Contributions of Motor Vehicles, Boats, and Airplanes,* to provide a CWA to the donor and must use it when reporting the same information to the IRS.

Penalties. A donee organization that knowingly provides a false or fraudulent acknowledgment or that fails to provide a CWA containing the required information within the prescribed timeframe will be penalized for each such act or failure (Code Sec. 6720). Those penalties are as follows:

- If the donee organization sells the qualified vehicle without any significant intervening use or material improvement, the penalty is the greater of

  - The product of the highest rate of tax specified in Code Sec. 1 and the sales price stated on the acknowledgment, or

  - The gross proceeds from the sale of the qualified vehicle;

- For any other qualified vehicle to which Code Sec. 170(f)(12) applies, the penalty is the greater of

  - The product of the highest rate of tax specified in Code Sec. 1 and the claimed value of the vehicle, or

  - $5,000.

STUDY QUESTION

---

1. A contemporaneous written acknowledgment (CWA) for a charitable donation of $250 or more can consist of:

   a. The recipient's Form 990

   b. A description of the property's value tied to the donor's Social Security or tax identification number

   c. An e-mailed acknowledgment to the donor meeting the information requirements of Code Sec. 170 information

   d. A statement attached to the donor's amended income tax return

---

Patents and Other Intellectual Property

The amount of a patent or other intellectual property (other than certain copyrights or inventory) contributed to a charitable organization is limited to the lesser of the taxpayer's basis in the property or the FMV of the property (Code Sec. 170(e)(1)(B)). This limitation applies to contributions of patents, certain copyrights, trademarks, trade names, trade secrets, know-how, certain software, or similar intellectual property or applications or registrations of such property.

Donee income from intellectual property. A donor is also allowed an additional charitable deduction for certain amounts in the year of contribution and in later tax years based on a specified percentage of the qualified donee income received or accrued by the charity from the donated property (Code Sec. 170(m)(3)). *Qualified donee income* is any net income received or accrued to the donee that is allocable to qualified intellectual property. For purposes of this additional deduction, *qualified intellectual property* includes patents, certain copyrights, trademarks, trade name, trade secret, know-how, certain software, or similar intellectual property or applications or registrations of such property but does not include such property donated to a private foundation, other than a private operating foundation or certain other foundations described in Code Sec. 170(b)(1)(E) (Code Sec. 170(m)(9)).

The amount of any additional charitable deduction is calculated as a sliding-scale percentage of qualified donee income received or accrued by the charitable donee that is allocable to the property to the applicable tax year of the donor (Code Sec. 170(m)(1) and Code Sec. 170(m)(7)).

Table 1 summarizes the percentage of the deduction available in the year of donation and subsequent years.

Table 1. Charitable Deduction Allocable to the Property for Donations of Intellectual Property	
Tax Year of Donor Ending on or After Date of Contribution	**Applicable Percentage**
1st	100
2nd	100
3rd	90
4th	80
5th	70
6th	60
7th	50
8th	40
9th	30
10th	20
11th	10
12th	10

The additional charitable deduction is allowed only to the extent that the aggregate of the amounts that are calculated with the sliding scale exceed the amount of the deduction claimed upon the contribution of the patent or intellectual property (Code Sec. 170(m)(2)). If the donor's tax year differs from the donee's tax year, the donor bases its additional charitable deduction on the qualified donee income of the charitable donee allocable to the donee's tax year that ends within the donor's tax year (Code Sec. 170(m)(4)).

CAUTION: The deduction is limited to 12 years and cannot be taken after the donor's 12th tax year ending on or after the date of the contribution, unless regulations are prescribed regarding short tax years (Code Sec. 170(m)(10)(C) and Code Sec. 170(m)(10)(D)).

COMMENT: In describing the apparent conflict of the 12-year limitation under Code Sec. 170(m)(7) and the 10-year limitation under Code Sec. 170(m)(5), a Department of Treasury attorney said, "Generally, the period for additional deductions is limited to 10 years. Each year, there is a deductible percentage of donee income declining from 100 percent in year 1 to 10 percent in year 10. Nevertheless, the table of donor taxable years under Section 170(m)(7) encompasses 12 years. The reason for the 12-year limitation is that that reflects additional time at the beginning and end of the decade to accommodate any lag between taxable years and the anniversary of the contribution. For example, a contribution may occur prior to the first complete taxable year of the donor, and those lead months, so to speak, would count 100 percent as would the first complete taxable year itself. On the other end, the taxable year of the donee organization in which falls the 10th anniversary of the contribution may end before the donor's taxable year end, and in that case, the donor would be allowed an additional 10 percent year at the end of the decade in which to deduct that final amount after that amount had been determined by the donee organization."

The taxpayer is required to inform the donee at the time of the contribution that the taxpayer intends to treat the contribution as a qualified intellectual property contribution (Code Sec. 170(m)(8)(B)).

No charitable deduction is permitted for any revenues or income received or accrued by a charitable donee after:

- The 10-year period beginning on the date of contribution of the property (Code Sec. 170(m)(5)); or

- The expiration of the legal life of the property (Code Sec. 170(m)(6)).

CAUTION: A contribution may end up costing the donor money. This would occur if the valuation of the property is less than the related costs made to ensure that the donee has the resources to further the technology.

Rev. Rul. 2003-28. Guidance from the IRS highlights important conditions and restrictions on charitable contributions that preclude their deductibility (Rev. Rul. 2003-28). The revenue ruling specifically addressed the contribution of a patent, but its fundamental principles are applicable to many other gifts. Especially in situations in which rights can be retained in contributed property, the danger arises that only a partial interest is transferred. Except in limited cases, Code Sec. 170(f)(3) denies a charitable deduction for contributions of partial interests in property.

The ruling considers the following three scenarios:

- Donor contributes a license to use a patent to a university. The donor retains the right to license the patent to others;

- Donor contributes a patent to a university. The university's use of the patent is contingent on the continued employment of a faculty member. If the individual ceases to be a member of the faculty before the patent expires, in 15 years, the patent reverts to the donor. The likelihood that the faculty member will no longer be employed is not so remote as to be negligible; and

- Donor contributes all of its interests in a patent to a university.

¶1004

The university agrees not to sell or license the patent for three years.

COMMENT: In all three scenarios the recipient of the contribution—the university—is a qualifying charity for purposes of the Code Sec. 170(a) charitable deduction.

The donor posed three questions to the IRS:

- Would the contribution of a license to use the patent be deductible if the taxpayer retained any substantial right in the patent?
- Would a condition placed on the contribution preclude deductibility?
- Would license or transfer restrictions on a patent affect deductibility?

The IRS observed that the first scenario is similar to an example in the governing regulations about contributions of motion pictures. For example, if the donor retains the right to reproduce films and exploit the reproductions commercially, the donor has made a partial contribution and cannot deduct it.

COMMENT: An exception to the partial interest ban exists. A deduction is allowed for a contribution not in trust of a partial interest that is an undivided portion of the donor's entire interest.

When a contribution is dependent on performance of a certain act or occurrence of an event, the contribution is generally only deductible if the act or event is so remote as to be negligible. In the second scenario, the contribution is contingent on the faculty member's continued employment for the remaining life of the patent. The IRS noted that the faculty member's continued employment is expressly not so remote as to be negligible. Consequently, the contribution is not deductible.

When a donor places a restriction on the marketability or use of a nonmonetary contribution, the fair market value of the contribution is determined in light of the restriction. Here, the restriction reduces the FMV of the contribution. It is not a restriction that can defeat the transfer itself and, therefore, only reduces the amount of the taxpayer's deduction rather than eliminating it entirely.

STUDY QUESTION

2. The deduction for contribution of intellectual property to a charity:

    a. May be claimed in later years for a percentage of qualified donee income from the property

    b. May be claimed even after the property's legal life expires

    c. May be claimed in most cases for transfers of partial interests by the donor

    d. May not be claimed when a donor places a restriction of use of a nonmonetary contribution

¶ 1005 RECORDKEEPING REQUIREMENTS

General Rules

Charitable contributions of $250 or more and *quid pro quo* contributions exceeding $75 are governed by substantiation and disclosure requirements.

Under these recordkeeping requirements, taxpayers are required to maintain receipts, canceled checks, or other reliable records to support claimed deductions for charitable contributions. Such evidence must show not only that the contribution was made but also that the amount claimed as a deduction was proper. Basically, the regulations (see Reg. § § 1.170A-1 and 1.170A-13) require that a taxpayer have:

- A canceled check;
- A receipt from the donee charitable organization; or
- In the absence of such original proof, some reliable written documentation for each charitable contribution made.

Money contributions. Donors of charitable contributions of cash, checks, or other monetary gifts must retain certain records of the gift, *regardless* of the amount. Specifically, the donor must maintain either:

- A bank record; or
- A receipt, letter, or other written communication from the donee indicating the name of the donee organization, the date the contribution was made, and the amount of the contribution.

If these records are not kept for each donation made, then no deduction is allowed for the charitable contribution (Code Sec. 170(f)(17)). The provision more closely aligns the substantiation rules for cash contributions with the substantiation rules for contributing other property to charitable organizations.

> **PLANNING POINTER:** The substantiation requirement may lead to increased contributions by check or credit card. Charities, including religious organizations, are establishing automatic donation programs online and include the proper documentation and receipts for donors.

> **COMMENT:** The deductibility of other small anonymous cash gifts, such as those to a Salvation Army kettle, has been eliminated.

Noncash contributions. Contributions of noncash property, such as land, antiques, and art objects, pose special problems for valuation and deductions. The main problem concerns the determination of the property's FMV, which is the key to the amount of the charitable contribution deduction that may be taken.

The FMV of noncash property generally is the price for which the property would sell on the open market on the date of contribution. It is the price that would be agreed on between a willing buyer and a willing seller, with neither being required to act and both having reasonable knowledge of the facts.

> **EXAMPLE:** Rebecca Worthington donates used clothing to a church rummage sale. The FMV would be the price that typical buyers actually pay for clothing of its age, condition, style, and use. The amount that buyers actually pay in a retail outlet for new clothing is not an appropriate amount to deduct.

The burden of establishing the FMV of a donated item falls on the taxpayer. In the case of donations of minor items, a taxpayer may be able to estimate the FMV at the time of the gift based on recent sales of similar items. Another possible method is use of replacement cost, i.e., the amount it would cost to replace the donated item on the valuation date. In either case, the taxpayer must take into account the amount of depreciation due to the physical condition and obsolescence of the donated item.

> **PLANNING POINTER:** Other ways donors can meet their responsibility to determine the value of noncash items is by using eBay, Craigslist, or garage sale prices.

In the case of donations of items of significant value, an appraisal may be the best method of establishing the item's FMV. In fact, if the amount of the donated item exceeds $5,000, the taxpayer must obtain a qualified appraisal of the item and attach a summary of the appraisal to the tax return (Reg. § 1.170A-13(c)).

A charitable deduction under Code Sec. 170(a) is denied to any individual, partnership, or corporation that fails to meet specific appraisal and documentation requirements (Code Sec. 170(f)(11)). An exception exists if the taxpayer fails to meet these requirements due to reasonable cause and not because of willful neglect (Code Sec. 170(f)(11)(A)(ii)(II)). For purposes of determining the threshold values for the various reporting requirements, all similar items of noncash property, whether donated to a single donee or multiple donees, shall be aggregated and treated as a single property donation (Code Sec. 170(f)(11)(F)).

Noncash contributions of $5,000 or less. If contributions of property (other than money or publicly traded stock) are made and the claimed value of the property does not exceed $5,000, the taxpayer should obtain and retain a receipt from the donee charitable organization. This receipt must show:

- The name of the donee;
- The date and location of the contribution; and
- A description of the property in detail reasonably sufficient under the circumstances.

Donors who value contributed property at $250 or more should ask the charity to comply with the *Omnibus Budget Reconciliation Act of 1993* (P.L. 103-66) substantiation and disclosure requirements. For *quid pro quo* contributions, the P.L. 103-66 requirements apply when donated property is valued at more than $75. Regardless of whether the P.L. 103-66 requirements apply, donors should maintain reliable written records that they can use later to establish the value of any property that they contribute to charity. When the P.L. 103-66 rules do apply, a charitable donee is not required to estimate the value of the contributed property. However, when the donor receives any goods or services in return in a *quid pro quo* contribution, the P.L. 103-66 acknowledgment should contain a description of those goods and services and a reasonable estimate of their value.

> **EXAMPLE:** Dillinger Larson contributes a painting that he values at $400 to his daughter's school and requests a written acknowledgment from the donee. The acknowledgment should describe the contribution and indicate whether Dillinger received goods or services in return. However, valuation of the donated property is Dillenger's responsibility.

When the property that a taxpayer contributes to charity is valued at less than $250, the P.L. 103-66 rules do not apply (unless a *quid pro quo* contribution is involved). With relatively small gifts, it may sometimes be impractical to obtain a receipt from a charitable donee. This would occur, for example, when the taxpayer leaves property at a charity's unattended drop site. Even for small donations, however, taxpayers should maintain reliable written records with respect to each item of donated property that could be included when the taxpayer claims a charitable deduction for the year.

Reliable written records. A taxpayer must maintain reliable written records to support the amount of the deduction. The burden is on the donor to establish the value of contributed property. The *Omnibus Budget Reconciliation Act of 1993* (P.L. 103-66) substantiation and disclosure rules apply to contributions valued at $250 or more and to *quid pro quo* contributions of more than $75. In *quid pro quo* situations, the donee organization must provide the donor a disclosure statement, including a good faith estimate of goods or services the donor received (Code Sec. 6115(a)(2)).

Factors supporting the reliability of written records include the contemporaneous nature of the written evidence of the contribution, the regularity of the taxpayer's recordkeeping procedures, and, in the case of small money gifts, the existence of such evidence of the donation that would not otherwise qualify as a receipt from the donee (for example, a tag, emblem, button, or other token traditionally associated with the charitable organization).

To be considered "reliable," written records should show the following:

- The name and address of the donee charitable organization;
- The date and location of the donation;
- A description of the donation in reasonable detail, including the value of the property;
- The FMV of the property at the time the contribution was made, the method used in determining the FMV, and, if the valuation was determined by appraisal, a copy of the signed report of the appraiser;
- In the case of ordinary income property (and also capital gain property held for 12 months or less), the cost or other basis of the property;
- If less than the entire interest in the property is donated, the total amount claimed as a deduction for the tax year and for prior tax years and the name of any person other than the donee charitable organization that has actual possession of the property; and
- The terms of any agreement that the taxpayer has entered into that relates to the use, sale, or other disposition of the donation (Reg. § 1.170A-13(b)(2)).

COMMENT: A doorknob hanger or blank receipt from a charity alone generally does not satisfy all the requirements listed above because it is not dated, not specific to the taxpayer, and does not describe the property contributed (see *K.J. Kunkel,* Dec. 60,284(M)).

Property donations in excess of $500. In addition to satisfying the recordkeeping requirement, a taxpayer must comply with the P.L. 103-66 substantiation and disclosure requirements when the value of donated property is $250 or more.

If the deduction for a property donation exceeds $500, the taxpayer must maintain a written record as to:

- The approximate date and manner of acquisition of the property (for example, purchase, inheritance, or gift) or the approximate date of completion if the taxpayer created the property; and
- The cost or other basis of property held for a period of less than 12 months immediately preceding the date on which the contribution was made (Reg. § 1.170A-13(b)(3)).

Individuals, closely held corporations, personal service corporations, partnerships, and S corporations must file Form 8283, *Noncash Charitable Contributions,* if the total claimed value of all contributed property (other than cash) exceeds $500.

For property valued at more than $500, the taxpayer (other than a personal service corporation or closely held C corporation) must include with its return for the tax year in which the contribution is made a written description of the donated property (Code Sec. 170(f)(11)(B)) and such other required information as the IRS may prescribe by regulation (Code Sec. 170(f)(11)(H)).

For property valued at more than $5,000, the taxpayer must include with its return for the tax year in which the contribution is made whatever information about the property and about the qualified appraisal of that property that the IRS prescribes by regulations (Code Sec. 170(f)(11)(C)). If the contributions are valued at $500,000 or more, then the qualified appraisal must be attached to the return when filed (Code Sec. 170(f)(11)(D)).

COMMENT: For property valued at $5,000 or more but less than $500,000, there is no change in the reporting requirements from those currently established under Reg. § 1.170A-13(c), but the door is left open for the IRS to amend this regulation and these reporting requirements.

These substantiation requirements for properties exceeding the $5,000 and $500,000 levels do not apply to donations of:

- Cash;
- Publicly traded securities;
- Inventory; and
- Any qualified vehicles sold by a donee organization without any significant intervening use or material improvement and for which an acknowledgment is provided (Code Sec. 170(f)(11)(A)(ii)(I)).

For partnerships and S corporations, these requirements are applied at the entity level. However, if the entities fail to meet these requirements, the denial of the deduction will be made at the partner and shareholder level (Code Sec. 170(f)(11)(G)).

Donee requirements. For *quid pro quo* contributions of more than $75, donees are obliged to comply with the disclosure requirements of Code Sec. 6115.

In addition, a donee that sells, exchanges, consumes or otherwise disposes of contributed property for consideration may be required to file Form 8282, *Donee Information Return*. Form 8282 must be filed within 125 days of the disposition if the property was valued at more than $500 at the time that it was contributed and if it was disposed of within two years of its original receipt. However, it is not necessary to file Form 8282 if an item is consumed or distributed without consideration in fulfilling the donee's purpose as a tax-exempt organization.

EXAMPLE: A tax-exempt relief organization that uses or distributes contributed medical supplies in aiding disaster victims need not file Form 8282, even though the supplies are consumed or distributed within two years of receipt.

When Form 8282 must be filed, a copy of the form must be provided to the donor. The obligation to file Form 8282 is imposed on an original donee or on successor donee organizations. The two-year period for determining whether a successor donee must file begins on the date that the original (predecessor) charitable donee received the property.

Form 1098-C. A donee organization may use Form 1098-C, *Contributions of Motor Vehicles, Boats, and Airplanes,* to provide a CWA to the donor and must use it when reporting the same information to the IRS. A separate Form 1098-C should be filed for each contribution of a qualified vehicle that has a claimed value of more than $500. A qualified vehicle is any motor vehicle manufactured primarily for use on public streets, roads, and highways; a boat; or an airplane. However, property held by the donor primarily for sale to customers, such as inventory of a car dealer, is not a qualified vehicle.

Charities are required to report vehicle donations to the IRS on Copy A of Form 1098-C. Copy B is given to the donor to attach to the donor's federal tax return. Copy C is for the donor's records, and Copy D is for the charity's records. Charities may use Copies B and C as contemporaneous written acknowledgments.

An acknowledgment is considered contemporaneous if it is provided to the donor no later than 30 days after:

- The sale, if it is an arm's-length sale to a third party; or
- The contribution, if the vehicle is transferred to a needy person for less than FMV or if the charity had to significantly intervene or improve the vehicle.

Donees can also file Form 1098-C electronically but are generally not required to do so. Only an organization that files 250 or more Forms 1098-C during the calendar year is required to file electronically. Donee organizations filing a paper copy must also include Form 1096, *Annual Summary and Transmittal of U.S. Information Returns,* along with Form 1098-C. The donee should check the box on Form 1096 indicating that Form 1098-C is being filed.

> **COMMENT:** One of the main advantages of electronic filing is that the deadline for reporting is extended. If the charitable organization files a paper copy, the report is due by February 28 in the year following the year in which the acknowledgment is provided to the donor. However, if a charitable organization files electronically, the deadline is March 31.

Penalty for Failure to Supply a Written Acknowledgment

Responsibility for providing a written acknowledgment in connection with *quid pro quo* contributions rests with the charity. A penalty of $10 per contribution, up to a maximum of $5,000 with respect to a particular fundraising event or mailing, can be imposed on a charity that fails to provide the required statement (Code Sec. 6714). However, the penalty will be waived if the charity can prove that there was a reasonable cause for its failure to comply with the substantiation requirements.

The general rule that a donor can only deduct the difference between a total payment to charity and the value of any goods or services that the donor receives in exchange applies to all charitable contributions, not just to *quid pro quo* contributions in excess of $75 (Rev. Rul. 67-246).

> **EXAMPLE:** In support of the annual fundraising drive of the Arlington Saves Charity, a local department store agrees to award a sweatshirt to each person who contributes $50 or more to the charity. The retail value of the sweatshirt is $15. Melissa receives one of the sweatshirts because of her contribution of $100 to Arlington Saves. Only $85 of her payment to the charity qualifies as a deductible charitable contribution. In determining the portion of the payment to a charitable organization that is deductible as a charitable contribution in these circumstances, the FMV of any consideration received for the payment from any source must be subtracted from the total payment.

Quid pro Quo Contributions in Excess of $75

The *quid pro quo* is the property or service that a donor receives in exchange for the payment portion to a charity: dinner, tickets to a professional sporting event, a video-tape, etc. The U.S. Supreme Court in **American Bar Endowment** set forth a two-part test for determining whether a payment that is made partly in consideration for goods or services is deductible under Code Sec. 170(a). For a charitable deduction to be allowed, the taxpayer must first intend to make a payment in an amount that exceeds the FMV of the goods or services received in return. Secondly, the taxpayer must actually make a payment in an amount that exceeds FMV (Reg. § 1.170A-1(h)).

When a *quid pro quo* contribution exceeds $75, the charity that receives the payment must provide the donor with a written statement that contains a good faith estimate of the value of goods and services that the charity has provided to the donor (Code Sec. 6115). The statement must also inform a donor that the donor's contribution is deductible only to the extent that the donor's payment exceeds the value of these goods and services. For example, a donor who writes a check for $1,500 to a charity and

¶1005

receives two $350 tickets to a benefit performance of a Broadway musical in return can deduct no more than $800.

PLANNING POINTER: If an exempt organization's website allows a donor to sign up for a fundraising event, the internet solicitation or receipt sent to the donor must show the nondeductible portion of the contribution.

CAUTION: If, due to an internet contribution, an exempt organization then sends a thank you note or asks for an additional contribution, the action may trip a state's solicitation statute.

No written statement is required if the goods provided by the organization are *de minimis*, token goods or services, such as inexpensive lapel pins, a newsletter that is not a "commercial quality publication," or unordered items that are mailed to potential contributors. Also, no written acknowledgment is required if the donor receives nothing but intangible religious benefits, such as admission to a religious ceremony, in exchange for a contribution of less than $250 (Code Sec. 6115(b)).

Tax Court reformulates *quid pro quo* test. The donation of a residence to a volunteer fire department for use and destruction in training was not a deductible charitable contribution because the value of the demolition of the home exceeded its value (*T.R. Rolfs,* Dec. 58,381). The proper test in a *quid pro quo* case was whether the FMV of the contributed property exceeded the FMV of the benefit received by the donor, not whether the value of the donation to the community exceeded the value received by the donor (*American Bar Endowment,* followed; *M.N. Scharf,* Dec. 32,243(M), distinguished).

In *Rolfs,* predonation estimates and a postdestruction building contract indicated the demolition was worth about $10,000, whereas the value of the residence was *de minimis.* The home had been severed from the land, IRS experts established that it was not feasible to move the house or salvage its contents, and the transfer to the firefighters was conditioned on their agreement to use the building only for training exercises that would destroy it quickly. The higher value determined by the taxpayers' appraiser was inaccurate because it was based on the "before and after" method commonly used for valuing easements.

The burden of proof as to the value of the house was not shifted to the IRS. The IRS's *quid pro quo* argument was not a new matter because it did not unfairly surprise or prejudice the taxpayers. Throughout the dispute, the taxpayers regularly cited *Scharf,* which had determined that a fire department's demolition of a donated building did not constitute a *quid pro quo* to the donors sufficient to disallow their charitable contribution deduction.

STUDY QUESTION

---

3. The FMV of noncash contributions such as art objects or used clothing is generally:

    a. The amount that the donor paid to acquire the contributed property

    b. The price for which the property would sell on the open market on the date of contribution

    c. The replacement costs of the property

    d. The donee's estimate of the value of donated property

¶ 1006 EXEMPT STATUS AND COVENTURES

Inurement to Private Individuals

An organization will lose its tax-exempt status if *any part* of the organization's net earnings inure to the benefit of any private shareholder or individual. The term *private shareholder or individual* refers to persons having a personal and private interest in the activities of the organization (Reg. § 1.501(a)-1(c)). Private inurement happens when an insider enters into an arrangement with an organization and receives benefits or something useful or beneficial greater than he or she provides in return. Inurement can be thought of as a subset of private benefit (see IRS Letter Ruling 201044025 and below), with the inappropriate payment to an "insider," someone who can exercise substantial influence over the affairs of an organization. One example of private inurement is the sale of charitable assets to an insider at less than FMV.

In another example, the Tax Court has held that a membership organization did not qualify as tax-exempt because there was an inurement of the organization's net earnings to a professional fundraiser (*United Cancer Council, Inc.,* Dec. 52,348). The contract awarded the fundraiser over 90 percent of the amounts contributed, plus permanent co-ownership of the organization's mailing lists and other controls over the organization's finances. The Tax Court held that such level of control made the fundraiser an insider. However, the appellate court reversed this holding, stating that no matter how unwise it was for the organization to enter into the contract, there was no private inurement because the fundraiser was not an insider (*United Cancer Council, Inc.,* 99-1 ustc ¶ 50,248). The contract was negotiated at arm's length, and the fundraiser had no personal or private interest in the organization and made no capital infusion to the organization; thus it could not be considered an insider.

The term "inurement" does not prohibit payments to stockholders or individuals. Rather, the inurement prohibition of Code Sec. 501(c)(3) is generally directed at payments that are made to shareholders or individuals for purposes other than as *reasonable* compensation for goods or services. The prohibition against private inurement, which has long applied to Code Sec. 501(c)(3) organizations, also applies to civic leagues and social welfare organizations.

The IRS has ruled that, in the case of organizations other than trusts, an organization's exempt status will not be affected if the organization accepts an income-producing asset from a donor and agrees to pay the donor the income from the asset for life or to award the donor a lifetime annuity specifically payable from the asset (Rev. Rul. 69-176). However, in the case of trusts, such payments are not permitted. In addition, see the rules for charitable remainder trusts under Code Sec. 664.

The inurement prohibition is, however, directed at many types of transactions. Examples of prohibited inurement include: the payment of dividends, the payment of unreasonable compensation to insiders, and the transfer of property to insiders for less than FMV.

> **PLANNING POINTER:** To prevent private inurement an organization should:
>
> - Segregate financial duties;
> - Require the signature of more than one financial officer on organization checks; and
> - Adopt a conflict of interest policy.

Private benefit. In addition, no part of a Code Sec. 501(c)(3) organization's net earnings may inure to the benefit of any private shareholder or individual. Thus, private benefit, unlike inurement, does not require an insider. This requirement must be met both in form and operation. It is not clear where the line lies between public and private benefit. Code Sec. 501(c)(3) does not define "private benefit." However, the regulations state that an organization is not organized or operated exclusively for exempt purposes unless it serves a public, rather than a private, interest (Reg. § 1.501(c)(3)-1(d)(1)(ii)).

PLANNING POINTER: If an organization provides more than incidental private benefit, its exempt status can be revoked. This is true even if the private interests served are unrelated to the organization. These rules help ensure that the charity truly serves the public, domestically and internationally.

Thus, an exempt organization's organizational documents must provide for distribution of the entity's assets for exempt purposes upon dissolution (Reg. § 1.501(c)(3)-1(b)(4)). Payments necessary to perform exempt functions, such as administrative expenses, are exempt unless the amounts paid are unreasonable.

EXAMPLE: Outcome is an educational organization the purpose of which is to study history and immigration. Outcome's educational activities include sponsoring lectures and publishing a journal. The focus of Outcome's historical studies is the genealogy of one family, tracing the descent of its present members. Outcome actively solicits for membership only individuals who are members of that one family. Outcome's research is directed toward publishing a history of that family that will document the pedigrees of family members. A major objective of the organization's research is to identify and locate living descendants of that family to enable those descendants to become acquainted with each other. Outcome's educational activities primarily serve the private interests of members of a single family rather than a public interest. Therefore, Outcome is operated for the benefit of private interests in violation of the restriction on private benefit. Based on these facts and circumstances, Outcome is not operated exclusively for exempt purposes and, therefore, is not an organization described in Code Sec. 501(c)(3).

The Tax Court has defined *private benefit* as "nonincidental benefits conferred on disinterested persons that serve private interests" (***American Campaign Academy,*** Dec. 45,704; also see *IRS Technical Instruction Program for Fiscal Year 2001,* Topic H, "Private Benefit Under IRC 501(c)(3)").

A penalty excise tax may be imposed on certain persons who improperly benefit from an excess benefit transaction with an exempt charitable or social welfare organization, as well as managers who know that the transaction is improper.

The IRS has written an article on beauty pageants, which "fulfill the traditional role of promoting the common good and general welfare of the community. Although the scholarships offer various contestants the chance to enhance their education, the opportunities for the winners to represent their communities and the sponsors of the pageants during their reigning year enhances their career aspirations as well as the economic prospects of the participating businesses." The IRS said that this duality—the public benefit coexisting with private benefit—will often defeat a claim for exemption under Code Sec. 501(c)(3), though supporting continued recognition of exempt status under Code Sec. 501(c)(4) (see *IRS Technical Instruction Program for Fiscal Year 2002,* Topic B, "Beauty Pageants: Private Benefit Worth Watching").

Private-purpose prohibition. Regulations clarify application of the Code Sec. 501(c)(3) prohibition against private benefit and the impact of the excess benefit excise tax upon enforcement of the rules (Reg. § 1.501(c)(3)–1(d)(1)(ii)). The regulations describe the interrelationship between sufficient justification to revoke a Code Sec. 501(c)(3) organization's exempt status and cause to impose intermediate sanctions under Code Sec. 4958.

¶1006

COMMENT: The IRS maintains that, through a more explicit explanation of what constitutes a violation and the application of penalties, the regulations will make it easier for tax-exempt organizations and the agency to ensure that Code Sec. 501(c)(3) organizations are operated for their intended purposes. Clearly, however, the rules also appear to place exempt organizations more at risk of losing exempt status because of benefits that may be obtained by disqualified persons.

Under the regulations, an individual's private benefit from a Code Sec. 501(c)(3) organization's transaction may jeopardize the organization's tax-exempt status, regardless of whether the benefits derived are economic or the extent to which the private interest is served. The rules explain that the imposition of the Code Sec. 4958 excess benefit excise taxes on the individual for the violation does not preclude the IRS from revoking tax-exempt status as well. The regulations further explain that each case will be considered on its facts and circumstances to make an individualized determination (Reg. §1.501(c)(3)-1(f)). The IRS provided a list of factors it would be considering, including:

- The size and scope of the organization's regular and ongoing activities that further exempt purposes before and after the excess benefit transaction or transactions occurred;

- The size and scope of the excess benefit transaction or transactions in relation to the size and scope of the organization's regular and ongoing activities that further exempt purposes;

- Whether the organization has been involved in multiple excess benefit transactions with one or per persons;

- Whether the organization has implemented safeguards that are reasonably calculated to prevent future violations; and

- Whether the violation has been corrected, or whether the organization is making a good faith effort to ensure its correction from the individual or individuals deriving the benefit.

"Multiple" in the third factor refers to both repeated instances of the same or substantially similar transactions, regardless of whether they involve the same or different persons and the presence of more than one transaction, and regardless of whether they are the same or substantially similar and involve the same or different persons. Implementation of safeguards will be treated as a factor weighing in favor of continuing to recognize exemption regardless of whether the safeguards are implemented in direct response to an excess benefit transaction or as a general matter of corporate/fiscal management.

COMMENT: In a teleconference, IRS officials stated that:

- The factors are to be considered in combination with each other;

- The factors are not equally weighted;

- The last two factors count extra, if done before the IRS arrives; and

- Correction by itself is not enough.

COMMENT: Some practitioners have complained that the regulations offer nothing but a double set of new restrictions: a noneconomic benefit test and an imprecise facts-and-circumstances determination.

Fundraiser as insider. Can a fundraising agreement be so one-sided that it, in effect, renders the professional fundraiser an insider, giving the fundraiser effective control over the charity? That's what the IRS contended when it retroactively revoked the United Cancer Council's (UCC's) exempt status, and the Tax Court agreed. The Seventh Circuit, however, in a strongly worded rebuke to both the IRS and the Tax

Court, overturned the Tax Court decision (*United Cancer Council, Inc.,* CA-7, 99-1 ustc ¶ 50,248).

> **COMMENT:** This decision allows—at least temporarily—a charity to be assured of its tax exemption despite being used by expensive fundraising organizations. The precedent protects both deductions for donors and the ability of failing charities to try rescuing themselves through aggressive fundraising.

A group of local chapters broke off from the American Cancer Society in 1963 to form the UCC. Its purpose was to emphasize cancer prevention, detection, and treatment rather than basic medical research. It was granted exempt status in 1969. In 1984, the UCC was on the brink of bankruptcy because several of its larger member societies had defected to the American Cancer Society. A committee of the board picked the fundraiser, Watson & Hughey Company (W&H), as the best prospect for raising the funds essential for the UCC's survival.

Another committee of the board was created to negotiate the contract. Because of UCC's perilous financial condition, the committee wanted W&H to front all the expenses of the fundraising campaign, though it would be reimbursed by the UCC as soon as the campaign generated enough donations to cover those expenses. W&H agreed, but demanded in return that it be made the UCC's exclusive fundraiser during the five-year term of the contract, that it be given co-ownership of the list of prospective donors it generated, and that the UCC be prohibited from selling or leasing the list, although it would be free to use it to solicit repeat donations.

The IRS revoked the UCC's exempt status in 1990, retroactively to 1984, when the contract was negotiated. The IRS contended that the retroactive revocation was proper because the organization's net earnings were inuring to the benefit of the professional fundraiser. For example, during the five-year term, approximately 90 percent of the contributions received were paid to W&H for fundraising costs ($26.5 out of $28.8 million).

> **COMMENT:** Although the UCC considered its experience with the fundraiser successful, it did not renew the contract when it expired by its terms in 1989. Instead, it hired another fundraising organization—with disastrous results. The following year, the UCC declared bankruptcy, followed within months by the IRS's retroactive revocation of the council's exempt status. The effect was to make the IRS a major creditor of the UCC in the bankruptcy proceeding. The retroactive revocation did not, however, affect the charitable deduction that donors to the UCC had taken since 1984.

The term "any private shareholder or individual" in the inurement clause of Code Sec. 501(c)(3) has been interpreted to mean an insider of the charity. None of the IRS's arguments impressed the appellate court. The IRS argued that since the inception of the contract, the UCC had no money to speak of, and because all the expenses of the fundraising campaign were borne by the fundraiser at the beginning, the fundraiser was similar to a founder of the charity. The court said that this has nothing to do with inurement and, pushed to its logical extreme, would deny exemption to any new or small charity that wanted to grow by soliciting donations, because it would have to get the cash to pay for the solicitations from an outside source, logically a fundraising organization.

Additionally, the IRS said, because W&H was the UCC's only fundraiser, the charity was totally at W&H's mercy during the five-year term of the contract-giving the fundraiser effective control of the charity. If W&H stopped its fundraising efforts, according to the IRS, the UCC would be unable to hire another firm until the contract with W&H expired, and thus might be completely cut off from funding. The court made two points with regard to this argument:

- W&H obtained an exclusive contract not in order to control the UCC but because it was taking a risk—the exclusive contract lent assurance that if the venture succeeded, the UCC wouldn't hire other fundraisers to reap where W&H had sown; and

- When a firm is granted an exclusive contract, the law reads into it an obligation that the firm use its best efforts to promote the contract's objectives. If the fundraiser walked away, it would be in breach and the UCC would be free to terminate the contract.

STUDY QUESTION

---

4. Code Sec. 501(c)(3) exempt organizations can prevent private inurement for insiders using all of the following *except*:

   a. Segregating financial duties

   b. Using only outside professional fundraisers for fundraising campaigns

   c. Requiring more than one financial officer to sign the organization's checks

   d. Adopting a conflict of interest policy

Affinity Programs and Member List Exchanges Between Exempt Organizations

Affinity programs—which usually consist of an arrangement between a tax-exempt organization and a service provider that allows the service provider to use the organization's name, logo, and membership list for a fee so that the provider can market services to the organization's members—can be a source of significant revenue. If the arrangement is structured properly, payments may qualify as royalty income not subject to the unrelated business income tax (UBIT).

Under Code Sec. 513(h), the exchanging or renting of member or donor lists between tax-exempt organizations to which deductible contributions can be made is not considered an "unrelated trade or business" for unrelated business income tax purposes.

> **PLANNING POINTER:** If an organization has many affinity programs, it should consider setting up a for-profit subsidiary and have the for-profit employees assist in marketing and providing other services. There would be two separate contracts—one going from the for-profit subsidiary to the service provider and a separate one from the exempt organization that owns the trademark for the right to use the trademark. Another way to structure the arrangement is separate contracts—one a plain, vanilla licensing agreement for the right to use the trademark and the other an agreement to provide certain services. A third way is to make an allocation of income received in the contract.

Cause-related marketing. A possible lucrative source of revenue for an exempt organization can come from cause-related marketing or a commercial coventure. The Foundation Center defines *cause-related marketing* as "the public association of a for-profit company with a nonprofit organization, intended to promote the company's product or service and to raise money for the nonprofit." Commercial coventures are also called *charitable sales promotions* or *charitable advertising campaigns*. The IRS has not issued much guidance on acceptable practices by nonprofits engaged in this area.

PLANNING POINTER: Organizations should consult with their tax advisors before entering into these transactions so that appropriate planning can be done. For example, it is important to allocate payments between royalty and services performed so that unrelated business income can be minimized.

PLANNING POINTER: Agreements between tax-exempt organizations and their cause-related marketers should consider indemnity obligations, compliance with the Internal Revenue Code, state charitable solicitation requirements, and prohibitions against fraudulent advertising.

PLANNING POINTER: New York Attorney General Eric T. Schneiderman has developed best practices guidance to promote transparency in cause-related marketing and to help ensure that consumers are properly informed and that charities receive what they have been promised (**www.charitiesnys.com/ cause_marketing.jsp**). The best practices are designed to increase the quality and consistency of disclosure to consumers, requiring participating companies to:

- Clearly describe the promotion;
- Allow consumers to easily determine the donation amount of any transaction;
- Be transparent about what is not apparent;
- Ensure transparency in social media; and
- Tell the public how much was raised.

Operational test. The law requires that an organization claiming exemption under Code Sec. 501(c)(3) also be operated exclusively for the prescribed exempt purposes. Under the "operational test" of Reg. § 1.501(c)(3)-1(c), an organization is regarded as operated "exclusively for" exempt purposes only if it engages primarily in activities that accomplish one or more of the exempt purposes. As with the "organizational test," an organization is not regarded as exempt "if more than an insubstantial part of its activities is not in furtherance of an exempt purpose." The operational test requires that no private inurement result from the net income of the organization.

Fiscal Sponsorship and Fiscal Agency

The terms *fiscal sponsor* and *fiscal agency* are not defined in the Internal Revenue Code or Treasury regulations. Fiscal sponsorship refers to a relationship in which one tax-exempt organization serves as the official recipient of charitable donations for another organization that is not yet recognized as tax-exempt. Fiscal sponsorship allows the exempt fiscal sponsor to provide financial or other support for the sponsored project, which usually does not have Code Sec. 501(c)(3) status, on the project's behalf. The sponsor accepts responsibility to ensure the funds are properly spent to achieve the project's goals. The sponsored organization usually looks for a fiscal sponsor that has a similar or consistent mission.

A fiscal agency refers to an arrangement with an established charity to act as the legal agent for a project. Fiscal agency generally involves one entity (the fiscal agent) acting as the legal agent of another entity (the principal). Thus, a fiscal agent does not keep the discretion and control that is a required factor of a fiscal sponsorship. A fiscal agent is not a fiscal sponsor. In a fiscal agency the Code Sec. 501(c)(3) fiscal agent must further the charitable and other tax-exempt purposes of the principal.

To maintain tax-exempt status under Code Sec. 501(c)(3), an organization must:

- Limit distributions to only those projects that further the organization's charitable purposes;
- Retain control and discretion as to the use of its funds; and
- Maintain records establishing that funds were used only for Code Sec. 501(c)(3) purposes (Rev. Rul. 68-489).

STUDY QUESTION

5. Marketing uses of a tax-exempt organization's membership list for a fee by a service provider is an example of:

    a. An affinity program

    b. A commercial coventure

    c. Fiscal sponsorship

    d. Fiscal agency

¶ 1007 UNRELATED BUSINESS INCOME TAX

General Rules

The income of an exempt organization is subject to the tax on unrelated business taxable income (UBTI) imposed by Code Sec. 511, if the income is from a trade or business regularly carried on and that trade or business is not substantially related (aside from the need of the organization for funds or the use it makes of the profits) to the organization's exercise or performance of the purposes of functions on which its exemption is based. Once the organization determines that these conditions exist, it is necessary to determine to what extent the income from the trade or business is subject to tax under Code Sec. 511.

Unless the organization is taxable as a trust, its UBTI is subject to the regular corporate income tax rates. Returns are made on Form 990-T, *Exempt Organization Business Income Tax Return.*

A supplemental unemployment benefit trust provided for in Code Sec. 501(c)(17) is included among organizations subject to tax.

The first $1,000 of unrelated business income is not subject to tax (taken as a specific deduction on Form 990-T, line 33).

Definition of *unrelated business income.* The income of an exempt organization is subject to the tax on unrelated business income imposed by Code Sec. 511 only if:

- The income is from a trade or business;

- Regularly carried on by the organization; *and*

- The trade or business is not be substantially related—aside from the need of the organization for funds or the use it makes of the profits—to the organization's exercise or performance of the purposes or functions on which its exemption is based.

A trade or business is "related" to exempt purposes, in the relevant sense, only when the conduct of the business activities has causal relationship to the achievement of exempt purposes (other than through the production of income). The trade or business is "substantially related," for purposes of Code Sec. 513 only if the causal relationship is a substantial one. Often, it can be difficult to distinguish which business activities are related and which are unrelated to an organization's exempt purposes. For the conduct of trade or business from which a particular amount of gross income is derived to be substantially related to purposes for which an exemption is granted, the production or distribution of the goods or the performance of the services from which the gross income is derived must contribute importantly to the accomplishment of those purposes. Whether activities productive of gross income contribute importantly to the accomplishment of any purpose for which an organization is granted an exemption depends in each case upon the facts and circumstances involved (Reg. § 1.513-1(d)(2)).

Definition of *unrelated trade or business*. Code Sec. 513 defines the term *unrelated trade or business* for Internal Revenue Code provisions involving the unrelated trade of business income of tax-exempt organizations. A business is exempt from the UBIT if the business is carried on by volunteers.

Code Sec. 513 defines the term *unrelated trade or business* with regard to tax code provisions involving the unrelated trade or business income of tax-exempt organizations. Code Sec. 512 defines UBTI, and Code Sec. 511 imposes the tax on this unrelated income. This tax is known as the UBIT.

The term *trade or business* has the same meaning as it has in Code Sec. 162(a), relating to trade or business expenses. Trade or business activities are "unrelated" if the activities are:

- Regularly carried on; and
- Not substantially related (aside from the need of the organization for income or funds) to the purpose or function constituting the basis for which the organization was granted exemption under Code Sec. 501 (Reg. § 1.513-1(a)).

> **COMMENT:** Providing goods and services at below-market prices does not make the income related. It is not relevant in determining whether the income from an activity is related to an organization's charitable purpose.

Exclusions from the definition. Code Sec. 513(a) states that the term *unrelated trade or business* does not include any trade or business:

- In which substantially all the work in carrying on the trade or business is performed for the organization without compensation (volunteer exception);
- Carried on by an organization described in Code Sec. 501(c)(3) or by a governmental college or university described in Code Sec. 511(a)(2)(B), primarily for the convenience of its members, students, patients, officers, or employees (convenience exception; Reg. § 1.513-1(c)(2)(ii)); or
- That consists of selling merchandise, substantially all of which has been received by the organization as donations from gifts or contributions (thrift shop exception; Code Sec. 513(a)).

Activities carried on for profit. An activity qualifies as a trade or business only if, among other qualifications, the taxpayer engages in the activity with the intent to make a profit. If an activity carried on for profit is an unrelated trade or business, no part of the trade or business is excluded from this classification merely because it does not result in profit (Code Sec. 513(c)).

> **COMMENT:** However, the IRS has stated that an activity must, at some point, produce a profit to be considered a trade or business.

> **COMMENT:** Startup losses or intermittent losses are probably less likely to attract IRS attention.

> **PLANNING POINTER:** To help protect against an IRS attack on a loss activity, an organization should have a business plan for the activity.

Corporate Sponsorships

Advertising revenue is generally considered unrelated business income. However, the mere acknowledgment or recognition of a corporate contributor does not ordinarily give rise to unrelated business income. Certain qualified sponsorship payments solicited and received by a tax-exempt organization are exempt from the UBIT under Code Sec. 513(i), which operates in addition to the other exceptions regarding UBIT (for example, the exceptions for activities for which substantially all the work is performed by volunteers and for activities that are not regularly carried on). The uncertainty that had existed under the facts and circumstances test used by the IRS prior to 1998 (see, for example, Announcement 92-15) has been reduced through the application of this safe-harbor definition.

> **PLANNING POINTER:** A corporate sponsorship arrangement, if properly structured, provides an exempt organization with tax-free income that is included as public support and gives the corporate sponsor a tax-deductible expense and an opportunity to keep its name in front of the public.

> **COMMENT:** A qualified sponsorship payment does not have to be a charitable deduction to the donor. The payment may be a marketing or other expense.

Definition of *qualified sponsorship payment*. A *qualified sponsorship payment* is a payment to a tax-exempt organization by a payor engaged in a trade or business, provided the payor does not expect any substantial return benefit (Code Sec. 513(i)(2)(A); Reg. §1.513-4(c)). For a payment to qualify as a sponsorship payment, there cannot be any arrangement between the payor and the tax-exempt organization under which the payor will receive any substantial return benefit. The use or acknowledgment of the payor's name, logo, or product lines in connection with the activities of the tax-exempt organization is not considered a substantial benefit in this context, and that use or acknowledgment will not prevent a payment from being a qualified sponsorship payment.

> **EXAMPLE:** Advet Inc., a manufacturer of pet food, contributes $10,000 to a tax-exempt organization that cares for abandoned cats and dogs. In return for the contribution, the tax-exempt organization agrees to include Advet's corporate logo in the published program the organization will distribute at its annual fundraising dinner. Based upon these facts, the $10,000 would not be subject to the UBIT because Advet will not obtain any substantial return benefit for its contribution.

In addition, *substantial return benefit* does not include goods or services that have an insubstantial value. The regulations disregard benefits having a FMV of not more than 2 percent of the payment. In determining whether the 2 percent threshold has been exceeded in any year, all return benefits (other than use or acknowledgment) must be considered. For example, if in exchange for a payment the exempt organization provides both a license and advertising the combined FMV of which does not exceed 2 percent of the total payment, the entire payment (even the portion attributable to the advertising) may be treated as a qualified sponsorship payment, and the entire amount (except any payment in the form of services) constitutes public support under Code Sec. 509 (T.D. 8991; Reg. §1.513-4(c)(2)).

The right to be the only sponsor of an activity—or the only sponsor representing a particular trade, business, or industry—is generally not a substantial return benefit. The portion of any payment attributable to the exclusive sponsorship arrangement, therefore, may be a qualified sponsorship payment. Unless the exempt organization agrees to limit distribution of competing products in connection with the payment, the exempt organization has not entered into an exclusive provider arrangement (Reg. §1.513-4(c)(2)(vi)).

When an exempt organization agrees to perform substantial services in connection with the exclusive provider arrangement, income received by the organization may be includible in UBTI.

> **EXAMPLE:** Assume the University of Iowa enters into a multiyear contract with a sports drink company under which the company will be the exclusive provider of sports drinks for the university's athletic department and concessions. As part of the contract, if the university agrees to perform various services for the company, such as guaranteeing that coaches make promotional appearances on behalf of the company (e.g., attending photo shoots, filmed commercials, and retail store appearances), assisting the company in developing marketing plans, and participating in joint promotional opportunities, then the university's activities are likely to constitute a regularly carried on trade or business. These activities are unlikely to be substantially related to the university's exempt purposes.

Advertising may be subject to UBIT. A qualified sponsorship payment does not include advertising of the payor's products or services. In this context, "advertising" includes messages that contain qualitative or comparative language, price information, an endorsement, or an inducement to purchase, sell, or use the payor's products and services (Code Sec. 513(i)(2)(A)).

> **EXAMPLE:** Assume the same facts as in the Advet pet food example above, except the tax-exempt organization also agrees to include an endorsement of Advet's pet food in its monthly newsletter. The endorsement will state that the tax-exempt organization uses Advet's pet foods exclusively because of the superior quality of the products. Based upon these facts, the $10,000 payment made by Advet would not qualify as a sponsorship payment. However, a portion of the payment might qualify as a sponsorship payment.

Allocation of payments. When a payor makes a single payment to a tax-exempt organization and a portion of the payment would have qualified as a qualified sponsorship payment if it had been made separately, the payment must be allocated between the nonqualified amount and the qualified amount (Reg. § 1.513-4(d)). According to the House Committee Report to the *Taxpayer Relief Act of 1997* (P.L. 105-34), the portion of the payment that is equal to the FMV of the benefit (for example, advertising) provided by the tax-exempt organization is subject to the UBIT (House Committee Report to P.L. 105-34).

> **PLANNING POINTER:** Before signing a sponsorship agreement, the organization should value the benefits and include that valuation allocation in the contract to reduce the risk that the benefits will be valued higher by the IRS.

Contingent payments. A qualified sponsorship payment does not include any payment if the amount of the payment is contingent upon:

- The level of attendance at one or more events;
- Broadcast ratings; or
- Other factors indicating the degree of public exposure to one or more events (Code Sec. 513(i)(2)(B)(i); Reg. § 1.513-4(e)).

The mere fact the payment is based upon the event actually taking place or being broadcast does not necessarily cause the payment to be subject to the UBIT. In addition, the mere distribution or display of the payor's products to the general public at a sponsored event will not necessarily subject a payment to the UBIT. Generally, the display or distribution of the products will not be considered advertising. It does not matter whether the products are given away free or sold at the event (House Committee Report to P.L. 105-34). For example, a soft drink manufacturer that has a sponsorship agreement that calls for the display of its logo on the scoreboard in a college gymnasium may sell its product or distribute free samples at collegiate sporting events.

Acknowledgments or advertising in periodicals. A qualified sponsorship payment does not include any payment that entitles the payor to an acknowledgment or advertising in regularly scheduled and printed material published by or on behalf of the tax-exempt organization. An acknowledgment in the form of displaying a sponsor's name, logo, or slogan is not considered an inducement to purchase and therefore does not return any substantial benefit to the sponsor. Because there is no substantial return benefit to the sponsor, the acknowledgment does not constitute advertising and will not prevent any corresponding payment to the exempt organization from being considered a qualified sponsorship payment. Use or acknowledgment may include:

- Exclusive sponsorship arrangements;
- Logos and slogans that do not contain qualitative or comparative descriptions of the payor's products, services, facilities, or company;
- A list of the payor's locations, telephone numbers, or internet address;
- Value-neutral descriptions, including displays or visual depictions, of the payor's product line or services; and
- The payor's brand or trade names and product or service listings (Reg. § 1.513-4(c)(2)(iv)).

If the publication is related to, and primarily distributed in connection with, a specific event conducted by the tax-exempt organization, the payment may be a qualified sponsorship payment (Code Sec. 513(i)(2)(B)(ii)).

Periodicals may include some forms of electronic publication. The term *periodical* means regularly scheduled and printed material published by or on behalf of the exempt organization that is not related to and primarily distributed in connection with a specific event conducted by the exempt organization. For this purpose, printed material includes material published electronically (Reg. § 1.513-4(b)).

> **EXAMPLE:** Parka Inc., a manufacturer of outdoor clothing, contributes $5,000 to the Save the Wolves Foundation, a tax-exempt organization. In return for the $5,000, an ad for Parka's products will run in the foundation's monthly magazine. Under these facts, no portion of the $5,000 payment could be excluded from the foundation's income subject to UBIT.

> **EXAMPLE:** Assume the same facts except that the $5,000 payment will entitle Parka Inc. to be acknowledged in a publication distributed by the foundation at its annual Wolf Day celebration at Yellowstone National Park. Based on these facts, the $5,000 payment would be considered a qualified sponsorship payment and not subject to UBIT.

> **PLANNING POINTER:** An acknowledgment that states "Buy a Product A" would constitute an advertisement. However, listing an internet address such as "**www.BuyaProductA.com**" is allowed.

Website hyperlinks and banners. Tax analysis of internet issues exists and can easily be applied to the unique features of the internet (see *IRS Technical Instruction Program for Fiscal Year 2002*, Topic I, "Tax-Exempt Organizations and Worldwide Web Fundraising and Advertising on the Internet").

Reg. § 1.513-4(f) contains examples of when sponsorship payments constitute unrelated trade or business. The last two examples relate to whether hyperlinks on an exempt organization's website to a sponsor's website constitute an acknowledgment of the sponsorship or, instead, are an endorsement qualifying as advertising. If the sponsor's website states that the organization endorses the sponsor's product(s), and the organization gave its permission for that endorsement to appear, then the endorsement is advertising, and only that portion of the payment, if any, that the organization can demonstrate exceeds the FMV of the advertising on the sponsor's website is a qualified sponsorship payment. However, if the organization posts on its website a list of its sponsors, hyperlinked to the sponsors' websites, without promoting them or advertising their merchandise, then the list merely constitutes an acknowledgment of the sponsorships, and the entire payments are qualified sponsorship payments that do not constitute income from unrelated business (Reg. § 1.513-4(f)).

Websites frequently contain banners, or areas that contain information separate from the general content of the webpage. These banners can appear anywhere on the page and usually contain information and links to somewhere else. Sometimes that "somewhere else" is another page within the same website. Sometimes the information is a commercial advertisement and the link is to the advertiser's website. According to IRS Letter Ruling 200303062, the sale of banner advertising is not periodical advertising provided the advertising is not a part of an online version of the organization's periodical.

COMMENT: The ruling does not entirely clarify whether the determining factor is if the banner appears on the same webpage as the periodical, or the banner appears within the text of the periodical instead of off to one side of the viewing area, or the advertisement also appears in the print version of the periodical, or the website as a whole is considered to be a periodical (instead of just containing content from the periodical). The actual determination probably depends on the specific facts and individual website design involved.

COMMENT: Using the general unrelated business income standards, it would appear that putting a sponsor's logo on an organization's website would constitute a qualified sponsorship.

PLANNING POINTER: To avoid unrelated business income, it is important for exempt organizations to review links and information on their websites, according to Steven Rutti, Ernst & Young, Phoenix. If an exempt organization allows its taxable entity to link to its website or provides promotional materials about the entity, income the exempt organization receives or is deemed to receive could be unrelated business income. Advertising is unrelated business income, he cautioned; however, qualified sponsorship payments are not taxable. If payments were made based on the number of clicks, these contingent payments could be subject to UBIT. In addition, direct sales from a nonprofit or third-party website could be unrelated business income. The IRS would look to the primary purpose of the sales, reviewing the nature, scope, and motivation of the sale.

Qualified trade show activities. A qualified sponsorship payment does not include any payment made in connection with a qualified convention or trade show activity. The term *qualified convention or trade show activity* is defined by Code Sec. 513(d)(3)(B) and refers to conventions or trade shows conducted by certain tax-exempt organizations that have as one of their purposes the promotion of interest in the products and services of the industry in general or the purpose to educate the attendees regarding new developments or products and services related to the exempt activities of the organization (see Reg. § 1.513-3).

Providing services or other privileges to the sponsor. If, in connection with a sponsorship payment, the tax-exempt organization provides services, facilities, or other privileges to a sponsor or the sponsor's designee, the furnishing of these privileges will not have any bearing on the determination of whether the payment is a qualified sponsorship payment. Examples of privileges the tax-exempt organization might provide include complimentary tickets or receptions for major donors (House Committee Report for P.L. 105-34).

However, the provision of privileges to the sponsor will be evaluated as a separate transaction in determining whether the tax-exempt organization has UBTI from the event. Generally, if the privileges do not provide substantial return benefits or if provision of such privileges is a related business activity, then the payments related to such privileges will not be subject to UBIT.

> **CAUTION:** Encouraging members to "like" a sponsor's Facebook page may be seen as a substantial return benefit.

Sponsor's receipt of a license. When a sponsor receives a license to use an intangible asset of the tax-exempt organization (for example, a logo, trademark, or designation), the receipt of the license will be treated as separate from the qualified sponsorship transaction in determining whether the tax-exempt organization is subject to UBIT (House Committee Report for P.L. 105-34).

STUDY QUESTION

6. A qualified sponsorship payment subject to the unrelated business income tax includes:

- **a.** Contingent payments for events
- **b.** Payments made to the exempt organization to acknowledge a sponsor at a specific event
- **c.** Acknowledgment for the payor in regularly scheduled and printed material of the Code Sec. 501(c)(3)
- **d.** A list of sponsors posted on the exempt organization's website that contains hyperlinks to the sponsors' websites and does not promote any sponsor merchandise

Advertising Revenue from Publications

Under Reg. § 1.513-1, the profits of an exempt organization from the sale of advertising in periodicals, journals, and magazines that the organization publishes are unrelated business income, unless the advertising activities contribute importantly to the accomplishment of an exempt purpose. For instance, advertising income would be related income in the case of a university newspaper that has a purpose of giving students training in journalism.

A unanimous U.S. Supreme Court ruled in *American College of Physicians* (86-1 ustc ¶ 9339), that a medical organization was liable for the UBIT on advertising revenue in its medical journal because the advertising was neither substantially related nor contributed importantly to the organization's educational purposes. The government's argument that the law required either the taxation or the exemption of income from all commercial advertising by exempt professional journals without specific analysis of the circumstances was rejected. The Supreme Court determined that judicial scrutiny in such cases should concentrate upon the conduct of an organization's advertising business rather than upon the quality of the advertisements.

> **PLANNING POINTER:** When a lawyer drafts an advertising agreement, the publishing team should consider confidential information, antitrust laws, retaining content ownership, and distribution of any advertisement.

Advertising revenues as unrelated income. Income from advertising in periodicals is generally deemed to be not substantially related to a publisher's exempt purposes. Reg. § 1.512(a)-1 sets forth rules relating to the UBIT on advertising revenues. Under these rules the amounts realized by an exempt organization from the sale of advertising in its periodical, which contains editorial material related to the accomplishment of its exempt purpose, constitute gross income from an unrelated trade or business activity.

Gross advertising income is all amounts derived from unrelated advertising activities of the periodical (Reg. § 1.512(a)-1(f)(3)(ii)).

Direct advertising costs are those costs directly connected with the sale and publication of advertising (Reg. § 1.512(a)-1(f)(6)(ii)). Expenses, depreciation, and similar items directly related to the advertising business activity are deductible to the extent they meet the requirements of Code Sec. 162 and Code Sec. 167 or other relevant tax code provisions. Thus, salaries of personnel employed full-time in carrying on the advertising activities are directly related to that activity and are deductible in computing unrelated business taxable income. Similarly, depreciation of a building used entirely in the conduct of the advertising activity is deductible. When facilities and personnel are used both to carry on exempt activities and to conduct the unrelated advertising activities, expenses, depreciation, and similar items attributable to such facilities (for example, items of overhead) must be allocated between the two uses on a reasonable basis.

If gross advertising income of an exempt organization periodical exceeds direct advertising costs, items of deduction attributable to the production and distribution of the readership content of the periodical may be deducted from the advertising activity in computing the amount of UBTI derived from the advertising activity to the extent such items exceed the income derived from or attributable to such production and distribution, but only to the extent such items do not result in a loss from such advertising activity.

Excess advertising costs. If direct advertising costs of an exempt organization periodical exceed gross advertising income, the excess costs are deductible in computing the unrelated business income from any unrelated business activity carried on by the organization. However, any excess deductions relating to the circulation of the periodical may not be taken into account in computing the unrelated business income from any trade or business other than advertising. Thus, if the circulation income of the periodical equals or exceeds the readership costs of such periodical, the unrelated business income attributable to the periodical is the excess of the gross advertising income of the periodical over direct advertising costs. However, if the readership costs of the periodical exceed the circulation income of the periodical, the unrelated business taxable income is the excess, if any, of the total income attributable to the periodical over the total periodical costs.

Allocating dues to circulation income. When periodicals are furnished to dues-paying members of the organization without further charge, a portion of the dues may be allocated to the circulation income of the periodical. Reg. § 1.512(a)-1(f)(4) sets forth three factors to be used in making this allocation:

- Subscription price charged to nonmembers;
- Subscription price charged to members; and
- Pro-rata allocation of membership receipts based upon cost.

Membership dues are allocated to circulation income based on total exempt function cost by multiplying membership dues by the following fraction: periodical total costs as the numerator and periodical total costs plus cost of other exempt activities as the denominator. The "cost of other exempt activities" is the total costs or expenses incurred by an organization in connection with its other exempt activities unreduced by any income earned by the organization from those activities (Rev. Rul. 81-101).

Consolidation of periodicals. Reg. § 1.512(a)-1(f)(7) permits the consolidation of two or more periodicals if such periodicals are published for the production of income. Consolidation is allowed when:

- The organization's gross advertising income from the periodical is equal to at least 25 percent of the readership costs of the periodical; and

- The publication of the periodical is an activity engaged in for profit.

Arkansas State Police Ass'n, Inc. A tax-exempt organization that maintained tight control over a magazine that bore its name could not avoid UBTI from advertising revenues simply by funneling the magazine's operations through a publishing contract (*Arkansas State Police Ass'n, Inc.*, CA-8, 2002-1 ustc ¶ 50,269). Although the association had set up its magazine operations to look like a nontaxable royalty arrangement by having a commercial publishing company bear all the costs of producing and distributing the magazine as well as soliciting all the advertising, the association remained too involved in significant aspects of the magazine's publication to escape the UBTI taint.

> **COMMENT:** Emboldened by several affinity-card cases in which exempt organizations were held to have nontaxable royalty income when lending their names to various credit card programs, the taxpayer in *Arkansas* failed to understand the line between passive and active participation. Nevertheless, the earlier Tax Court decision had recognized that it is a fine line to draw and refused to sustain penalties against it.

> **COMMENT:** The taxation of tax-exempt organizations' UBTI was undertaken in order to end abuse when charities conduct commercial enterprises that compete with corporations whose profits are fully taxable. When computing UBTI, all royalties are excluded (see Code Sec. 512(b)(2) and Reg. § 1.512(b)-1(b)).

In the *Arkansas* case, the taxpayer, a nonprofit and tax-exempt state police association, entered into an agreement with a publishing company to publish its magazine three times each year. The publishing company paid the taxpayer an annual fee and a percentage of advertising revenues. The magazine's cover indicated it was the taxpayer's official publication.

> **COMMENT:** Under Code Sec. 513(a), an organization that is otherwise tax-exempt will be taxed on business income from conducting business not related to "the exercise or performance of its charitable, educational, or other purpose." The taxpayer did not contest that the magazine operation was unrelated to its tax-exempt purpose.

On its tax forms, the taxpayer treated the amounts received from the magazine's publication as nontaxable royalty income. The IRS, however, characterized the payments as UBTI and the Tax Court agreed.

The payments were not passive royalty income even if the taxpayer spent small amounts of time working on the magazine. A royalty does exist when A uses B's name for the promotion of A's products. However, unlike the affinity credit card cases relied on by the taxpayer (see *Oregon State University Alumni Ass'n, Inc.*, CA-9, 99-2 ustc ¶ 50,879; *Mississippi State University Alumni, Inc.*, Dec. 52,229(M); and *Sierra Club, Inc.*, CA-9, 96-2 ustc ¶ 50,326), no royalties were involved in the present case because the publishing company used the taxpayer's name to promote the taxpayer instead of to promote itself or its product.

Also, as in *National Collegiate Athletic Ass'n* (Dec. 45,512), the core of the taxpayer's and publishing company's agreement was for the imposition of a duty on the latter for the performance of publishing services on behalf of—and under the control of—the taxpayer. Through its publication of the magazine, the publishing company acted on the taxpayer's behalf for the taxpayer's benefit.

> **COMMENT:** The IRS has not acquiesced in court cases regarding passive income and royalties.

Internet advertising. In determining what on an organization's webpage is advertising, a rough rule of thumb is that if it is an active or passive placard, or a running banner and income is being derived, it is advertising. If the webpage shows merely a displayed link, then it may not be advertising, but only if related to activities or purposes of the organization (*IRS Technical Instruction Program for Fiscal Year 1999,* Topic C, "Internet Service Providers: Exemption Issues Under IRC 501(c)(3) and 501(c)(12)").

STUDY QUESTION

7. Direct advertising costs of an exempt organization's periodical:
    a. Include salaries of full-time advertising personnel for the periodical
    b. Are not deductible if facilities and personnel are used to conduct exempt as well as nonexempt advertising activities
    c. Do not reduce unrelated business income from any of the organization's trade or business other than advertising
    d. Are excluded from calculations of gross advertising income of the periodical

Travel Tours

Tax-exempt organizations increasingly offer travel and tour activities to raise funds to carry out their tax-exempt missions. However, if the tour is not substantially related to tax-exempt purposes, the income will be classified as UBTI, and the organization may be subject to income tax. But whether a travel tour makes an important contribution to an organization's tax-exempt purpose depends upon the particular facts and circumstances in each case. IRS regulations explain when a tax-exempt organization's travel and tour activities are substantially related to its tax-exempt purposes (Reg. § 1.513-7). Further, the regulations explicitly state that the fragmentation rule in Code Sec. 513(c) and Reg. § 1.513-1(b) applies to travel tours (Reg. § 1.513-7(a)).

Facts and circumstances test. The final regulations follow the general facts and circumstances approach of the proposed regulations issued in 1998, despite requests by some practitioners for specific standards. The IRS said that no one set of factors could be sufficiently comprehensive to deal with the variety of exempt organizations subject to the travel tour regulations. However, the final regulations do contain new examples that explain whether educational and noneducational travel tours are related to an organization's exempt purposes (Reg. § 1.513-7(a)).

> **EXAMPLE:** Discover Antiquity, an ancient history organization offers expeditions to archaeological sites featured in a foreign national museum. On the trip, tours of the site are conducted by the organization's archaeologists. Participants receive educational materials, including the layout of the sites and descriptions of the research and discoveries. The IRS says this is not an unrelated trade or business.

Tour development, promotion, and operation. Under the regulations, new relevant facts and circumstances include, but are not limited to, how a travel tour is developed, promoted, and operated. The regulations include new examples that illustrate the relevance of these factors (Reg. § 1.513-7(b)).

¶1007

EXAMPLE: A performing arts educational organization offers trips to major cities, providing tickets to evening plays, concerts, and dance programs. The promotional materials describe sightseeing and opportunities to socialize. No educational materials are prepared. The final regulations say that the tour does not "contribute importantly" to the organization's educational purpose.

Related activity hours. Some practitioners were concerned that the IRS did not specify how many hours of related tax-exempt activities must be offered in a travel tour. The final regulations provide that the number of hours spent on any tax-exempt related activity is only one factor in determining relatedness of the tour as a whole to an organization's exempt purposes. In addition, the hours during which the activity normally would be conducted must also be taken into account.

EXAMPLE: Healthy Avians, an environmental research organization, conducts a long-term study of the effect of pesticides and fertilizer on birds. Nonscientists are invited to collect data during the same hours as, and under the supervision of, the organization's biologist. Rustic accommodations with few amenities are provided to the group. Promotional materials describe the work schedule. The IRS says that this activity is substantially related to the organization's purpose (Reg. § 1.513-7(b), Example 5).

Tour industry concerned. Tour industry representatives asked that the final regulations include provisions that prevent tax-exempt organizations from unfairly competing with taxable travel businesses. The IRS refused to do this, pointing out that the proper test is the tour's substantial relatedness to an organization's exempt purposes, not the presence or absence of unfair competition.

No specific recordkeeping requirements are provided, aside from what is required of every Code Sec. 501(a) exempt organization (e.g., Code Secs. 6001 and 6033). However, it is clear that contemporaneous documentation demonstrating how an organization develops, promotes, and operates each travel tour it sponsors will greatly increase the likelihood of that activity being determined to be substantially related to the organization's exempt purposes.

Volunteer Labor

A business is exempt from the UBIT if substantially all of the work in carrying on the business is performed by volunteers (Code Sec. 513(a)(1)). The regulations do not specify a particular percentage as satisfying the substantially all requirement exception. However, the term "substantially all" is found elsewhere in the Internal Revenue Code and has been interpreted to be 85 percent or more (*IRS Technical Instruction Program for Fiscal Year 1996*, Topic D, "Update on Gaming Activities").

This exception applies to the following activities performed for the organization without compensation:

- A retail store operated by a tax-exempt orphanage open to the general public when substantially all the work is performed by unpaid individuals (Reg. § 1.513-1(e));

- A weekly public dance held by a volunteer fire department with substantially all volunteer labor (Rev. Rul. 74-361);

- A thrift shop when substantially all labor is uncompensated (Rev. Rul. 80-106); and

- Bar and catering services offered to the general public by volunteers at the organization's banquet facility (IRS Letter Ruling 9605001).

The term "compensation" has broad application. For example, when free drinks are provided to volunteer collectors and cashiers in connection with a bingo game, the exemption for volunteer labor is denied because the drinks are considered compensation. Also, payment to a volunteer of an hourly rate with deductions for taxes constitutes compensation rather than a reimbursement for expenses.

Compensation also includes any tips the workers may receive from patrons at a gaming session. Many local jurisdictions strictly prohibit tipping at gaming functions. If tipping is allowed, the exception for volunteer labor does not apply. If tips are prohibited by the local jurisdiction and the organization is conducting bingo and the workers receive tips, the exception for certain bingo games may be inapplicable.

> **CAUTION:** Organizations should be careful not to unintentionally convert their volunteers to employees. This could occur, for example, if an organization gave a volunteer a $500 gift card, which is taxable compensation, according to Peter Lorenzetti, IRS, EO Area Manager, NY, speaking at an AICPA Not-For-Profit Industry Conference. There is no such thing as a *de minimis* gift card amount, he said. However, a "thank you" dinner would be allowed without affecting the exempt status.

> **COMMENT:** The *Volunteer Protection Act of 1997* (P.L. 105-19) provides limited protections to volunteers, nonprofit organizations, and governmental entities in lawsuits based on the activities of volunteers. The stated purpose of the act is to promote the interests of social service program beneficiaries and taxpayers and to sustain the availability of programs, nonprofit organizations, and governmental entities that depend on volunteer contributions by reforming the laws to provide certain protections from liability abuses related to volunteers serving nonprofit organizations and governmental entities.

STUDY QUESTION

8. Which of the following is ***not*** a factor in determining whether a travel tour creates UBTI by an exempt organization?

   a. The number of tour hours spent on a tax-exempt related activity

   b. The extent to which the tour's development, promotion, and operation reflect the educational purpose of the organization

   c. Facts and circumstances of whether the tour is substantially related to the organization's exempt purposes

   d. Special recordkeeping requirements to substantiate the relatedness to the exempt purpose

¶ 1008 GAMING

General Rules

A common misconception is that the conduct of gaming by an exempt organization is a charitable activity. There is nothing inherently charitable about gaming. The conduct of gaming is no different than the conduct of any other trade or business carried on for profit. The fact that an organization may use the proceeds from its gaming to pay for the expenses associated with the conduct of its charitable programs will not make the gaming a charitable activity (IRS Pub. 3079, "Gaming Publication for Tax-Exempt Organizations"). Organizations can conduct activities such as gaming as long as the activities are not substantial in relation to the organizations' exempt function activity.

COMMENT: It is a common misconception that proceeds from gaming that further an organization's charitable purpose is a charitable activity. Gaming does not further the exempt purpose of most organizations. The conduct of an activity, not the proceeds raised, has to further the organization's exempt purpose.

The term *gaming* includes activities such as:

- Bingo;
- Beano;
- Lotteries;
- Pull-tabs;
- Pari-mutuel betting;
- Calcutta wagering;
- Pickle jars;
- Punch boards;
- Raffles;
- Scratch-offs;
- Texas Hold-Em Poker and other card games;
- Tip boards;
- Tip jars; and
- Certain video games.

COMMENT: Pull-tab gaming includes games in which an individual places a wager by purchasing preprinted cards that are covered with pull-tabs. Winners are revealed when the individual pulls back the sealed tabs on the front of the card and compares the patterns under the tabs with the winning patterns preprinted on the back of the card. Included in the definition of pull-tabs are "instant bingo," "mini bingo," and other similar scratch-off cards.

PLANNING POINTER: All exempt organizations conducting or sponsoring gaming activities, whether for one night out of the year or throughout the year, whether in their primary place of operation or at remote sites, must be aware of the federal requirements for income tax, employment tax, and excise tax.

PLANNING POINTER: Officers of the exempt organization should:

- Supervise the conduct of the gaming operation;
- Choose the gaming location;
- Review and approve leases;
- Assign multiple persons to the sale of games; and
- Monitor serial numbers of the games.

Code Sec. 501(c)(3) organizations must be organized and operated for charitable purposes listed in the tax code. Therefore, the sole purpose of a Code Sec. 501(c)(3) organization cannot be to conduct charitable gaming. Also, an organization's exemption may be jeopardized when the gaming results in inurement or private benefit to individuals, or when funds from the activity are diverted for private purposes.

Tax-exempt organizations involved in gaming may be subject to UBIT. In addition, to avoid tax problems, records of gross revenue and expenses from the activities must be maintained.

EXAMPLE: A volunteer fire company regularly holds a bingo night that is open to the public to attend. The income from the wagering is not considered unrelated business income because of the volunteer labor exception.

COMMENT: Most states require that an organization be recognized by the IRS as exempt from federal income tax before issuing a license to conduct charitable gaming. Many states limit licenses to organizations recognized under specific subsections for Code Sec. 501(c).

COMMENT: Raffle tickets to be mailed as part of a raffle conducted by a nonprofit organization do not violate the proscription against mailing lottery tickets set forth in *USPS Domestic Mail Manual* 601.12.3 (USPS Customer Support Ruling PS-307 (March 2002)).

Bingo Games

Income derived from bingo games conducted by certain types of "exempt" organizations is not subject to the unrelated business income tax if certain conditions are met (Code Sec. 513(f)). Bingo is a game of chance played with cards that are generally printed with five rows of five squares each. Participants place markers over randomly called numbers on the cards in an attempt to form a preselected pattern such as a horizontal, vertical, or diagonal line, or all four corners. The first participant to form the preselected pattern wins the game.

The term "bingo game" means a game in which:

- The wagers are placed;
- The winners are determined; and
- The distribution of prizes or other property is made, in the presence of all persons placing wagers in the game (Code Sec. 513(f)(2)(A)).

Reg. § 1.513-5 defines bingo and indicates that "no other games of chance (including, but not limited to, keno games, dice games, etc.)" are covered by the exclusion.

Two other crucial requirements must be met so that bingo game income can be excluded from the UBIT. First, the game must be conducted in a state where bingo games are ordinarily not carried out or conducted on a commercial basis. Second, the game must be conducted in a locality where such games are not illegal under either state or local law. The determination of whether bingo games are conducted on a commercial basis is made solely on the basis of the state law where the game is conducted and not on the basis of the laws of other states. Further, it would seem that both of these requirements are met in those states whose laws restrict the operation of bingo games to exempt organizations (see Code Sec. 513(f)(2)(B) and Code Sec. 513(f)(2)(C)). If bingo is expressly prohibited under state or local law, it is immaterial whether state or local officials enforce the law.

It should be noted that Code Sec. 513(f) does not change the existing rules that deal with the qualification of organizations as exempt organizations under the primary activities test. Accordingly, if an organization's principal activity is the operation of bingo games on a business basis, the organization will not be treated as an exempt organization for purposes of the Internal Revenue Code. However, the mere fact that an organization receives most of its funds from bingo games, or the mere fact that its members devote substantial time to the operation of the games, or both, would not jeopardize the organization's tax-exempt status.

EXAMPLE: Church of the Valley, a tax-exempt organization, conducts weekly bingo games in Florida. State and local laws in Florida expressly provide that bingo games may be conducted by tax-exempt organizations, but proceeds are taxable.

Bingo games are not conducted in Florida by any for-profit businesses. Because Church of the Valley's bingo games are not conducted in violation of state or local law and are not the type of activity ordinarily carried out on a commercial basis in Florida, that church's bingo games do not constitute an unrelated trade or business.

> **EXAMPLE:** Rescue Squad X, a tax-exempt organization, conducts weekly bingo games in State M. State M has a statutory provision that prohibits all forms of gaming, including bingo games. However, that law generally is not enforced by state officials against local charitable organizations such as X that conduct bingo games to raise funds. Because gaming is prohibited under state law, the bingo games are illegal, and X's bingo games constitute an unrelated trade or business, regardless of the degree to which the state law is enforced.

STUDY QUESTION

9. Gaming activities held by an exempt organization are ***not*** subject to UBIT if:
   - **a.** Conducting charitable games is the exempt organization's only activity
   - **b.** Only volunteers receiving no form of compensation carry on the activities
   - **c.** Activities are limited to conducting bingo games in a state allowing commercial bingo games
   - **d.** The gaming revenues further the organization's exempt purpose

¶ 1009 CONCLUSION

The charitable fundraising tax rules are abundant and detailed. Shortcuts in the pursuit of revenue are not recommended. It is important for taxpayers and practitioners to understand federal tax laws to comply successfully with all the charitable fundraising rules set forth above. Not following the rules could result in no charitable deduction being allowed to the taxpayer or, more seriously, revocation of an organization's exempt status.

CPE NOTE: When you have completed your study and review of chapters 8-10, which comprise Module 3, you may wish to take the Final Exam for this Module. Go to **CCHGroup.com/PrintCPE** to take this Final Exam online.

¶ 10,100 Answers to Study Questions
¶ 10,101 MODULE 1—CHAPTER 1

1. a. *Correct.* **A foreign estate is not a U.S. person under FATCA, although other estates are.**

b. *Incorrect.* A domestic corporation or partnership is considered a U.S. person under FATCA.

c. *Incorrect.* A domestic trust is considered a U.S. person under FATCA.

d. *Incorrect.* Any domestic entity serving to hold specified foreign financial assets is a specified person.

2. a. *Incorrect.* Under FATCA requirements, unless the account is owned by a bona fide resident of the U.S. territory, it is subject to reporting on Form 8938.

b. *Incorrect.* A currency swap and similar agreements with a foreign counterparty are other specified foreign financial assets.

c. *Correct.* **The stock is not reportable on Form 8938 if a bona fide resident of Guam (a U.S. possession) is the owner.**

d. *Incorrect.* An interest in a foreign entity is reportable on Form 8938 even if the account is not maintained by an FFI.

3. a. *Correct.* **Each spouse includes just half of the value of the jointly owned assets in his or her foreign financial assets for reporting.**

b. *Incorrect.* Each of the owners not married to each other must list the entire value of the jointly owned asset in determining his or her total assets.

c. *Incorrect.* A parent electing to include a child's unearned income by filing Form 8814 lists the jointly owned asset's value on the parent's Form 8938.

d. *Incorrect.* When one spouse is not a specified person, each spouse includes the entire value of the jointly owned asset in determining the total specified foreign financial assets.

4. a. *Incorrect.* The limitations period is extended to six years even for classes of assets that the IRS excepts from the reporting requirements if the assets increase gross income by $5,000 or more.

b. *Incorrect.* The statutory period is extended to six years even when omissions of gross income of more than $5,000 are properly reported.

c. *Correct.* **If the omitted income is less than $5,000, the normal three-year limitations period applies.**

d. *Incorrect.* The duration of the limitations period is extended to six years even when the assets' value is less than the reporting threshold if gross income from the assets increases by at least $5,000.

5. a. *Incorrect.* The maximum fine for tax evasion is $250,000.

b. *Incorrect.* Filing a false return incurs up to a $250,000 fine, which is half as much as the fine for another individual tax violation.

c. *Correct.* **Failure to file an FBAR carries a fine of up to $500,000, double the fine applied to other individual tax law violations.**

d. *Incorrect.* Defrauding the government carries a fine of up to $250,000; the violation's maximum prison term is five years.

6. a. *Incorrect.* Preventing treaty abuse is Action 6 of the project, and an output report was issued regarding the action in September 2014.

b. *Incorrect.* Making dispute resolution mechanisms more effective is Action 14 of the project and is one of the 2015 deliverables.

c. *Incorrect.* Strengthening CFC rules is Action 3 of the project and was one of the 2015 deliverables.

d. *Correct.* **The project seeks to prevent the artificial avoidance of the permanent establishment status.**

¶ 10,102 MODULE 1—CHAPTER 2

1. a. *Correct.* **The initiative focuses on improving taxpayer services, better equipping employees, and achieving better outcomes for business taxpayers.**

b. *Incorrect.* Staffing levels in the LB&I Division has decreased substantially since 2010 for revenue agents trained in domestic and international issues.

c. *Incorrect.* Large business audits have declined by more than 20 percent, whereas the number of taxpayers filing returns has increased.

d. *Incorrect.* The Future State Initiative, under the ConOps system, includes centralized work and issue selection.

2. a. *Incorrect.* The division is moving away from exams that focus on individual large taxpayers.

b. *Incorrect.* IPUs have become an important knowledge management tool of LB&I since December 2014 as an issue framework for agents.

c. *Correct.* **The issue focus is reflected by the use of Issue Practice Groups and International Practice Networks.**

d. *Incorrect.* In FY 2016, offshore compliance and FATCA oversight remain priorities for overseas bank accounts and investments.

3. a. *Incorrect.* The revised structure replaces separate deputy commissioners for International and Operations groups with one deputy commissioner.

b. *Correct.* **Under the new structure, ADCs for International and Compliance Integration functions report to the deputy commissioner.**

c. *Incorrect.* The nine practice areas (PAs) replace industry groups in the revised structure.

d. *Incorrect.* The LB&I Division's reorganization aligns the structure to employ a strategic approach to effective tax administration.

4. a. *Incorrect.* The QEP was involved in examinations prior to initiation of any appeal.

b. *Correct.* **QEP set the foundation for improved communications, but the agents and exam teams retained authority to determine the issues and required documentation.**

c. *Incorrect.* It was the role of the taxpayer to orient the exam team about the taxpayer's business and tax strategies.

d. *Incorrect.* Such disputed issues were addressed in the initial planning meeting to initiate the exam process.

5. a. *Incorrect.* The exam team uses a return survey to evaluate the audit potential and resources through a risk analysis.

b. *Correct.* **A timely response to the** *Notice of Proposed Adjustment* **fosters an early resolution of the examination.**

c. *Incorrect.* The exam team evaluates materiality of tax items, considering qualitative as well as quantitative factors.

d. *Incorrect.* The exam team issues the IDRs for taxpayers to complete but does discuss the information requested with the team before the IDRs are created.

6. a. *Correct.* **In the Fast Track process, the taxpayer, issue team, and Appeals Office all agree to participate and to agree to a mutual resolution of the issue.**

b. *Incorrect.* The taxpayer, not members of the exam team, can contact the Appeals Office for unresolved issues or adjustment notices received.

c. *Incorrect.* Tax Court is not a resort for the IRS when unagreed issues remain after the exam.

d. *Incorrect.* The issue manager oversees the issue and manages one of the technical team managers, and so is already involved in attempts to resolve the issue.

¶ 10,103 MODULE 1—CHAPTER 3

1. a. *Incorrect.* CPEOs are being certified by the IRS.

b. *Correct.* **The CPEO must provide the customer and the IRS with information the customer needs to claim the employment credits.**

c. *Incorrect.* The IRS will quarterly publish and update the list of those certified.

d. *Incorrect.* The IRS has released temporary regulations that describe requirements for qualifying as a CPEO.

2. a. *Incorrect.* IRS personnel who maintain the denial will forward the review request and case file to the OPR.

b. *Correct.* **The applicant has 30 days from the date of the** *Notice of Proposed Denial* **to request a review through the CPEO program office.**

c. *Incorrect.* Although additional documentation may be needed for arguing that certification should be granted, the applicant does not have to submit a replacement application.

d. *Incorrect.* If the application is denied or withdrawn, the $1,000 user fee remains nonrefundable.

3. a. *Incorrect.* An applicant must authorize the IRS to conduct personal and professional background checks and waive confidentiality.

b. *Correct.* **A CPEO cannot be an individual, trust, or disregarded entity.**

c. *Incorrect.* Such knowledge or experience is one of the suitability requirements for CPEOs.

d. *Incorrect.* The CPEO applicant must consent to allow the IRS to disclose such confidential tax information as necessary to the CPEO's customers and others as necessary.

4. a. *Correct.* **In such a case, the financial statements are required for all the applicants and CPEOs in the controlled group.**

b. *Incorrect.* Unless the applicant's financial position is unclear, separate financial statements are not required for the applicant in a controlled group.

c. *Incorrect.* The opinion of the independent CPA auditing the statements must be unmodified.

d. *Incorrect.* The statements of the controlled group must be presented in accordance with GAAP.

5. a. *Incorrect.* Failure to meet the surety bond and any strengthening bond requirements is cause for suspension or revocation of the certification.

b. *Correct.* **The exception to the positive working capital requirements would not be met if there were failure in three or more consecutive fiscal quarters, not just one quarter (assuming the exception's other requirements are also met).**

c. *Incorrect.* The CPEO must meet the independent financial review requirements, including a CPA's unmodified opinion of the CPEO's financial statements.

d. *Incorrect.* Regular reporting is required to both the IRS and CPEO's customers.

6. a. *Correct.* **Each customer must be notified of the suspension or revocation.**

b. *Incorrect.* The CPEO provides supporting information necessary for the customer to claim the credits.

c. *Incorrect.* The agreement is not nullified; however, the CPEO must notify the customer that it may also be liable for taxes or remuneration the CPEO had paid for the former worksite employee.

d. *Incorrect.* The CPEO must provide financial statements and the CPA's opinion to the IRS, not to customers.

¶ 10,104 MODULE 1—CHAPTER 4

1. a. *Incorrect.* Section 1245 property installed in a remodel-refresh project is not taken into account under the safe harbor and is instead separately depreciated.

b. *Incorrect.* Any costs of a remodel-refresh project that qualify for deduction under Section 179 and are deducted by the taxpayer under Code Sec. 179 are excluded from the remodel refresh safe harbor.

c. *Incorrect.* Costs of an initial build-out for a new lessee of a building do not qualify for a safe harbor.

d. *Correct.* **The cost of 15-year qualified leasehold improvement property that is not expensed under Code Sec. 179(f) as qualified real property is included in the cost of the remodel-refresh project that is subject to 25 capitalization and 75 percent deduction.**

2. a. *Incorrect.* Rev. Proc. 2016-29 applies to accounting method changes filed on or after May 5, 2016, in tax years ending on or after September 30, 2015.

b. *Correct.* **The advance consent procedure must be used to change from an impermissible method of computing depreciation to a permissible method (Change #7) if the taxpayer claimed any type of federal tax credit on the property. A similar rule also applies if a taxpayer is filing an accounting method change under the repair regulations to change from capitalizing an asset to depreciating it.**

c. *Incorrect.* The waiver, which was scheduled to apply to changes filed for tax years beginning before January 1, 2015, was extended one year to apply to changes filed for tax years beginning before January 1, 2016.

d. *Incorrect.* Rev. Proc. 2016-29 no longer includes the method change allowing a late GAA election because the deadline for making the election has expired.

3. a. *Incorrect.* Unless Congress passes another extender, bonus depreciation is due to expire after 2019.

b. *Correct.* **The 50 percent rate applies only through 2017 and is reduced by 10 percent each year through 2019.**

c. *Incorrect.* Long production property placed in service in 2020 will continue to qualify for the 30 percent bonus depreciation even though bonus depreciation expires for other types of bonus depreciation property after 2019.

d. *Incorrect.* Such qualified improvement property has been approved for bonus depreciation by the PATH Act amendment of Code Sec. 168(k)(2)(B)(ii).

4. a. *Correct.* **Bonus depreciation may be claimed for specified plants when they are planted or grafted instead of the year that they are placed in service by becoming productive.**

b. *Incorrect.* Plants qualifying for the 50 percent deduction as specified plants must generally have a preproductive period exceeding two years

c. *Incorrect.* Specified plants must be planted or grafted in the United States.

d. *Incorrect.* The election to claim bonus depreciation on specified plants is made annually by taxpayers who qualify as farmers.

5. a. *Correct.* **The PATH Act makes permanent the rule allowing taxpayers to make, change, or revoke the Section 179 expense deduction without IRS consent on an amended return. The rule is not removed.**

b. *Incorrect.* Both the $500,000 dollar limitation and the $2 million investment limitation will be indexed for inflation beginning in 2016.

c. *Incorrect.* The PATH Act makes permanent the rule allowing taxpayers to expense off-the-shelf software (but not databases or similar items).

d. *Incorrect.* The PATH Act allows portable air conditioning and heating units to be expensed as Section 179 property.

6. a. *Incorrect.* Act Sec. 169(d)(3) of the PATH Act allows the election to productions that begin before January 1, 2017.

b. *Correct.* **The act extends the election for four years for most property placed in service through 2019, except for LPP, for which the election extends through 2020.**

c. *Incorrect.* The PATH Act extends the three-year MACRS recovery period for race horse property placed in service before January 1, 2017.

d. *Incorrect.* The PATH Act amendment to Code Sec. 168(e)(3) seven-year recovery period for property placed in service before January 1, 2017.

¶ 10,105 MODULE 2—CHAPTER 5

1. a. *Correct.* **A C or S corporation having assets of $10 million or more must file its Form 1120 or 1120S electronically.**

b. *Incorrect.* All members of a controlled group must file electronically if the aggregated number of its returns exceeds 250 for the tax year.

c. *Incorrect.* Filing requirements for S corporations are determined by their assets; all S corps are required to distribute information from Form 1120S to shareholders regardless

d. *Incorrect.* U.S. partnerships must file Form 1065 electronically if they have more than 100 partners.

2. a. *Correct.* **The maximum six-month extension for filing Form 3520-A remains the same.**

b. *Incorrect.* The previous three-month extension period for the forms is extended to six months under the act.

c. *Incorrect.* The act lengthens the extension period from five months to six.

d. *Incorrect.* The extension period for filing Form 8870 increased from three to six months.

3. a. *Correct.* **Starting with 2016 tax filings, the due date for FBAR is April unless the taxpayer receives an extension to October 15.**

b. *Incorrect.* June 30 was the filing deadline for tax years prior to 2016.

c. *Incorrect.* The filing deadline without an extension is earlier than September 30, 2017.

d. *Incorrect.* The FBAR deadline is earlier in 2017 even with a six-month filing extension.

4. a. *Incorrect.* Annual payments and wages do not have to be reported by January 1 of the following year.

b. *Correct.* **The filing deadline to all recipients for all three forms was accelerated to January 31 under the PATH Act.**

c. *Incorrect.* The February deadline for filing Form 1099-MISC was changed by the PATH Act.

d. *Incorrect.* The filing deadlines for all three forms, which previously were staggered, were made the same under the PATH Act.

5. a. *Correct.* **The extended due date for Form 5500 returned to 2½ months, as that in effect before the Surface Transportation Act changes.**

b. *Incorrect.* For calendar year taxpayers, the extended due date is October 15.

c. *Incorrect.* Both single-employer and multiemployer private pension plans must file Form 5500.

d. *Incorrect.* The plan sponsor is still required to maintain a signed paper copy of Form 5500 in the plan records.

6. a. *Incorrect.* Form 1095-B, not the offer and coverage form, was due to employees by March 31, 2016.

b. *Incorrect.* An earlier deadline applied to providing Form 1095-C to employees.

c. *Correct.* **A May 31 deadline had previously applied to electronic filings. However, the IRS also announced that its ACA Information Returns (AIR) system would remain up and running after the June 30, 2016, deadline.**

d. *Incorrect.* Different deadlines applied to providing the form to employees and to the IRS.

¶ 10,106 MODULE 2—CHAPTER 6

1. a. *Incorrect.* Errors or omissions of any monetary amounts are not inconsequential.

b. *Correct.* **If the payee can report the statement's information properly or put the statement to its proper use, the error is generally considered inconsequential. No misstatement of monetary amounts or the payee's address is inconsequential, nor is use of an inappropriate form for the statement.**

c. *Incorrect.* The payee statement must include information required by any administrative pronouncement, such as revenue rulings and revenue procedures.

d. *Incorrect.* Errors or omissions regarding the payee's surname could prevent the IRS from correlating the information on the statement with the payee's tax return.

2. a. *Incorrect.* The start date of the delinquency period is not limited to when the IRS receives the return.

b. *Incorrect.* A penalty is due only if the taxpayer owes tax at the time the return is due over and above amounts already paid or withheld.

c. *Correct.* **Code Sec. 6072 states this timeframe as the period in which the FTF penalty is imposed.**

d. *Incorrect.* The FTF penalty does not apply to information returns.

3. a. *Incorrect.* Inconsequential errors or omissions may not even be subject to penalties if the information may yet be correlated by the IRS.

b. *Correct.* **Gross understatements are generally subject to a 40 percent penalty, whereas substantial understatements incur a 20 percent penalty.**

c. *Incorrect.* Substantial understatements of income tax generally are not subject to a 40 percent accuracy penalty.

d. *Incorrect.* An argument of a tax position may be considered as nonnegligent if it meets the reasonable basis standard.

4. a. *Incorrect.* Taxpayers commit fraud by treating ordinary income as capital gains, which are taxed at a lower rate.

b. *Correct.* **Fraud often consists of omitting income rather claiming income more than that substantiated by the payor to the IRS.**

c. *Incorrect.* Taxpayers fraudulently claim credits, frequently the earned income tax credit, to which the taxpayers are not entitled.

d. *Incorrect.* Taxpayers commit fraud by claiming more deductions than ones to which they are entitled.

5. a. *Incorrect.* The penalty for an erroneous refund or credit claim does not apply to any portion of the amount subject to the accuracy-related penalty.

b. *Incorrect.* A reasonable claim exempts the taxpayer from the penalty.

c. *Incorrect.* The penalty does not apply if the EITC is the basis of the erroneous claim.

d. *Correct.* **The penalty is imposed if a transaction lacks reasonable basis because an excessive amount claimed arises from a transaction that lacks economic substance.**

6. a. *Incorrect.* Such a delay is a ministerial act by the IRS.

b. *Incorrect.* Shifting priorities in workloads is a ministerial act at the IRS.

c. *Correct.* **A personnel management issue for IRS staff constitutes a managerial act that may abate imposition of interest.**

d. *Incorrect.* Such a delay in handling the audit process is a ministerial act of the IRS.

¶ 10,107 MODULE 2—CHAPTER 7

1. a. *Correct.* **The assessment may be immediate and need not be issued with a notice of deficiency.**

b. *Incorrect.* The IRS is not required to issue a notice of deficiency and treats the underpayment as a mathematical or clerical error.

c. *Incorrect.* The partner in such a case has no right to petition the Tax Court for a redetermination.

d. *Incorrect.* A petition for abatement, which generally is allowed under Code Sec. 6213(b)(2), may not be filed to abate the underpayment.

2. a. *Incorrect.* The principal place of business of the partnership does not affect deductibility of required income tax payments.

b. *Correct.* **Code Sec. 6241(4) states that no deduction is allowed for any payment required to be made by a partnership.**

c. *Incorrect.* Partners are still taxed on their distributive share of income, gain, loss, deductions, or credits.

d. *Incorrect.* A partnership adjustment may occur for an item of income, gain, loss, deduction, or credit and does not determine the required tax payments.

3. a. *Correct.* **The partners are liable for interest on an imputed underpayment as determined at the**

partnership level.

b. *Incorrect.* The partnership may make the alternative election up to 45 days after the date of the adjustment notice.

c. *Incorrect.* Tax attributes must be adjusted for tax years subsequent to the reviewed year.

d. *Incorrect.* The election may be revoked with the IRS's consent.

4. a. *Correct.* **The partnership, not the IRS, files the AAR**.

b. *Incorrect.* The administrative proceeding is initiated for items at the partnership level or for any partner's distributive share of the item.

c. *Incorrect.* The proposed adjustment results from the administrative proceeding.

d. *Incorrect.* The final adjustment is mailed at least 270 days after the mailing of the proposed adjustment.

5. a. *Correct.* **If the partnership petitions the U.S. District Court or Court of Federal Claims, the amount of imputed underpayment must have been deposited with the IRS.**

b. *Incorrect.* The court's determination is treated as a final judgment but may be reviewed.

c. *Incorrect.* The window for filing a petition for readjustment is 90 days.

d. *Incorrect.* The court, not the partners, has the jurisdiction to determine the allocation of the items.

6. a. *Incorrect.* The BBA rules provide that the partnership can pay the full amount of the imputed underpayment under Code Sec. 6225(a).

b. *Correct.* **Partnerships may be more likely to use the Code Sec. 6226 mechanism as the preferred method to avoid double taxation.**

c. *Incorrect.* Under Code Sec. 6225(c)(2), one or more partners can submit payments by means of filing amended tax returns.

d. *Incorrect.* Reviewed year partners can elect to push out the FPA to those partners.

¶ 10,108 MODULE 3—CHAPTER 8

1. a. *Incorrect.* Such acts are subject to penalties enhanced by the *Identity Theft Penalty Enhancement Act,* enacted in 2004.

b. *Correct.* **The 1998** *Identity Theft and Assumption Deterrence Act* **criminalized production and possession of false identification.**

c. *Incorrect.* Stealing someone's Social Security benefits is subject to enhanced penalties under the act.

d. *Incorrect.* The act enhanced the penalty for assuming an individual's identity to violate immigration laws.

2. a. *Incorrect.* This type of fraud is not the focus of the directive, but identity thieves often use victims' SSNs during the crime.

b. *Incorrect.* This type of fraud involves leaving an unpaid income tax bill on the victim's account but is not the subject of Directive 144.

c. *Correct.* **The department's Tax Division advisory board is developing and implementing uniform national policies for fighting stolen identity refund fraud (SIRF) crimes.**

d. *Incorrect.* Ghosting, or assuming the identity of deceased individuals to access their financial records, is not the subject of Directive 144.

3. a. *Correct.* **The https indicates the message comes via the Hypertext Transfer Protocol Secure web source.**

b. *Incorrect.* Such e-mails that seem urgent may indicate a scammer hopes the recipient will be threatened into providing PII.

c. *Incorrect.* Usually such messages indicate that the source is not a legitimate organization requires PII.

d. *Incorrect.* Scammers may be representing themselves as sources, such as the IRS, that do not request PII on the internet.

4. a. *Incorrect.* The TAS is not the issuer of any federal tax refunds.

b. *Incorrect.* The TAS is not the office that rejects returns of SIRF victims

c. *Correct.* **The TAS can help individuals to use a refund trace or delayed refund.**

d. *Incorrect.* The TAS does not process appeals but helps individuals understand IRS actions generally and for identity theft issues.

5. a. *Incorrect.* The fraud alert is a 90-day limitation requiring lenders and creditors to verify an applicant's identity before opening new accounts, revising accounts, or granting credit cards, but the alert does not block access to the report.

b. *Incorrect.* An extended fraud alert is a fraud alert limiting banking and credit account revisions for up to seven years but does not block access to the report.

c. *Correct.* **The security freeze prohibits credit lenders and outside companies from accessing an individual's credit report without his or her consent.**

d. *Incorrect.* The IRS Form 14039 is a report files with the IRS, not credit reporting agencies.

6. a. *Incorrect.* Such a piece of photo identification must be submitted to the IRS with other proof that the taxpayer is a victim of tax identity theft.

b. *Correct.* **A CAP document is not used to respond to an IRS notice or letter of income reporting and tax liability.**

c. *Incorrect.* The IRS form is part of the documentation that reports tax identity theft to the IRS.

d. *Incorrect.* This document, a combination of the FTC *Identity Theft Affidavit* and police report, is submitted to the IRS in response to notice or letters informing an individual of issues with his or her return.

¶ 10,109 MODULE 3—CHAPTER 9

1. a. *Correct.* **In elective deferral arrangements the employee decides whether and how much to contribute, often to reduce current taxable wages.**

b. *Incorrect.* In a money purchase plan the employer is required to contribute a fixed amount annually to employees' accounts.

c. *Incorrect.* Employers fund defined benefit plans, or pensions.

d. *Incorrect.* Employers fund profit-sharing plans as a percentage of employees' compensation, but the percentage contributed annually may vary.

2. a. *Incorrect.* The maximum an employee can defer in 2016 is $15,500 per year (if he or she is at least age 50) for a SIMPLE IRA but $24,000 for a SARSEP plan.

b. *Correct.* **Employers can contribute 100 percent of an employee's compensation up to $53,000 for a SARSEP but only up to 3 percent of compensation for a SEP plan.**

c. *Incorrect.* The opposite applies: employer matching is allowed up to 3 percent for a SIMPLE IRA but not a SARSEP.

d. *Incorrect.* Both plan types allow salary deferrals.

3. a. *Incorrect.* A 403(b) plan participant may be eligible for a separate 15-year catch-up contribution of up to $3,000 annually and a last 3-year catch-up contribution for the 457(b) plan.

b. *Correct.* **The annual deferral limit applies separately to each plan.**

c. *Incorrect.* An individual whose 457(b) plan allows both types of catch-up contributions must choose one (that which allows a larger deferral).

d. *Incorrect.* He or she can defer $18,000 to each plan plus a $6,000 catch-up to each plan, or $48,000 ([$18,000 + $6,000] × 2).

4. a. *Correct.* **This special rule prevents participants from rolling over amounts from a non-SIMPLE plan account into their SIMPLE IRA within two years of starting participation.**

b. *Incorrect.* Rollovers from a Roth IRA can only be made to another Roth account.

c. *Incorrect.* Married spouses can roll over twice in 12 months if one account belongs to each of them.

d. *Incorrect.* Rollovers may be made from IRAs, 401(k) plans, 403(b) plans, and 457(b) plans, but the amounts are subject to taxation when made from non-Roth plans.

5. a. *Incorrect.* If the participant has a single IRA in which he or she has no basis, simply transferring a distribution does not create basis.

b. *Incorrect.* Simply transferring amounts through a trustee does not create basis.

c. *Correct.* **Because the individual takes no current year deduction, the amount of the contribution is basis nontaxable upon later distribution.**

d. *Incorrect.* Withholding 20 percent of the actual distribution does not create basis in the account.

6. a. *Incorrect.* Distributions from an ongoing SEP are ineligible for tax-free distributions that count toward an individual's RMD.

b. *Incorrect.* The individual may not use such amounts as qualified charitable distributions that count toward his or her annual RMD.

c. *Correct.* **Such donations are not taxed as distributions but do count toward meeting the annual RMD.**

d. *Incorrect.* Because no RMD is necessary from a Roth account, the taxpayer should use amounts from that which would be taxed, up to an exclusion of $100,000 for the year.

¶ 10,110 MODULE 3—CHAPTER 10

1. a. *Incorrect.* Chief Counsel Advice 201120022 states that reference to the charity's Form 990 return does not qualify as CWA.

b. *Incorrect.* No SSN or tax ID number is required on the CWA for the contribution.

c. *Correct.* **An e-mail can constitute a CWA as well as can a letter, postcard, or computer-generated form if the donor provides a description and estimated value of goods or services provided.**

d. *Incorrect.* The CWA from the donee must be obtained by the time that the donor's income tax return for the tax year is filed.

2. a. *Correct.* **The additional deduction is allowed in the year of contribution as well as subsequent tax years up to a maximum of 12 years.**

b. *Incorrect.* Code Sec. 170(m)(6) does not permit a charitable deduction after the legal life of the property expires.

c. *Incorrect.* Rev. Rul. 2003-28 disallows a charitable deduction if the donor retains rights in the property or places contingencies on the donation (unless they are negligible).

d. *Incorrect.* The restriction reduces the fair market value (FMV) of the contribution but does not eliminate it altogether.

3. a. *Incorrect.* The original acquisition cost is not used to determine the donation's FMV for the donor's deduction.

b. *Correct.* **Checking the prices of comparable property using eBay, Craigslist, or garage sales may help donors to determine the FMV.**

c. *Incorrect.* The FMV of used property is not comparable to the price the donor would pay to acquire the item currently.

d. *Incorrect.* The donor, not the donee, is responsible for determining the value of the contributed property.

4. a. *Incorrect.* Segregation of financial duties helps to prevent parties from becoming insiders who receive inurement.

b. *Correct.* **As in the *UCC* Tax Court case, professional fundraisers can be considered insiders for private inurement.**

c. *Incorrect.* Requiring multiple signatures helps to keep one officer from awarding benefits to insiders.

d. *Incorrect.* Practicing vigilance over potential conflicts of interest can help prevent insiders from receiving inappropriate financial payments.

5. a. *Correct.* **The arrangement enables a service provider to use the exempt organization's list for payments that constitute royalty income not subject to tax for the Code Sec. 501(c)(3) organization.**

b. *Incorrect.* A commercial coventure or cause-related marketing is intended to promote the for-profit company's products or services through sales promotions or advertising that may be conducted on the exempt organization's website, not just by using a membership list, and income may require allocation between royalties and services performed.

c. *Incorrect.* Fiscal sponsorship entails a Code Sec. 501(c)(3) organization receiving charitable donations for another organization not yet recognized as exempt.

d. *Incorrect.* Fiscal agency arrangements involve an established charity serving as the legal agent for a principal's project for tax-exempt purposes.

6. a. *Correct.* **Payments contingent on attendance levels at events, broadcast rating levels, and degree of public exposure to the event would trigger UBIT.**

b. *Incorrect.* The acknowledgment is not considered advertising subject to UBIT.

c. *Incorrect.* Such displays and acknowledgment offers no substantial return benefit to the sponsor and thus are not subject to UBIT for the exempt organization.

d. *Incorrect.* If the acknowledgments on the exempt organization's site do not endorse sponsors' products or services, the banners or links do not constitute advertising subject to UBIT.

7. a. *Correct.* **The salaries are directly related to carrying on the advertising business activities and deductible for UBIT.**

b. *Incorrect.* In such cases items of expenses are allocated between exempt (untaxed) and nonexempt activities (deductible from UBIT).

c. *Incorrect.* Excess deductions for direct advertising costs of the periodical do not affect the amount of unrelated business income from other activities of the organization.

d. *Incorrect.* If the gross advertising income exceeds the periodical's direct advertising costs, deductions attributable to the readership content may be deducted from the advertising activity.

8. a. *Incorrect.* Reg. § 1.513-7 in the final regulations provides that related activity hours is a factor in whether the tour as a whole relates to the purposes of the organization.

b. *Incorrect.* The final regulations consider how the tour is promoted and conducted as facts and circumstances testing relatedness to the organization's exempt mission.

c. *Incorrect.* Facts and circumstances test whether the tour activities are related to the organization's tax-exempt purposes.

d. *Correct.* **Reg. § 1.513-7 regulations do not include special recordkeeping requirements for the travel tours.**

9. a. *Incorrect.* A Code Sec. 501(c)(3)'s sole purpose cannot be to conduct charitable gaming.

b. *Correct.* **The volunteers may not receive compensation such as tips, gift cards, or free drinks.**

c. *Incorrect.* Bingo games are not subject to UBIT only if they occur in a state where commercial bingo games are not ordinarily conducted.

d. *Incorrect.* The conduct of an activity, not revenues raised, has to further the exempt purpose to exclude the proceeds from UBIT.

Index

References are to paragraph (¶) numbers.

¶ 10,200 Final Exam Instructions

Completing your Final Exam online at **CCHGroup.com/PrintCPE** is the fastest way to earn CPE Credit with immediate results and no Express Grading Fee.

This Final Exam is divided into three Modules. There is a grading fee for each Final Exam submission.

Processing Fee:	Recommended CPE:
$113.94 for Module 1	6 hours for Module 1
$113.94 for Module 2	6 hours for Module 2
$132.93 for Module 3	7 hours for Module 3
$360.81 for all Modules	19 hours for all Modules
IRS Program Number:	**Federal Tax Law Hours:**
4VRWB-T-01812-16-S for Module 1	6 hours for Module 1
4VRWB-T-01813-16-S for Module 2	6 hours for Module 2
4VRWB-T-01814-16-S for Module 3	7 hours for Module 3
	19 hours for all Modules

Instructions for purchasing your CPE Tests and accessing them after purchase are provided on the **CCHGroup.com/PrintCPE** website.

Alternatively, you may scan and submit your completed Final Exam Answer Sheets for each Module by emailing **CPESubmissions@wolterskluwer.com**. Each Final Exam Answer Sheet will be graded and a CPE Certificate of Completion awarded for achieving a grade of 70 percent or greater. The Final Exam Answer Sheets are located at the back of this book. To mail your Final Exam, send your completed Answer Sheets for each Final Exam Module to **Wolters Kluwer Continuing Education Department, 2700 Lake Cook Road, Riverwoods, IL 60015**,

Express Grading: Processing time for your emailed or mailed or faxed Answer Sheet is generally 8-12 business days. To use our Express Grading Service, at an additional $19 per Module, please check the "Express Grading" box on your Answer Sheet and provide your Wolters Kluwer account or credit card number **and your email address**. We will email your results and a Certificate of Completion (upon achieving a passing grade) to you by 5:00 p.m. the business day following our receipt of your Answer Sheet. **If you mail your Answer Sheet for Express Grading, please write "ATTN: CPE OVERNIGHT" on the envelope.** NOTE: We will not Federal Express Final Exam results under any circumstances.

Recommended CPE credit is based on a 50-minute hour. Participants earning credits for states that require self-study to be based on a 100-minute hour will receive 1/2 the CPE credits for successful completion of this course. Because CPE requirements vary from state to state and among different licensing agencies, please contact your CPE governing body for information on your CPE requirements and the applicability of a particular course for your requirements

---

Date of Completion: If you email or mail your Final Exam to us, the date of completion on your Certificate will be the date that you put on your Answer Sheet. However, you must submit your Answer Sheet for grading within two weeks of completing it.

Expiration Date: December 31, 2017

Evaluation: To help us provide you with the best possible products, please take a moment to fill out the course Evaluation located after your Final Exam. A copy is also provided at the back of this course if you choose to email or mail your Final Exam Answer Sheets.

Wolters Kluwer, CCH is registered with the National Association of State Boards of Accountancy (NASBA) as a sponsor of continuing professional education on the National Registry of CPE Sponsors. State boards of accountancy have final authority on the acceptance of individual courses for CPE credit. Complaints regarding registered sponsors may be submitted to the National Registry of CPE Sponsors through its website: www.learningmarket.org.

One **complimentary copy** of this course is provided with certain copies of Wolters Kluwer publications. Additional copies of this course may be downloaded from **CCH-Group.com/PrintCPE** or ordered by calling 1-800-248-3248 (ask for product 10024491-0004).

¶ 10,301 Final Exam: Module 1

1. FATCA currently requires all of the following specified persons with foreign assets exceeding the threshold to file Form 8938 *except*:

   a. Specified domestic closely held corporations and partnerships

   b. Domestic entities indirectly holding specified foreign assets

   c. Nonresident aliens electing to be resident aliens to file joint returns

   d. Any individual who is a resident alien for any part of the year

2. If a foreign financial institution (FFI) fails to meet FATCA requirements, a U.S. withholding agent must withhold _____ on any withholdable payment to the FFI.

   a. 10 percent

   b. 20 percent

   c. 30 percent

   d. 40 percent

3. Under FATCA requirements, _____ is a reportable specified foreign financial asset.

   a. A financial accounts in a domestic branch of a foreign bank

   b. A security issued by a person other than a U.S. person

   c. All assets in a financial account subject to the mark-to-market rules

   d. An account at a foreign branch of a U.S. financial institution

4. Specified persons who are joint filers living abroad are subject to FATCA requirements when their specified foreign assets exceed _____ on the last day of the year or _____ anytime during the year.

   a. $50,000; $75,000

   b. $100,000; $150,000

   c. $200,000; $300,000

   d. $400,000; $600,000

5. To report the value of a specified foreign financial asset for Form 8938, the taxpayer:

   a. Lists its total worth in the currency type used for the account without converting it to U.S. dollars

   b. Identifies the value in the foreign currency, then converts it to U.S. dollars using the averages of the monthly or quarterly exchange rates used for paying estimated tax

   c. Identifies the value in the foreign currency, then converts it to U.S. dollars using the Treasury Department's year-end spot rate

   d. Identifies the beginning value of the asset for that tax year, then converts it to U.S. dollars using the Treasury Department's year-end spot rate for the immediately preceding year

6. An accuracy-related penalty of _____ applies under FATCA to tax underpayments involving undisclosed foreign financial assets.

   a. 10 percent

   b. 20 percent

   c. 30 percent

   d. 40 percent

7. For purposes of the FBAR rules, a U.S. person can have a financial interest in a foreign account unless he or she:

    a. Is a deemed owner of the financial interest's account

    b. Is a constructive owner acting on behalf of the U.S. person who owns the foreign account

    c. Is a discretionary beneficiary in a discretionary trust

    d. Is the owner of record or holder of legal title of the foreign financial account

8. Which officers or employees are subject to FBAR requirements?

    a. Ones with signature or other authority of a bank-owned account

    b. Ones having a financial interest in an account of the institution

    c. Ones registered with and examined by the Commodity Futures Trading Commission

    d. Ones of an entity with a class of security listed on any U.S. national securities exchange

9. An exception to FBAR reporting applies to:

    a. Employee welfare plan accounts of government entities

    b. Annuity policies with cash value

    c. Mutual fund accounts issuing shares to the general public

    d. Accounts with brokers or deals for futures or options

10. The 2014 Offshore Voluntary Disclosure Program imposes an accuracy-related penalty for offshore taxpayers' noncompliance of:

    a. 10 percent

    b. 20 percent

    c. 30 percent

    d. 40 percent

11. Which of the following is **not** a ConOps theme named by the IRS?

    a. Strategic workload application

    b. Reduced interactions among stakeholders

    c. Compliance risk-focused operations

    d. Data-centric operations

12. As a result of a 2015 survey of LB&I employees, the division seeks to improve information sharing through all of these methods **except:**

    a. Town hall meetings

    b. Coordinated Industry Case program

    c. Getting It Right Together website

    d. Two-way communications

13. In its restructuring, the LB&I Division moved toward:

    a. Shared economic characteristics

    b. Common geographical locations

    c. Unified compliance function

    d. Similar tax issues

14. The restructured LB&I Division:

    a. Has a single deputy commissioner position

    b. Implemented an international deputy commissioner

    c. Created deputy commissioner positions based on shared economic characteristics

    d. Developed leaders based on industry groups

15. In the revised LB&I structure, a(n) _____ is a group of employees who focus on specific areas of expertise, creating a compliance plan.

    a. Practice area

    b. Industry group

    c. Enterprise group

    d. Risk group

16. The LB&I Division is building a new, principles-based examination structure named:

    a. The Enterprise Risk Management Approach

    b. The Agile Model

    c. The Coordinated Examinations Model

    d. The Specialty Practice Area Approach

17. In 2015, the LB&I Division replaced the former Coordinated Industry Case (CIC) Model for selecting entities to audit with:

    a. Quality Examination Process

    b. Continuous Auditing Model

    c. Enterprise Risk Management program

    d. Rules of Engagement Process

18. The new examination process measures performance of the exam team:

    a. By the number of case openings and time spent on each case

    b. By the number of case closures

    c. By the amount of tax revenue received per team member

    d. By the subsequent risk analysis results

19. In the new exam process, a(n) _____ is an analysis and evaluation completed by the exam team describing a case's audit potential and resources.

    a. Scope statement

    b. Initial notice

    c. Return survey

    d. Resource allocation statement

20. Informal claims for refund should be provided to the exam team within _____ of the opening conference.

    a. 10 days

    b. 30 days

    c. 60 days

    d. 90 days

21. All of the following are tax credits given special treatment for *customers* of a certified professional employer organization (CPEO) ***except:***

    a. The work opportunity credit (Code Sec. 51)

    b. The excess employer Social Security tax credit (Code Sec. 45B)

    c. The *Federal Unemployment Tax Act* credit (Code Sec. 3302)

    d. The small employer health insurance credit (Code Sec. 45R)

22. Excluded employees for the purposes of the service contract are employees who:

    a. Work during not more than eight months during any year

    b. Have not yet completed six months of service

    c. Are younger than age 30

    d. Work less than full time

23. Under the proposed CPEO regulations, a self-employed individual:

    a. May not be considered a covered employee for the CPEO's customer

    b. Is considered a worksite employee

    c. Cannot be counted in determining whether the 85 percent threshold is met.

    d. Cannot perform services on the customer's worksite

24. Accompanying the CPEO application is a _____ user fee.

    a. $100

    b. $500

    c. $1,000

    d. $2,500

25. Which of the following is required within 30 days from the date of the notice of CPEO certification?

    a. Letter from a qualified surety that the surety agrees to issue a bond to the applicant

    b. Proof of a surety bond

    c. An unmodified opinion from an independent CPA that the financial statements meet GAAP standards

    d. An assertion that the applicant has withheld and deposited all federal employment taxes for which it is liable

26. A CPEO ***cannot*** be:

    a. A sole proprietorship

    b. A disregarded entity for federal tax purposes

    c. A business entity

    d. A trust

27. For federal employment taxes, a CPEO must annually post a bond of up to:

    a. $10,000

    b. $50,000

    c. $1 million

    d. $5 million

28. A CPEO applicant's financial statements must each carry an independent CPA's opinion that is:

    a. Qualified

    b. A disclaimer of opinion

    c. Reviewed but not audited

    d. Unmodified

29. Related party rules prohibit CPEO treatment between a corporate CPEO and a customer who is an individual, if the individual owns more than _____ in value of the corporation's outstanding stock.

    a. 10 percent

    b. 20 percent

    c. 25 percent

    d. 51 percent

30. Negligent failure of a CPEO to meet reporting responsibilities incurs an IRS penalty of _____ per report.

    a. $10

    b. $50

    c. $100

    d. $500

31. The per-item deduction limit for a taxpayer without an applicable financial statement was increased from $500 to _____ effective for tax years beginning in 2016.

    a. $1,000

    b. $1,500

    c. $2,500

    d. $3,000

32. Under the remodel-refresh safe harbor, _____ of qualifying remodel-refresh costs are deducted and the remaining costs are capitalized.

    a. 15 percent

    b. 35 percent

    c. 55 percent

    d. 75 percent

33. The remodel-refresh safe harbor does not apply to _____.

    a. Gasoline service stations

    b. Restaurant buildings

    c. Grocery stores

    d. Shoe stores

34. The advance consent procedure must be used to file an accounting method change from capitalizing an asset to deducting its cost as a repair expense if the _____.

    a. Taxpayer claimed a federal tax credit on the capitalized asset

    b. Taxpayer did not depreciate the capitalized asset

    c. Accounting method change is filed for a tax year beginning after 2014

    d. Taxpayer is a corporation

35. The eligibility limitation that prevents a taxpayer from using the automatic consent procedure to make the same method change for the same item in the five-year period ending in the year of change was waived an additional year for changes made under the repair regulations for changes filed for tax years beginning before _____.

    a. January 1, 2014

    b. January 1, 2015

    c. January 1, 2016

    d. January 1, 2017

36. The bonus depreciation rate for qualified property placed in service in 2018 is _____.

    a. 30 percent

    b. 40 percent

    c. 50 percent

    d. 60 percent

37. Bonus depreciation on specified plants is claimed in the tax year that the specified plants _____.

    a. Are placed in service

    b. Bear crops in commercial quantities

    c. Are planted or grafted

    d. Are purchased

38. Qualified improvement property that is eligible for bonus depreciation consists of internal improvements to _____.

    a. Residential rental property

    b. Nonresidential real property

    c. Section 1245 property

    d. Motorsports entertainment complexes

39. The 15-year recovery period for qualified leasehold improvement property, retail improvement property, and restaurant property was extended _____.

    a. Through 2015

    b. Through 2016

    c. Through 2017

    d. Permanently

40. The maximum deduction for Section 179 qualified real property for a tax year beginning in 2016 is _____:

    a. $250,000

    b. $500,000

    c. $2,000,000

    d. $2,010,000

¶ 10,302 Final Exam: Module 2

41. Under the combined annual wage reporting (CAWR) system, the Social Security Administration (SSA) and the IRS have an agreement, in the form of a Memorandum of Understanding (MOU), to:

    a. Share wage data

    b. Provide for substitute return preparation

    c. Outsource tax collection

    d. Process tax refunds

42. The Affordable Care Act's medical device excise tax has been suspended effective for sales on or after January 1, 2016, and before:

    a. January 1, 2018

    b. January 1, 2020

    c. January 1, 2030

    d. Indefinitely

43. Any administrator or sponsor of a plan covered by ERISA must file information about it every year on:

    a. Form 1065, Schedule L, *Balance Sheets*

    b. Form 5500, *Annual Return/Report of Employee Benefit Plan*

    c. Form 1120S, Schedule K-1, *Shareholder's Shares of Income, Crediting, Deductions, Etc.*

    d. Form W-2, *Wage and Tax Statement*

44. The FinCEN Report 114 (FBAR) is:

    a. Filed directly with FinCEN, not the IRS

    b. Attached to Form 1040, 1065, or 1120 returns

    c. Required if account totals exceed $100,000

    d. Not required if a financial account is held in a savings account

45. The Surface Transportation Act changed FBAR filing requirements by, among other changes:

    a. Allowing waivers of the penalty for failure to timely request an extension for first-time filers

    b. Eliminating the requirement to file Form 8938 in addition to the FBAR

    c. Allowing paper filings of the FBAR

    d. Revising the filing deadline to November 30 for the 2016 tax year and beyond

46. The PATH Act changed filing requirements for employers by:

    a. Eliminating the requirement to file Form-2 if the employer has fewer than 10 employees

    b. Raising the paid total compensation requiring filing to $950 for the tax year

    c. Providing that Form W-2 no longer qualifies for the extended due date of March 31 for filing electronically

    d. Eliminating the requirement to submit Forms W-2 to the Social Security Administration

47. Rather than using an employee's Social Security number (SSN) on Form W-2, the PATH Act authorizes employers to use:

    a. A bar code

    b. A password

    c. An "identifying number"

    d. Monochromatic icons

48. The PATH Act changed the refund date of the earned income tax credit for calendar year taxpayers to no earlier than:

    a. January 31

    b. February 15

    c. February 28 or 29

    d. March 15

49. The EFAST2 filing system is used by all of the following to share private pension plan information *except:*

    a. The IRS

    b. The Commerce Department

    c. The Department of Labor

    d. The Pension Benefit Guaranty Corporation

50. Which of the following forms is *not* used by employers or insurers for ACA information reporting purposes?

    a. Form 1094-B, *Transmittal of Health Coverage Information Returns*

    b. Form W-3, *Transmittal of Wage and Tax Statements*

    c. **c.**Form 1095-A, *Health Insurance Marketplace Statement*

    d. Form W-2, *Wage and Tax Statement*

51. At tier 3 penalty rates for 2015 information returns and payee statements not filed on or before August 1, the maximum penalty a small business may incur is:

    a. $75,000

    b. $250,000

    c. **c.**$ 532,000

    d. $1,064,000

52. A failure to file penalty is not imposed if certain corrected information returns are filed on or before:

    a. April 15

    b. August 1

    c. September 30

    d. December 31

53. Informational return penalties under Code Secs. 6721, 6722, and 6723 do *not* include:

    a. Failure to timely comply with specified information reporting requirements

    b. Failure to file an informational return

    c. Failure to investigate credits, exemptions, or deductions

    d. Failure to furnish or file a correct payee statement

54. The nonfraudulent failure to file penalty for tax returns may reach a maximum of _____ of the tax that is underpaid.

    a. 5 percent

    b. 10 percent

    c. 25 percent

    d. 50 percent

55. If a taxpayer's return does not disclose foreign financial assets that are understated, the accuracy-related penalty under the income tax provisions generally equals _____ of the tax underpayment.

    a. 40 percent

    b. 25 percent

    c. 20 percent

    d. 10 percent

56. A negligence penalty applies to all of the following types of disregard of the tax code rules and regulations *except:*

    a. Careless

    b. Disclosed

    c. Reckless

    d. Intentional

57. A substantial understatement of income tax that triggers an accuracy-related penalty is an understatement that exceeds the greater of 10 percent or _____ for individuals and _____ for corporations.

    a. $5,000; $10,000

    b. $10,000; $20,000

    c. $15,000; $25,000

    d. $25,000; $50,000

58. *Knowingly* claiming false tax credits, exemptions, or deductions is evidence of:

    a. Negligence

    b. Civil fraud

    c. Inadvertent fraud

    d. Undisclosed fraud

59. A fraudulent failure to file a return carries a maximum penalty of the lesser of _____ of the tax liability or _____ each month not filed.

    a. 10 percent; 2 percent

    b. 25 percent; 5 percent

    c. 75 percent; 15 percent

    d. 100 percent; 20 percent

60. The interest rate charged on underpayments of tax and erroneous refunds is _____ over the federal short-term interest rate for most taxpayers.

    a. 1 percent

    b. 2 percent

    c. 3 percent

    d. 5 percent

61. Under the new audit rules of Code Sec. 6221(a), under the BBA, a partnership may elect to opt out o6f the audit rules if it has:

    a. A single partner

    b. 10 or fewer partners

    c. 50 or fewer partners

    d. 100 or fewer partners

62. The duty of consistency rules apply to partnership tax years beginning after:

    a. December 31, 2016

    b. March 15, 2017

    c. December 31, 2017

    d. April 15, 2018

63. Under the BBA, each partnership must appoint a(n):

    a. Partnership representative

    b. Audit liaison

    c. General partner

    d. Partnership examiner

64. Generally, the new audit rules will apply to adjustments made for returns filed for partnership tax years after:

    a. January 1, 2016

    b. December 31, 2016

    c. April 15, 2017

    d. December 31, 2017

65. All of the following are factors relevant to determining imputed underpayments *except:*

    a. Adjustments to items of credit

    b. Netting all adjustments and multiplying the net by the highest rate of tax

    c. Aggregating the adjustments for all partners

    d. Treating the net increase or decrease in loss as a decrease or increase in income

66. A partnership can elect within _____ of the date of the notice of final partnership adjustment to apply the adjustment rules at the partner, rather than partnership, level.

    a. 10 days

    b. 45 days

    c. 60 days

    d. 90 days

67. If a partnership petitions for judicial review of an adjustment, under Code Sec. 6234:

    a. The partnership is required to pay the adjustment while the court reviews the petition

    b. No assessment of a deficiency may be made until the decision of the court becomes final

    c. The partnership is assessed additional penalties if the amount is due to mathematical error

    d. Interest continues to accrue while the issue is pending

68. A petition for readjustment following receipt of a notice of final partnership adjustment must be filed within _____ after the notice is mailed.

    a. 30 days

    b. 60 days

    c. 90 days

    d. 270 days

69. Computation of imputed underpayments does ***not*** account for:

    a. Any influx of new partners

    b. Future contributions of capital or services by partners

    c. Partnership level adjustments with individual partners' other tax attributes

    d. Current partners' accountability for underpayments by former partners

70. The New York State Bar Association recommends implementing the BBA's provisions for addressing imputed underpayments through:

    a. The withholding tax approach

    b. Correct return position

    c. Final partnership adjustment approach

    d. TEFRA FPAA approach

¶ 10,303 Final Exam: Module 3

---

71. Consumers are entitled to a free credit report from the three credit reporting agencies under the:

    a. *Identity Theft and Assumption Deterrence Act*

    b. *Fair and Accurate Credit Transactions Act*

    c. *Fair Credit Reporting Act*

    d. *Identity Theft Penalty Enhancement Act*

72. Restitution in an identity theft case may include the value of the victim's time remediating the associate harm under the:

    a. *Identity Theft Enforcement and Restitution Act*

    b. *Fair and Accurate Credit Transactions Act*

    c. *Fair Credit Reporting Act*

    d. *Identity Theft Penalty Enhancement Act*

73. For any knowing or reckless disclosure or use of tax return data, under Code Sec. 7216 preparers may be penalized:

    a. $250 per person

    b. $1,000 and one year in prison

    c. $500 per return if they are CPAs or $250 per return if they are enrolled agents

    d. At the state level for civil penalties but at the federal level for criminal penalties

74. The IRS maintains that all of the following are methods that should be used to help prevent tax identity theft *except:*

    a. Obtaining an IP PIN

    b. Filing tax returns early in the tax season

    c. Filing returns by mail, not electronically

    d. Not responding to e-mail information requests labeled IRS

75. A strategy for preventing business tax identity theft is to:

    a. Change the organization's employer identification number annually

    b. Conduct an identity theft action plan assessment

    c. Provide only electronic copies of Form W-2 to report wages

    d. Install antiphishing software

76. U.S. Postal Service communications are subject to identity thieves if:

    a. Outgoing mail is given directly to a letter carrier

    b. The recipient has mail delivered to its general office's mail slot

    c. Incoming mail is held at the post office when the recipient is away

    d. The recipient uses a post office box for deliveries

77. The federal repository for complaints about and resources for resolving identity theft is:

    a. The Federal Trade Commission

    b. Social Security Administration

    c. U.S. Department of the Treasury

    d. U.S. Trustee Program

78. If a furnisher of information to a credit reporting agency is notified that a debt is the result of identity theft:

    a. The furnisher may not sell, transfer, or place the debt in collection

    b. The furnisher may automatically close the victim's account

    c. The furnisher must provide the account holder all of the records of the identity theft transactions

    d. The debt is automatically canceled

79. A fraud alert placed on an individual's credit report requiring identity verification lasts for:

    a. 30 days

    b. 60 days

    c. 90 days

    d. 6 months

80. An Identity Theft Report used to address tax identity theft comprises:

    a. The FTC *Identity Theft Affidavit* and IRS Form 14039, *Identity Theft Affidavit*

    b. IRS Form 14039, *Identity Theft Affidavit* and a police report

    c. The *FTC Identity Theft Affidavit* and police report

    d. The FTC *Identity Theft Affidavit* and state's equivalent report form

81. A 401(k), 403(b), or 457(b) plan is a type of:

    a. IRA

    b. Profit-sharing plan

    c. Elective deferral arrangement

    d. Defined benefit plan

82. A plan that allows flexibility from the employer's perspective in the amount an employer contributes annually to an employee's account is the:

    a. Defined benefit plan

    b. Profit-sharing plan

    c. Elective deferral arrangement

    d. Matching contribution arrangement

83. The portion, if any, of a traditional IRA distribution that is not taxed is the:

    a. Employer contribution

    b. Basis

    c. Elective deferral

    d. Annuity rollover

84. The maximum employers can contribute to a SEP or SARSEP plan for an employee for 2016 is:

    a. $5,500

    b. $12,500

    c. $25,000

    d. $53,000

85. A maximum of $1,000 catch-up contribution for a plan participant who is at least age 50 in 2016 is available for:

    a. A traditional or Roth IRA

    b. A SIMPLE 401(k) plan

    c. A SIMPLE IRA

    d. A 403(b) and 457(b) plan

86. A governmental 457(b) plan may feature a(n):

    a. Last 3-year catch-up contribution

    b. Double annual addition limit

    c. Early required minimum distribution rule

    d. Higher salary deferral option

87. A self-employed individual who has a profit-sharing/401(k) plan can deduct up to _____ of net profit minus self-employment tax of contributions for 2016.

    a. 10 percent

    b. 20 percent

    c. 50 percent

    d. 100 percent

88. An account in a _____ is ineligible for rollovers.

   a. SEP IRA

   b. 457(b) plan sponsored by a nongovernmental organization

   c. Profit-sharing plan

   d. Qualified annuity plan

89. An owner must begin to take required minimum distributions (RMDs) from a traditional IRA by April 1 of the year following the calendar year when he or she reaches age:

   a. 59½

   b. 66

   c. 70½

   d. 72

90. RMDs during the lifetime of the taxpayer are not required from a:

   a. 403(b) plan

   b. 457(b) plan

   c. Roth IRA

   d. Nondeductible IRA

91. A donor must file a tax return including Form 8283, *Noncash Charitable Contribution,* for a tax year when the donor's contributed property exceeds:

   a. $250 in value

   b. $500 in value

   c. $1,000 in value

   d. **d.$** 5,000 in value

92. A written acknowledgment from the donee is required to allow deduction of a cash charitable contribution of at least:

   a. $250

   b. $500

   c. $1,000

   d. $5,000

93. A "qualified vehicle" under Code Sec. 170 does *not* include:

   a. A motorcycle to ride on public highways

   b. A sailboat used primarily for racing

   c. A used car with a claimed value of $400

   d. A 737 jet airplane

94. The donee organization that receives a donated vehicle whose estimated value is $9,000 provides a contemporaneous written acknowledgment to both the donor and IRS using:

   a. Form 990, *Return of Organization Exempt From Income Tax*

   b. Form 1098-C, *Contributions of Motor Vehicle, Boats, and Airplanes*

   c. Form 8282, *Donee Information Form*

   d. Form 8283, *Noncash Charitable Contributions*

95. *Quid pro quo* contributions are enforced under the *Omnibus Budget Reconciliation Act of 1993* for contributions of more than:

    a. $75

    b. $250

    c. $500

    d. $1,000

96. The penalty per contribution for failure to provide donors with a written acknowledgment in connection with a *quid pro quo* contribution is a maximum of _____, per donor and event/mailing.

    a. $10, up to a maximum of $1,000

    b. $10, up to a maximum of $5,000

    c. $50, up to a maximum of $10,000

    d. $50, up to a maximum of $25,000

97. An organization risks losing its tax-exempt status if _____ of its net earnings inure to the benefit of a shareholder or individual.

    a. Any part

    b. 10 percent

    c. 25 percent

    d. 51 percent

98. An arrangement between a tax-exempt organization and service provider to obtain royalty income not subject to UBIT from the use of the organization's logo or membership list is a(n):

    a. Trademark license

    b. Affinity program

    c. Fiscal agency

    d. Legal project agency

99. A maximum of _____ of unrelated business income in a charity's tax year is not subject to UBIT,

    a. $50

    b. $250

    c. $500

    d. $1,000

100. All of the following are "unrelated" trade or business activities of an exempt organization *except:*

    a. Activities not connected in a major way to the function for which the organization was granted tax exemption

    b. Activities that the organization conducts on a regular basis

    c. Selling goods or services at below-market prices

    d. Selling merchandise paid for by the organization to publicize its cause

101. A qualified corporate sponsorship for a charity:

    a. Generates UBTI regardless of how the arrangement is structured

    b. Grants the sponsor a tax-deductible expense for the sponsor if properly structured

    c. Creates a substantial return benefit to the sponsor, generating UBTI

    d. Can include use of a charity's license with a FMV of up to 10 percent of the total payment

102. Which of the following factors is *not* used to allocate dues to the circulation income of a charity's periodical?

    a. Pro-rata allocation of membership receipts based on cost

    b. Gross income from advertising in the periodical

    c. Subscription price charged to members

    d. Subscription price charged to nonmembers

103. The income generated by a tax-exempt organization that conducts travel tours is not UBTI if:

    a. The tours include nonmembers of the organization

    b. The tours are substantially related to the organization's tax-exempt purposes

    c. The tours are conducted on a breakeven basis

    d. The tours require extensive tax-exempt related activities for nonmembers

104. Compensation of volunteer labor that would disqualify an activity from exemption from UBIT includes all of the following *except:*

    a. Tips

    b. "Thank you" dinner for volunteers

    c. Gift cards

    d. Free drinks

105. Bingo games conducted by a tax-exempt organization are generally *not* considered subject to UBIT if:

    a. The organization's principal activity is operating bingo games

    b. The games are conducted in localities where they are not considered illegal

    c. The games are carried out on a commercial basis

    d. Proceeds of the games are given to tax-exempt organizations

¶ 10,400 Answer Sheets

¶ 10,401 Top Federal Tax Issues for 2017 CPE Course: MODULE 1

(10014583-0005)

A $113.94 processing fee will be charged for each user submitting Module 1 for grading. If you prefer to mail or email your Final Exam, remove both pages of the Answer Sheet from this book and return them with your completed Evaluation Form to: Wolters Kluwer Continuing Education Department, 2700 Lake Cook Road, Riverwoods, IL 60015 or email your Answer Sheet to Wolters Kluwer at **CPESubmissions@wolterskluwer.com**. You must also select a method of payment below.

NAME _____

COMPANY NAME _____

STREET _____

CITY, STATE, & ZIP CODE _____

BUSINESS PHONE NUMBER _____

E-MAIL ADDRESS _____

DATE OF COMPLETION _____

PTIN ID (for Enrolled Agents or RTRPs only) _____

METHOD OF PAYMENT:

☐ Check Enclosed ☐ Visa ☐ Master Card ☐ AmEx

☐ Discover ☐ Wolters Kluwer Account* _____

Card No. _____ Exp. Date _____

Signature _____

EXPRESS GRADING: Please email my Course results to me by 5:00 p.m. the business day following your receipt of this Answer Sheet. By checking this box I authorize Wolters Kluwer to charge $19.00 for this service.

☐ Express Grading $19.00 Email address: _____

* Must provide Wolters Kluwer account number for this payment option

 Wolters Kluwer

Module 1: Answer Sheet

(10014583-0005)

Please answer the questions by indicating the appropriate letter next to the corresponding number.

1. _____	9. _____	17. _____	25. _____	33. _____
2. _____	10. _____	18. _____	26. _____	34. _____
3. _____	11. _____	19. _____	27. _____	35. _____
4. _____	12. _____	20. _____	28. _____	36. _____
5. _____	13. _____	21. _____	29. _____	37. _____
6. _____	14. _____	22. _____	30. _____	38. _____
7. _____	15. _____	23. _____	31. _____	39. _____
8. _____	16. _____	24. _____	32. _____	40. _____

Please complete the Evaluation Form (located after the Module 3 Answer Sheet) and return it with this Final Exam Answer Sheet to Wolters Kluwer at the address on the previous page. Thank you.

¶ 10,402 Top Federal Tax Issues for 2017 CPE Course: MODULE 2

(10014584-0005)

Go to **CCHGroup.com/PrintCPE** to complete your Final Exam online for instant results and no Express Grading Fee.

A $113.94 processing fee will be charged for each user submitting Module 2 for grading. If you prefer to mail or email your Final Exam, remove both pages of the Answer Sheet from this book and return them with your completed Evaluation Form to: Wolters Kluwer Continuing Education Department, 2700 Lake Cook Road, Riverwoods, IL 60015 or email your Answer Sheet to Wolters Kluwer at **CPESubmissions@wolterskluwer.com**. You must also select a method of payment below.

NAME _____

COMPANY NAME _____

STREET _____

CITY, STATE, & ZIP CODE _____

BUSINESS PHONE NUMBER _____

E-MAIL ADDRESS _____

DATE OF COMPLETION _____

PTIN ID (for Enrolled Agents or RTRPs only) _____

METHOD OF PAYMENT:

☐ Check Enclosed   ☐ Visa   ☐ Master Card   ☐ AmEx

☐ Discover   ☐ Wolters Kluwer Account* _____

Card No. _____   Exp. Date _____

Signature _____

EXPRESS GRADING: Please email my Course results to me by 5:00 p.m. the business day following your receipt of this Answer Sheet. By checking this box I authorize Wolters Kluwer to charge $19.00 for this service.

☐ Express Grading $19.00   Fax No. _____

* Must provide Wolters Kluwer account number for this payment option

Wolters Kluwer

Module 2: Answer Sheet

(10014584-0005)

Please answer the questions by indicating the appropriate letter next to the corresponding number.

41. _____	49. _____	57. _____	65. _____
42. _____	50. _____	58. _____	66. _____
43. _____	51. _____	59. _____	67. _____
44. _____	52. _____	60. _____	68. _____
45. _____	53. _____	61. _____	69. _____
46. _____	54. _____	62. _____	70. _____
47. _____	55. _____	63. _____	
48. _____	56. _____	64. _____	

Please complete the Evaluation Form (located after the Module 3 Answer Sheet) and return it with this Final Exam Answer Sheet to Wolters Kluwer at the address on the previous page. Thank you.

¶ 10,403 Top Federal Tax Issues for 2017 CPE Course: MODULE 3

(10014585-0005)

Go to **CCHGroup.com/PrintCPE** to complete your Final Exam online for instant results and no Express Grading Fee.

A $132.93 processing fee will be charged for each user submitting Module 3 for grading. If you prefer to mail or email your Final Exam, remove both pages of the Answer Sheet from this book and return them with your completed Evaluation Form to: Wolters Kluwer Continuing Education Department, 2700 Lake Cook Road, Riverwoods, IL 60015 or email your Answer Sheet to Wolters Kluwer at **CPESubmissions@wolterskluwer.com**. You must also select a method of payment below.

NAME _____

COMPANY NAME _____

STREET _____

CITY, STATE, & ZIP CODE _____

BUSINESS PHONE NUMBER _____

E-MAIL ADDRESS _____

DATE OF COMPLETION _____

PTIN ID (for Enrolled Agents or RTRPs only) _____

METHOD OF PAYMENT:

☐ Check Enclosed   ☐ Visa   ☐ Master Card   ☐ AmEx

☐ Discover   ☐ Wolters Kluwer Account* _____

Card No. _____   Exp. Date _____

Signature _____

EXPRESS GRADING: Please email my Course results to me by 5:00 p.m. the business day following your receipt of this Answer Sheet. By checking this box I authorize Wolters Kluwer to charge $19.00 for this service.

☐ Express Grading $19.00   Fax No. _____

* Must provide Wolters Kluwer account number for this payment option

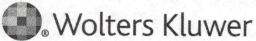

Wolters Kluwer

Module 3: Answer Sheet

(10014585-0005)

Please answer the questions by indicating the appropriate letter next to the corresponding number.

71. ___	78. ___	85. ___	92. ___	99. ___
72. ___	79. ___	86. ___	93. ___	100. ___
73. ___	80. ___	87. ___	94. ___	101. ___
74. ___	81. ___	88. ___	95. ___	102. ___
75. ___	82. ___	89. ___	96. ___	103. ___
76. ___	83. ___	90. ___	97. ___	104. ___
77. ___	84. ___	91. ___	98. ___	105. ___

Please complete the Evaluation Form (located after the Module 3 Answer Sheet) and return it with this Final Exam Answer Sheet to Wolters Kluwer at the address on the previous page. Thank you.

¶ 10,500 Top Federal Tax Issues for 2017 CPE Course: Evaluation Form

(10024491-0004)

Please take a few moments to fill out and submit this evaluation to Wolters Kluwer so that we can better provide you with the type of self-study programs you want and need. Thank you.

About This Program

1. Please circle the number that best reflects the extent of your agreement with the following statements:

		Strongly Agree				Strongly Disagree
a.	The Course objectives were met.	5	4	3	2	1
b.	This Course was comprehensive and organized.	5	4	3	2	1
c.	The content was current and technically accurate.	5	4	3	2	1
d.	This Course content was relevant and contributed to achievement of the learning objectives.	5	4	3	2	1
e.	The prerequisite requirements were appropriate.	5	4	3	2	1
f.	This Course was a valuable learning experience.	5	4	3	2	1
g.	The Course completion time was appropriate.	5	4	3	2	1

2. What do you consider to be the strong points of this Course?

3. What improvements can we make to this Course?

THANK YOU FOR TAKING THE TIME TO COMPLETE THIS SURVEY!